A

The Rabbi as

"Jack H Bloom has written the best book I have ever read about the contemporary rabbinate. Well-written, insightful, compassionate, yet devoid of specious sentimentality, Bloom, a rabbi and a trained psychotherapist of national standing, explores the complex motivation involved in selecting this problematic but important vocation and the emotional conflicts the choice is likely to engender. Bloom not only recognizes the problems inherent in the role of the rabbi but offers much sage advice concerning how to overcome them."

—Richard L. Rubenstein, Ph.D., D.H.L., L.H.D.,
President Emeritus and Distinguished Professor of Religion,
University of Bridgeport

"This is an exceptional and inspiring book on the spiritual journey of a beautiful human being. Dr. Bloom shares his own trek into the desert and back, illuminating how such a soul-searching path can bring one into a profound connection with spiritual truth and cultural identity. His description of the need for blessings in each of our lives is deeply moving, as are his accounts of the trials and tribulations of those who are called to give them. The book is an exceptional blend of spiritual love, conceptual clarity, and heart. I highly recommend it."

—Stephen Gilligan, Ph.D., Psychologist
and Author, *The Courage to Love*

"In this brave and insightful book, Jack Bloom reminds us that even in these laid-back times, there are limits to how much a rabbi can be 'one of the guys/gals.' Yes, congregations want to be closer to their rabbis, but only up to a point. For the rabbi can never simply be a person; he or she is a living Torah, a fearless advocate of Torah values, and above all a symbol of all that Jewish tradition represents. According to Bloom, only by accepting this reality as the starting point for its relationship with its rabbi can a congregation develop a realistic set of expectations for its spiritual leader. Similarly, only by accepting his or her role as Symbolic Exemplar can the rabbi develop a sense of self and meet the needs of his or her family. For congregants who want to understand their rabbis and for rabbis who want to understand themselves, this book is must reading."

—Rabbi Eric H. Yoffie, President,
Union of American Hebrew Congregations

THE RABBI AS SYMBOLIC EXEMPLAR

By the Power Vested in Me

THE HAWORTH PRESS
New, Recent, and Forthcoming
Titles of Related Interest

Shared Grace: Therapists and Clergy Working Together by Marion A. Bilich,
Susan T. Bonfiglio, and Steven D. Carlson

A Memoir of a Pastoral Counseling Practice by Robert L. Menz

The Pastor's Family: The Challenges of Family Life and Pastoral Responsibilities
by Daniel L. Langford

A Theology for Pastoral Psychotherapy: God's Play in Sacred Spaces by Brian W. Grant

Pastoral Counseling: A Gestalt Approach by Ward A. Knights Jr.

THE RABBI AS SYMBOLIC EXEMPLAR

By the Power Vested in Me

*For rabbis, other clergy, and the laity
who care about them and their sacred work*

RABBI JACK H BLOOM, Ph.D.

The Haworth Press®
New York • London • Oxford

This book was set in 12 pt. Perpetua by Alpha Graphics of Pittsfield, NH.

Published by

The Haworth Press, Inc., 10 Alice Street, Binghamton, NY 13904-1580.

AUTHOR'S NOTE
The case study of Mr. Wright, appearing in Chapter 11, pages 226–228, copyright 1957 B. Klopfer. Anyone with contact information for Klopfer, please contact the author at <JackHBloom@aol.com>.

Cover design by Marylouise E. Doyle.

Cover illustration by Mish Kinsella.

Library of Congress Cataloging-in-Publication Data
Bloom, Jack H, 1932–
    The rabbi as symbolic exemplar: by the power vested in me / Jack H Bloom.
        p.   cm.
    Includes bibliographical references and index.
    ISBN 0-7890-1865-9 (hardcover: alk. paper)—ISBN 0-7890-1866-7
(softcover: alk. paper)
        1. Rabbis—Office.   2. Pastoral theology (Judaism)   I. Title.

BM652.B48 2002
296.6'1—dc21   00-056546

To my father,

who paved the road

To Joe Glaser, cherished friend,

who opened the door

To my beloved *schatz*, Ingrid,

who by being exactly who she is

made room for this Bloom to blossom

Contents

USING THE POWER
OF SYMBOLIC EXEMPLARHOOD

THE RABBI AS SYMBOL
IN THE PUBLIC ARENA

Foreword

BY DR. NEIL GILLMAN

Let me say it at the outset. The author of this volume and I have been friends for over forty years. We've known each other since the fall of 1954 when we both entered the Rabbinical School of the Jewish Theological Seminary, and we have kept in touch since then.

The Jack Bloom whom I knew back then was an imposing student. I entered the school with a minimal background in formal Jewish studies. He had spent ten years in what was then (and probably remains) the best Jewish day school in the country. He was fluent in Hebrew; I could only stammer a few sentences. He had graduated from Columbia. I had graduated from McGill University in Montreal—a fine school, but not quite an Ivy. He was on the Seminary's most advanced program of studies; I was on the beginners' level.

But I quickly caught up, and for the remaining years of the program, we took most of our classes together. Even more important, we became part of a mini-community of students, one of several that developed in the Seminary's dormitory, enjoying much of what Manhattan had to offer to young, Jewish graduate students.

Subsequently, in Jack's senior year, I urged him to apply for a particularly attractive assistantship in a nearby pulpit, only to be devastated to learn that another colleague whom I then considered far inferior to him got the job. This was my introduction to the vagaries of congregational decision making, and it left a memorable impression. From then on, on principle, I have refused to predict what will happen when a congregational search committee meets behind closed doors. I also began to appreciate what was to become one of the central messages of Jack's subsequent work: despite the power and authority vested in the institution of the rabbinate, hovering over the career of every rabbi is a pervasive sense of insecurity. After all, it is the lay congregation that hires and fires.

After serving for a decade as a congregational rabbi, Jack decided to pursue training in clinical psychology. (I decided to complete my own doctoral work in philosophy and remained at the Seminary, first, in a series of administrative positions and, later, on its teaching faculty. I have been here ever since.)

The unifying theme of this collection of papers is the complementarity of religion and psychology. On the face of it, that such a complementarity exists should not be surprising, especially if one begins with a naturalist understanding of religion. If, that is, religion emerges as a totally natural and intuitive creation of human beings and their societies—an assumption which both Jack and I share wholeheartedly—then the discoveries of both religion and the social sciences must illuminate each other, simply because their common point of departure is the nature of the human person and of the communities these persons create. We learned this approach to religion from our teacher, the late Mordecai M. Kaplan, the most controversial member of the Seminary faculty, but one who had an enduring impact on our thinking.

But if the two disciplines are complementary, why the palpable, mutual mistrust that we typically encountered five decades ago? Why did some therapists dismiss religious commitments as illusory, neurotic, or worse? Why did some believers avoid badly needed personal psychotherapy on the assumption that therapists always begin with a deep-seated prejudice against any form of religious commitment? There is no simple answer to these questions, but it is clear, at least to this writer, that the problem was less with the disciplines and much more with some of their practitioners. Not all religiously committed Jews shared the naturalist understanding of religion. To them, Judaism was created by a supernatural God who revealed its truths to our ancestors at Sinai and are thus eternally binding. If you begin with this assumption, then the social sciences can only subvert religious claims. Many psychotherapists, on the other hand, remained influenced by Freud's pioneering work which viewed religion as an illusion—possibly a valuable illusion, but an illusion nonetheless.

Happily, much of this mistrust has faded in recent years. A simple glance at the citations in this volume will reassure us that competent therapists no longer automatically view religion as a symptom of mental illness.

The first paper in this collection, the author's frequently painful but remarkably candid autobiographical statement, includes an accurate description of the minimal place assigned to courses in rabbinic counseling in our rabbinical curriculum. The reason for this was not a prejudice against psychology—the Seminary leadership in those days was remarkably sophisticated on this count—but rather a more generalized prejudice against spending too much curricular time on what they dubbed "practical" or professional training courses. Our school's curriculum was heavily weighted on the side of rigorous textual study—of the Bible, Talmud, Midrash, Codes of Law, and the rest. Skills such as homiletics (how to construct and preach a sermon), education, counseling, and the "how to do its" of performing weddings and funerals would be developed on our own when we entered the field. They were just too trivial to waste valuable curricular time.

Happily this too has changed. Our rabbinical students are now required to take a number of such practical courses and enroll in a series of clinical internships in the "real world" as part of their training. In addition, the Rabbinical Assembly, the association of Conservative rabbis, provides ample settings for further in-service training in the distinctive psychodynamics of the rabbinic role—many of which were inspired by Jack Bloom's work and continue to feature his active participation. It is worth noting that his work in this area also bridges the denominational divide between the Conservative and the Reform rabbinate. Jack is one of a handful of rabbis who is a full member of the Central Conference of American Rabbis (Reform), and of the Rabbinical Assembly (Conservative). In addition to his work with Conservative rabbis, especially in the Rabbinic Training Institutes sponsored by his alma mater, he has served for a quarter of a century as Director of Professional Career Review for his Reform colleagues.

Jack Bloom knows Judaism and psychology, not only from books, but from the inside, from life. He is a practicing psychotherapist who has also served as a congregational rabbi and remains deeply involved in the life of a congregation of Jews. He is in the unique position of studying rabbinic functioning from three distinct perspectives: as a rabbi, as a psychotherapist, and as a congregant. Not only has he functioned in these roles, he has felt himself enriched by all three. In one of the more mind-boggling claims in this anthology, the author confesses, "I did more important work during the ten years I was a pulpit rabbi than I will do the rest of my career. Unquestionably! I have no doubt about it. I touched more lives, I affected more people, I made more Jews, and I was a much more effective kind of person in terms of my impact on others. I have no question at all about that." This from a man who has been a practicing psychotherapist for three decades!

There are two themes running through this collection that I have long identified with Jack Bloom's work and that have influenced my own thinking to this day. The first theme that has become closely identified with Jack Bloom and his work is his notion of the rabbi as "symbolic exemplar: The rabbi is a walking, talking, living symbol."

Much has been written in recent decades on the nature and role of symbols, but the core notion remains that a symbol points beyond itself to some other reality from which it draws its power. Thus a national flag is not simply a colored piece of cloth; it represents, nurses from, directs our attention to the "country for which it stands." To use a recent example, the fuss over the Confederate flag that flies over the South Carolina State House is not about the piece of colored cloth itself, but rather about its different meanings which it calls forth: Is it a symbol of racial oppression? Or of the glorious heritage of the American South?

If the rabbi is a symbol, then what you see when you look at a rabbi is not what you get. You see a human person, but what you get, in a concise, vivid, and distilled way, is a reading of the world, precisely that second-order, Jewish reality which you assume the rabbi stands for. With that kind of "seeing," you trigger the waves of emotion associated with it.

This symbolic role is precisely the source of the rabbi's authority and power. But it has its inevitable trade-offs. The instance of the Confederate flag captures that ambiguity. Bloom's point is precisely that in the process of seeing the rabbi as a symbol, you have effectively dehumanized this human being. This rabbi is no longer simply a person, a man or a woman, mother or father, with feelings, foibles, talents, idiosyncrasies, neuroses, character flaws, and the rest. He has become more than he is. The tension between the rabbi as a human being and as a symbolic exemplar accounts perfectly for the sense of set-apartedness, isolation, loneliness, and vulnerability that pervades the career of so many rabbis, and that Bloom traces with such masterful precision. He's been there. But if the rabbi tries to give up that symbolic role, must he or she then surrender the authority so central to the institution?

The unpacking of this dilemma is precisely what Bloom pursues in his therapeutic work with rabbis and in the rabbinic career reviews that he conducts.

The second theme is that each of us constructs his or her own reality, both what he calls the "first order of reality," and also the "second order of reality." The notion of this second order, the one that ascribes meaning to our experience of the world, is crucial. What is given to us is far from a meaning-laden world; if anything it is a blooming confusion. Our intuitive human role is to shape the given, to structure it so that it becomes a single, coherent whole and makes it possible for us to survive. In effect, we impose cosmos on the chaos of our experience; we create meaning out of what we are given. Religion is one way of doing that. Or, more precisely, whatever does that for a human community is by definition its religion.

Judaism represents one such second order of reality. Its canonical version appears explicitly in Jewish scriptures and in the rituals and liturgies of Jewish life. No one second-order reading of the world is inherently more true or more false than another; they are just different. But support for this Jewish second order may call upon this pragmatic criterion: it has worked superbly well for thousands of generations of people much like you and me, through millennia and in strikingly different cultural and historical contexts.

As Bloom argues, the task of psychotherapy is not to upset this reading, but rather to help someone reconstruct it or to offer some alternative when it has become discordant, when it no longer works. But crucial to this work is the gift of awareness—awareness that we do create our own realities, that we are responsible for how we choose to read the world, and that we are free to embrace or reject that reading. With awareness comes liberation.

Along the way, we learn a great deal more from this book. We learn, for example, in the most technical contribution to this volume, about the issue of qualifications for admission to rabbinic education and of the value of psychological testing prior to admission to the school—an issue that has roiled at least our faculty deliberations for decades and remains far from resolution. We learn also about the often painful impact of the rabbi's symbolic role on the rabbinic family, on the spouse and children. To my amazement, we have a number of what we popularly call "P.K.'s" (Preachers' Kids) in our school, and if the walls of my office could speak, they would report eloquently on the pain they suffered growing up in the hothouse of a rabbinic home.

This book should be required reading for rabbis, rabbinical students, and particularly for congregants. The rabbi's symbolic role is not only of his or her making; it requires the collaboration of the lay community. To the extent that the lay community helped create the dilemma, it can help dissolve it as well. The key remains awareness, and this book should be viewed as a resource for promoting this awareness.

If the lay community learns only one truth from this collection, namely that no rabbi has it all together, that just as much as the congregant is in search of meaning, so is the rabbi, that the only difference between the two is that the rabbi may be slightly more advanced in the process, have a touch more awareness of the ambiguities of the rabbinic role, then this extraordinarily insightful anthology will make a major contribution to our understanding of American Jewish religious life.

Dr. Gillman is the Aaron Rabinowitz and Simon H. Rifkind Professor of Jewish Philosophy at the Jewish Theological Seminary in New York City.

Acknowledgments

My thanks to Stephen Gilligan, Ph.D., whose Irish twinkle lights the way to the heart of an exemplar *mentsch*. Years of friendship, affection, and learning with Steve have been a gift beyond compare. His thinking, and defining himself in his own truly unique way, has challenged me to do the same. Self-Relations, which is his creation, pervades significant portions of this book. He has helped me be more of who I am. I am in his debt.

Thanks to Bertha Harrison, whose truly tireless efforts to get this book ready for the publisher, whose unflagging energy and calm steadying demeanor have made working under difficult time constraints so much easier. Her fastidious removal of my excessive use of semicolons taught me once again the vagaries and beauty of English grammar. Most of all, she has assured me that her Mah-Jongg group will buy six copies of this book.

It is with pleasure that I acknowledge Arnie Sher and Paul Menitoff of the Central Conference of American Rabbis, and Steve Shaw and Bill Lebeau, of The Jewish Theological Seminary of America. They have provided live settings in which I could teach much of what is in this book. Elliot Stevens has in his inimitable fashion made sessions of the Professional Career Review program pleasant and incredibly easier. They need to know that those priceless opportunities have brought me incredible joy. Their loving concern for Jewish life reminds me once again that God's words are spoken and heard in multiple ways. David Szonyi encouraged me at an early point that there was indeed a book in all my writings. He suggested the autobiographical chapter which deals with the formation of an "Athletic Coach for Rabbis."

I also want to acknowledge my colleagues on Hucalum, Ravkav, and Ravnet, Internet rabbi discussion groups, for being willing to share their both thrilling and vulnerable experiences as rabbis. They demonstrate great courage. They have also served as a ready and almost instant font of knowledge, when sources were unavailable to me. Among them I want especially to thank Rabbi Allan Lehmann, whose encyclopedic knowledge was always there when information was needed.

Thanks to all the folks at The Haworth Press who restored my faith that a publishing house, from top to bottom, could exemplify *menschlichkeit* (human "being" at its best). And thanks to Norm Tuttle of Alpha Graphics whose unflagging patience and support helped me ride the inevitable and sometimes dangerous rapids of publishing.

I love rabbis and the work they do. Without my colleagues in the Central Conference of American Rabbis and the Rabbinical Assembly, this book would be greatly diminished. It has been a joy to know them in ever-increasing numbers. I have learned more from them than I ever taught.

My hopes are with my children, Rachel, her husband Oren Faiga, and Rebecca, who are the next links in the chain. Their Jewish lives demonstrate the strength and fragility of our tradition. May they and my grandchildren, Ben and Lee Faiga, cherish our past, making it a present to our future. My stepchildren, Kirsten, her husband Phil Lambert, and Kenneth Baker, whom I love and who have reciprocated in kind, remind me daily that the [*Tzelem*⇔*Neshamah*][1] is not limited to my people alone. My stepgrandchildren, Spencer, Jake (not named after me), and Riley, are a constant source of joy to their Omi and Jack.[2]

Above all, I thank the Holy and Bountiful One, who has both put up with and blessed this "recalcitrant servant" and given me life and strength to reach this day.

---

1. See Chapter 6.

2. The above acknowledgment should also serve to notify R and R and K and K that all future contributions will be gratefully accepted.

Introduction

One of my hopes for this book is that it will be used in the education of rabbis, and the laity who care about them and their work. A number of my previously published articles have found their way into the curricula at our seminaries. Each chapter, though part of the whole, focuses on a different aspect of being a rabbi. Each is written so that it can stand alone. That has necessitated some redundancy and repetition of similar ideas. For example, my thinking about the rabbi as Symbolic Exemplar is basic to each "stand alone" article. I ask the reader to understand when reading more than one article that some of the exposition may indeed repeat itself. The reader is hereby reassured that neither you nor I is suffering from short-term memory loss. This is intentional and in the service of assuring that each article can stand on its own, and so be of greater use.

I try to deal with the gender revolution in writing by including both genders wherever possible, sometimes by alternating gender in different paragraphs, sometimes by being aware as I wrote the not previously published pieces that both genders need some space. I have found constricting the constant use of he/she, herself/himself, and having to avoid all words that indicate gender for words that are gender neutral. In the previously published material, gender is as it was published. I have done my best. I beg your forgiveness for places I may have inadvertently failed.

In Chapter 1, "An Athletic Coach for Rabbis," I have woven into the narrative a number of pieces that were published before.

It is my fervent wish that this book be useful to all those concerned with the important and sacred work our clergy do.

Jack H Bloom with his father circa 1937

1

An Athletic Coach for Rabbis: The Path I Have Come?!

"Jake!! Who are you kidding? We can't put that in." Well, that was the best I had to offer. A joking throwaway line. The deadline passed. I didn't come up with anything better, so that's what my Ramaz High School Yearbook lists as my ambition. There was more truth in it than I knew. It is the road I have taken, wandering from it, losing my heading, often blown off course, yet the way I have trudged in becoming, what some have flatteringly called, a rabbi's rabbi. It is an odyssey I want to share so you can understand how, and perhaps why I have made this work the passion of my life. To tell this odyssey I will include memoirs written at different times. They give some perspective on this autobiographical religious quest and help capture the terrain and the twists in the religious road that I have taken.

I am told that like the biblical Jacob, I was a pain in the heels of my brothers almost from birth. Though my mother wanted a girl, there I was, a four-and-a-half-pound boy, born on the anniversary of the creation of the world,[1] in, of all places, Christ Hospital, Jersey City, New Jersey. My father had my brothers *walk* ten miles with him from West New York, New Jersey, to visit me and our mother. It was the first day of Rosh Hashanah

---

1. The twenty-fifth day of Elul. According to Jewish tradition, Rosh Hashanah took place on the first Sabbath.

5693, Saturday, October 1, 1932, a day when riding was prohibited. My b'ris[2] followed a couple of days later. I don't know if my brothers were there, or who did it. I have no recollection of the day. But I know they complained often about that trek. Sol, my older brother by eight years, nicknamed Ace, recalls searching under the hospital bed for a reward that Dad had hidden there—a package with chocolate in different shapes: cigar, cigarette lighter, etc. On the way home a nail pierced the heel of Sol's shoe, causing significant pain. Dad had to stop and ask a stranger for a hammer to straighten the errant nail out and ease Ace's pain.

First, just to get it out of the way—about my name. All family members, following the lead of those who knew me when I was a little kid, refer to me to this day as Jackie, the familiar, affectionate diminutive of Jack. When my father started to "get religion" in the late 1930s, I was summarily notified that my name was no longer Jackie. I was now Jacob Hirsch, named for Dad's maternal grandfather, Yaakov Hirsch Cohn/Catz. It was OK with Dad if I didn't have that whole sobriquet, especially the "non-American" Hirsch. Harold would be my English middle name. And it was as Jacob Harold Bloom that I entered Ramaz, though most often listed as Jacob H. Bloom. All teachers from then through the end of high school referred, and where still around refer, to me as Jacob. In high school after having seen the play *Harvey* about an invisible rabbit, I took Harvey as my middle name and so affected for a while Jacob Harvey Bloom or, even a bit more pretentiously, J. Harvey Bloom. On my high school diploma I am Jacob Harvey Bloom. My summers were spent at Camp Massad where, though officially I was Yaakov, I became, for reasons I do not grasp, Jake. This filtered back to high school. So Jake I was informally, to all who knew me right through my Seminary years. Try as I might, I could not change it. When I showed up at Columbia in the fall of 1950, I was determined to introduce myself as Jack (probably with the Harvey). That lasted a couple of days until Gerry Kaufman, who knew me from Massad and Ramaz, came into the dorm hall and yelled out, "Jake, How are ya?" That ended that. And so it was Jake to friends, Jacob to Seminary professors, and Jack to no one until I got to Fairfield, Connecticut. There, though my first checkbook reads Jacob H., I decided to go with Jack H. Upon Dad's death in October 1961, rummaging through a whole bunch of documents, as one will do at times like that, I came across *two* birth certificates: one from Christ Hospital, Jersey City, New Jersey, and the other from the

---

2. The ritual circumcision on the eighth day, marking entrance to the Covenant.

County of Hudson, New Jersey. They proclaimed my name to be Jack H (without a period). My father, repenting his action, had drawn a line through that and penned in Jacob Hirsch. Somehow I had stumbled back to Jack H, my given name, sort of like Harry S Truman. When Columbia, collecting data for inscribing my Ph.D., decreed that no initials were allowed, I filled in the space with "Aitch." They responded with an ordinary H. However all that may be, I know immediately from what era a friendship dates and what the relationship is by whether I'm called Jackie, Jake, Jacob, or Jack. This may sound all too trivial, but in some ways it is a metaphor for my religious quest. If the name is one's identity, searching for who I really am religiously has been beset by obstacles often parading as blessings.

Whatever I was called, I was the youngest son of a youngest son, and for reasons formerly unfathomable to me, my father's unabashed and absolute favorite. His darling Jacob. Dad was an overpowering father to my older brothers, an impossibly strict single-minded disciplinarian, possessed of an awesome temper. He "kidnapped" me from my mother, determined to raise "this one" himself. Convinced that the methods he and my mother had used were lacking, and that my mother was less than useless in this endeavor anyway, he altered many of his ways. Though no less controlling, he was incredibly more gentle with me. Not having hesitated to use the belt with my brothers, he never once physically disciplined me. Nonetheless, I was petrified of him. He heaped mounds of nurturing love upon me. All the experiences children associate with their mothers are linked in me to him. He cooked breakfast for me every day (hot oatmeal, Wheatena, Cream of Wheat, made from scratch—no "instants" for him), followed before leaving the house with Cod Liver Oil, which for some inscrutable reason I liked. He gave me baths; clipped my toenails with his pocket knife (a sometimes harrowing experience); sang lullabies ("Rozhinkes mit Mandlen"[3] was my favorite); climbed into bed in the morning to read *Black Beauty* and *Uncle Tom's Cabin* to me; bought my clothes; enjoyed being with me, whether in a rowboat on Central Park Lake or partaking in multiple food treats. We had Sunday meals at Garfein's Kosher Restaurant on the Lower East Side, open *only* on Sunday so "you can be sure the food is fresh," or at the cafeteria on Broadway and 125th Street for pancakes and genuine maple syrup, preceding and softening the impact of the Sunday morning cello lessons I detested. He was limitless in physical affection ("What's a kiss without a hug?"). My mother,

---

3. "Raisins and Almonds"—a Yiddish folk song.

who resigned or was "fired" from raising me, went to work in the family business. A black maid, Wilhemina, was hired to care for me when I was six months old. She remained my female caregiver until we moved to Palisade, when I was four and a half. My mother, whether to deal with her guilt or to assuage me, would tell me repeatedly, "But your father loves you so much." It was true. His love was an awesome burden and also my salvation.

My earliest remembered "religious" experiences took place in 1938–1939 after we moved to the house on Inwood Terrace in, at the time, suburban Palisade, New Jersey.

Christmastime 1938. I am taken to Macy's and get to meet Santa. I'm not sure what I asked for, though following that encounter a ping-pong table appeared in the garage on Christmas Day. It was the same table on which I played a great deal later in my early teen years and got to be pretty good. It was also the last time I visited with Santa.

A Saturday night. After closing the store, we drove home on Bergenline Avenue in a 1938 Dodge Panel truck with the Dodge Ram on the hood in exuberant jumping posture. The truck developed an ignition fire of some kind, and we went into a Chinese restaurant at "Nungessers," which was the boundary between Hudson and Bergen Counties, to get something to eat. It was the last time I had Chinese food until 1952.

A friend (perhaps it was Toodles, who lived down the block and was killed in a gas explosion the summer I was away at Camp Dalmaqua in 1941) shared with me a part of a sandwich his mother had prepared. I told my mother that it was delicious and asked her to make me one like that. She discovered that it was ham salad and warned me that I was *never, ever,* to eat *that* again!

The first two certainly had to be before the Lichtensteins entered our life on Purim[4] eve 1939. Their arrival changed the kashrut (kosherness) of our kitchen and many of Dad's habits.

WHOSOEVER SAVES A SINGLE LIFE,
SAVES A WORLD ENTIRE[5]

It was April 1938. Having just passed through "Anschlussed" Austria in a sealed railway car, my mother, Sally, was returning from a visit to

---

4. Joyous holiday marking the saving of the Jews from the wicked Haman, as told in the Book of Esther.

5. Avot DeRabbi Natan; 31:2.

her aged mother in Rumania. Seated at the kosher table aboard the French liner *Ile de France*, she was joined for dinner by one Martin Lichtenstein of Breslau, Germany. As the great ship crossed the Atlantic, the conversation that unfolded the next few days revealed that Mr. Lichtenstein had, after much effort and interminable waiting, obtained from the United States Consulate in Berlin an immigration number for his family. The number would enable them to enter the United States and so escape the storm gathering over Germany's Jews. Immigration numbers alone were not enough. They were less than useless if the lucky possessor did not have certain affidavits from bonafide American relatives. The affidavits signed by these American citizens affirmed that not only was there a family relationship but these relatives had the means and agreed to support the new immigrants for up to five years. This was to ensure that the new refugees would not become a public charge, and a drain on the United States of America. Martin had an aunt in Detroit and was headed west after docking to ask her if she would sign for him and his family. At some point in their shipboard conversations, my mother gave Martin Lichtenstein this business card:

 PALISADE 6-9849 Estimates Cheerfully Given
We Measure Free of Charge

GO WHERE THE THRIFTY GO TO SAVE !

BIG   **BLOOM'S**   SMALL

SALES   BARGAIN·FLOOR·COVERING·STORE   PROFIT

LINOLEUMS, RUGS, CARPETS, FURNITURE

684 BERGENLINE AVENUE

WEST NEW YORK, N. J.

A month or so later, Mr. Lichtenstein showed up at the store. He was distraught and depressed. The aunt in Detroit was unable or unwilling to sign the affidavits. It was, after all, Depression time. And besides, no one in their right mind had the temerity to predict what was about to happen in the land of Bach, Goethe, and Schilling. Then began a redemptive moment. My parents, Sam and Sally, told Martin Lichtenstein that they would be his family's sponsors. They would say that they were his cousins. They would open their books and their Internal Revenue Service records to the Immigration authorities to demonstrate that they not only were related but had the wherewithal to sponsor this escaping family. They agreed to support the Lichtensteins for as long as was needed. They would sign any and all of the crucial affidavits. According to the Lichtensteins' son, Kurt, "They signed whatever was put in front of them."

On Friday, March 3, 1939, the ship's manifest of the *SS Manhattan*, passing the Statue of Liberty in New York harbor, listed four Lichtensteins. It was some eleven months after Sally had inadvertently met Martin Lichtenstein and barely six months before the German invasion of Poland. Sam Bloom got in his truck, with the *Go Where the Thrifty Go to Save* logo emblazoned on its side, crossed the Hudson, and went to the pier at 18th Street to pick up the immigrant family he had sponsored and was now responsible for. Martin and Katie and their two children, Irma and Kurt, and their belongings awaited their American benefactor eagerly and with some trepidation arriving in this strange new land. It was a winter Friday and the ship arrived at 9:30 P.M. The Sabbath[6] had in its inexorable way begun eighteen minutes before sunset. The Lichtensteins were new refugees. They were also observant Jews. Despite Sam's pleas, despite the fact that this was their first day in the United States, and their patron had come to fetch them, and everyone would have understood anyway, they politely, but steadfastly, refused to ride in the truck on the Sabbath. What to do? Sam Bloom resourcefully escorted them to the nearest hotel. There they refused even to sign the hotel register. That experience marked a turning point for Sam. He gradually, over the next years, returned to the traditions of his ancestors and became more and more personally observant. Sam signed the register for them, returned home, and came back with the truck Saturday night after the Sabbath was safely over. He took them to the new family home in Palisade. After a Sunday's R&R, he spent the next week finding and renting an apartment for them on 58th Street in West New York, New Jersey. Then he went on to obtain, using any contact he knew and with his own persistent style and after much effort, an Edgewater, New Jersey peddler's license for Mr. Lichtenstein, so that he might begin earning a living. Those were the days of the Great Depression and a peddler's license was no small thing.

---

6. Orthodox Jews do not ride on the Sabbath, which lasts from before sunset Friday to the appearance of three stars Saturday evening.

I was a little boy back then. From my child's perspective, the Lichtensteins were the source of great bounty. They gave me a mechanical toy car they had brought with them from Germany. The car had a long wire attached to a small module that I could hold in my hand. The module had a steering wheel on it and a miniature gear that could propel this wondrous toy forward or backward and in any direction I wished to steer it. A marvel of German technology! The Lichtensteins gave the family a Zeiss Ikon camera, a bellows model, with an eyepiece through which, by looking down, one would frame the picture. It served as the family camera for many years. There were also some little silver whiskey goblets—a few of which I still have. But the pièce de résistance was a scooter that had a floorboard with a ratchet that was attached to the rear wheel. By shifting your weight back and forth you could make it go without *ever* putting your feet on the ground. I loved it, and was heartbroken when my father inadvertently drove over it and bent the rear wheel. I have never seen anything like it in the United States.

The families became and remained good friends for a long time afterward. Indeed the Lichtensteins virtually became our "cousins," visiting back and forth and attending each other's *simchas*.[7] I remember spending a full Sabbath at their home in West New York in a very observant Sabbath atmosphere, an atmosphere almost too intense for me. I remember Irma's marriage at the Broadway Central Hotel in New York City. And so the years passed. In October 1961 Sam Bloom died. At his funeral the rabbi of the West New York synagogue, where he regularly attended morning services, seemed to have a score to settle with the Lichtensteins. In his eulogy he mentioned that even though Sam had done this saintly act of saving this family from the Holocaust, those he had saved were not even present at the funeral. It turned out that the Lichtensteins indeed were there. Nonetheless, without Sam Bloom around, and with his beloved Sally going through difficult times, and my own preoccupation with my studies, my new spouse, and beginning career, the two families lost touch.

Fifteen years later, on a shopping expedition to Orchard Street on New York's Lower East Side, I walked into a store called Charlie's Place. Whom should I see behind the counter, seated with a yarmulke (skullcap) on his head, but Kurt Lichtenstein. I recognized him immediately, walked over to him, and said, "Kurt, I'm Jack." There was no recognition.

"Kurt, I'm Jack Bloom," and still no recognition.

---

7. Joyous occasions. Originally a Hebrew word, taken over by Yiddish.

"Kurt, I'm Sam Bloom's son." Kurt's eyes lit up and he blurted out, "*Jackie!*"

It was the first time we had seen each other in years. We inquired into the usual things. Are you married? How many kids? Where do you live? Before parting, we exchanged addresses. Having Kurt and his wife Brocha's address meant that they were on our list to receive our High Holyday cards, each of which included a family photo.

Sometime thereafter, Kurt invited us to the Bar Mitzvah[8] of his fourth son in Monsey, New York. My wife and my daughter Rebecca went to the Bar Mitzvah, and were seated in the women's section. I was honored with an *aliyah*[9] among the men. Afterwards there was a *kiddush*,[10] where we were seated at long tables, laden with potato and noodle *kugels*, nestled in the aluminum containers they had been baked in, large bottles of soda, bowls overflowing with chopped liver, pickles, cole slaw, and potato salad, all the appurtenances of a lavish *kiddush*, that paid little attention to presentation, but ensured that no one would go away hungry. As fortune would have it, I was seated across from the Lichtensteins' fifth son, who was less than ten years old. He was looking around when suddenly his gaze fell upon me and his eyes went wide. He said to me, "*You're* the man in the picture."

"Yes, that's right, I'm the man in the picture."

"*You* saved my father from Germany."

"No, I didn't save your father from Germany. My father saved your father from Germany."

"*Your* father, saved *my* father from Germany?"

"That's right!"

He stood up, grabbed a full potato *kugel*, lifted it high, and pushed it towards me.

"MISTER—HAVE THE *WHOLE* PIE!!"

I left the Bar Mitzvah with a radiant inner glow. That Sabbath day I reaped what my parents had sown with a spontaneous decision back in 1938. Long before that it was written that "whosoever saves a single life saves a

---

8. At age thirteen, a young person is obligated for the fulfillment of God's commands. The occasion is marked by being called to the reading of the Torah, and participating as an "adult" in the service.

9. Congregants are honored by being called to and reciting blessings for a portion of the Torah being read at the service.

10. Collation following the service. Jewish life is intimately linked with food.

world entire." My parents saved a family they did not know from a destiny they could not have imagined. They gave life to Kurt and Brocha's five sons and all their descendants for generations to come, thirty-three from Kurt alone as of 2002. His sister, Irma, has thirteen grandchildren. There was no pie big enough. Their act is an inheritance I did not earn and will always treasure.

In addition to the Lichtensteins, my religious life was profoundly influenced by a man named Adolf, whom I am thrilled I never met, my grandparents, whom I wish I had met, and especially my paternal grandmother, who was channeled to me through Dad.

Grandmother Miriam was known for acts of charity, goodness, and obsessional rigidity. My father's elder sister, Leah,[11] recounted how her mother baked for anyone in the community who needed it for Shabbat,[12] and how generous she was with the poor. Leah told a story of a poor *ba'al agolah* (a drayman), who had gotten a young woman pregnant and chose not to honor his obligation to marry her. Miriam pawned her own jewelry telling the young fellow that if only he would marry and set things right, she would buy him a horse and a wagon so he could earn a living.

A further confirmation of her nature came years later from a Mrs. Clara Beraru of Beersheba, Israel, whom I met while doing the wedding of good friends' daughter to her grandson. During the wedding festivities, I discovered that she was from Frumusica, Romania, the hamlet that was home to my grandparents. Spiriting her away from the reception, I took her to my home to see an 1899 wedding photo of my family. She recognized all the people in the photo and described my grandmother in the following words:

"She would feed the entire town, giving food to anyone who needed it; even though others would try to get her to do less. She would gather the other women around her in the synagogue and during the service. She would explain to them what was going on and lead the service for them. She made sure that brides had dowries for their weddings. She always wore a kerchief on her head." Mrs. Beraru pointed to the picture of the wedding and said, "Here she had a *sheitel* (wig), but later she always wore a kerchief with a very nice little lace design in front."

She repeated over and over again what a wonderful woman my grandmother was and all the acts of kindness, generosity, and piety she did.

---

11. Personal interview, Leah Meirovici, Dad's sister, 1976.

12. Depending on context, Shabbat (Hebrew) or Sabbath (English) will be used.

My ninety-four-year-old cousin Iris, born in Romania, testifies to what she perceives as my grandmother's rigid religious nature by exclaiming that she "even had a blessing for going to the bathroom."[13]

Dad repeatedly demonstrated both her generosity and her rigidity. Though Dad did not talk incessantly about his father, whose early death left him at age twelve the sole male family breadwinner, he clearly loved him and exemplified many of his attributes. Yekutiel Zalman was also very religious, an appropriate match for Miriam Catz, a *schochet's* (ritual slaughterer) daughter. Antiphonally, Miriam's brother, the legendary Ephraim Catz, was an atheist Zionist who celebrated Yom Kippur[14] with a holiday feast. He was the first settler in what later became the city of Kiryat Bialik in Israel. Against all odds, the opposition of the Zionist establishment, Arab raids and destruction, he established what he hoped would be a self-sufficient family farm named for his wife Sabinia. Their farmhouse is now a community center and her name adorns the sign on the Haifa to Akko highway. Single-mindedness and courage seem to have been family traits.

GRANDPA ZALMAN'S *CHUTZPAHDICK*[15] PUSHINESS[16]

At the end of the nineteenth century, all Jews were banned from public schooling in Romania. Yekutiel Zalman Blum, known to all as Zalman, was the unofficial "Mayor" of the small Jewish community (perhaps a hundred or so Jews) of Frumusica (in Romanian, Pretty Little Place). Frumusica consisted of houses on either side of a road leading elsewhere, or as my father put it, "The horse was at one end of town and the wagon at the other." On one occasion the Romanian Metropole (the Bishop or Archbishop of the Romanian Orthodox Church) came to town—whether to inspect a church or just on his way elsewhere is not known. Zalman went forth to greet him with bread and salt, as was appropriate, and to intercede with him on behalf of Jewish students. Leah, his daughter, reported, with some glee, that in speaking with the Metropole, her father opened the conversation in *Loshon Kodesh* (Hebrew). In

---

13. What Iris did not, and does not, know is that this is one of the most meaningful of prayers, a part of the morning devotions.

14. Day of Atonement on which one abstains from all food and drink for twenty-five hours.

15. A Yiddish word conveying a combination of moxie and guts.

16. Personal interview, Leah Meirovici, Dad's sister, 1976.

a way both ingenuous and ingenious, *chutzpahdick* in its brilliance, to which the Metropole could not object. Zalman established his total equality with the Metropole. That this changed what was going on in Romania is doubtful. That it showed his self-respect, courage, and knowing that he was any man's equal is for sure. That my father had all three of these is also for sure.

It is also told about Zalman that when Theodore Herzl spoke in the area, Zalman traveled the ninety kilometers to hear Herzl and, in the enthusiasm after the speech, lifted and carried Herzl on his shoulders. Zionism was also Dad's passion. He had lifelong regrets that in 1914 he headed west to the "golden land" rather than east with his best friend to be a *chalutz*.[17] Sending my brother Ace, immediately upon his 1946 discharge from the United States Army, to Palestine to study agriculture at the Hebrew University, was considered by my dad as one of the great achievements of his life.

His very pious widowed mother did her level best to dissuade Dad from going to America. With some prescience she feared for his religious future. When he became eligible for the Romanian army, she offered to buy him a horse, so he could be in the reserves rather than the regular forces. Thus he could stay home in Frumusica, gathering produce from the peasants for resale in the larger town of Hirlau, my mother's birthplace, and home to the Blum clan. She wanted to ensure that he would not join his much older brother and cousins who had left for *goyishe* (gentile) America.

Despite his mother's repeated admonitions, Dad dropped his *tefillin*[18] into the middle of the Atlantic on the way over. He became a secular Zionist Jew and was in the 1920s and 1930s a member of the Workmen's Circle (Arbeiter Ring), socialist and secular in orientation. It always was a bit peculiar to hear Dad, who by then was a budding capitalist and landlord, and Mr. Sol Star, owner of the local dairy/grocery, greet each other as "Chover" (Comrade) Star and "Chover" Bloom. Given all this, Hitler, Nazism, and, especially, the German-American Bund were the catalysts in Dad's return to parental ways.

During first and second grades I walked to School No. 4, along Route 5. Mr. Woodward, the principal, and Dad had a run-in about the pictures of the German-American Bund,[19] which we were busily pasting into

17. The name given the pioneers who went to Palestine to work the land, to achieve personal transformation and national redemption.

18. Phylacteries—with which traditional Jews wrap head and arm at morning services.

19. Pro-Nazi organization of the middle and late 1930s.

scrapbooks. Mr. Woodward apparently told Dad, "People like you, Mr. Bloom, shouldn't stick their noses in where they're not wanted." Dad quoted Mr. Woodward often when retelling that encounter. That, plus Adolf and the Lichtenstein arrival propelled Dad back to his parents' patterns and forward to getting me a Jewish education. My previous formal Jewish education during the first and second grades involved going to Sunday school in neighboring Cliffside Park and coming home with a coloring book festooned with people in long robes and odd hats who were named Abraham, Isaac, and Jacob.

Observance was instituted incrementally—first we observed Friday night. Then my father would go to synagogue Saturday morning and to the store on Shabbat afternoon. Then he would stay home all day and Mom would go in. Then both of them stayed home and the help ran the store. Eventually the store followed the lead of the Fasses, owners of New Jersey Carpet, those most vile of competitors directly across Bergenline Avenue. The Fasses were Orthodox Jews who had always kept their store closed. Now Bloom's Bargain Floor Covering joined them in closing on Shabbat.

The change was not an easy one to impose on the family. Dad's creeping campaign to have the family become observant had its share of unruly lurches and bumps, some due to my brothers, eight and eleven years older, respectively, who had been raised with a very different set of commitments.

THE RADIO THAT WAS DEMOLISHED
FOR NOT OBSERVING SHABBAT

The radio at Inwood Terrace was located in the finished basement, where the family ate and lived. The kitchen, dining room, and living room on the first floor were used only for company and as a passageway to the second-floor bedrooms. A 1930s-style radio console only recently had been placed on its shoulders, a newfangled combination table model that incorporated a 78-rpm record player. Listening to a Beethoven symphony required Herculean efforts in lifting and moving. One day in the early 1940s when my father was returning to religion, but the store was still open on Shabbat, I was outside playing stoopball on the front steps while my brothers were inside listening to classical music, when I heard Dad's car coming. Dad was a terrible driver who had countless fender benders, and I could hear the rambling wreck arriving blocks away. I ran inside to warn my brothers. But Dad, clear about what I was up to, and perhaps wanting to provide a Shabbat atmosphere for his youngest, beloved Jacob, stormed into the house and tore the radio apart, ripping its guts out. It was an awesome display of his temper, which though I witnessed it often, always would instill anew the fear of the Living God. The radio survived, was repaired, and unrepentantly resumed its non-observant ways. I could cheat and listen, if I kept its volume low to the "old red head," Red Barber, describing the exploits of my beloved Brooklyn Dodgers, even as my father took his Shabbat nap two flights up.

THE CHECKERS THAT FLEW ON HIGH

I was eleven years old. Yom Kippur day's *Yizkor*[20] was being recited at Temple Israel Community Center in Cliffside Park. I was downstairs with the other kids, whose parents' being alive disqualified them from attending *Yizkor*. We had a checkers game going.[21] The game extended beyond the conclusion of *Yizkor*. My father raced downstairs, temper flaring, and with a quick upward sweep of his hand dispatched the religiously non-caring checkers to their destiny in every corner of the hall. I was mortified! There was no help for it!

RAMAZ

Unhappy with Public School No. 4, pursuing a Jewish education for me became Dad's top priority. Dad, wanting a modern school, found his way to the Jewish Education Committee in New York City. Dr. Alexander Dushkin, its head, told him that there was a school just started by a Rabbi Joseph Lookstein called Ramaz. It apparently was begun for his son "Hackie" when Haskell[22] was of kindergarten age. The school was modern, very "up to date," and, best of all for Dad, had no sessions on Sunday. Sundays were very special to Dad. Sunday was family day. And family, especially his relation with his Jacob, was very special to him. Six days a week in the store till ten every night was more than enough. My father did not want me to go to school on Sunday. Because of that, I thankfully was not enrolled, though it would have been logistically much simpler, at the Yeshiva of Hudson County,

---

20. Memorial service for the departed. Those who had living parents were traditionally exempted.

21. I had been the checkers champion of Ramaz in third or fourth grade. As an award, they gave me a book called *How to Play Chess*. I often wonder about the message.

22. Today Rabbi Haskell Lookstein, his father's worthy successor, a prominent and courageous leader of modern Orthodoxy and lover of all his fellow Jews.

a "down at the mouth" school that, like every other yeshiva, had Sunday sessions. Ramaz's meld of Americanism and Judaism also met my father's needs precisely. He had become, from April 1, 1914, his first day in America, a fervent patriot, in love with everything American. Now he could return himself and his youngest to the traditions of his people, without compromising either of his loyalties.

After an evaluation which included an IQ test by Dr. Benjamin Brickman, the educational administrator of the school, I was accepted to Ramaz.

So in 1940 at age eight, a third-grade student, I became an out-of-state commuter to Ramaz from what was then the far reaches of New Jersey. I took a bus, the 125th Street ferry, a subway, and a cross-town bus to get there. It took well over an hour and I commuted both ways. My father taught me the commuting thing by putting me on the Third Avenue trolley at 86th Street and telling the trolley driver to let me off at 125th Street. He went up to the Third Avenue elevated train, which was quicker if you timed it right, and was there at 125th Street to meet his eight-year-old.[23]

At Ramaz, my third-grade English teacher was Mrs. Needleman, whom all of us adored. I spent my first year at Ramaz catching up in Hebrew. With the help of Miss Zabadavsky, in one year of private tutoring and make-up work, I was brought up to snuff so that I was able to be in the regular fourth-grade religious studies class with Mr. Kest. Miss Buchwald was my fifth-grade teacher. And it was in fifth grade that I met Ray Arzt, who at 110th Street joined me on the upper deck of the No. 4 Fifth Avenue bus. It was the start of a lifelong friendship. Though I didn't know it then, by meeting the Arzts, I was introduced to another way of being Jewish. In sixth grade we ran through a bunch of English teachers until Mr. Ira Sherman settled in for the long haul. In Hebrew studies we adored Mr. Neiman and then in seventh and eighth grades had the legendary Mr. Rappoport, whose solution to any and all discipline difficulties was the hall, preceded by the feared "*just get out* ___," the blank being filled in with the name of the violator—Merims, Berkowitz, Bloom, or whoever.

A benign side benefit of Dad's controlling ways was that he would generously and graciously do a lot for his Jacob that other dads did not do. That ranged from getting tickets for me and my friends to the New York

---

23. This was not the route eventually used, perhaps because crossing 125th Street meant traversing the center of Harlem.

University vs. Notre Dame basketball games, when none were available, to providing hats for the team we organized in sixth grade called the *Hornets*, to putting up a backboard and regulation ten-foot-high basket on the street outside our house so I could practice my basketball shooting, no matter what the weather. There wasn't much he wouldn't do for his Jacob. Jacob's part of the job was to be a cooperative, good, religious (or acting religious) little boy.

My Bar Mitzvah took place on Shabbat Shuvah,[24] September 15, 1945, at Temple Israel Community Center, Cliffside Park, New Jersey, with Rabbi Joseph Spevack officiating. It was followed at home by what was at that time a fairly lavish *kiddush*.

The reception, at the Paramount Kosher Caterers, 45th Street right off Broadway, followed the actual Bar Mitzvah by exactly a month due to the Jewish holidays occupying each Saturday and Sunday. Thanks to Dad's inveterate desire to photograph with the latest in technology, a film record of that momentous event remains for posterity. What occurred off camera was more interesting at the time.

The 1946 Ramaz eighth grade had seventeen boys and four girls. So if the hormones were raging, one's aim had to be very good. A group of us, probably all the girls and some of the boys, moved to the stair landing outside the room where the *simcha* was taking place and decided to have a game of "spin the bottle" with all of its 1945 excitement. Not much happened, but word got back to Rabbi Lookstein, who was present in the other room. The following Monday, we were called into his office, told that we had disgraced the honored name of Ramaz, and were, therefore, banned from any extracurricular activities for the foreseeable future. I was embarrassed that this had happened at my Bar Mitzvah and relieved that it was a group punishment and not mine alone.

A DIFFERENT TAKE ON THAT EVENT, WRITTEN FIFTY YEARS LATER[25]

He was thirteen and pudgy, standing in a suit that itched, bought from Bobby's Clothing Store on Canal Street. Bobby's specialized in outfitting husky boys. He was thinking more about the *kiddush* that was to follow

---

24. Repentance Sabbath preceding Yom Kippur, the Day of Atonement.

25. J. Grishaver and S. Kelman, eds. *Haazinu, Learn Torah with . . . 1995–1996*. Los Angeles, CA: Alef Design Group, 1996, pp. 385–387.

than what he was doing. It was his Bar Mitzvah day and he was reading (or, more accurately, reciting from memory) the Torah portion *Haazinu*. Thank God and his birthdate—it was *really* short. The *aliyot* were just a few verses long. He was doubly lucky, because Mr. Rappoport had insisted, in his antiquated way, that the entire seventh grade, each and every one, learn *Haazinu* by heart. As classmate after classmate struggled to recite the right words, he could, with just the inkling of a smirk, rattle it off. To be fair to him, he had to learn a special trope for *Haazinu*. That was burden enough. But it had become part of him. And every year thereafter, when he could, he would chant the poem in any synagogue that would have him.

He was chanting Moses' great ode, *Haazinu*. "Give ear, O heavens, let me speak; Let the earth hear the words I utter!" A visionary's poem! Breathtaking scope! People's destinies decided! The fate of nations hanging in the balance! The Bar Mitzvah boy understood little of it. *Everyone* said it was too tough to understand anyway. Even Mr. Rappoport said so. Maybe Mr. Rappoport had assigned it by heart, because of the verses at the end of *Haazinu*, "Take to heart all the words with which I have warned you this day. Enjoin them upon your children, that they may observe faithfully all the terms of this Teaching. For this is not a trifling thing for you; it is your very life."

Mr. Rappoport took such things seriously. This was no trifling matter. He would have it be part of us. Memorized.

When Moses delivered *Haazinu*, *he* didn't have to learn it by heart. He *knew* it by heart. The words came from his heart. They were his. Moses just spoke the poem, teaching as he went. Moshe Rabbeinu, our peerless teacher who against all odds, had brought the people Israel to the very edge of the Promised Land. Moses, who maneuvered between an ingrate people and their explosive ally who had more than once threatened to destroy them all. Moses, master mover of men and, yes, let it be said, of God. God's friend and intimate; awesome leader of God's People. Yet at the end of the ode, in full view of the promise about to be realized, Moses hears the fateful words the Bar Mitzvah boy dares in his ignorance recite, "You shall die on the mountain that you are about to ascend . . . for you broke faith with Me among the Israelite people, at the waters of Meribath-Kadesh in the wilderness of Zin, by failing to uphold My sanctity among the Israelite people. You may view the land from a distance, but you shall not enter it. . . ."

He didn't understand it when he stood in his Bobby's suit and he doesn't understand it now. How could Moses who envisioned the whole thing, who led the trek through the desert for forty years, be turned away on account of such trivia! OK, so he hit the rock (probably hurt his hand) instead of talking to it, to get water for his people. Big deal! A small thing! Too great a punishment for a trivial offense, not forgotten by the God of justice, nor forgiven by the God of compassion. He is denied the prize for not having sanctified God's name in the midst of the people Israel.

He didn't know if he would understand it if he lived to Moses' 120. Nor did he care. It was enough just to get to the end of the Torah portion without any mistakes. And to get downstairs for the herring in sour cream.

Fifty years later he understands a bit more, though not very much. There have been glimpses of meanings. Learning it by heart did something. It comes in his dreams and enters his musings from time to time. He knows that though the big vision is crucial, little things matter. They count big time. Kind words he said to others, words others offered him, made a difference. A smile, a note, a bit of praise and appreciation all lingered. He knows he liked them when he got them, but though it was so easy, he often failed in giving them. He's learned that though he needs to keep his eye on the goal, he needs to attend to the little things at the same time. And that's a tough balancing act. He's learned that we fail when success is in our grasp and succeed when failure is at the door. And that we are magnificent in both. He's seen that we're both holy and mundane, saint and sinner, generous and stingy, incredibly vicious and supremely kind, each of us and all of us. He's recognized that though we get lost in the little things, we dare not ignore them. For it's in the little things that we sanctify God's name in the midst of our people.

He understands a bit more and then only sometimes; like Moses we're destined to die without the prize; and that the prizes we do get are often not worth the pursuing. He has seen big prizes lost by small acts. He's noticed that for brief shining moments we succeed, and that we make promises to ourselves that we intend to keep and don't. That things we can't help impede us. And that that's just the way it is. We're more human than not. Over the fifty years he had learned something—sometimes.

He had learned *Haazinu* by heart. Mr. Rappoport's pedantic vision and the luck of his birthdate had seen to that. Long after his Bar Mitzvah, he was reading *Haazinu* in synagogue with the confidence of having done it fifty times. Pretty soon it would be *kiddush* time and he could have some herring in sour cream. But now his wife's caring concern about animal fat would deny him that prize too. Still, he could taste the herring as the words, planted in him long ago, came out of his mouth. He had never guessed, and didn't know now, how they would bloom.

HIGH SCHOOL

At the end of eighth grade a decision had to be made about high school. I took the test for Stuyvesant, an elite public high school, though how I would fake a New York address was never really decided. My cello and I were taken by Dad to Music and Art High School for an audition. That would have been a sad joke. I went through times when I fancied that I would go to Fort Lee High, our New Jersey town's high school. Dad in his single-mindedness, "Your choice is to do it my way," prevented that debacle. When all was said and done, I found myself that fall attending Ramaz High School in its second year, in the freshman class known rather elegantly as the First Form. Hackie Lookstein, for whom Ramaz was really founded, was in the second form and that's all there was.

Ramaz High School was a good experience for me. I got to play varsity basketball and become president of the Student Organization. Dad did not come to basketball games, but when I ran for president, he did not hesitate to have campaign buttons made that read *Bloom for President* or photo tags with me posing impressively in front of an old blanket. I did my part by campaigning wisely, targeting and cultivating the First Form as the swing vote, and defeating Arnold Smith for the job. Though he was 6'3" and center on the basketball team, I was second high scorer and president of the school.

Ramaz was deeply committed to its pursuit of integrating Americanism and Judaism. It was concerned with how we students appeared in public and wanted to make sure that we had the social skills to behave appropriately in private. Ramaz discouraged us from wearing *yarmulkes* (skull-caps) in public. In ninth grade Ramaz taught us social dancing. We learned the all-purpose box step for the fox trot, the Rhumba, which was fashionable back then, and the waltz. Ramaz-sponsored dances often took place after basketball games and were the envy of the all-male Yeshivas of Yaakov Yoseph, Manhattan Talmudical Academy, Brooklyn Talmudical Academy, and Mesivta Torah ve Daat, who were our basketball competition. When we chose our school colors (to the best of my recollection the suggestion of blue and gold was mine), we bought reversible warm-up jackets (I still have mine) with gold on one side and blue on the other and were sternly instructed that the less flashy blue jacket with gold RAMAZ on the back was to be worn in the street. The brazen gold jackets with blue RAMAZ lettering were to be used only during basketball games.

Today, Ramaz will not sponsor a prom. Back then it was one of the ways it used to demonstrate how up-to-date Orthodoxy could be.

At the Ramaz senior prom in 1950 Raiselle Sorscher was my date. A photo of us and the couple we were with was taken at Bill Miller's Riviera in Fort Lee, New Jersey, where Tony Bennett was featured. When the photo was included forty-eight years later in a coffee table book,[26] I contacted Raiselle. Married with grandchildren, she was living in Detroit. On the phone she reminded me that she and a number of her "Orthodox" friends had in the early 1950s attended the Jewish Theological Seminary's College of Jewish Studies and then switched to the Teacher's Institute. That is something that would not happen today. She offered that though it was a sweet thing I did, submitting the photograph, she was not sure she was so pleased about it because, "You know we're quite Orthodox, and my sons-in-law will razz me about it."[27] I was somewhat stunned to be reminded of something I knew, which was how far to the right Orthodoxy has moved over the past fifty years. The world has indeed changed.

Ramaz prided itself on providing a second-to-none secular education, and succeeded in doing that. In choosing colleges, Ramaz was clearly proudest of those of us who made it into the "Ivies." Its Jewish education, in my later view, had one foot in the twentieth century and one firmly planted in the seventeenth century. How good it was depended on where one's own feet were standing.

MASSAD

Though Ramaz was special, Massad was the most formative influence on who I am as a Jew. More than any other experience, it shaped me as far as my attitude and commitments to my people, Hebrew, and *Eretz Yisrael*[28] are concerned.

My father had already made camping part of my brothers' Jewish education, having sent them to Kindervelt[29] in the 1930s. My first sleepaway

---

26. Allon Schoener. *New York—An Illustrated History of the People.* New York: W.W. Norton, 1998.

27. The "razzing" issue being that of "negiyah"—for a man and woman who are not married touching one another is prohibited. It was not an issue for us back in the 1949–1950 school year.

28. The Land of Israel.

29. A leftist, Yiddish-speaking camp. At least my brothers knew Yiddish from my immigrant parents.

camp bore an Indian name, Dalmaqua, whose season was truncated by polio that summer of 1941. In 1942 it was Surprise Lake Camp sponsored by the 92nd Street YMHA. Sometime in fifth grade my father heard of Massad. I have no idea how. He took me to 145 West 46th Street to Camp Massad's office where I met Shlomo Shulsinger for the first time.

My father and Shlomo shared some personality characteristics. Kindred souls, each qualified as a monomaniac, in Hebrew, *Meshugah ledavar echad*. There was no idea that was too bizarre for my father. It was bizarre to have a camp where they spoke Hebrew, but he certainly liked the idea and wanted that for his son. Massad had started as a day camp on Long Island in 1941. They had shared a facility in Monticello, New York, in 1942. Now it was 1943. It was to be Massad's first year as a two-month sleepaway camp located, as Shlomo and Rivkah (his wife and co-director) would say, *Beharei Ha-Pocono* (the Pocono Mountains).

I didn't dare risk any serious objections. Few people, even grownups, did that with my dad. Being his favorite, I got some things, but the crucial ones were in his hands alone. If my father wanted it to happen, it happened! So his Jacob had become a commuter from New Jersey to Ramaz at age eight and went to a crazy Hebrew-speaking camp called Massad at age ten. A regular *chalutz*.

It became clear to me early that *everyone* in camp was scared of Shlomo. Being scared of a monomaniac was not an unfamiliar feeling for me. From the point of view of a little kid, he was a *much older* man, a distant, to-be-feared figure with his jacket draped over his shoulders, sleeves hanging, walking stick in hand, obsessed with rooting out those who dared speak anything but Hebrew. A significant dramatis personae.

A REMINISCENCE SAYS IT ALL[30]

It was the spring of 1982. I was driving west on Route 80, to Hershey, PA, when my car, seemingly on its own, gravitated towards an exit on the road. I was nearing Tannersville, PA, where from 1943 through 1954 with a break of one year in Israel, I spent eleven years of my young life at Camp Massad. With iron discipline, I straightened the car out, knowing that first I

---

30. Published as "Reminiscences," in *Avar ve' Atid*, Vol. 1, No. 1, September 1994, pp. 51–54, Herzl Fishman, ed., the Joint Authority for Jewish-Zionist Education.

had to get to Hershey for the rabbi's conference I was leading. Inexorably I returned the next afternoon to Tannersville and Camp Massad, *Beharei Ha-Pocono* (in the Poconos).

When I arrived at the camp, the caretaker refused to allow me in. I protested to him as to how I had been there for the first time almost forty years before and that there was no way he could keep me out. He then allowed me to walk up that steep hill that marked the entrance, and to take a look around. "But not too long," he called after me. The camp had just been closed and sold to Camelback, a ski resort—an odd name, I thought, since I had known the small mountain that "towered" over the camp, as *Rosh Hahar* (top of the mountain) where the *Pasei Harakevet* (railroad tracks) used to be, and where we sometimes trudged on a Thursday which was *Yom Tiyul* (hike day), which gave the *mitbach* (kitchen) a day off and meant that we made *krichim* (a Massad word for sandwich, later supplanted by the "linguistically purer" *sendvichim*).

I walked around the campgrounds which looked like a Hollywood set devoid of actors. Everything I remembered, and more, was there, but no people. Bunk A-3, better known as *Dekel* (date palm), where I had started as a camper in *Geza*, in 1943, hadn't changed a bit. (*Ivri Tzair* [Young Hebrew], abbreviated, spelled *Etz* [tree]. The camp population by age, in ascending order, was made up of *Shoresh* [root], *Geza* [trunk], *Anaph* [branch], and *Tzameret* [crown of the tree].) Of such metaphors was the iconography of the place created. *Chadar ha-Ochel* (the dining hall) was still there, adorned with its *pitgamim* (pithy sayings of the Zionist fathers). "*Im tirzu en zu agadah*" ("If you desire it enough, it is no dream"—Theodore Herzl) was still there—seemed like it had always been. I walked through the camp, mostly in the *Emek* (valley of Jezreel—the boys' campus) though I bravely ventured into the *Galil* (Galilee—the girls' campus) despite having been sternly warned years before that it was off limits to boy campers. The two were appropriately named, the *Emek* being quite deep and the *Galil* at the very top of the hill.

I was flooded by thoughts of what this place had meant to me, how it had shaped my identity in a most profound way. How its almost absurd dedication to Hebrew and to the creation of an environment of *Eretz Yisrael* had molded my character forever. Those years at Massad had formed my identity as an American Jew, more than my day school education at Ramaz, more than my becoming a conservative rabbi, surprisingly even more than stays in *Eretz Yisrael* itself.

A flood of memories . . . odd memories . . . disconnected, yet each profound. This was the place that first taught me classical music. I had in my head Hebrew words for Brahms' first symphony,[31] Shubert's ninth, Dvorak's New World, Hebrew lyrics for Mendelsohn's wedding march,[32] and even for a conflation of "Whistle While You Work" and "Dixie."[33] All used for anthems, pep songs, and marches for the *Maccabiah*, the high point of the season when the camp was divided in two, given names from the *Eretz Yisrael* experience, *Ir* (city) and *Kfar* (village), *Chayalim* (soldiers) and *Chalutzim* (pioneers), *Haifa* and *Jerusalem*, etc., and then competed in everything from sports to song, drama to cleanliness. (A minor oddity: I had the dubious distinction from 1943 through 1951 of never having been on a winning side in a *Maccabiah*. Finally, as *Rosh Pelugah* (chief honcho of *Kfar* in 1952) I achieved my minor nirvana.)[34] So much of classical music and some popular music

---

31.   אורים השמים הופך אבניך בהיר. את עבריה, רבת היצירה, את נס התחיה מלהיב
לך לאומה, לאומה לאדמה, את גבולותיך נרחיב, עד שכל הארץ תל אביב

The lights of heaven turn your stones bright, you are Hebrew, creative, the banner of rebirth. For the sake of land and people we will expand your boundaries that all the land be Tel Aviv.

32.   חיפה וירושלים אנו רוצים בשידוך עלו נה, כל הערים בינתים לחגיגת התווך,
כלתינו בלה בלה היא עטרת הכרמלה החתן חסון לב בחורה מזעזע, חיפה וירושלים. . .

Haifa and Jerusalem [the names of the two teams], we would see you wed, let all the cities come to the nuptials. Our bride is beautiful, the crown of the Carmel, the groom in his strength stirs the heart of his beloved . . . Haifa and Jerusalem. . . .

33.   For this song the two teams were city (*Ir*) and village (*Kfar*). This is *Kfar*'s song:
אחד מכם נמצא, לפני שבוע בא, לא מאמינים העירונים אז הנה מה קרה

Up to here, "Whistle While You Work." Now "Dixie."

היה היה בן כרך אחד, לכפר הוא יום אחד ירד וראה אדמה היא תחית האומה
זה רק קרה אחר יומים, אחז קרקע מלא חפנים וראה אדמה היא תחית האומה
לכן בני העיר עלו וראו שכאן בכפר אין רק עפר, הכפר עתיד עמינו,
עלו וראו תקות מדינתנו, הכפר הכפר הכפר עתיד עמנו.

One of you is here, came a week ago, the city folks don't believe it, so here is what happened.

There was a city guy, who came to the village, and realized that land was the life of the nation.

It took two days, he held a fistful of earth, and realized that land. . . .

So, you city folk, come see that here there's not just earth, but the future of our people. Come see the hope of our state, the village is our future.

34.   There is a photo in *Kovetz Massad* (a collection of photos of camp life) of the giving of trophies at the end of the *Maccabiah* in which I emerged triumphant. In that photo Shlomo appears, along with Chayah Angstreich, the head of the other team. I remain unidentified. So much for Shlomo's vaunted recollection of everyone who went to Massad. Or perhaps I was just written out of the history of the place when I "defected" to Ramah.

from the 1940s and 1950s is etched in my mind in Hebrew. I spent winters looking for appropriate melodies for marching songs for the *Maccabiah*. I thought that Gershwin's "Strike Up the Band," would be terrific but to my regret never got a chance to use it. In 1948, the first year of *Massad Bet* (the idea was so successful that there was a second camp and later a third), I was part of what was arguably the best *kevutzah* (bunk) ever, named *Merchavia* (a kibbutz in *Eretz Yisrael*). We had learned well, and used the Coast Guard anthem to extol our being last to *tefillot* (prayers) and yet always first to breakfast.

My mind flashed to years later when Israelis would ask me where I learned my fluent Hebrew and would look at me curiously when I said that I had learned it in a summer camp run by a man who was *meshugah ledavar echad*, a monomaniac. His dream was a camp for American Jewish children where only Hebrew was spoken. He turned his dream into reality, realizing Herzl's dictum in another area, and made the "impossible" happen, and *that* I told the curious inquirer is where and how I learned my Hebrew.

I walked to the flagpole, where *Mifkad* (the assembly) which began and ended the day took place. I saw in my mind's eye and heard in my inner ear, a counselor stepping out front and saying, *"K'vutzat Dekel, arba'ah mishemonah kiblu ayin hayom"* ("In Date Palm Tree [the name of our bunk], four out of eight campers received *ayin* today")—*ayin* being the first letter of *Ivrit* (Hebrew). This was the daily reward if your counselor thought you were making an effort at speaking Hebrew on any given day. If your bunk got more *ayins* than any other bunk over a whole summer, the lot of you got *degel Ben Yehudah* (the Ben Yehudah pennant) in honor of the creator of modern Hebrew, a true exemplar of *meshugah ledavar echad*. If a bunk was incorrigibly derelict in getting *ayins*, they risked Shlomo's personal attention, an outcome not greatly to be desired.

My mind recalled *tekasim* (pageants) held most often on Wednesdays, when dressed in blue shorts and white shirts with the *Ivri Tzair* patch on the left breast pocket (I still have one), we marched to one or the other flagpole, to witness a presentation about some Zionist accomplishment or other. My mind wandered to mock radio broadcasts, describing the news of the day in Hebrew and almost always ending with the baseball scores. I thought of the time in the dining hall where we learned "The Partisan Song" with Hebrew lyrics[35] rather than the Yiddish "jargon" which was held in such contempt, a reflection no doubt of the Kulturkampf which had shaken the *Yishuv* thirty or so years earlier. A contempt which did not reckon with

35. Don't say, "This is my final road," though the clouds have covered the sun's light. The day we have longed for will yet come, and for our part we will shout, "We are here!"

the tragic end happening, as we sang, to the great community who spoke "jargon."

I thought of all the leadership that came out of this place. I recalled that first *Maccabiah*, in 1943 when Gershon Cohen *z"l*[36] and Gershon Winer, both later to be heads of Jewish institutions of learning, headed the two teams. I remember how that first *Maccabiah* ended in a tie. *Tayku*—we were disappointedly told—only Elijah himself could figure out how Shlomo arranged for that to happen. "Hackie" Lookstein and "Louie" Bernstein, Orthodox leaders; Sam Karff,[37] destined to be president of the Central Conference of American Rabbis (Reform), to whom I played backup first base, and who revealed to me years later that he envied me my first baseman's mitt; the Rudavskys, the Gamorans, the Feinsteins, Alvin Schiff, later head of the Jewish Education Committee of New York, who was *madrich* (counselor) in A-4 when I was in A-3; my own counselor, David Lifschitz *z"l*, known familiarly as *Lamed* (the letter of the Hebrew alphabet with which his name began), later head of Shaare Tzedek Hospital in Jerusalem; the counselor in A-2 was Carmi Charney, later T. Carmi the great poet, and even a later rebel from Hebraism, Noam Chomsky; a mere smattering of the cornucopia of Jewish leadership who shared summers in this curious place.

I continued wandering for longer than the custodian would have liked, my mind constantly lighting on the profound impact this place had on me. Virtually all of the campers were obsessed with Shlomo Shulsinger, who created and ran the place with an iron Hebrew hand. I remembered Ray Arzt tell what was perhaps a true story. In the midst of contract negotiations, Shlomo told him that Charles Kadushin, Ray's very good friend, spoke Hebrew better than Ray, and Ray was said to have responded, "And Bialik [the poet of the Hebrew renaissance] spoke Hebrew better than you." We laughed heartily when we heard that story. Shlomo had been bested not only at his own game but on his home field, Hebrew.

I recalled my first interview in the office on 46th Street where my father had brought me to sign up for this strange Hebrew-speaking camp. I started to cry, wondering if they played baseball at this weird place and, if so, what did they call a ball and bat. Little did I know that Shlomo and his entourage had created a Massad dictionary full of arcane Hebrew terms for the nomenclature of baseball.

---

36. An abbreviation for the Hebrew *zichrono leverachah*. May his/her memory be a blessing.

37. Upon saying to Sam over forty years later, "*Heveh muchan*" (be prepared), he will instantly respond, "*Tamid muchan*" (always prepared).

My mind flashed to 1955 when I left Massad for Ramah and didn't know what Shlomo's response would be. I received the following letter from Shlomo. Curiously enough, a letter whose Hebrew words I have remembered verbatim over the years.

יעקב

איני מתרעם לגמרי על שאתה עוזב את מסד.

אני תקוה שתחדיר לתוך רמה את הקוים האידיאולוגיים של מסד.

שלמה

"Yaakov,

I am not at all angry that you are leaving Massad. It is my hope that you will infiltrate Ramah with the ideological convictions of Massad.

Shlomo"

This was a special place. This place with names from a far-off land, this place where the leaders' obsession with us all speaking Hebrew permeated down the levels, so that one felt an almost joyous guilt in violating that structure, but also learned to treat Hebrew as something very special. This place where Reform, Orthodox, and Conservative, in those years, could work and play together and participate fully in their identity as Jews with all of the variations involved.

I took my fill as I wandered around that day of the soon no longer to be place of my youth. It curiously had not changed in the thirty years since I had been there—at least not physically. It bore the same slogans, the same standards, and the very bunks in which I had slept, and it had been a place that changed and shaped my life. As it came time for me to get back to Hershey to continue teaching, I found myself wanting in some way to say *kaddish*[38] for the place. And yet, at the same time, to say *hallel*[39] for what it had done for me and for so many others in its own peculiar and unusual way.

It was time. I turned to reassure the custodian that I was not going to stay, walked back down the hill, got into my car, and headed west on Route 80.[40]

---

38. The doxology used as a memorial prayer.

39. A prayer of praise and gratitude.

40. After Shlomo got the Reminiscences, he was thrilled with them and carried a copy with him everywhere. I come home one Sunday and my wife Ingrid says to me, "A Mr. Shulsinger called and you have to call back before four o'clock because he is leaving for Israel." So I sit down at my desk and call and suddenly in the middle of the conversation I become

Massad infiltrated and pervaded my consciousness and loyalties. Ramaz provided a lot for me, but the deepest visceral loyalties came out of the Massad experience. It is linked to everyday life and peak experiences such as the following.

PARTITION DAY: NOVEMBER 29, 1947

As I write this, it is fifty years plus one day after the United Nations' vote on partition of the Holy Land. It was one of those occasions, indelibly inscribed on one's memory, as to where you were at the moment. It is Saturday afternoon, around 5:30 P.M. Dad and I are listening to the radio and the United Nations General Assembly partition debate. I'm not sure why Dad permitted listening to the radio that day. Perhaps it was because of the importance of the event. The radio was in the totally fixed-up finished basement, equipped with bookcases, kitchen, eating table, and the radio. We had not yet started using the upstairs kitchen, dining room, and living room, which lacked a radio (the main floor was still for guests only), when we heard that the United Nations had just voted to partition the Holy Land. Dad and I exuberantly hugged each other and danced a hora around the room, with a sense of ecstatic joy, matched but few times in a lifetime. Just the two of us responding to the fulfillment of that two-thousand-year-old dream. Mom is not there because she is at the store. Ace was in Tel Aviv at that time, fulfilling Dad's Zionist dream, and dancing there.

That experience and so many more came out of that really odd educational web Shlomo and Rivkah had created. When I first heard a news report on Kol Yisrael, Israel's radio station, on my first visit to Israel in 1953, my whole associative structure went back to hearing headlines—the Shidurei *Chadashot* after supper at Massad—"*Achshav neshader et ha-chadashot mi . . .*" ("Here are today's headlines") which then described events in Yugoslavia, France, New York, and of course what really mattered to me, the results of the Brooklyn Dodgers/St. Louis Cardinals "crucial" baseball series.

Massad pushed Hebraism, suffused in the environment of *Eretz Yisrael*, manifested by language spoken and names given to places and things. Massad was summer camp for American Jewish kids in a Hebrew/Israel frame. *Chalutziyut* (pioneering) was honored for those already there, but there was

---

aware that here I am, a man of sixty talking to a man of eighty, and I'm still worried about whether my Hebrew is good enough. Still worried! Yes! Some things never change.

little talk about *aliyah*.[41] Massad was the embodiment of informal education without sound modern educational principles, both ahead of its time and behind its time. Probably least useful in Massad were the *sichot* (discussion groups) held twice a week. This was as close as Massad got to formal education. Massad did not push *datiyut* (religious observance) in a formal sense. No case was made for it. Morning services and other observances were simply presumed. What was crucial in Massad were the people, the language, and the environment that enveloped you.

On a visit to Shlomo and Rivkah's apartment[42] (a miniature Massad museum) in 1995, my closing words before the door shut behind me were,

> "I am truly grateful for what you did for me, knowingly or not knowingly."

Among the photos in a Massad album, the 1944 camp photo shows my brother Norman in army uniform in the background and my mother and father. In a photo of a Torah dedication at Massad, there in the back is my father. It was he who gave me over to Massad that it might be foreground in my life. That strange place that changed me forever.

A DECADE FULFILLING DAD'S DREAM: COLUMBIA AND THE JEWISH THEOLOGICAL SEMINARY OF AMERICA

At the end of high school, the choice had to be made as to where I was to go to college. There were five choices: Columbia, University of Pennsylvania, Syracuse, Temple, and Rutgers, the State University of New Jersey. I took Dad's 1949 Chevrolet station wagon to look at Temple, and was joined by Warren Brown, a Ramaz classmate. We had supper at Old Bookbinders in Philadelphia, and I was impressed with how good a fish restaurant could be, so Temple was OK if that's where I ended up.

---

41. In this context, "going up" to settle in The Holy Land. The "going up" is a positive value judgment.

42. Looking for Shlomo and Rivkah's home on Jabotinsky, I got lost by looking for their apartment on Tschernichovsky. (Those knowledgeable in the history of Zionism will know the immense ideological divide between the two.) When I finally arrived I jokingly said in Hebrew, "I really got mixed up. You failed to educate me properly as to the difference between Tschernichovsky and Jabotinsky. I thought that Jabotinsky was Tschernichovsky." That banter came directly out of Massad.

Perhaps it was the residual influence of those twin imposing statues, one female representing "letters" and the other male representing "knowledge,"[43] who presided over the entrance to Columbia at 116th Street and Broadway, that I had passed countless times headed home on the trolley, but for whatever reason, I wanted to go to Columbia. Dad wanted me to go to Columbia. Ramaz wanted me to go to Columbia. Its Ivy League status aside, Columbia was tough to get into. It was 1950 and the flood of World War II veterans at Columbia was just beginning to ebb. I was placed on the waiting list. I don't remember what happened to Syracuse, Penn, and Temple. I think I made two out of the three. But Rutgers accepted me and that was it. It was relatively close to home and, as the State University, was cheaper and closer to Dad's purview. Dad, concerned about my Jewish observance, had made arrangements with a brassiere manufacturer in New Brunswick, New Jersey, for me to stay at his house and eat my, for sure, kosher meals there.

I would have rather stayed in the dorms at Rutgers. I could no more tell Dad that than I could have said to him that I wanted to stop keeping kosher. Many times on my way home from high school, I had ingested, with amazing rapidity, fearing discovery and death by lightning, a hot dog and orange drink at the Nedicks at 8th Avenue and 50th Street, near the Greyhound terminal from where I took the Orange and Black bus home to New Jersey. But Rutgers and the brassiere manufacturer's home it was to be.

Just days before starting, a special delivery letter from Columbia notified me that I had been admitted and that an immediate response and registration were required. I was thrilled that I had gotten into my first choice. Dad was thrilled because to him it meant I would live at home, the better to monitor my religious life. So my life as a commuter student continued, this time at Columbia. It was decidedly closer to home than Ramaz and now Dad provided a car to navigate the distance. I stayed in the dorms for freshman orientation and regretted not living on campus. I did apply for dorm status. Out-of-town students were given priority in the very grungy rooms. It was not to be. Dad, I am sure, did not want it to happen. He wanted me home for Shabbat, though Shabbat observed alone in Palisade was a deadly experience.

As a freshman at Columbia I went through a period of "licentiousness" as far as observance was concerned. Dad's reaction was mixed. The first Rosh Hashanah eve,[44] that of 1950, I walked home with a friend from *shul* (synagogue) a mile and a half away. Instead of walking along Anderson Avenue, the

---

43. Columbia University press release, July 20, 1967.

44. The Jewish New Year, which is either always early or late, that year September 11, 1950.

usual route, I walked along Palisade Avenue, a longer route, accompanying him to his home. Waiting for me, Dad, wondering what sin I was committing, lost his temper and bolted out of the house searching for me. When our paths crossed a couple of blocks from home, I self-righteously yelled back at him, proclaiming that I had indeed *walked* and in no way was to be accused of any "sin." Such "sins" in multiples did take place, such as the first Chinese food since 1939, when I was not in Dad's purview. Yet by the beginning of my sophomore year, a member of the glee club, I drove down to concerts in New Jersey, in my first self-owned car, a 1937 light blue four-door Chevrolet, leaving from home on Shabbat with no hint of any objection on Dad's part.

During my years at Columbia, I earned my living teaching religious school. While a freshman, I taught Sunday school at the newly formed Jewish Community Center of Fort Lee, New Jersey. Towards the end of the year I discovered that it was Dad who was paying my salary. Even after all of these years, I still feel duped and angry. As a sophomore I got a bonafide job teaching religious school Sunday and two afternoons at Temple Israel Community Center with my own Rabbi Henry O. Griffel z'l. I enjoyed doing it and was terrific at it. Teaching enabled me to pay my own way at Columbia. Tuition at the time was $375 a semester. Dad could easily have paid, but that discussion never came up between us. Teaching gave me a fair amount of pocket money and enabled me to buy my first new car, a 1952 four-door standard-shift green Chevrolet, practical for getting everyone into and costing all of $1875. Junior and senior years, I added the two remaining afternoons to my teaching load.

During those years, the spring semester at Columbia concluded at the end of May. Until camp began in July, I soda jerked at the new Dairy Queen Dad had built at 72nd Street and Bergenline Avenue in North Bergen, New Jersey. During the Columbia years I was a closet *treyf*[45] eater, and the Dairy Queen gave me another way to indulge. I would cross the street to the luncheonette next to the Embassy Theater, where I could see the Dairy Queen from the counter and wolf down a double cheeseburger, asking the owner to let me know if he saw my father and praying that my dad did not show up there. The Dairy Queen was a dangerous place to work, what with my propensity for imbibing the product faster than it could be produced. Cones went for ten cents, sundaes were twenty and thirty cents, and a Blizzard went for a quarter. I would, of course, bring my friends from New York over to the Dairy Queen when I was not working. They (Ray Arzt, Larry Kobrin, Chuck Kadushin, and many others) remember many a trip over the

---

45. The diametrical opposite of kosher.

George Washington Bridge, when we could not decide what else to do on a Saturday night.

I was at Columbia during the Korean conflict. My eligibility for the draft risked an outcome that did not seem desirable. Besides which, I must have been scared. There were a couple of ways to avoid the draft. Maintaining an adequate college rank and doing well on a test offered to college students made deferment possible. Deferment would also happen if I became a pre-theological student. I was encouraged by my rabbi, Dad, and others to apply to be a pre-theological student at the Jewish Theological Seminary. Acceptance would confer the treasured "4D" draft status. I imagine that my combined Ramaz and Massad background made me in some way desirable, and indeed I was accepted. How this happened in the light of my religious observance beats me. I *was* attending the Seminary College of Jewish Studies, though in a half-hearted way. Since I was attending the Seminary College anyway, and didn't perceive myself as being able to quit, it didn't seem to matter much. I think I convinced myself that it couldn't hurt.

Driven by my at best mixed and more often negative feelings about religiously observant Jewish life, I decided to sign up anyway for the college draft deferral exam. Maybe that would open new options and I could drop out of the Seminary, forfeiting my "4D" status. During the summer of 1952, I drove home from Massad to spend the night at home and go to Columbia in the morning where the test was offered. My father, an early riser who was fastidious about waking me on all other occasions, did not wake me up that morning. I slept in. I did not get to the city for the 9 A.M. test. I was *furious*. I accused him of Machiavellian[46] manipulation to force me to become a Rabbi. It took me some twenty years to realize that I could have set my own alarm clock.

Doing a lot of things at the same time, my schedule was full to bursting. Despite myself I had inherited my father's ability for hard work. I carried between fifteen and eighteen credits at Columbia and a full academic load at the Seminary College of the Jewish Theological Seminary. Sundays, I taught Hebrew school from 9 A.M.–noon and drove across the George Washington Bridge to 122nd Street for Seminary classes from 1 P.M.–6 P.M. Monday through Thursday, I taught Hebrew school from 3:30 P.M.–5:30 P.M. and Tuesday and Thursday evenings returned to the Seminary from 6:30 P.M.–9:30 P.M. As a freshman and sophomore, teaching *only* two afternoons, I was able to be in the

---

46. Probably only recently taught me by the "Contemporary Civilization" program at Columbia.

Columbia Glee Club.[47] Later on, teaching four times a week made that impossible. I often regret the toll exacted by my second academic program and my work. They thinned out my Columbia experience which I loved dearly.

THE ZIONIST CURE

As a result of just not being mature enough, I did not do as well as I could have the first two years at Columbia. I did the minimum needed for a B average. But that was head and shoulders above what I achieved by attending and rebelling simultaneously at the Seminary College. My first trip to Israel in August 1953 turned things around. It also confirmed and solidified my (Dad's?) career choice.

What was later to become the Hayim Greenberg Institute was offered to students at Hebrew teachers' colleges across the United States. Students of the Seminary College, administratively part of the Teacher's Institute were eligible. I, with some trepidation, approached Sylvia Ettenberg, dean of the Teacher's Institute, told her that I heard that people were going to *Eretz Yisrael*, and asked her if I might go. She took a chance on me and supported my going though my record at the Seminary College left something to be desired. Dad, thrilled, offered to pay my car payments while I was gone. To get the OK from Columbia and still graduate with the bicentennial class of 1954, I took nine credits that summer of 1953, breaking my Massad continuous attendance record. I got an A+ in French that summer, replacing the failing grade I had earlier underachieved in the same subject. It marked a symbolic turnaround in my academic achievements.

Thirty budding Hebrew teachers embarked that August aboard the *SS Constitution* for nine glorious fun-filled days. For a soon-to-be twenty-one-year-old, it was unbelievable that one could order sandwiches from the galley for all of us at 2 A.M. if that was what we wanted. Chaperoned by Professor Chaim Dimitrovsky, who was very observant, the great divide and controversy in the group was between those who ate warm meals, especially fish prepared by the kitchen staff, and those whose kashrut dictated that they eat out of cans. Arriving in Naples, we visited Pompeii and Rome, had real Ital-

---

47. A high point was our presenting Handel's *Messiah* with Mom and Dad in attendance and with Dad's love of culture superseding any concern he might have had with where the lyrics were inexorably heading. We did it with the all-female Hunter College Chorus. It led to my first and only college date with a non-Jewish woman who was quite beautiful.

ian pizza (a disappointment), and then boarded the flagship of the Israeli navy, the *SS Jerusalem*. Built in 1912 as the *SS Argentina*, the *Jerusalem* was something else again. Its main task was bringing immigrants from Morocco to Israel. The ship was overpopulated, undermaintained, and generally impossible. Bedbugs occupied our beds. Slop thrown in a bucket overboard cascaded into our porthole, soiling our cabin beyond further use. The only working toilets were technically off limits, located as they were in first class. We ate *third* shift: breakfast at 9:30 A.M., lunch at 2:30 P.M., and dinner at 8:30 P.M. To avoid sleeping in our cabin we searched for any and all horizontal locations. One night, asleep on a bench in the first-class lounge (a location we were not permitted in vertically but especially horizontally) a lurch in the ship knocked dishes, glasses, and cutlery out of their cabinet, spreading the shards all over the floor. We rapidly escaped that "safe" haven fearing that we would be caught, blamed, and perhaps thrown overboard. One cannot imagine how grateful we were after four sleepless nights to see through the haze the morning sun reflected on the golden dome of Haifa's Bahai Temple.

On the ensuing trip to Jerusalem, a "Massad" peak moment happened. A rickety old bus took us up the Judean Hills on the old winding road. As we ascended, we got used to and even a bit bored by the repetitive view of the neatly terraced hills. Abruptly the driver negotiated a hairpin turn and Jerusalem in all its splendor stood suddenly and startlingly in front of us. With no advance planning for a moment our entire young lives had readied us for, we burst out singing a song we had all been raised with, "Me'al pisgat Har Hatzofim, Shalom lach Yerushalayim," "From the top of Mount Scopus, I greet you, Jerusalem." Tears rolled down my cheeks, a shiver seized my spine. It was a moment that has lasted a lifetime.

In Jerusalem, we were put up at the Hotel Salvia, across from what is today Beit Hanasi.[48] Our stay was blighted by two deaths. Moshe Cohen z"l, my roommate, came down with hepatitis, was taken to the hospital, there only to get worse and die. Because one is prohibited from keeping the dead overnight in Jerusalem, his funeral, a truly eerie experience, took place in the middle of the night on Givat Shaul to torchlight. Joel Kraemer moved into the room. I was astounded at his courage sleeping in the same place and the very same bed Moshe had occupied. Joel and I, both New Jersey natives, became and remain friends to this day. Later, the trip was

---

48. The graceful building, across from the president of Israel's residence, as of this date remains.

further marred by the unexpected death of our *madrich* (chaperone), Moshe Feinstein's wife.

It was *Tzena*[49] time in Israel, so we were allowed a limited amount of eggs and meat per week. That we did not feel deprived was in part due to Dad's having shipped with me a larger-than-steamer-trunk–sized container of canned meats and other goodies. His Jacob was not to be deprived of anything if he could help it. I went to spend Yom Kippur with Chaim Tirer, my very observant new immigrant cousin, who lived in Hadera. Conditions were difficult. Their bathroom and kitchen were both outside the house. As a house gift, I brought twenty-four cans of beef. I imagined that they would well nourish the family until my next visit. I later discovered that Chaim sold them on the black market. Perhaps he needed the cash more than the calories. Or maybe he just didn't trust the signatures of rabbis in far-off America who certified that these cans contained bonafide kosher meat.

We were blessed to have Zev Vilnay, the father of all guides in Israel, to take us on our trips, and to tell the women in our group if they needed to relieve themselves and no appropriate facilities were available, to do what Sarah our Matriarch had done. Having no sisters, it took a while until I understood what he meant. When we traveled we went luxuriously, it seemed to us, in buses. Those Americans who were training to be group leaders, etc., traveled piled on the back of trucks. We considered ourselves lucky. A high point was going to visit Kibbutz *Sdeh Boker* in the Negev[50] sitting, talking, and being photographed with Ben Gurion, who at the time had given up the premiership and "retired" there.

It was during the trip that the track I was on anyway became OK. When I returned to the United States, I had decided to devote whatever contributions I had to *Am Yisrael* (the Jewish people). To serve the Jewish people, the rabbinate seemed the best way. I was still not at that point a profound fan of the Holy One Blessed be He. I was no more "religious" than I

---

49. Austerity: "To the Israeli resident, austerity means that he must surrender ration coupons for almost all foods and get along each week on such rations as one-fifth pound of frozen meat, one-half pound of chicken, two pounds of potatoes, one-half pound of plums." Alvin Rosenfeld and Judy Shepard, "Ticket to Israel: An Informative Guide 1952." *Jerusalem Report*, March 27, 2000. The immense box of food Dad sent with me must have been worth half the gross national product (GNP) of Israel that year.

50. The southern, mostly desert part of Israel, which Ben Gurion envisioned as the future of the Jewish State, and setttled there to serve as both *chalutz* and exemplar.

had been. Even though I was to go on to be a rabbi, I was an agnostic rabbinical student. I was a cultural Zionist who got into American Jewish religion that way. I flirted with going reform, but ended up where I was. Becoming a devotee of Mordecai M. Kaplan's brand of liberal, naturalistic Judaism seemed a good way to go. That was the only way of expressing my commitment that made some sense to me. I did not see any other possibility than the rabbinate. It was also my father's direction. Dad probably would have preferred that I went to Orthodoxy's Yeshiva University, but this was good enough for him. His Jacob would be a rabbi. His dream was realized.

Finishing both Columbia (BA) and the Seminary College (BHL)[51] in June 1954, with an academic flourish, I entered the Jewish Theological Seminary, ambivalently at best, as a four-year student. That was the shortest program and was geared for those who were well prepared. Overall I had done well. I had a good background Hebraically and Judaically. The Seminary charged no tuition and provided full room and board. Taking an extra year before graduating was encouraged, and I did so. I was ordained and received my MHL in 1959.

THE JEWISH THEOLOGICAL SEMINARY

What follows, a response to an article in *Conservative Judaism,*[52] conveys something of the ambiance at the Rabbinical School of the Jewish Theological Seminary in those years of the middle and late fifties.

Reading Michael B. Greenbaum's article[53] about Professor Finkelstein jogged my memory to a Friday evening eons ago, when along with a couple of other students I was invited to Professor Finkelstein's home for Shabbat dinner. Shabbat dinner at Professor Finkelstein's apartment was legendary in an inverse sort of way. It consisted week in and week out of a very tired, diminutive piece of chicken and some canned green peas. Hardly hearty Shabbat fare for young strapping students! Certainly not the kind of "world to come" feast that we experienced at other professors' homes! Yet what was served did not matter. We were all in a state of *suspended awe*. And if my own inner experience reflected that of other students, *we were frightened out of our*

---

51. Bachelor of Hebrew Letters.

52. In a more limited form, this appeared in *Conservative Judaism,* Vol. XLIX, No. 1, Fall 1996, pp. 91–96, as a letter to the editor.

53. "Finkelstein and His Critics." *Conservative Judaism,* Vol. XLVII, No. 4, Summer 1995, pp. 3–78.

gourd! We reassured ourselves that this encounter could be survived. Others had done it before us! Professor, which is what we *always* called him (not Rabbi or Doctor, or Moreh, almost never using his last name, or, God protect us, Louis), moved the conversation along that evening by asking if we thought that *history made leaders* or on the other hand did *leaders make history*. I don't remember my garbled response, clouded as it was by my anxiety that my answer meet his approval. I was only distantly concerned with having it reflect anything that I might have thought, even had I given any thought to that momentous issue. It would have been *truly* considerate when the invitation was offered by phone to include *the question* that would be used to move the conversation along. At least then I might have prepared with the hope that the Professor would mark on a curve.

Reading Greenbaum's thoroughly researched article some forty plus years later, it seemed clear that had he been with us that evening, he would have confidently asserted that history and trends, ideas and the zeitgeist make and shape leaders and only secondarily the other way around. In his section on Understanding Finkelstein and the Seminary[54] Greenbaum covers *almost* all the bases *except one that is crucial*.

> To understand why Finkelstein pursued the path that he did, it would be helpful . . . to look at . . . the early legacy of presidential leadership which he inherited as well as the zeitgeist . . . the Seminary's mission and the institution's relationship to the Conservative Movement . . . etc.

The one base not covered is the effect of Professor Finkelstein's idiosyncratic personality and character on what happened in those years. In keeping with Gregory Bateson,[55] I suggest that an overwhelming factor that influenced the events of those times, and the history of the Conservative movement was the personality, political operating style, and methodology of the Professor himself. With a different chancellor there would have been significantly different outcomes. And his style can only really be known in

---

54. Ibid., pp. 53–54.

55. Gregory Bateson. *Mind and Nature*. New York: E.P. Dutton, 1979. ". . . it *does* matter who starts the trend. If it had been Wallace [an early evolutionist] instead of Darwin, we would have had a very different theory of evolution today. . . . It is, I claim, nonsense to say that it does not matter which individual man acted as the nucleus for the change. *It is precisely this that makes history unpredictable into the future.*"

the fullness of direct experience; in having watched him deal with friend and foe, and those between; in dealing with him head on, as difficult as that often was; in fulfilling orders; in attempting to provide feedback and struggling to interact, as we referred to it back then, "man to man," and indeed even in hearing that high-pitched voice, so easy to mimic, yet so profoundly persuasive. Though it is the stuff of historical dissertations, the Finkelstein "style" factor is only opaquely realized in memos and letters sent to him and received from him.[56] To take for historical truth speeches delivered by Seminary board members as being their own creation is questionable. That they jotted them down, yellow pad in hand, while relaxing at their swimming pools on a Sunday afternoon, thinking about the past, present, and future of Schechter-Adler's Seminary, is doubtful at best. The Professor was not of a mind to let others say things at Seminary occasions of which he did not approve. The speeches, understandably enough, most likely had a different origin.[57] I held some of them in my hands.

If you do read on, you should know that my credentials are limited and unsung in such trenchant historical essays. I was a very minor figure in the ranks at the times described in the article. I was a rabbinical student at the Jewish Theological Seminary of America from 1954 through 1959. Having had an extensive Judaic background, Ramaz, Massad, and Seminary College of Jewish Studies, I entered as a four-year student. I took an extra year, probably due to my analysis, being single, and wanting to delay a career decision. It was quite fashionable back then to take a year to devote to the "heavy" stuff, during which one studied only Talmud and Bible. I actually had Professor ("Read You, Bloom") Lieberman for Talmud for all five years. After a stint as student body president and including three summers at Camp Ramah in Wisconsin, I worked for a couple of years as an assistant in the Office of the Chancellor.

I did mostly administrative work, which in the world of Talmud research was a competency not overly valued. I was an administrative or-

---

56. Still I do take the liberty of including such a letter from myself to him, to buttress my point. Even there, the distinction between the written and oral word remains thirty years later astounding!

57. Greenbaum, "Finkelstein and His Critics," p. 60: "In a commencement address . . . Stroock was proud of the fact, therefore, that the Seminary had been, and was being, 'sponsored by men and women of varied degrees of adherence to traditional Jewish practices. Finkelstein was no less taken with this reality'." (Probably because he had more than a hand in writing the speech or at the very least approving its content.)

ganizer of the September 1957 Convocation when Chief Justice Earl Warren came to visit the Seminary for a weekend, to "study" Talmudic Ethics.
That certainly was a Finkelstein coup, a high point in what Greenbaum
describes as Finkelstein's "bridge building." It made the front page of the
New York Times with a photograph of the Chief Justice and the Chancellor.[58]
One of my assignments that Shabbat involved greeting the limousine in
which the former Chief Justice was to arrive at the Seminary. When the
rear door opened, I discovered to my surprise and dismay (*it had not been
planned for*) that next to the Chief Justice sat former President Harry S
Truman and Mrs. Truman.[59] The Trumans'[60] presence, a delightful surprise, had a downside. It upset the seating plan for lunch. Only one seat
was left at the table. It was my good fortune that Shabbat afternoon to be
the perfect solution to a politically sensitive issue of protocol. Every big-
wig and faculty member coveted a place at that table. The past president
of the student body, who was also helping administrate the weekend, would
do just fine! So it came to pass that I had Shabbat dinner with Professor
Finkelstein, Chief Justice Earl Warren, President and Mrs. Harry S Truman,
and Professor Saul Lieberman.[61] I watched in horror as Professor Lieberman
sucked tea through a sugar cube (*Mah yomru hagoyim?!*)[62] and heard President Truman, clearly oblivious to Professor Lieberman's indiscretion,

---

58. Saturday, September 14, 1957. The *Times* photograph was clearly prepared in advance
of the Sabbath, probably Friday afternoon before sundown. Professor Spiegel's "Amos vs.
Amaziah" speech was delivered at Saturday luncheon, in the presence of the surprise guest,
President Truman.

59. Legend has it that Chief Justice Warren had said to HST, "Harry, I've been invited
uptown for a good Jewish meal. Want to come along?" This demonstrates yet again the
crucial place kashrut has had in determining Jewish destiny.

60. There is some disagreement as to the presence of Mrs. Truman. Both Marjorie Wyler
z'l, at that time Director of Public Relations, and myself do *not* recall her being there. But
Professor Finkelstein's letter of September 19, 1957 to HST reads, "Dear President Truman:
Professor Shalom Speigel will share my great appreciation of your cordial letter which arrived this morning. Needless to write, your presence and that of *Mrs. Truman* added immeasurably to the weekend for all of us." As one of the "People of the Book," I will go here
with the written text, although that does not account for there being only *one* extra seat."

61. Due to Shabbat restrictions there were no photographs, so my children and grandchildren will no doubt refer to this as one of the stories told in my dotage.

62. "What will the gentiles think of us?!"

praise Professor Shalom Spiegel's magnificent speech "Amos vs. Amaziah" as being the best talk he had ever heard.[63]

I later ran the graduations of 1958 and 1959. In 1958 a serendipitous perk of being a student/administrator happened while walking along the sixth floor, where the administrative offices including Professor Finkelstein's were. Marjorie Wyler z"l, Director of Public Relations, approached and offered me the chance to be in the December 1958 edition of *Cosmopolitan* magazine, as the Jewish exemplar in their Christmas article, "Who Goes into Religion." Actually, another student, Henry Sosland, was her first choice, but his family lived in Kansas City. That was a bit rich for *Cosmo*'s budget. Palisade, New Jersey, right across the George Washington Bridge, would do just fine! So there I was in *Cosmo* sans cleavage.

In 1964, while a pulpit rabbi in Fairfield, Connecticut, Professor Finkelstein called me from retirement and asked me to help organize and direct the Herbert H. Lehman Institute of Ethics. The topic I proposed, The Role of the Rabbi, reflected my concern for an issue I later expanded in my own Ph.D., and which has been a focus of many of my efforts since. I was asked to do the following Lehman Conference, but more about that later.

So I was *not* a mover and a shaker. My memos did not have to do with the momentous issues of the Conservative movement such as, Who should sit on the law committee? or What should our relationship be to the world around us?, but concerned themselves with more mundane topics like, What do we do in case of rain on graduation day? Are the graduation gowns clean? Are there enough of them? Who will hood whom? Who will hand whom the diplomas? and that most elegant of instructions: "Tip right—grab left—shake right."[64] Is the prepared speech to be delivered by a member of the board ready? How is it to be gotten into the hands of the orator? etc. I was a foot soldier in the ranks, at most a lowly noncommissioned officer. Yet such underlings often do have a distinctive view of what is going on.

---

63. After reading Harry S Truman's biography by David McCullough I realized that HST meant what he said and said what he meant. I contacted McCullough, who said he did not know of that weekend and referred me to the Truman Archives in Independence, Missouri. I offered them a copy of "Amos vs. Amaziah" which I had saved all these years, in return for whatever they had about that weekend. I now have in my possession copies of the correspondence between Professors Finkelstein and Spiegel, and later Chancellor of the Seminary Gershon Cohen and President Truman.

64. The instruction meant that the graduate was to tip his mortarboard with his right hand, reach for the diploma with his left, and shake hands correctly.

It is with some trepidation, even now, that I offer these observations/ remarks. Professor Finkelstein was in many ways a great man, possessed of vision, charisma, and dedication. As Lord Hailsham said of Churchill, "He was a man of genius and like all men of genius, there are dark patches and there are bright patches."[65] Like each of us, Professor Finkelstein was a "both-and" experience, possessed of great virtues and great flaws. Much of what went on in those years and our inheritance from that time was a reflection of and a response to who Professor Finkelstein was, and how he chose to run things and interface with the Seminary he led, the Rabbinical Assembly he parried with, and the world around him in which he longed to be a potent force.

The Seminary in Professor Finkelstein's era was a very *Byzantine* place.[66] Indirectness and often intrigue were dominant modus operandi. Open and direct communication, meaning communication that was somewhat consistent over time and similar with different people, was a rarity. There were layers upon layers behind other layers intertwined with still other layers in virtually every message. Messages given to one person were often quite different in content and mood than those given to another. A careful reading of many of the events that Greenbaum describes from that period testifies to that. There were power ploys that involved flattery, people being told what it was thought useful for them to hear, co-opting and then neutralizing any opposition that *seemed* to threaten the Seminary's position at the apex of the triangle that was the Conservative movement. Even letting everyone on the elevator before you,[67] though it may have been genuinely well intended, did not necessarily convey a message of respect. A greater feeling of respect might have been engendered had Professor Finkelstein had a different, more direct style, and had the people he dealt with had the experience of being treated as ends as well as means.

---

65. Public television's *The Churchills*. Boston, MA: WGBH and Brooks Associates.

66. That Byzantine was not a synonym for Jewish, I learned years later when I became involved through the gracious good offices of Rabbi Joseph Glaser *z"l* with the Central Conference of American Rabbis. I was astonished that Jewish organizations did not have to be marked by intrigue, expediency, dissimulation, and Machiavellian strategies. One could be clear, differ with, yet respect one's "adversaries" and work with them. It was an interesting lesson in man making history.

67. Part of the legendary Finkelstein persona.

Given that Byzantine atmosphere, there *were* a number of messages that were extremely clear. Their meaning was the opposite of respect.

Pulpit rabbis, as a group, though educated by the Seminary, were *not* respected. The Seminary certainly took little responsibility for producing those who aroused Professor Finkelstein's fears[68] of being "at the mercy of people who know nothing." The unknowing included virtually all those Seminary graduates who struggled in the vineyard, and certainly those who hoped to do so. It is a curious comment on the education the Seminary provided and the purpose of that education. The usefulness of the "unknowing," as Greenbaum correctly points out, was in providing financial support for the Seminary. It is remarkable that the pulpit rabbis even raised as much as they did, given the contempt in which they were held. It is interesting to note that a number of times the relationship between the Seminary and the Rabbinical Assembly is described as that of mother and child [69] with the hope that mother would treat the child, who wanted to be seen as a grown-up, in a more respectful manner. Mother was gracious, though unbending, as long as she was deferred to.

If Seminary graduates were not treated with respect they at least were perceived as a potential danger, which I suppose is respect of a certain kind. Students, on the other hand, knew up close what it was to be infantilized by "mother." First, we were told over and over and over again, in more ways than we could count, that what we were studying for, i.e., the Pulpit Rabbinate, was a second- if not third-rate occupation. It was clear that "mother" did not love or respect all her student children equally. Those who showed promise as world-class scholars got the cream skimmed off the milk. Professor Lieberman was at best if not contemptuous at least condescending towards the students he taught and the ordination diplomas he signed. And Professor Finkelstein seemed to revere Professor Lieberman and all he stood for.

When I entered graduate school in psychology and was told by our professors at orientation that they hoped we would all be published by the end of the first year, I almost fell through the floor! At the Seminary we joked that we were not to publish until we were eighty-five, and then *only* in mimeograph.

Our Seminary curriculum, even with its Wissenchaft imprint, was almost completely unrelated to the pulpits and people for whom we were

---

68. Greenbaum, "Finkelstein and His Critics," p. 57.

69. Ibid., pp. 31, 32.

ostensibly being trained. Being on the faculty at a Rabbinic Training Institute years later, it was mind-boggling to discover as I sat in on courses that Talmud, Bible, and, yes, even modern Hebrew literature could be taught with integrity for the text, respect for those learning, and in a way in which the pulpit rabbi might make good use of the material in the work in which he/she was engaged. Among the great courses we had back then, only a few (most notably Professor Shalom Spiegel's Prayerbook course) were directly relevant to our future work. Even Spiegel's Jeremiah and medieval Hebrew poetry, great as they were, and models as they were of how to think and study, were usable mostly if one tried to teach them in miniature as it were. They remain high points in my life. I would not have missed them for the world, yet they were only obliquely oriented towards what we would be doing when we got out.

When I think of a teacher whose work could be crucially useful in the pulpit and who later "built bridges" to the wider world around the Seminary, I remain astonished at the implicit disrespect in which Professor Abraham J. Heschel was held in those days. He was allowed to teach a great deal in the Seminary College, where as an undergraduate, I had him often. In the Rabbinical School, where the prestige was, he was limited to a total of forty-five minutes in one of our four years. Students read *Time* magazine, opened their mail, and otherwise demeaned the man and his teachings in a way they would not have dared with other professors who were held in higher institutional respect.

What was then the purpose of our education? For the scholarly, it was to be in a yeshiva, albeit a Wissenschaft yeshiva. That was not a bad purpose in the context of the immediate post–World War II world. We all received in many ways a superb Jewish education for which I remain eternally grateful.[70] But it was not an education tailored to meet the world mission of the Seminary or the Jewish mission exemplified in Greenbaum's article by the Rabbinical Assembly. To believe the public hype and to ignore the fact of what was really going on inside the institution is to be unduly influenced by outdated press releases. The Institute for Religious and Social Studies might have been useful in keeping the trustees interested and happy

---

70. It is interesting to note that we spent at minimum four years, and for some six, and with ordination got a master's degree. It took me five years to get a Ph.D. in Clinical Psychology and that included a thesis that was supposed to be an original contribution to science. Perhaps this is another indication of the fear of the "unknowing."

and giving the Seminary a place in the broader world. It had little or nothing to do with the student body.

It is remarkable that the world-shaking things being done by the Institute for Religious and Social Studies and the Conference on Science Religion and Philosophy were shielded from and largely irrelevant to the student body. If Judaism was to be a force in the world, we clearly were not to be a part of that force. The closest we came to the work of the Institute for Religious and Social Studies was literally a fence. On Tuesdays we were aware that the Institute was in session when the dining room was partitioned off by screens demarcating the boundary between the Institute participants and the students. A couple of tables were left for the students on one side of the partition. We were instructed to come to the cafeteria early so we might find a seat and eat behind the partition, without disturbing the Institute's proceedings.

It is mind-boggling to imagine how an idealistic student body told that the pulpit was not the meaningful place to be might have been inspired if Professor Finkelstein had enlisted it in the Seminary's crucial mission to the world. Imagine the excitement that could have been ignited in the student body if we would have had posed to us the task of making Judaism a vital force in the western world. That would have been a challenge worthy of young idealistic rabbinical students. That what we were being trained to do was diminished and that what the Seminary said it was doing was kept from us, bespeaks either a lack in leadership, dissimulation of serious proportions, or, more benignly, an inability to make any sort of link between goals and the means whereby those goals might be achieved. Thus we were a student body taught disrespect for our chosen profession and kept from what was *ostensibly* the mission of the institution.

Magnificent opportunities were wasted in those years. The opportunity for the Seminary to work hand in respectful hand with its own graduates in the Rabbinical Assembly to plant and shape the future of Conservative Judaism in America was lost at a time when the soil was most fertile. The opportunity to inspire the generations of students who went through the Seminary at that time, most of whom had *significantly* wider and deeper Jewish backgrounds and educations than later generations, and to use them in the "bridge building" mission to the wider world was also lost. For failing in these, leadership has to take its portion of responsibility. And Professor Finkelstein was at the apex of that leadership. Those missed opportunities were more a result of Professor Finkelstein's personal leadership style than of the zeitgeist or trends.

Professor may have had a sense of his own responsibility in these matters. In a speech[71] delivered at the Herbert H. Lehman Institute of Ethics in 1964, Professor Finkelstein offered:

> Well, somewhere along in 1950, I lost my nerve . . . I somehow felt that this was not something that I could see through, and there I stopped pressing for it really. I kept on talking about it, . . . but I didn't press for it very hard any more after about 1952 or 1953. . . . I know one of the reasons that I lost my nerve was—when I say "I," I put it in the first person . . . the Seminary wouldn't do it if the man who happened to be the chief clerk felt his hands heavy. So, we didn't do it. But, . . . one of the reasons that it fell through was because I had taken the short road instead of the long road . . . the long road would have been to try to persuade the members of the Rabbinical Assembly of the importance of what we were trying to do, of what it really meant and then, to do it. I tried to do the short road so we could call the first steps, but we couldn't do the main step because the whole Rabbinical Assembly had never been persuaded.

As I read the words thirty years later, I wondered, what was his purpose? Was it a straight message, or was it just another? . . . He clearly believed that leaders make history and not the other way around. More than history influenced the man, he influenced the history of his days and ours.

The following personal experience and proof texts are testimony what it was like for a foot soldier to deal with the Professor's Byzantine leadership style.

In early 1963 Professor Finkelstein asked me to organize the Herbert H. Lehman Institute of Ethics Conference on the Moral Implications of the Rabbinate, scheduled for that December. The topic I proposed and approved was "On Being a Rabbi." It went off very well and was considered a great success.

I later received the following letter, dated April 8, 1965, from Dr. Finkelstein.

> Dear Jack,
>
> It is important for us to have a conversation so that we can begin planning for the next Morals Conference which I hope will take place this

---

71. Pp. 11–13 of a carbon copy transcription. To the best of the author's knowledge, this was never published.

September. I would appreciate it very much indeed if you came in to see
me and would suggest Thursday, April 15th at 2:30 P.M. as a convenient hour.

With best wishes,

Affectionately, as ever,

Louis Finkelstein

Expecting to discuss the topic and format for the next conference, I
was sandbagged instead by being told that Professor Finkelstein wanted Rabbi
Eugene Wiener[72] to do the next conference with me. I had no idea why. Nor
was I enlightened as to what the motive might be. I wondered what was
wrong. Had I made some gross mistake? What was going on anyway? It felt
like a familiar maneuver, setting two young rabbis in competition with each
other, but beyond that I was totally puzzled as to what was in it for the Professor. I told him that if he wanted Gene to do the Conference that would be
OK with me, but it was one or the other and not both of us. I was asked to
continue the planning, but the conference had its own Byzantine denoue-
ment. I was very puzzled and wrote Professor Finkelstein the following letter, which I submit in its entirety:

October 15, 1965, *Chol HaMoed Sukkot*[73]

Dear Professor:

I was dismayed and more than a little surprised by what happened in
your office the other evening. There may indeed be reasons, human and
financial, for what happened that I do not know about, but that does not
change what happened, and how it happened.

If it is your desire that I continue to have the responsibility for the
forthcoming conference, I shall of course do all in my power to guarantee
its success. I do wish first to explain my understanding of what took place
prior to Wednesday evening.

When I originally accepted the responsibility for the first conference,
I did so for a number of reasons. Firstly, I believed the conferences to be
of great benefit to the men of the Rabbinical Assembly, whom I respect
greatly, and with whom I am privileged to work closely. If there was anything I could do to help the conferences be even better, I wished to do it.

---

72. Later to become Professor of Sociology at Haifa University. We had prepared for
Professor Lieberman's Talmud sessions together and had become good friends.

73. *Chol HaMoed*: The middle days of the Jewish festival of thanksgiving, in the fall, which
follows the High Holydays.

Second, I hold you personally in great respect and wished to be of assistance in forwarding the work you are doing. (I must say that I considered it a great boon to have been able to work out a number of things that had been problems in our relationship from years back, and to establish a relationship marked by trust and loyalty.) I accepted your gracious offer of responsibility for the second conference, because the first went well, and I thought that more could still be done.

After accepting the task of the conference I set about thinking about what kind of conference it should be, keeping in mind your own expressed desire to involve men from the academic community. I thought that a conference could be held which would reflect well on the Seminary and benefit my colleagues, if we could help the men meet some of the challenges we face in the day-to-day pulpit. What came forth after a great deal of thinking and discussion was a conference in which our men would be helped to meet the challenge of changing the community in the light of the teachings of Judaism. This was the plan that was brought to you, and after a number of meetings, the last with Prof. Sol Levine,[74] an outline of the conference was decided upon and it was that outline that Renee[75] and I were working on in good faith. Renee and I were told that we had a specific budget to work with and we proceeded upon that understanding. Prof. Levine, who was quite impressed with meeting you, and who is and remains an unusually capable person, involved himself quite enthusiastically in doing what he could to help the conference proceed. I had made the suggestion that he serve as a co-chairman of the conference along with one of our men, such as Rabbi Everett Gendler. As agreed upon in your office the conference was to have two parts. First, there would be a presentation by those working with the disadvantaged, of what the problems were, what the expectations of the disadvantaged were, and what the solutions might be. The second part was to involve experts from the academic community who knew community organization and structure, and who could help the men explore ways in which they could move ethical ideas into practical application in their own communities. The job of these experts was not to lead discussion groups, but share their depth of knowledge with the men of the Rabbinical Assembly. Certainly such interdisci-

74. Sol Levine, at that time Professor at Harvard, later at Johns Hopkins, had been a keynote speaker at the previous Herbert H. Lehman Institute of Ethics Conference, run by the author.

75. Renee Gutman, a Seminary administrator, assigned by Dr. Finkelstein to work with me.

plinary sharing of knowledge is nothing new in our country. Many business executives and other highly trained specialists return to institutes such as Aspen and others in order to perfect their ways of viewing and moving.

Wednesday evening the carpet was pulled out from under this particular conference structure. A structure which I still believe would have made the conference unusually fruitful and a credit to the Seminary.

I still do not understand why what happened Wednesday happened. I can only surmise that there may have been reactions and possible repercussions elsewhere within the Seminary.

It would seem to me that there are at least two alternatives at the present time. First, would be the availability of $1000 which would enable the conference to go on as originally planned. If that is not within the realm of possibility, then I would suggest that we have six presentations, with an open discussion to follow each. This would enable the men to have some contact with each of our academics and would mean that they could spend more time with a larger group.

I shall of course make myself available if you wish to discuss this further.

Looking forward to hearing from you, I remain

Sincerely,

Jack H Bloom

I was certainly not the only one ever to be confronted by Dr. Finkelstein's Byzantine indirectness. If members of the Rabbinical Assembly had a myopic view of things,[76] it may have been the result of sand being repeatedly thrown in their collective face. Promises were made, assurances given, perhaps all in good faith, but then were not kept, perhaps because something else interfered. This often led to the sense of having been coopted, infantilized, and manipulated.

The Professor was a great man, driven by a grand personal vision. Yet what he did on one hand, he often undercut with the other. Perhaps that was an outcome of always gazing forward and backward simultaneously. How else to explain his vision of reaching out to the world, and yet considering one of his great achievements, bringing to the Seminary the man he personally adored, Professor Saul Lieberman, whose parochial interests were not in sync with Professor Finkelstein's "bridge building." Hadassah Davis,[77] his

---

76. Greenbaum, "Finkelstein and His Critics," p. 64.

77. Louis Finkelstein. "My Father." *Conservative Judaism*, Vol. XLVII, No. 4, Summer 1995, p. 80.

daughter, put it quite touchingly, "My father would not embarrass a student, yet how does one fathom his 'I want to make the world a better place!'[78] and yet demeaning as 'unknowing' those he was responsible for educating to do the task. It is a mystery and a reflection of the idiosyncrasies of his personhood."

Winston Churchill was correct: *History is biography.*[79] The Conservative movement is the inheritor of Professor Finkelstein's biography. It is a notable and distinguished biography, of which we may be proud, and at the same time, we can wish it had been different.

For my part I wish I had the answer that Shabbat eve so many years ago. I might have at least *sounded* intelligent.

Let his memory be a blessing.

THE BIG BAD FOX AND THE GOOD LITTLE FOX WHO OUTFOXED HIM

With the exception of a few pleasantries when our paths inadvertently crossed, I have not spoken with Seymour Fox since the spring day in 1958 when I told him, following three summers at Ramah, that I would not be going to Ramah in the Poconos as Assistant Director and *Rosh Machon*.[80] Fox was a critical person in my days at the Seminary. He was a brilliant, controlling, often charismatic, generally feared, and sometimes detested figure. At the end of my first year in rabbinical school, I was elected treasurer of the student body on an anti-Fox platform in what otherwise amounted to a Fox sweep. He soon enough converted me so that I became one of his "fair-haired" disciples. Going to "his" camp Ramah Wisconsin became a foregone conclusion the summer of 1955. I succeeded him the following year as president of the student body. In September of 1957, I was selected by him as his assistant in the Office of the Chancellor, at the munificent sum of $2500 per annum. I was coming off a diet supported by speed pills and had lost thirty-five pounds. I went from a 48 long to a 44 long suit size, and was trim for the first time in my memory. Getting off the Dexedrine added to feelings of depression and I spent long periods of time, during the summer of 1957, hating what I was doing as *Rosh Machon* and taking extended naps. I had taken

---

78. Davis quote, in ibid.

79. Public television's *The Churchills*.

80. In charge of the high school teenage program.

the following year as an extra year with just Talmud and Bible classes.[81] I was also coming off a failed romance with Sarah Fisher. Sarah and I were really good friends and had developed a somewhat romantic relationship. We broke off, and I went with Marcia Bender, who was only nice to me. Then, under Seymour Fox's guidance and tutelage, he clearly instructed me to go back with Sarah, and I took his direction. With a total lack of grace and decency, I broke off with Marcia, who was to spend the summer at Camp Ramah and whom I treated as if she was not there.[82] The second time with Sarah didn't work. Though at one time I asked Sarah to marry me, she showed good judgment, doing us both a great favor, by turning me down. Though a good friendship, it would not have been a good match.

My psychotherapy began soon after I started working with Fox. The working relationship with Seymour was tumultuous and degrading, as the personal relationship had been. I often felt both abused and crazy. Fox had earlier suggested that psychotherapy might be appropriate (he was right!) and wanted to suggest the therapist. I knew that made no sense. I turned instead to Rebecca Imber, who had been the camp psychologist the previous summer and with whom I had talked a good deal. She suggested Seymour Fuchsman, with whom I spent the next five and more years in therapy.[83] At my first interview, the good Seymour determined that we would see each other three times a week at a fee of $15 per session, close to $200 per month, no insurance, nothing. How I would pay I did not know. What I did know was that I needed it. Therapy with Seymour Fuchsman was a terrific experience. I am eternally grateful to him.

We spent the first year and a half exploring my relationships with my father and with Fox, which were inextricably intertwined. My father could be overwhelming and I perceived Fox as doubly and triply so. The working relationship with Fox ended with an "almost" confrontation in front of the Chancellor when Fox accused me of lying about some letters that the Chancellor had asked me to bring into his office for his signature. It was the first time I confronted Fox, saying, "If you don't believe me that he asked for them,

---

81. Due to this quirk, I had Professor Lieberman as Talmud professor for all five years I was at JTS.

82. Forty years later, I apologized to Marcia for my terrible behavior and she shared with me how much it had hurt her at the time, and the effects it had. It took a long time. I'm glad we got to do it in this lifetime.

83. Odd that the nemesis and the cure both had essentially the same name.

let's go in and find out." He refused to do that. From that moment I was cut off by Fox, given absolutely nothing to do. I sat at my desk empty-handed until I was asked to do the graduation of 1958 under the administrative direction of David Kogen[84] and Harriet Catlin.[85] The graduation of 1958 was immensely successful. It was the smoothest, most efficient the Seminary had experienced in many years. Running it restored my self-respect and my sense of my own competency. It also put me in touch with all levels of the Seminary hierarchy who respected my work greatly and made me realize that there was life without Fox.

I was the first of the Fox entourage to break with him and to demonstrate, as ridiculous as it sounds, that one could survive the break. Fox was utterly vicious in maintaining that if you were with him a golden future awaited you, but if you broke with him there would be no future for you in the American Jewish Community, certainly the Jewish educational community. You were a dead duck.[86]

I spent hours talking to Carl Friedman *z"l*, roommate of Ismar Schorsch[87] and my bathroom mate, who was later killed in an automobile crash, reassuring him that there was a future after Fox. "Hey you can survive in Jewish education without Seymour. Look at me! I'm doing OK. He doesn't control everything and everyone."

RAMAH

I spent the summers of 1955–1957 before breaking from Fox at Camp Ramah in Wisconsin. Wisconsin was the camp the Fox loyalists went

---

84. David, whom I remembered from when I was a little boy at Massad, always a true *mentsch*, later became a Vice-Chancellor of the Seminary. He was at the time a redemptive figure for me.

85. The Seminary's Director of Special Projects. Our relationship was superb. Forty-two years later her response to my High Holyday card was, "I remember you as my favorite student at JTS."

86. Fox indeed did blackball me from any Ramah employment until the mid-1960s. My good friend Ray Arzt, head of Ramah in Palmer, Massachusetts, who lived in Fairfield, Connecticut, when I was rabbi there, got the OK to bring me back innocuously as head of *Tarbut* (culture) for the waiters. It was a politically safe sinecure that allowed our families, always close, to spend the summers together.

87. At the time of this writing, Chancellor of the Seminary.

to. They were important years, but not nearly as formative as my Massad years. They were also marked by burgeoning internal conflict.

Fox, influenced by Dr. Joseph Schwab[88] of the University of Chicago, instituted a dynamic, supposedly egalitarian model, centered on "self-government" and espousing a "non-competitive" environment. The major competition in camp was evaluating which counselor created the most non-competitive bunk.

Ramah was an attempt to deal with a totally different population than Massad. It was about creating a renaissance in American Jewish life in a conservative mold. At its best, Ramah imparted to its campers a sense of being a revolutionary. But Hebrew and *Eretz Yisrael* were not what the revolution was about. It was about what campers were going to do in the Conservative American Jewish synagogue they were returning to in a few weeks. How they would maintain the religious changes, prayer, and keeping kosher back home, given the home and synagogue mores they were returning to, was what was on the agenda. Not having the critical mass of day school attendees and kids from intense Hebraic backgrounds, Ramah was dealing with, at best, the products of the three-day-a-week Hebrew school of the 1940s and 1950s. These youngsters had only the bare rudiments of Hebrew. They knew precious little of what it meant to be an observant Jew. The discussion about how and where and when to be kosher never existed at Massad. Keeping kosher was a given. At Ramah you were talking about what you were going to do when you went back to your family, and you want to keep kosher and Mom and Dad don't. What are you going to do when you go back to your *shul* and the rabbi has readings in English and you want to have a service just like you had at Ramah. How are you going to forward your Jewish education over the winter when you know more than any of the kids in your Talmud Torah, and there are no facilities available. Massad never faced that challenge.

The staff were Seminary students, largely ex-Massad types. There *was* disquiet about the downgrading and subsequent lack of Hebrew. The concern for Hebrew was a remnant brought over by those who came from Massad. In the early years there was a prohibition on English in the public arena at Ramah and announcements were in Hebrew with the tacit under-

---

88. Dr. Joseph Schwab was William Rainey Professor of Natural Sciences and Professor of Education at the University of Chicago, in the 1950s. He served in Fox's time as a consultant to Camp Ramah.

standing that counselors would translate for the campers. Ramah's understandable position was that English was imperative to reach the population attending. English was also a statement about "religion" being moved to the top of the pyramid, far above Hebrew. A part of me bought that. A part of me had trouble with it. In Massad "religion" and prayer were background. In Ramah it was very much foreground. That change brought me some discomfort. My initial response was, as it was a few years later, to make every effort to beautify and make prayer more relevant. It was a way of dealing with my inner struggle.

Great things did happen at Ramah. I was destined to use Ramah extensively in my pulpit work, though a good deal of what I did came from Massad.

INDECISION

During my Seminary career there were times when I thought I did not want to be a pulpit rabbi. The tenor of the Seminary demeaned the pulpit rabbinate. A career as scholar and even one in administration within the Seminary hierarchy seemed more greatly to be desired.

I spent some time one summer trying to sell Rassco[89] shares to rabbis. Hated it. Nothing came of it.

I applied to the William Alanson White Institute for their Analytic Training Program and was interviewed by no less than the great Rollo May. He came to the correct conclusion that I was not clear enough about what I wanted and was inappropriate for acceptance.

I took a six-credit summer psychology course at Columbia. To my surprise it was all about eyes and ears and how the brain works and none of that good stuff I was involved with in therapy. I stood one day that late summer at 121st Street and Broadway with the catalogs of New York University, Columbia, and City University in my hands. Each listed statistics among the courses one would have to take to get a Ph.D. in Clinical Psychology. Statistics gave me agita. One by one I ceremoniously dropped the catalogs in that big wire wastebasket and gave up going into psychology. Ten years later it would be a different story. If other so-and-so's could get through statistics, so could I.

By 1958 psychotherapy had "freed" me to become considerably less observant in terms of diet and driving on Shabbat. With what I perceived to

---

89. An Israeli building corporation.

be Fuchsman's advice,[90] I would not park the car too close to the Seminary, nor bring a cheeseburger into the dorm. I avoided doing anything to provoke the religious establishment at JTS. An example: In the late summer of 1958, I was invited to a Saturday night Labor Day weekend dance at Birchwood Country Club in Westport, Connecticut. I rented a tux, but chose to go home to get dressed and leave more inconspicuously from there. To my surprise, I discovered that though I left for Connecticut long before Shabbat was out, Dad had no trouble with my setting my own parameters for observance. As I write this, I'm aware of its importance in my life since I do remember it.

Instead of Ramah that summer I spent most of the summer in the city, with the exception of ten glorious days at Fire Island. I went alone. Nobody, but nobody, knew me. Anonymity reigned. I rented a little room. When asked the usual, "What do you do?" I said I was a low-level administrator at the Seminary, which was partially true, but carefully omitted that I was a soon-to-be ordained rabbinical student. I ate hamburgers and cheeseburgers with abandon. I heard "Volare"[91] sung a million times. I took a game of Scrabble along with me as a way of meeting women on the beach. This was how I met Muriel, a schoolteacher, ten years older than I, who by my limited standards was quite a hot dish. I dated her from Fire Island to sometime into my weekend pulpit in Ramsey, New Jersey.

The year 1958–1959 was a year that shall live in indecision. For my senior year I took a weekend pulpit at the newly formed Jewish Community Center in Ramsey, New Jersey.[92] It was my first pulpit experience and I *loved* it. On the way up to Ramsey for Friday night services, I would meet my brother Norman and we would eat at a diner with my hoping not to be noticed or identified there, since it was, after all, Shabbat. I was put up at a

---

90. It is of interest to note that all the time I worked with Fuchsman, I perceived him to be a totally secular Jew, who cared *nothing* for ritual and observance. Years later in 1969 when I was a psychology intern at the Veterans Administration Hospital in Montrose, New York, I went to visit Seymour who lived nearby and was terminally ill on a Friday afternoon. To my great shock there were candles and challah ready for Shabbat and bookshelves full of Jewish books. So much for perception.

91. A song, excruciatingly popular that summer.

92. Kind of interesting—Ramaz, Ramah, Ramsey—oh well! In 1997 my stepdaughter and her family moved to Ramsey. I looked up the Jewish Community Center of Ramsey. No Jewish community existed in Ramsey. Sic Transit Gloria.

motel in Ramsey, did services on Friday night and some tutoring, and a very occasional service on Saturday morning. I cheated on observance that year, riding on Shabbat and doing all sorts of illicit things. But I liked being a weekend rabbi, so going into a pulpit did not look too bad.

It was December of that year that the *Cosmopolitan* article "Jack Bloom Future Rabbi" appeared. I learned that a short article distilled from a two-hour interview could reflect the interviewer and not the interviewee. An offhand remark plucked out of context by the interviewer could take on a life and have an effect all its own. I had said in response to the question "What is practical theology?" that our teacher, Max Arzt, taught us "not to sit crosslegged in the pulpit." I meant it as a throwaway charming line. Max, father to my lifelong friend Ray Arzt, felt diminished and was deeply hurt. Wherever he is studying and teaching in the Academy on High, I ask his forgiveness and want him to know that I learned from that experience to be more careful in the future.[93]

The "voluntary" draft, run by the Rabbinical Assembly to provide chaplains for the armed services from among the seniors to be ordained, still existed. So while moving towards graduation, I simultaneously moved toward becoming a chaplain in the U.S. Navy.[94] I was in the middle of my therapy at that time which further complicated things. Though all the paperwork and everything was done, and I had even been interviewed by Rear Admiral Joshua Goldberg, who until then was the highest-ranking Jewish military chaplain, at the last moment I decided to ask for and got a one-year deferment.

One day, I was approached by Wolfe Kelman at the door to the sixth-floor elevator saying he wanted to talk to me about coming to work for the Rabbinical Assembly. After mentioning it to me, Wolfe never said another word. I assume I was blackballed by the aforementioned Seymour Fox who hung out with Wolfe.

I was also applying to be assistant rabbi at the Society for the Advancement of Judaism. I often wonder how my life would have been differ-

---

93. Not careful enough. In June 2000, attending a family Bat Mitzvah at Congregation Kehillath Israel in Boston, MA, I was innocently sitting on a pulpit chair, waiting to be called to lift the Torah, when one of the officers raced breathlessly over to me and notified me that "at *KT*, we don't sit crosslegged on the pulpit." I meekly straightened my legs as Max Arzt's lovable face filled my memory.

94. I sometimes wish I had done that, as I sometimes wish that in 1952 I had gone into the six-month U.S. Army program that I was eligible for and which would have solved my Korean War problem. So be it. Life is where we end up while going somewhere else.

ent if what was supposed to happen did happen. I liked the thought of getting a job in New York City, so I could continue my therapy. The Navy processing could continue, even if I got a deferment, which was to be for one year only. The SAJ was looking for an assistant rabbi for Jack Cohen. The assistant's job description was to be in charge of youth work. This was the mother congregation of the Reconstructionist movement, founded by Mordecai M. Kaplan[95] with whom I had a good relationship. I was the perfect candidate. They wanted someone with youth experience. I had been head of the *Machon*, the teenage program at Ramah, and had a lot of youth experience. Everyone assumed they wanted a Reconstructionist. I was the outspoken Reconstructionist in the student body. The other applicant was shy to the point of being reclusive, very traditional with virtually no experience in youth work. He was a most unlikely candidate. Anticipating my new role, I rented a newly built apartment on Columbus Avenue near 96th Street. It all seemed set: Assistant at the SAJ, my list of single women in New York City still viable, continuing my psychotherapy, and a two-year deferment (one at a time) in hand. Soon after ordination, I was an officiant on July 3, 1959, at the wedding of beloved friends Joel and Ann Zaiman at Congregation Beth El in New Rochelle, New York. That was also the night of the SAJ board meeting ratifying my new position. Calling Jack Cohen ruined a perfectly nice wedding reception with wonderful hors d'oeuvres. The board had chosen the other guy. (To the best of my recollection he lasted three months!) Stunned, I asked Jack Cohen, "Why? Why? Why?" His answer, elegantly simple, was, "That's how boards are!" It may be how boards are, but it sure changed the direction of my life. I was scheduled to go to St. Louis the next day to court my future wife. When I got back in mid-July with the High Holydays approaching, there I was, unemployed.

PAYING OFF MY DEBT TO DAD:
TEN YEARS IN THE PULPIT

The Rabbinical Assembly office, where Wolfe Kelman, Executive Vice President and at the time placement director reigned, had a map which showed how far every town in the United States was from Times Square. There were three geographically desirable locations: Port Washington and Smithtown on Long Island, and a job as assistant to Rabbi Harry Nelson at

---

95. Kaplan was the only professor at JTS who began each class with a prayer.

Congregation Rodeph Sholom in Bridgeport, Connecticut. Sam Klein, a slightly more senior colleague was interviewing there, so I was prohibited from calling. It was late in the season and getting later. One day Wolfe Kelman walked by me in the cafeteria and, without breaking stride, gave me the OK to call Harry Nelson. Nelson told me that a board meeting was imminent that would change the job definition. And so it was. At that fateful board meeting the job title was changed from Assistant to Rabbi Harry Nelson in Charge of Suburban Congregation in Fairfield, to Rabbi of Fairfield Jewish Community Group and Assistant to Rabbi Harry Nelson. Only words. But words make a difference.

I drove up to Bridgeport for the interview. The route Nelson had me take led me to believe that Bridgeport was a bucolic New England town. Partial images can deceive. The two boards who interviewed me were strikingly different. The Rodeph Sholom Board was decked out on a sultry summer night in jackets and ties. The Fairfield Jewish Community Group Board (it wasn't Beth El yet—I chose that name later) in slacks and polo shirts. The interview went OK. I had to handle one curve ball about whether I would ride to the beach on Shabbat. I'm not sure exactly what I answered but I didn't get impaled on my answer. I met briefly with Harry Nelson in his office, presumably to avoid his veto. While the boards were conferring as to my suitability, Chuck Engelberg of the Fairfield Community Group took me to see their "facilities." I was horrified to see a derelict, rodent-infested building in the midst of overgrown vegetation. My first thought was, "My God, they expect me to mow the lawn." But it was mid-summer and the job met enough of my criteria. It *was* a job. It was an *hour* from New York City, my therapist, and those young women who had won a place in my datebook. It was a *one*-year job, as the Navy still awaited me. The school was to be run by the educational director of Rodeph Sholom so I *wasn't* going to be the principal, or so I thought. About all the Fairfield group with its 110 members had was a relationship with Congregation Rodeph Sholom and not much else. So we settled on $7500 a year, half paid by each group, and away we went.

I also met Harry Nelson's main criterion, which was staying out of his hair. It became increasingly clear as time went on that Nelson did not want an assistant. An assistant had been forced on him by his board after he suffered a massive heart attack.

As the rabbi of the suburban congregation I had my own place, where I was for Sabbath and Holidays. As his assistant I visited the hospital, though he felt he had to visit it immediately after me, a stance which I now understand, though at the time resented as a comment on my inadequacies. It of course had nothing to do with that. I taught adult education and was to be involved with the adult singles group, a responsibility which ended abruptly when I came back from Thanksgiving weekend in St. Louis, engaged. I attended staff meetings at Rodeph Sholom, and learned something about how this master rabbi operated. Nelson would make a program suggestion. The staff member at whom it was directed would respond by saying that it was impossible to implement. Two or three weeks later, that staff member would suggest the very same program and Nelson would compliment him on his originality and creativity. I did deliver one or two sermons at times when Beth El was not having services. I didn't diminish his work load. Nor did he really want it diminished. I turned out to be quite popular and as Harry weakened this became a problem for him. Harry was one of America's great pulpit rabbis. Since coming to Bridgeport in 1934, he had built a congregation of over twelve hundred families, which was a truly quality institution in every way. But after his heart attack, he was never the same. He died much weakened in 1964, awaiting surgery which might have saved a great man.

The first congregational affair I went to was a *Selichot*[96] night celebration held by the Fairfield Group, at the uniquely inappropriately named, "Porky Manero's." I was offered a choice that night which determined my behavior for the next ten years. "Rabbi, do you want fish or prime rib?" Calculating my position as an assistant rabbi, I answered after some moments of hesitation, "Fish." The dinner was followed by everyone attending Selichot services at Rodeph Sholom, where I delivered my first sermon. When Harry Nelson berated the congregation for having a non-kosher affair at Porky Manero's, I could at least claim that I opted for fish.

Being the rabbi of Congregation Beth El, 1959–1969, was an interesting though mixed experience. My paternal ancestry seemed to determine that I would be single-minded in some ways, while conflicted religiously in others. Overall, I enjoyed my first years in the pulpit. Despite occasional bloopers,[97] I was good at the work. In a difficult situation with a young con-

---

96. A Saturday night penitential service that ushers in the High Holydays.

97. Doing my first wedding back in 1960, I began my wedding talk to Harold and Anita Rappoport with, "*Harriet* and Anita." In doing the seven blessings in English, I solemnly intoned, "Grant perfect joy to these loving companions, as you did to Adam and Eve in the garden of *evil*." I followed those two with, "Therefore by virtue of the authority vested in me by the State of *Israel*, I now pronounce you . . ." Three bloopers in a single wedding! Despite these, Harold and Anita Rappoport of Fairfield, Connecticut, are still happily married, and it was never mentioned during contract negotiations.

gregation not knowing what either party expected we somehow moved along. Without a usable building, High Holyday services were held at the Masonic Temple. Our ritual chairman's main qualification for that illustrious post was that he had a truck with which folding chairs could be moved from one location to another and being a contractor he had no objection to the loading and "schlepping." Religious school was at Osborn Hill, a local public school, courtesy of the generosity of Miss Elizabeth Banks, the principal. We had to be very careful not to test her generosity too much by how we left the place each day.

We started building a structure at the site of the derelict shack, which ended up costing $275,000. As decisions about the building took place, my belief in congregational autonomy, democracy, and that this was really their synagogue and not mine was gradually undermined. Doubts about the congregational polity crept in. Who did the congregation *really* belong to? Was the rabbi an insider or an outsider? What is the rabbi's role in decisions that are not solely "spiritual," yet whose impact affects everything that is done? I noted that congregants acted with little concern for the consequences of their decisions. These doubts were magnified by the congregation's "considered" decision to have the building designed by a rather journeyman architect, whose main qualification was that he was a member. It was assumed that he would kick back a large part of his fee. What democracy gave us was a poorly designed building with the roofs of one section not meeting the other, kitchy stars of David on the large windows facing the street, and, worst of all, no kickback. There were two clearly better plans. I had believed that the decision was really theirs to make. Yet I was the one who had to live with the outcome.

The relationship of Rodeph Sholom to the newly renamed Beth El was described in the *United Synagogue Review* in its Spring 1960 issue as "A Spiritual Marshall Plan." It did not last long. Rodeph Sholom soon regretted their decision not to grow unwieldy by referring potential new members to their "satellite." Watching some of their "young'uns" join Beth El may have contributed to the ultimate separation of the two congregations after the first two years of my tenure. Beth El, for its part, felt aggrieved that Rodeph Sholom did not come through with help for the building. After some Sturm und Drang the two split off from each other and an attitude of covert animosity rather than overt cooperation ensued.[98]

---

98. Although when I was leaving in late 1968, the two congregations considered a total merger, which was surprisingly turned down by Rodeph Sholom at the last minute.

My main initial thrust was to get kids to continue beyond Bar/Bat Mitzvah and to build a Hebrew High School from ground zero. Before my arrival, each child's Jewish education ceased the moment the reception began. I cajoled two boys and four girls of that first year's Bar Mitzvah crop to continue beyond the "big day" and finish eighth grade. The six with some coaxing and much praise hung in there and we had an eighth-grade graduation, a photo of which hangs proudly on Beth El's wall to this day. Once that happened, I got five[99] of the six to agree to serve as an example and continue for the first year of Hebrew High School.

I had some of the monomaniacal qualities of both my father and Shlomo Shulsinger. Every resource, honorable and questionable, was thrown into the struggle. I was single-minded! One Sunday morning while the heroic, lonely five were in class, the United Synagogue Youth group decided to have a car wash on synagogue grounds. I threw them out, saying, "You don't *have* to come to study after Bar Mitzvah, but as long as there are some kids who *do*, no other activities will take place which might draw anyone away from studying." I caught a good deal of flak for that, but defended it as an important priority. At some level I felt like a New Testament figure who, given my Jewish loyalties, shall remain nameless.

I created and used the vaunted "Bar Mitzvah Pledge." A Bar Mitzvah did not *have* to take it, but was under very strong pressure to do so. I publicly reported on Bar Mitzvah day with great hoopla that the new teenager had in *my* presence, in *my* study, pledged to continue his/her Jewish education beyond Bar/Bat Mitzvah. When the pledge was not announced, it was very clearly perceived as missing. I did not go to any Bar Mitzvah reception if the kid had not pledged to continue his/her stay at Beth El. It wasn't elegant, probably unfair, but altogether it worked and it became de rigueur at Beth El to continue one's Jewish education.

The Beth El High School as an institution treated itself with respect. We set high standards, expecting them to be lived by. It was crucial that the kids treat the high school with respect. We passed and failed kids, refused to promote them if they didn't do their work, made attendance vital, and did not let them go to Ramah, or be honored by the congregation in any way, if they were not up to snuff. We responded to their cooperation and dedica-

---

99. Their names deserve a footnote: Diane Baron, Cheryl Cole, Elaine Dommu, Elliot Friend, and Francine Pareles. The five, founders of the Hebrew High School, hung in there to become its first graduates.

tion by showering them with all the benefits the pulpit and the congregation could offer. It was made clear in every way that Beth El took them seriously and that they had the single-minded concern and attention of the rabbi. No opportunity passed without mentioning and honoring the kids in some way. I brought the full weight of the pulpit to bear, relentlessly teaching and preaching, honoring and praising the high school students and publicizing their activities. Ray Arzt[100] often said that I used the pulpit irresistibly and integrated what was said on the pulpit Saturday morning with what went on the rest of the week in the congregation. The boys were asked to be Torah readers, each doing the minimum three verses. They were not very good, but not many in the 1960s were doing very much of that, so what we were doing was way ahead of the game. We provided the kids, who were with us, with challenging volunteer activities in the community, ranging from working with the retarded at a local center to creating programs for Jewish residents at a state institution for the retarded. We would take them to Midnight Mass Christmas Eve and to visit the Bethlehem, Connecticut, monastery where one sister Miriam built an ongoing relationship with them. We regularly took the Hebrew High School away for Shabbat weekend retreats which were great fun. Those weekends bound the kids together.

We called our committed high school students, *LTFers*, The *L*eaders *T*raining *F*ellowship, having been the creation of Mordecai M. Kaplan. In the context of a small congregation we did some great things. The local press was full of articles about what our kids were doing in the community. I was known as the Teenagers' Rabbi, though with some resentment by those whose teenagers had, despite the pressure and the blandishments, dropped out after Bar/Bat Mitzvah or after eighth-grade graduation. I countered such complaints by saying that I was committed to those who were committed. It was very much an elitist position, one which I think we ignore at our peril.

---

100. That Ray and Roz Arzt decided to move to Fairfield was a lucky break for me. We had been buddies since fifth grade at Ramaz. As the director of Camp Ramah in New England, he could live anywhere. A relationship was created between our wives and our families that duplicated ours. Later, Ray offered me a summer job as Educational Consultant to the waiters, a cushy job. The job was a sign, as Ray told me later, that I was no longer on Seymour Fox's blacklist for my rebellion against his authority ten years earlier. Early in the 1960s, Joe (later Professor of Education at the Jewish Theological Seminary) and Betty Lukinsky and family moved to Fairfield. We helped them find a house, hopeful that would lead to a Ramah-type community, but they lasted six months and returned to Boston.

Camp Ramah was a major tool in making the high school happen. I was constantly pushing Ramah, trying to get kids there in any way I could. When Zev and Mira Raviv, lifelong friends,[101] came to the congregation as principal and teacher, I got Zev to direct, as I produced, the play *Tevya and His Daughters*, the same Shalom Aleichem story that later became *Fiddler on the Roof*. I used the ensuing profit as scholarships for Camp Ramah. The scholarships, a very small portion of the tuition, were used as a wedge, to flatter and cajole the parents and the kids to go. It was hard for the parents not to come up with the balance of the tuition when their child was being honored with a scholarship. I tried to get kids to Ramah any way I could, whether as campers, or baby-sitters, administrative assistants, or whatever.

During the ten years at Beth El, from a congregation which never was over 175 families, we succeeded in getting forty-five kids each summer to Ramah and finally had a high school of sixty kids, attending six hours per week. One year in cooperation with Rodeph Sholom, we even had a bus going to New York to allow our best students to attend the Prozdor[102] of the Jewish Theological Seminary.

Two laypeople need to be mentioned. In very different ways, they helped make all of the above possible. For all my efforts, it would not have been done without them.

The first was Charles Feld, who became over the years, Cantor Feld. Charlie had officiated without compensation at the first services of the Fairfield Jewish Community Group back in 1954. Dealing with Charlie in those years was both wonderful and not too easy. He was one of the first people I met when we had to work out the High Holyday service. In the early years Beth El had a choir and an organist, John Alves, who would show up in August, drill the choir, and accompany them on the High Holydays.

Charlie, at age fifteen, had saved himself and his younger brother during the Anschluss.[103] Coming to the States, he served in the U.S. Navy Seabees and married Phyllis Lebowitz, whose father owned Ostermoor Mattress. As head of the company, Charlie was one of the more wealthy members of the congregation. In those years, though he took no salary, he was

---

101. I met Zev and Mira at Massad in 1950. They have had long and distinguished careers in Jewish education, assets to any community they have worked in.

102. The very intensive high school program of the Seminary, which drew on day school graduates.

103. The German annexation of Austria in March 1938.

concerned with how he was seen as Cantor and once got the congregation to buy a $15,000 organ as a token of respect and appreciation for his work. The organ was seldom used.

Charlie's serving as Cantor (and he later took voice lessons to help his range) enabled Beth El to focus its limited financial resources on getting educators. When one thinks that this congregation in 1962–1963 was able to have Zev and Mira Raviv and later Stuart and Vickie Kelman[104] to work with me on the educational end, all of that was made possible by Charlie. Years later, I wrote him the following:

> December 6, 1992
> Cantor Charles Feld
> Congregation Beth El
> 1200 Fairfield Woods Road
> Fairfield, Connecticut 06430

Dear Charlie:

You were one of the very first people I met upon arriving at Beth El in the summer of 1959, fresh out of rabbinical school. I remember well going to your home on Short Hill Lane and starting to prepare our first High Holiday service, to take place in the illustrious premises of the Masonic Temple. We worked together for the next ten years side by side and I have many wonderful memories of those years. They were years during which Beth El was struggling to build a building, a congregation, but even more, a set of standards upon which the future could be built. I do not know if the Congregation is fully aware of how crucial your contributions were during those ten years.

Our goal back then was to build a Congregation committed to Jewish education, with an emphasis on the high school years. For a congregation of limited membership, we succeeded beyond our wildest expectations. At our zenith, we had a six-hour-per-week Hebrew High and forty-five kids at Ramah. As I often told people—it was Charlie Feld who made it possible. You fully gave of yourself, with no financial compensation, and thus enabled us to devote financial resources that would have

---

104. Stuart, a product of Congregation Rodeph Sholom, Bridgeport, CT, got his start in Jewish Education at Beth El. He is now one of America's finest Jewish educators and an innovative rabbi. Vickie, who spent many tearful hours in my office during her first year teaching, is now a renowned Jewish family educator.

gone to having a Cantor to educational personnel. It was a glorious achievement that you made possible during those formative years.

You have over the years, before I arrived and after leaving the pulpit of Beth El, exemplified the very best in Yiddishkeit. You are a tribute to your parents, a protector to your brother, a special gift to a generation of children you have trained and loved, a credit to this congregation, a sweet singer in Israel, and one who I am honored to have carry my prayers on high.

May the Almighty who gave you to us in His inscrutable fashion give you, together with Roberta[105] and all those you love, years of health, happiness, and song.

Sincerely and in great affection,
Jack H Bloom

It could not have been done without Trudy Engelberg. It was her husband Chuck, the caring and loving veterinarian, who had taken me on my first ride through Fairfield. But it was Trudy who supported anything that needed to be done for the Jewish education of our children. Nothing was beyond her ken. Nothing was impossible. Ingenuity ruled. That included moving old, inappropriate, wrong-sized school furniture from the old Nathan Hale school over to the spanking new building built on Fairfield Woods Road, which had nothing in it. It included constant budget battles and support beyond measure. Upon her resignation I wrote:

July 31, 1968
Mrs. Charles Engelberg
116 Beechwood Lane
Fairfield, CT 06430

Dear Trudy:

This letter has been long in formulation. To one to whom words are a regular thing, in this situation words do not come easily. What can I say to nine years of close, intensive work together with you; to the ins and outs and the ups and downs of trying to create with paper clips, spit, and adhesive tape a Jewish education that would be meaningful for our young people? How does one sum up the intermixing of personal and public encounters, private sadness, public frustration, shared joys and all the work, relationship, and affection that two human beings have for one another

---

105. Charlie had remarried.

over almost a decade? . . . As my mind wanders over these nine years, I think of principals hired, of troubles we had, . . . of people who complained at ungodly hours of the day and night . . . of budgets prepared and of budgets presented and of extra expenditures that had to be met, of all the battles that had to be waged, to try to build some Jewish education in our Congregation. . . . I think of a truly unusual and outstanding woman. A woman whose desire to create a meaningful Jewish education, whose selflessness knew no bounds or limits, who did all that must be done and more for the realization of an ideal. . . . How does one indeed weigh all that you have done? . . . In the final analysis, I have only one measure and that measure is the fact that through your efforts and through all that you have done, the lives of many young people have been changed Jewishly . . . and if there is a reward for all the years and for all the sweat, these young people are that reward. They have been changed. They have arrived at new commitments, at new ways of looking at the world, . . . at new loyalties and the link has been forged in the eternal chain that is our people. . . .

God bless you now and always, Trudy. You are an outstanding woman.

Sincerely,
Jack Bloom
Rabbi

SOME GOOD ENDS AND SOME ODD ONES

Back when I started at Beth El, all Bat Mitzvahs in the Greater Bridgeport area took place on Friday night. Neither Orthodox nor Reform had them. Since Rodeph Sholom was *the* Conservative congregation, all the Bat Mitzvahs were there. Because I did not like Friday night services anyway, and in the name of all that was good, having the girls be on equal footing with the boys, I was determined to move Bat Mitzvahs to Shabbat morning, thus accomplishing two goals with one move. How was I going to do it? It was not the norm either in the country or in Connecticut. Since the Torah was not read on Friday night, Conservative congregations could finesse the reading of the Haftorah, but would not dare call a woman to the Torah on Shabbat morning. The way I handled this "difficulty" would have the National Organization for Women incensed if I tried it now. Back then, it was radical. Utilizing a gap between Bat Mitzvahs, I checked around the country as to what other avant-garde congregations were doing. I checked out the Halachic considerations. What came up repeatedly was something about *kavod hatzibur,* the "honor of the congregation." This prevented women from being called to the Torah. What this meant was not fully clear but Rabbi David Aaronson *z'l* had figured a way of getting around this in Minneapolis. I thought it might work in Fairfield. The civilized world's custom was that women were escorted by men. So what I suggested and then happened was that each Bat Mitzvah was escorted to the pulpit for the *Maftir,*[106] by her father, or if there was no father, by me, and the blessings were recited in unison. Halachically there would be no problem, since the "male" blessings of the father would "count." The young girl would then read the Haftorah by herself, since this did not have the importance of the Torah reading. The girl would then say *Ashrei* (Psalm 145), and as the Cantor led the procession for the return of the Torah, sing the appropriate psalm. This was considered avant-garde back in 1961. Yet it did not even occur, during all those years, to have the young teenage women read Torah with their male cohort. I didn't want to be burdened by reading Torah regularly so I organized a whole group of teenagers who read Torah those years, but not a one of them female. Times have changed.

THE CANDLELIGHT PARADE

At the first Yom Kippur *Ne'ilah* service,[107] I wanted the day to end in dramatic fashion. Most congregations hardly made use of what was a very powerful moment. Immediately following the sounding of the last shofar[108] blast, they would race through *Ma'ariv* (the evening service). It was totally anti-climactic. Reaching back into my Massad experience, I borrowed a ceremony whole, cut and pasted it into the *Ne'ilah* service, and did something which was a first in that context, but which later spread nationwide. I had the lights shut, and had a children's procession enter, led by two children, one holding a cup filled with wine, the other a spicebox, followed by as many children as I could muster, with each holding a lit multi-wicked *Havdalah* candle.[109] We then proceeded to sing the plaintive *Eliyahu*

---

106. The final *aliyah.* The person honored with this usually reads the Prophetic portion which follows.

107. The Fast Day's final service as darkness approaches, symbolized by the closing of the gates.

108. The ram's horn used during the High Holydays to proclaim God's kingdom and call the listener to repentance.

109. Implements for the Havdalah service, which marks the end of a Holy Day and the return to the weekday.

HaNavi,[110] recite *Havdalah* followed by the very dramatic shofar blowing in the dark with the lights abruptly going on as the last sound of the shofar ended, then shouting out *Leshanah haba'ah b'Yerushalayim*.[111] This meant passing up *Ma'ariv*, which in light of my own history, I didn't mind too much, but it sure made the conclusion of the service glorious and dramatic, which I did like a great deal.

THE RED LIGHT AND THE BLUE-EYED GLARE

I am still noted among those with long memories for the red light. I was a strict disciplinarian. I had a red light installed over the door through which one entered the Sanctuary and was operated by a button on my pulpit. When it was lit, no one dared enter the sanctuary. If kids made noise, their parents were asked to remove them. If congregants dared chat during the service or the sermon, my piercing light blue eyes bore down on them. On one level it may have been youthful rigidity. On another it was a time which required that people start to treat what was going on in the synagogue with respect. However that might be, when Rachel and Rebecca were born and started to scamper up to the pulpit, I softened more than a bit.

THE GREAT *KITTEL* CAPER

I also instituted one of the least popular programs ever. Back around 1966, a consultation with my friend and colleague Ray Arzt resulted in the idea that it would be meaningful, appropriate to the holiness of the day, and a great equalizer if *everyone* came to the *Bimah*[112] on the High Holydays wearing a white *kittel*.[113] We had a man in the *shmata*[114] business create *kit-*

---

110. Elijah the Prophet, who will announce the coming of the Messiah.

111. "Next Year in Jerusalem"—the oath that concludes both the Passover Seder and Yom Kippur's end. This continued until 1999 when neon lightsticks replaced the candles and killed the drama. Our seminaries need to teach our rabbis more about using ritual in a dramatic fashion.

112. The front of the synagogue where the Rabbi and Cantor officiate.

113. The *kittel*, a white garment symbolic of purity, was traditionally worn on solemn Jewish occasions and is the garment in which the dead are buried.

114. A Yiddish colloquial expression meaning rag. In popular parlance, used to describe anyone involved in almost any business using fabric.

tels in three sizes: small, medium, and large. Each congregant prior to doing anything that involved ascending the *Bimah* went to the small cloakroom outside the sanctuary, donned the appropriate-size *kittel*, went for their honor, *aliyah*, reading, ark opening, or whatever, and when finished returned the *kittel*. There was a good deal of commotion in that cloakroom, checking of sizes, etc. This went on for a couple of years. I thought it was great! It really added to the spirituality (a word we didn't use then) of the service. When I left the congregation in 1969, they incinerated the *kittels*, even as I boarded the plane for Tel Aviv. No word about them or remnant of them has ever been revealed. Maybe I was before my time. I still think it's a great idea.

BEYOND BETH EL

During those years I was quite busy beyond the congregation. I was brought back to the Seminary on a part-time basis to run the first two Conference(s) on the Moral Implications of the Rabbinate, held under the auspices of the Herbert H. Lehman Institute of Ethics in the fall of 1963 and 1965. Already interested in the role of the Rabbi as Symbolic Exemplar, a concern which has permeated my career, I proposed to Dr. Finkelstein a conference on "The Role of the Rabbi." For the first conference Richard Rubenstein wrote a psychoanalytically oriented and highly controversial paper, "Death of a Rabbi," which Dr. Finkelstein wanted to ensure would not be published. The 1963 conference followed the trip the previous May of nineteen members of the Rabbinical Assembly, who volunteered to be dispatched by the Assembly's convention to go to Birmingham, Alabama, to support Dr. Martin Luther King in his struggle. It was from a Birmingham jail that his famous letter had been written and it was in Birmingham that the confrontation between civil rights activists and the dogs and hoses of Bull Conner's police force was riveting the nation. I was a member of that delegation, and used the experience to write my own paper[115] for the conference I was running. Being there was a highlight of my life[116] and the article is

---

115. "Journey to Understanding." *Conservative Judaism*, Vol. XIX, No. 4, Summer 1965, pp. 11–16. See Chapter 14.

116. While bringing some material about Birmingham to the Seminary archives, I did a brief imitation of Dr. Finkelstein's high-pitched voice for the young woman I was dealing with. She said, *"Really? Is that really how he sounded?"* I was aware that I was at the brink of being a relic from what was to her the ancient past and to me still current events.

suffused with my concern for the symbolic aspects of the rabbinic role, a concern which was to culminate in my Ph.D., almost ten years later. The article is included in this book as Chapter 14.

I was discovering that being a symbol could indeed be positive. It was also becoming a great burden.

After some exciting and quite satisfying first years, I grew increasingly antsy about being a rabbi. Gradually I was feeling more and more isolated and alienated. I was feeling lonely, wondering sometimes aloud, why people couldn't just treat me (and my wife) as just regular folk.

When I would go to laypeople and risk whining a bit about how lonely we felt, they would respond, "But we love you, rabbi. We don't understand how you can say that." Attempting to console, they would offer, "You are at every Bar Mitzvah, every wedding, how can *you* feel lonely?" And then back to "We love you." All I did was make them feel guilty. I soon learned to keep my mouth shut about that at least.

In therapy I tried to tell my shrink how lonely things were getting, how difficult it was to live behind a glass wall. That somehow it wasn't the usual kind of life. He responded with a wise look on his face: "You *are* getting older. You're *married* now. Things *aren't* the way they were when you were a graduate student. It's *different*." I said, "No, there's something else going on." He replied, "No, it's not so." There was something going on. What it was was destined to occupy much of my life.

He was a sensitive, progressive man who helped me in more ways than I can count. I am in his debt. He meant a great deal to me. He clarified and fortified my life. About this he was of no help. He couldn't understand. I understood something about my shrink later on. When he was terminally ill after I was into clinical psychology and hadn't been a pulpit rabbi for a number of years, his soon-to-be widow called me and said, "Seymour is on his death bed and asked if you would say Kaddish[117] for him at his funeral." I realized at that moment that there was no way I could explain my position to him. *I had become his rabbi* and he needed to keep me there. Clergy, whether Protestant, Catholic, or Jewish, understand instinctively, and resonate to that sense of loneliness, isolation, and alienation. Living in a pulpit makes it visceral all too quickly.

I was of course deeply ambivalent about prayer. Leading prayer felt fraudulent. I had solved the problem in Massad by becoming a monitor at services and at Ramaz, by staying silent, daydreaming about shooting hoops

---

117. The memorial prayer recited for the dead.

in gym period which took place after *Mincha* (afternoon prayer) was over. At the Seminary, I avoided it when I could and did my best to fake it when I couldn't. I hassled with it over the years. In a curious way that led to my being, what I consider in the context of the early sixties, quite creative. An article I wrote for the *Reconstructionist Magazine* in 1962 was titled "Is Prayer-book Revision Enough?" In some ways still cogent after all these years, it indicates clearly how I felt about the whole endeavor of routinized prayer.

> Rabbis . . . are often "bored stiff" with the endless repetition of the same formulas over the years. And time and repetition have not endeared the service to us. . . . For most of us Rabbis, satisfactions come in areas other than prayer. We see ourselves as teachers, pastors, counselors, administrators, fund-raisers, community statesmen, and much else. Few of us would recommend prayer to a person who came for counseling. Few of us, deep down, see ourselves as especially adept at prayer. We are supposed to be the prayer leaders. Our training and our role have made us that. But our doubts remain. . . . Are we, ourselves, moved by it? Does it lead to piety? And, because we are not convinced, we find it hard to convince others. . . . If a congregant should happen to leave *shul* better than when he came in, we do not really believe that it had anything to do with his reciting the *Shemoneh Esreh*,[118] the *Shema*,[119] or *Alenu*[120] with special fervor . . .
>
> Is the expenditure of time and effort on a liturgy of regular, routinized prayer in all its forms moving us significantly in [the direction of piety]? . . .
>
> I think the answer is no. The prayer service, even as it has been revised, cannot move us significantly toward these goals.
>
> The liturgy presupposes that man can speak directly to a personal God. Furthermore, it assumes that God not only can, but, given the right circumstances, will answer. Twenty centuries ago and two centuries ago, this was accepted as fact. And it was basic to our religious experience. Today it is, at best, "a manner of speaking." What we mean when we say that God answers prayer is ". . . ," and off we go into what are often very clever rationalizations. One thing is certain: We do not mean what our ancestors meant, that God could and would answer prayer quite directly,

---

118. The 18, the silent devotion, on weekdays consisting of eighteen prayers, hence the name.

119. "Hear O Israel the Lord is One, The Lord alone"—watchword of Jewish belief.

120. *Alenu* concludes most services, proclaiming our duty in bringing the Kingdom of God.

if need be by interfering with natural law and human affairs; we do not mean that God personally listens to the entreaty of man. . . .

To meet the problem of meaningful Jewish worship head on we will need more than a revision of the words of the past, more than a new sentence here, a new introduction there, or comments in passing. We will have to thoroughly reevaluate the very presuppositions of our service and its function today. . . .

Prayer will, no doubt, remain within our new form of worship . . . But there will have to be a *strong shift in emphasis away from the services which consist of routinized prayer repeated day by day, week by week.* Prayer will occupy a smaller place in our worship service. . . . Study is perhaps the primary area; not just study, but *Talmud Torah*, studying in order to act, studying as an act of worship.

I spent gobs of time and energy struggling to make prayer meaningful. I wrote introductions and filled the front cover and the back cover of our prayerbooks with material. I had preludes and postludes to prayer. I created a service that was all singing. When Neil Gillman, a beloved friend, came to Beth El two and a half decades later, as scholar in residence, he said, "Wow, this service! They sing this service from beginning to end! The whole thing." Laybel Waldman, my successor, responded, "This is Jake Bloom's service." I circumvented my prayer fraud thing by having a service totally sung. Hebrew singing I liked. That, I could live with.

Some of what I did was good and lasted, some was terrible and lasted. I am amazed at how even bad innovations can become a congregation's tradition. One day, bored to distraction with the "Ashrei" that I had heard intoned over and over and over again all my years at Massad and Ramah, I appropriated the classical melody for "Anim Zemirot,"[121] twisted and turned the words of "Ashrei" to fit the melody that I did not think would ever be heard in the confines of a Conservative congregation. I do mean twisting and turning. Once I instituted it, it became holy writ at Beth El. One Sukkot day, not a Shabbat, Zev Raviv and I decided that we could not sing the Sabbath psalm, had no melody for the weekday holiday psalm, but still wanted to carry the Torah around. We dug back in our Camp Massad experience and came up with "Torat Emet,"[122] which has become tradition and which I do think

---

121. "The Hymn of Glory" attributed to R. Yehudah ha Haasid. Used intermittently, but less often now.

122. A traditional melody.

works rather well. After visiting Camp Ramah in Connecticut at the behest of Ray Arzt and meeting Zalman Schachter,[123] I brought the idea of colored *taleisim*[124] to Beth El. We taught some kids to tie *tzitzit*[125] and encouraged all the mothers of Bar Mitzvahs to make *taleisim* for their husbands and sons. Pretty soon the sanctuary was a fairly colorful place. We even experimented with *davening to nusach*[126] in English, which did not take root.

None of all this resolved my discomfort with the world of prayer. I felt I was a total fraud. My discomfort showed through after my dad's death when some congregants started a daily minyan for me to say Kaddish and I effectively sabotaged it by my sporadic attendance.

Beyond loneliness and fraud, there were three paradigmatic events that hastened my leaving the pulpit.

First, was the birth of my daughter Rachel. With her birth in 1964 the energy I expended in being the father of the congregation started to dissipate. At some level I had apparently decided to out-father my own father. Now that I was father to a daughter of my own, I found myself not calling my answering service from New York to find out if there was something I needed to attend to, someone I needed to call, some way I needed to "father" the congregation.

Second, also in 1964, was Harry Nelson's death. He had been a great rabbi. Part of my megalomania was that I too would sacrifice myself for them (as he did), and in return after my time, they would lionize me, perhaps build monuments, etc. At Nelson's funeral, the Governor, the Senators, the Congressman, the Mayor, you name it, had all been present. The crowd filled the sanctuary, the social hall, and spilled out the door and down the steps and engulfed Park Avenue. I was asked to deliver a talk on the *Shloshim* (thirtieth day) following Nelson's death. That came out on Thanksgiving morning. I prepared a fine talk titled "Thirty Years and Thirty Days," comparing how things were in Jewish life in Bridgeport when Nelson had arrived and how they were at his recent death. I assumed that the sanctuary, on a day

---

123. A founder of the Jewish renewal movement.

124. *Taleisim*: Yiddish/Hebrew plural of *tallis/tallit*—prayer shawl.

125. Fringes of the *tallis/tallit*, which Jews are to note as reminders of God's commandments.

126. Praying with the traditional melodic modes that are different for each service.

when people would not be working, would be full to overflowing. A meager group showed up. The empty pews far outnumbered those occupied. That morning put a pinprick in the balloon of my megalomania, and it leaked and leaked and leaked. Such deals were fool's gold.

The third occurred when I was back being a student once again, taking a Master's in Pastoral Counseling at the Postgraduate Center for Mental Health. Ray Arzt came over to the house. He was hungry. I made him a hamburger and inadvertently (or advertently) left the tinfoil which was under it in the oven. The next day when my wife discovered it, a major fight ensued. The kitchen was, after all, her domain, and she did always want things neat. In the therapy group experience at the Postgraduate Center later that same day, I recounted the hamburger incident. How the discussion moved from beginning to end I had no idea then or now, but the outcome an hour and a half later was that *I could get more out of life*. At a level deeper than I fully know, that influenced my decision to go into clinical psychology.

The Postgraduate Center for Mental Health Program in Pastoral Counseling was an attempt to deal with my disquiet. It was suggested to me by Stanley Rosner, a local clinical psychologist, who himself was in training there as an analyst. I applied, was accepted, and ended up with a Master of Sacred Theology in Pastoral Counseling from New York Theological Seminary, a fundamentalist Christian institution which had a working agreement with the Postgraduate Center. That added STM to the parade of initials which follow my name.

Though it was a good experience, it did not dispel the darkening cloud gathered around me. I had gotten to a point where what I liked about being a rabbi was inundated by my experience of being a rabbi. I liked the teaching. I liked the Jewish studies part. I liked the educational part. I liked being part of determining the Jewish future. I did not like being a Symbolic Exemplar. And prayer remained as always a troublesome area.

THE PSYCHOLOGICAL SOLUTION

One night coming home from New York with the Rosners, Stan mentioned that he wanted to begin a Postgraduate Center for Mental Health in Fairfield County and that he intended to hire me as Director of Clergy Affairs or something. The Rosners got off at Exit 42 on the Merritt Parkway to head home to Weston. We were headed to Exit 46. Between those two exits a light went off in my head. If he hired me and I had no viable credential, I would be stuck. *"I'll get a Ph.D. in Clinical Psychology."* I had no idea what was involved. But I went on a single-minded manic surge and in three weeks or a month, thanks to some winter storms, which closed the Beth El Religious School, got applications into seven institutions; took the Graduate Record Exams which I prepared for by revisiting high school algebra and geometry which I abhorred; and had interviews at five or six institutions, determined that one way or another, I was going to get a Ph.D.[127]

I first assumed that Yale would be only too glad to accept this "fair-haired," young, and reasonably well-known rabbi. Though applications had been formally closed a few days earlier, I got an interview with a Dr. Levine. He asked me, "What do you think about research?" Research—Research—Research—What is that? I had not the foggiest. "I think you'll be happier at Adelphi," he graciously offered. Adelphi apparently had a program focused on therapy and not research. I went to see Gordon Derner, who headed up the Adelphi program, meeting him at the Veterans Administration at 23rd Street and 1st Avenue in New York. I would have met and seen anybody at any place to make my getting into graduate school happen. But more important I developed with astonishing rapidity a keen interest in research, especially on moral development in teenagers. I wrote some useful essays on that subject that I included in my applications. It was a wild time. I was working on this from 7 A.M. to midnight.

When I went in to see Seymour, my therapist, he shared with me that he knew some faculty at Columbia and at New York University and Fordham. Using Seymour's name to gain entrance, I wangled interviews with them. It was meeting Dr. Rosalea Schonbar, Professor at Columbia, that made the difference. Rosalea was senior faculty there. It was clear that she liked this young rabbi and we really hit it off. During the course of the interview I dared suggest that my psychology GREs[128] would not tell them much about

---

127. It is interesting to note that the thought that went through my head was, "Dad, I've paid my debt, now it's my turn."

128. The verbal GREs were another story. They changed my inner life forever. The family myth was that my brother Norman was an absolute genius—a failed genius but a genius nonetheless. My father would often say, "If I hadn't ruined Norman, he would have been the salvation of Israel." Sol was credited with a tough behind, able to study long and diligently, work hard, but was not thought of as a first-rate intellect—though indeed he was. Not knowing where I fit in, I was convinced that I wasn't as smart as Norman and certainly was lazier than Sol. Though my father favored me, I didn't think highly of my abilities—I was at best a sports freak. This self-evaluation withstood my attending an Ivy League college, which neither of them had done; my being president of the student body at Ramaz

me, since I had never had undergraduate psychology. By this time I understood something about research, but nothing compared to what the youngsters I was competing against knew. I offered that I was counting on Columbia to teach me psychology. Rosalea summoned Professor David Ricks (I did not know that he was new to the faculty and therefore was assigned to admissions) and suggested to him that *Mr.* Bloom's files should exclude his GREs in psychology. Ricks was of course in no position to contradict her.

Getting in was tough. I applied to Columbia, Adelphi, New York University, Fordham, City University, Boston University, and Yale. Besides Yale, Columbia was logistically the easiest, though I would have done anything I needed to do, even if it meant commuting by flying to Boston. April 15 was the acceptance date. Around April 1, I came home and my wife told me that the answering service had a call from Columbia from the selfsame Professor Ricks. When I returned the call, he immediately launched into asking me if I wanted a VA stipend or a Mental Health stipend. I was busy calculating in my head which one would give me a leg up on being accepted, telling him that any stipend or none at all would be OK, when I suddenly realized, despite his total silence on the subject, that I *had* been accepted, and we were just talking about details. I had the presence of mind to choose the Veterans Administration program, got off the phone, grabbed my wife, lifted her in the air, spun her around, and let out a shout heard down the street. *It was a great day!* The odds against getting in had been severe. Columbia took fifteen out of 450 *final* applicants. As I discovered later, the class was composed mostly of young, bushy-tailed psychology undergrads and two old fogies, each thirty-five, a rabbi and a nurse. WHOOPEE! I made it.

That summer at Columbia's suggestion, to give me some background in psychology, I took Experimental Psychology at City University. Luckily because it was summer session, we did not have to "run rats." The Evelyn Woods Rapid Reading course I took in Bridgeport turned out to be a lifesaver. I had immense reading to do, a congregation to run while doing it, and as it turned out, a Veterans Administration Hospital to work in, in addi-

---

and then at the Seminary; my growing proficiency in two civilizations, etc. When I shared stuff I had published and others thought it good, that too did not penetrate. The GRE results changed all that. I remember vividly removing from the mailbox the letter from the Educational Testing Service. I took it to the green counter, next to the phone in our kitchen, opened it, and noted that on the verbal score, mine was off the chart. I was declared to be in the 99-plus percentile. I blurted out, "Shit! I'm as smart as Norman." I never believed it before and never doubted it after.

tion to a family. Rapid reading, working eighteen hours a day, and the loyalty and competence of Anne Tyler, my sixty-five-year-old secretary at the synagogue, made getting through the first two years possible. Wherever she abides in the great beyond, she has my thanks and has earned at least one of the three letters in Ph.D.

Considering what I later learned and instinctively knew about the symbolic nature of the rabbinate, I then did what in retrospect I consider a stupid act. I was in the middle of a contract at the synagogue which was going to end up in its last year paying me $15,000. I went to them and said that I would be away three days a week. They did the math, realized I would be available four days and offered me 4/7 of my salary. I came back and said if all the days were equal, I would be out of town on Shabbat and Yom Kippur. We finally settled on $11,000. My mistake was saying I would be worth less.

The Veterans Administration internship paid $4500 a year, *tax free*, so the first two years were financially viable. I was assigned to Montrose Hospital, just outside Peekskill, New York. Montrose, built during the New Deal, was an inpatient, long-term hospital. There were a dozen or so buildings. One was for women. I was luckily assigned there. The care was better and the patients a bit less hard core. I began there in the summer of 1968, working a full forty hours. That fall, beginning my second year, my triangle route day began on the road by 6:15 A.M., wired for sound, listening to lectures and notes of lectures on a tape, and arriving at Montrose at 8:15 A.M. At 4:30 P.M. I headed down to Columbia, to take whatever courses were required, and then either stay over in New York City for next morning's course work or head back home about 10 P.M. to drive the sixty miles to Montrose the next morning. It was a grind. After doing the Montrose gig for about a year, I asked to be assigned to the Psychology Department at the West Haven Veterans Administration Hospital, which was a great place in those days. The transfer was granted and that made things a bit simpler. I would drive sixty miles to New York and then eighty miles, past Fairfield, to West Haven and then twenty miles back home.

I made it through those years a day at a time. I never thought about the overwhelming tasks that lay ahead, only about what I had to do this day and get done by the end of the week. Difficulties I processed as being just a part of jumping through the hoop. One of the hoop jumps I remember well. We had to have a paper in the Columbia offices at 3 P.M. on Friday, December 22. Anne Tyler got the paper done that morning. I called New York, asking if I could send the paper Special Delivery, making sure the postmark indicated a time before 3 P.M.; after all, with the Christmas break faculty was not going to read any of the papers for a while. I was told NO WAY. I got in the car, drove to 120th Street, put the paper on the appropriate desk, and drove back. Just another hoop.

During the second year, I was a full-time student, working at the VA, in West Haven, a full-time rabbi, though admittedly running the congregation out of my hip pocket, doing no community invocations and benedictions, attending no committee meetings. Things were only repeats, nothing new or original. At one meeting in dealing with financial negotiations, Bud Loewith, a congregant, is supposed to have said, "If he gives up the clinical psychology stuff, a life contract, if not, nothing." Though I was very upset by that back then, he was really quite right.

Oddly, this gave me more evenings at home than I remembered in years. Time at home was spent working on reading, paper writing, testing. Evelyn Lula, our devoted baby-sitter, single-handedly provided me with three of her younger siblings to test for the Wechsler Intelligence Scale for Children, and herself and two older siblings for the Wechsler Adult Intelligence Scale,[129] all of which were part of my Columbia requirements.

I have virtually all my High Holyday sermons except for those from 1968, my last High Holydays there. They were marked by anger and vitriol, for no reason probably, except that I had trouble handling the transition in any other way.

I had decided that 1968–1969 would be my last year at Congregation Beth El. It was clear to me *and* to them that I was no longer interested in the pulpit and that psychology graduate school was a way of getting out. I pondered going to Israel. It was after the Six-Day War, and a lot of my friends had gone on *aliyah*. If I could realize that long-held dream by doing an internship, it would also serve as a way of getting out of Beth El gracefully. I needed Columbia's OK, since all internships had to be American Psychological Association approved. An internship was 2500 hours, a year's work, and it turned out that I had already logged that many hours at the VA. This gave me the freedom of presenting my time in Israel as a second internship

---

129. Those tests changed Evie's life. They indicated that Evie had a quite high IQ, much higher than her siblings. Evie had very limited educational goals. The test results led to a sequence of events beginning with a remedial summer program at the University of Connecticut, and concluding in her getting a Bachelor's in Nursing. Her father, an impoverished itinerant painter petrified of any government involvement, would not sign for or back her, so I had to become her sponsor.

and made it easier to get permission. After much correspondence back and forth, Professor Joel Shanan, a Czech-born psychologist, trained at the University of Chicago, offered me a one-year internship at the Hadassah Hebrew University Medical Center Department of Psychiatry.[130] The internship was not going to be on his budget line, but was supported to a limited degree by the Jewish Agency. My munificent salary was zero, but I was able to get a stipend as a possible new immigrant of 600 lira[131] a month and a loan from the Jewish Agency of $900 to get the family there.

So I was set to go to Israel. The papers published an article that Rabbi Bloom was leaving Beth El in order to volunteer in Israel. It was the truth but not the whole truth. At the affair marking my tenth anniversary and my leaving for Israel as a volunteer, I was given a purse of $800 and a wooden box. My beloved friend Joel Zaiman vindicated my choice of him as best man at my wedding some ten years earlier. Joel invited me to be third rabbi for the High Holydays at Providence, Rhode Island's Temple Emanuel, where he served with the late deservedly beloved Eli Bohnen. The fee was a providential $1200. With the rental of our house on Woodside Circle and the sporadic sale of some Israel Bonds I had bought over the years, and the High Holyday jobs bracketing the year, we managed. So at the end of July 1969, ten years after I came to Fairfield, I left the congregation and pulpit life. Immediately after Yom Kippur, we flew to Tel Aviv.

What follows is my farewell letter upon leaving Beth El.

Jack Bloom
171 Woodside Circle
Fairfield, Conn. 06604

Rabbi
Congregation Beth El
Fairfield, Conn.
June 13, 1969

Dear Friends;

As you know, a decade of association with Congregation Beth El and with Greater Bridgeport Jewry as the Rabbi of Congregation Beth El is coming to a close for me. The years have been full, exciting and meaningful in a great many ways. The trials and tribulations of being a rabbi can-

---

130. It was to turn out that my "office" was right next to the Chagall windows.

131. The Israel currency at the time, worth about $180.

not diminish the significance of the experience. It was, all in all, a good decade. During these years I had the chance to work with some of you, to know many of you, and to share the experience of building a Congregation in our community. I had the opportunity at Beth El to try to do some things that are important and that will affect the future of Jewish life in America. I was able to teach (a task I enjoyed greatly), to help set standards for a Congregation, to help people, and to learn from them.

There were many satisfying moments provided by people's willingness to share a part of their lives, both joyous and sad, with me. In some ways this is one of the most satisfying and frustrating parts of the Rabbinate. Any rabbi both is and is not a part of his congregation. He is in it and essential to it, but ultimately is an outsider. He is in the community, but never fully a part of it even if he has been there for thirty years. Yet that fact, inherent as it is in congregational life, cannot diminish the luster of the joyous and fulfilling moments. There were times when I felt that the work I was doing was of consummate importance and that I did that work reasonably well. No man can ask for more.

Part of the work that meant a great deal to me was the creation and building of our Hebrew High School into one of the finest in the country. The High School became a vehicle for touching and changing the lives of a number of our young people. Some of those who came through High School are already educating other young people Jewishly. Others retain memories of their High School years at Beth El which will influence them all their lives. Many long and hard hours were spent with these, our young people. They were some of the best moments of the past decade. My only regret is that some of the young people in our Congregation did not have the opportunity to be exposed to this experience.

Over the years I gave a good deal of my time to persuading, cajoling, and raising scholarship money to encourage as many of our young people as possible to attend Camp Ramah, an institution which I believe is a keystone in the future of American Jewish life. The pictures of the large Ramah contingents that adorn the Synagogue walls testify to your cooperation in helping me make this possible. Not all my priorities were your priorities; a man has to choose his priorities, and I could do no different. There are things I might do differently today if I were to do them again. The emphasis I placed on teenage education and Camp Ramah *are not* among them.

During the past ten years the Greater Bridgeport area has become my home. Whatever roots I and my family have, we have here. During the coming High Holy Days I will be serving as a Rabbi in Providence,

Rhode Island. Next year Meryl, Rachel, Rebecca, and I will be in Israel. I shall be volunteering my services at the Hadassah Medical Center, Department of Psychiatry. In addition to any help that I may be able to bring there, I see the year as a sabbatical, a learning experience and a transitional year for me. For all of us I hope it will be a year of fulfillment and joy, a year in which we will realize every day the hope "next year in Jerusalem." Following that year we will return to our home here and try to make the transition to being private citizens in this community. That will not be an easy transition. I hope that with my own understanding of the difficulties involved and with the help and cooperation of others, it will be possible.

Beyond being part of this community, it has been and remains my hope to continue to use a portion of my talents towards the betterment of Jewish life in this country. As you know, I am currently working toward my Ph.D. in Clinical Psychology and hopefully within a year after my return from Israel will have concluded my studies. In addition to any other work, I hope to become involved working with pulpit rabbis, helping them be more effective. The congregational structure of American Jewish life presents great difficulties to men whose careers are dependent on it. The "flight from the pulpit" of many men deeply committed to Jewish life testifies to that. My Ph.D. dissertation will deal with the problems of the clergy generally and the Rabbinate specifically. I hope to become a resource for men who have chosen the pulpit, helping them appreciate their difficult role as men "set apart"; assisting them in dealing with their families, their staff, their congregational boards, and the congregation itself; and consulting with them on ways in which they can increase their effectiveness and protect their own well-being. It should be exciting work. I look forward to it.

For your many kindnesses to me these past ten years, I thank you. May God bless you now and always.

Sincerely,
Jack Bloom
Rabbi

POSTSCRIPTS

Those ten years, I sometimes realized and sometimes had not the faintest idea and all too often was dreadfully uncomfortable with the special power and effect I, God's decidedly recalcitrant servant, had being a rabbi, and a Symbolic Exemplar.

P.S.#1: THE HATS THAT SAID THANKS[132]

Back in my last days in the pulpit, Mildred Swist was dying of cancer. Her husband Herman and two adult children, both in their early twenties, were keeping the seriousness of her situation a "secret" in order to "protect" her. I went to St. Vincent's Hospital to visit her and entered a room full of friends and relatives all chatting happily away. All knew the "secret" but were acceding to Herman's wish to protect Millie. "Don't worry, Mildred, you'll be fine; everything will be OK; don't worry about it." There was a feigned and forced optimism. Mildred was going home the next day. There was nothing else that could be done in the hospital.

When I went over to her bed Millie asked, "Rabbi, so are you going to tell me stories too?" I said, " No stories Millie, but if you want to talk, I'm available."

After some pleasantries with her visitors, I left.

A couple of days later Millie called the synagogue office, asking me to come visit. When I arrived at their home, Herman was there with her son and daughter. I went upstairs to Mildred's bedroom. She made it clear that she knew what was wrong with her, that she was very ill, despite all the lies she was being told. I said, "Yes, I know. That's very clear." She said, "You know I am going to die," and I said, "Yes, that's true."

That moment began a most moving experience. She started to talk (the first visit was two hours) about her feelings, about dying, and not being able to see the weddings of her two kids, leaving her husband, and about the fulfillments and losses in her life.

I went downstairs and said to her family, "You can talk to Mom truthfully. No secrets! She knows how ill she is and that she is going to die." The family made contact and Mildred was no longer isolated from those she loved best and who loved her most. We had a number of other visits, in which she was able to be straight and talk about what was really happening to her. She died shortly thereafter.

---

132. This story appears in a slightly altered version in Chapter 11.

There were maybe a couple of other things in my ten years in the pulpit that were as important as that. Certainly, to that family there was nothing as important as that one statement that made that possible. The statement was simple: "No stories, but if you want to talk, I'm available."

For years following her death, Herman, a hat salesman, would appear at our door once a year. In his hands, he always had two funny hats, one for Rachel and one for Rebecca. Refusing our pleas to come in, he would just hand me the hats, say "Thank you," and depart into the night.

Sometime during my divorce, the early spring of 1982, Herman died in Florida. A couple of months later, June or July 1982, a memorial service was held for him at Beth El. I was at home in the sunroom crying about my divorce and totally missed it. I have felt bad about that to this day. I sometimes wonder how the hats feel.

P.S. #2: THREE THANKS IT TOOK
THIRTY YEARS TO HEAR[133]

Having served in a congregation for ten years, I quickly learned that a rabbi is a walking, talking, living symbol of the best that is in humankind. Being credited with superlative inner qualities and inordinately deep-set commitments makes life difficult for those who have chosen the pulpit. Trying to live up to high standards, calling upon others to do the same, serving a congregation full of individuals who are testing, testing, testing whether those ordained are really what they "should" be, all these make life tough. In working with rabbis I find that as they move toward mid-career, their symbolic exemplarhood is a drain on them and often the root of their discontent. Rabbis complain about the gap between them and their congregants: living in a "glass house," loneliness in the midst of the crowd, always having to be "on," and even being treated differently than anyone else. Rabbis want to hold their spouses' hands, and not have congregants offer, "Oh, what a cute couple they are; look at how they kiss each other." Having picked one of the most public of callings, rabbis yearn for anonymity. They are relieved when going to the movies, they find no congregants present. Paradoxically, they often expect people to treat them with deference and respect befitting those who exemplify moral, ethical, and spiritual values. Symbolic exemplarhood gives their work its power and their lives its frustrations. In the mael-

---

133. "On Being a Rabbi." Reprinted from the *Rabbinical Assembly Newsletter*, September 1997.

strom it's hard for them to see the powerful effect they do have. It was hard for me to see it back then.

It took almost thirty years for three seemingly minor incidents in which I unknowingly participated to demonstrate how my being a rabbi touched others in ways unknown to me.

While I was officiating at his mother's marriage, Danny Paul, whom I had known as a little boy, introduced me to his ten-year-old daughter. "Do you know who this man is?" he said to her. She shrugged. "What is it that we do every night when I put you to bed?" "Every night, Daddy, you ask me what I learned that day." "Well this is the man who taught me that. He said that a Jewish child should learn something new every day!"

I had no recollection of ever having said anything like that. Maybe it was a throwaway line; maybe it was something I read. Yet, because the rabbi said it, Danny heard it and shaped his daughter's life with that statement.

A week or two later I was listening to a speech at the local Jewish community center. Cindy Dimenstein *z"l*, director of the Bureau of Jewish Education, reached over, tapped me on the shoulder, and said, "There's something I have to tell you, something that I've been waiting over thirty years to tell you. Do you remember when my family and I were members of your congregation, back around 1966 or '67? I was six or seven. Remember how you did birthday blessings, with all the kids standing under the tallis?" I nodded politely. (I remembered that I hated doing them. I only did them because another rabbi was doing them and my congregants wanted me to do the same.)

"I was standing under the tallis—By the way, what day is your birthday?" I responded, "September 26." "Mine is September 27 and you asked each kid what his or her birthday was, and when you came to me you said, 'September 27! Cindy that's a really important birthday, cause that's the day right next to my birthday.' Well, I felt so big, so puffed up, so important that I never forgot it. My birthday right next to the rabbi's! WOW! And every birthday since, I have that wonderful feeling of being someone important."

Returning to synagogue, on his parents' forty-fifth wedding anniversary, Dr. Brian Meyer called me aside and said, "There's something I have to share with you." He told me how I called him into my office one day when he was nine years old, and said to him, "'Brian, you're a bright and special student and we are going to send you to Camp Ramah.' That day changed my life. What you said that day and my going to Ramah was a turning point in who I am today. I wanted to thank you for it." A rabbi does more than he or she realizes, yet seldom knows what he or she is doing that makes a difference.

I have always maintained that my ten years in a congregation changed more lives than all the years working as a psychologist. And I had no idea. I was focused on congregants' attendance, on stray remarks they made to me, on their response at salary time, on whether they invited my wife and me to go to the movies with them. In weighing how much they loved, respected, and listened to me I never really knew the impact I had. Perhaps there was no really obvious way of measuring it. Perhaps I was looking in the wrong place. However it is, it happened one person at a time, often in the least expected places. It's a pity I was conflicted about it and felt uncomfortable with the power that being a Symbolic Exemplar gave me. Looking back, I'm in awe at what can happen.

OPENING THE DOOR: THE BENEFITS OF PIDYON SHEVUYIM[134]

Well, there I was in Israel. And there began a treasured friendship that changed my life and for which I am eternally grateful.

Joe Glaser *z"l* with his wife Agathe and family were spending 1969–1970 in Rehavia prior to Joe's taking up his duties as Executive Vice President of the Central Conference of American Rabbis. Our kids (my Rebecca and his Jackie) constituted two-thirds of the Anglo-Saxon Landsmanschaft at the little *gan* (nursery school) located next to Ray and Roz Arzt's house on Keren Kayemet Street. (The Arzts' daughter Ilana was the third member of that triumvirate.) One day, the three Anglo-Saxons "ran away" from the *gan*. To great parental relief and rejoicing they were soon found unscathed. Their retrieval led to my meeting Joe for the first time and warranted an invitation to the Glaser apartment. Seated across from each other, sharing a coffee, we shared our dreams. Joe's dreams concerned leading and caring for his fellows in the Conference. I had just completed my "review of the literature"[135] titled, "Who Become Clergy?"[136] which had been accepted for publication on its own. I was planning to write the rest of my dissertation on "The Pulpit

---

134. Literally, Redeeming the Captive. A duty that trumps all others. The kids weren't technically captive, but lost they were, though they didn't know it.

135. The required opening chapter of every Ph.D. dissertation.

136. Chapter 3 in this book.

Rabbi as Symbolic Exemplar," and the effect that has on rabbis' lives. I also shared my seemingly paradoxical dream of working with rabbis to make their lives easier and strengthen them in their rabbinate to ensure that fewer would do what I did and abandon the pulpit. We were to become fast friends. He charged my daughters at each of their Bat Mitzvahs, was one of the first to know of and officiated at my marriage to Ingrid. He was always a close, loving "straight on" confidant who did not mince his words. On regular visits to Tanglewood, we joked about our both having blonde *yekkeh rebbitzens*.[137] He made it possible for me to be a rabbi's coach. I am in his debt always. I miss him greatly.

In 1974, Joe called and asked in his own inimitable style if I knew anything about "Mid-Life Crisis."[138] He said that the Conference had received a grant from the Merrill Foundation to do work on Mid-Life Crisis and Rabbis.[139] I hemmed and hawed, but sensing a door opening said, "Joe anything you need, I'll be glad to do." Out of our deliberations came an innovative pioneer program dealing with the very real needs of modern rabbis: The Mid-Career Review Program of the Central Conference of American Rabbis. The first Review met in December 1995 at Mohonk Country House in New Paltz, New York. It ran from Sunday evening to Wednesday after lunch. Sixteen rabbis from all over the country attended. I was at that point president of the Gestalt Institute of Connecticut and ran the workshop as an extended Gestalt group. We were in session from 9 A.M.–10 P.M. I was assisted by a pair of rabbinic advisors, chosen by Joe, who did individual consultations with each rabbi during meals and breaks. I found myself very comfortable and felt very much at home with my Reform colleagues. I had long been aligned with their struggle dealing with Judaism in modern terms and found the ideas of personal autonomy in confronting our tradition very much in keeping with my

---

137. *Yekkeh* is Israeli slang for Jews of German descent, *rebbitzen*, a yiddishism for rabbi's wives.

138. Mid-Life Crisis was created as a condition by the fact of being named. It did not exist before and has not ceased existing since. Its existence as an entity demonstrates the power of language.

139. As fate would have it, apparently sent their way by another longtime friend with whom I had been in Birmingham—Richard Rubenstein, who, from his Harvard days, was a friend of Charles Merrill, Chairman of the Board of the Trust. He suggested the idea of Mid-Life Crisis work for clergy, strongly recommending the project to him and through him to the Board.

own.[140] My teacher Mordecai M. Kaplan's words about the past having a vote, but not a veto, still echoed in my mind. I was not beyond some residual religious culture shock when I first heard *HaMotzi* and *Birchat HaMazon*[141] done bareheaded. The subsequent move of Reform to more traditional ways dovetailed nicely with what was evolving in my own religious life. I have often thought of the difference between the two groups that commanded my loyalty as being an institutional relic rather than a needed reality. There is much more that unites us than divides us.

The first Career Review was immensely successful. The group was live, open, and honest, willing to share and to deal with their own frustrations in the rabbinate and work on what they wanted for their future. A high point was the work centering around Fred Pomerantz and his vision of what his rabbinate might be by using his musical abilities in pursuit of his dream. Minutes after returning to Fairfield, Joe called, telling me that many of the participants had called him telling him about their experiences at the Career Review. Joe asked me, "What have you done with these guys?! They are crying, exultant, telling me that it was a life-changing experience."

I was invited to be keynote speaker at the 1976 Central Conference of American Rabbis convention in San Francisco. There, sharing my then recent dissertation, I spoke about the rabbi's family and what effects being a rabbi, a walking, talking, living symbol, has on the rabbi's family. I shared how the rabbi is a hostage of his family and their behavior, and the resultant loneliness and set-apartness of the pulpit occupant and family. I received an extended, prolonged standing ovation from the 700-plus audience.[142] I coined the term Symbolic Exemplar, which provided a name and a framework for the rabbinic experience. It has since become common usage. My very description, drawn from my own experience of what it was like to be a rabbi, touched a very sensitive chord. The tape of the speech was distributed by a number of rabbis to their new congregants, in the hope that congregants might better understand what it is like to be their rabbi.

---

140. In later correspondence with my good friend Rabbi Elliot Dorff, a prominent Conservative thinker, I offered that my dual membership in the Central Conference of American Rabbis and the Rabbinical Assembly gave me the special prerogative of being Reform when it was a matter of personal autonomy and Conservative in matters of community.

141. The prayers before and following eating.

142. An ovation on tape that I can turn to if I am ever feeling doubtful about the nature of my work.

Joe had opened the door, giving me entree to the Central Conference. I became Director of Professional Career Review, and eventually a full member of the Conference. I started to do Mid-Career Reviews around the country and was invited back to various conventions. That began my career as consultant and rabbi to rabbis. Joe and Stanley Dreyfus, Placement Director of the Conference, would send rabbis to Fairfield for one- or two-day individual Career Reviews when that seemed appropriate. The program was described by participants as one of the finest the Conference had ever done for its members. Reviews were run in Illinois, Mississippi, Florida, Georgia, and California, among other places. When the grant ran out, they eventually stopped. They have resumed recently as self-supporting projects in Atlanta, Georgia; Camp Kutz, New York; Malibu, California; and Oconomowoc, Wisconsin.

It took the Rabbinical Assembly, my original rabbinic home, a number of years to catch up. They invited me to deliver an address on "The Inner Dynamics of the Rabbinate" at their 1980 convention. It was essentially the same talk delivered a couple of years earlier in San Francisco. In 1987, I delivered a talk at the Rabbinical Assembly convention in Atlanta, on "Communication Strategies in the Rabbinate for the Next Century." In that talk I reiterated a suggestion that I had made in my dissertation. In the dissertation I offered that

> rabbis need situations where they can experience themselves as just men. . . . In such enclaves the rabbi will not have to be a symbol in order to exist. These enclaves could be of short or long time span. . . . These could range from short-term groups for rabbis . . . to multi-day retreats, to longer enclaves where the rabbi's anonymity insofar as his being a symbol can be guaranteed.[143]

At the convention I suggested that

> I want to encourage the Rabbinical Assembly to start to create ways rabbis can be with each other outside their symbolic exemplarhood. Many young people have come to the rabbinate through the Camp Ramah experience, where they found themselves in an environment, a support sys-

---

143. The Pulpit Rabbi as Symbolic Exemplar, Ph.D. dissertation, Columbia University, 1972, pp. 207–209.

tem that allowed them to really be themselves. Thinking mistakenly that being in a congregation would be the same as being in Camp Ramah, they went on to become servants of the Jewish people. We have to go back to creating, for these servants of the Jewish people, the kind of support system that enables them to spark the idea of being in Jewish service for their entire lives. It means creating groups of rabbis, places where rabbis can be with one another as brothers and sisters,[144] in a way in which they do not have to be "on" all the time.

Rabbi Steve Shaw, newly appointed Director of Community Affairs for the Jewish Theological Seminary, heard my talk, pulled me aside, and for three hours, in his inimitable way, pumped me for anything and everything I knew.[145] Out of that came my participation in the Rabbinic Training Institutes sponsored by the Jewish Theological Seminary for the members of the Rabbinical Assembly. Since the first one, I have been a faculty member in the fulfillment of my dream. Steve brought his own magnificent talents, experience, and creativity to those institutes. That they have been and continue to be a magnificent success is due overwhelmingly to Steve, one of the Jewish community's most unrecognized talents.

THE LITTLE METAPHOR THAT BLESSED ME

A number of years ago, at a Rabbinic Training Institute, I had the chance to co-lead an evening workshop with my old friend Neil Gillman. We had often worked in parallel sessions, but never together. Neil was doing his metaphor gig, helping rabbis clarify what their theology really was. I was there to use trance to solidify each person's work. The participants were asked to present their Metaphor for God. Metaphors poured forth. God was the sun; God was a Jewish Mother; God was a locomotive; and on and on. Each metaphor creative and unique. Neil's metaphor portrayed God as his older brother who never taught him baseball and left him home while he went and played with his friends.[146] Mine, which just popped up in me at the time,

---

144. By 1987 women were being ordained by the Jewish Theological Seminary.

145. Since I had accepted the non-paying invitation to speak only to spend time with my old buddies, I first, until I picked up Steve's enthusiasm, felt resentful of the time being stolen from my visit.

146. Gillman's recollection is that I reframed that metaphor for him by saying, "Perhaps he was off playing with the other kids because he knew you could take care of yourself."

I had never thought of before. I later discovered that it wasn't unique. It was that God was my "hide and seek" partner. Inexplicably one of us initiated a round, decided who was "it," who would pursue whom, who would flee and hide, who would chase and search for the other. Occasionally one of the partners discovered the other's hiding place and made contact. For those brief periods the game was exciting, though each of us did not know where the other was hiding until briefly touched. More often, we were just plain bored, and sat around dozing or scratching our navels. At those times the game could not be more meaningless.

This metaphor resolved my lifetime conundrum of prayer. Prayer was no longer a problem. It had unlocked something profound in me. It took me a number of years intellectually to figure out what had happened. But prayer was no longer a problem. I later grasped that the metaphor blessed who I was, and the way I was. It welcomed that struggling recalcitrant part of me, blessed it as being of integrity, and as a treasured part of my relationship with God. There was room in God's world for that part to be blessed just as he was. That part of me that struggled for expression had human and divine presence. And it was in the Buberian [I–Thou] relationship between them that something new could emerge. The ability to pray. Took a long time but it happened.

Shortly after returning to Fairfield, I was asked to pinch-hit leading services for Laybel Waldman, my successor who was away on sabbatical. I had for years obdurately refused to lead services. I went so far that at one point at the funeral of my beloved elder cousin Sol, I agreed to do the eulogy, but told my family that they would have to get a different rabbi to recite the psalms and lead the service. I am embarrassed today that I behaved that way. At the time it seemed a position of integrity. It seems absurd now. I found myself saying yes to the congregation's request. I wondered if I could be comfortable leading services. To my surprise it turned out to feel good, even fun.

The following week, the Ten Commandments were read. In commenting on the reading, I noted that the first wasn't even a commandment. It was in the words of my colleague and friend, Larry Kushner, God's calling card. I offered that the tenth commandment was impossible to fulfill. God might command identifiable, verifiable acts—observing the Sabbath, honoring one's parents—or the absence of certain acts—not killing, stealing, or committing adultery—but *not coveting*. That is an impossible commandment. How can you command what is in one's mind, and is as natural as daybreak? The really tough part isn't about houses or spouses or asses or Mercedes.

The tough part is the indeterminate "anything that is your neighbor's." What we humans most covet are the indefinables: our neighbor's personality, talents, perceived self-confidence, personal capabilities, the quality of their relationships with their spouses, their family life, etc. What not coveting directs us to is accepting that *we are who we are, that we cannot be different from who we are, and that by valuing and being in relationship with the wounded, often rejected parts of us, we can make something wonderful happen—returning us to who we are—God's creation—made in the Image, blessed with neshamah.* I ended then and now by saying,

> I couldn't be the rabbi my father wanted me to be.
> I couldn't be the rabbi my seminary wanted me to be.
> I couldn't be the rabbi this congregation wanted me to be.
> I have had to be the rabbi I am.
> Some folks like that.
> Others not at all.
> But that's who I am.
>
> God's recalcitrant servant. An Athletic Coach for Rabbis.

2

*Psychotherapy and Judaism Today: The Interface**

As Rabbi/Psychologist, Psychologist/Rabbi, having both feet planted firmly in both camps, I have been intrigued about the interface between Judaism and psychotherapy and the gifts each might bring the other, in creating a mutually beneficial relationship.

The line drawn between psychotherapy (psychology's healing sibling) and religion, which in the past had full responsibility for human mental health, is of recent vintage, as such things go.

Before psychotherapy was split off, it was the religious officiant who was responsible for healing one's emotional life, which was undifferentiated from one's spiritual life. Mental illness as a separate entity did not exist. The term itself is a neologism of the past 100 years. When we look back from the perspective of psychology/psychotherapy upon past behavioral aberrations, we as it were project mental illness backwards. People had physical illness, but there was no such thing as mental illness. From a religious point of view, what we call mental illness was often spirit possession, which the religious officiant could exorcise, resolve, or alleviate by religious, ritual means and restore the sufferer to spiritual wholeness.

---

*This paper, in a somewhat different form, was first delivered as the keynote address of the Chesky Institute of the Central Conference of American Rabbis, and later published in the *CCAR Journal: A Reform Jewish Quarterly*, Summer/Fall 1995, pp. 59–74.

Psychotherapy has become a separate field, named, differentiated, and with a framework of its own. It is only the religious fundamentalist who maintains that religion can do all the mental and emotional healing human-kind requires. During this last century Freud, his disciples, and those who broke from discipleship, crowned psychology and its operational tool psychotherapy "queen of the ball." Religion became the superannuated relative who, though related, was an embarrassment to the bright sparkling and attractive young queen who held such promise for human well-being. Religion initially rejected its renegade daughter. Psychotherapy was the province of the godless. Only those lacking religious faith and practice were involved in psychotherapy. And if it didn't start out that way, atheism for sure was how it would end. Despite the objections of the traditional religions, their renegade daughter made immense progress. The traditional religions were like immigrant parents in a new land, watching as their children assimilated, being "with it" by taking on the culture, the "new" language, and rejecting parental mores, their arcane accents, and "weird" behavior. Some traditional religions fought the new ways, by insisting on the old. Some saw some worth in the new ways and struggled to adapt while not losing their integrity.

Less traditional religions often deferred to the daughter and with the zeitgeist assumed that somehow the daughter knew more about the world of human understanding than religion did. This was implicit in the training of an entire generation of theological students. Pastoral psychology meant a bit of Freud, a smidgen of psychopathology, and how to be a good referral source. Rabbis were to deal with "religious" issues. Mental illness was the province of the mental health professional. The implicit message in Seminary training of that generation was, "You guys are all right for what you're doing but don't get in over your head. You'll do great damage." It was a demeaning message about the inadequacy of religion, Judaism, and us as rabbis in doing the very work we were being trained for. We were *not* taught about using the psychotherapeutic potencies of our role as symbolic exemplars, as spiritual leaders. We were *not* taught how as rabbis we could communicate wellness, heal and create wholeness in the people we would be working with. The rabbi was left in care of the religion for those, often of course "unanalyzed," who might therefore need it, but it was a religion largely shorn of its spiritual and emotional healing potential.

Perhaps psychotherapy, religion's child, needed to go through its own adolescent rebellion, and break away so as to establish its own identity. Perhaps only after standing on its own two feet could a rapprochement take place after years of estrangement. There was more than some surprise when the grandchildren raised on psychotherapy looked back to their grandparents' religion for emotional sustenance—the very same religion their parents had rejected.

Psychotherapy discovered that the ignored grandparents still had a great deal of wisdom to offer, and a mutually respectful adult relationship was possible. To use a metaphor from our own religious myth: though Eve was taken from Adam's rib, once she was differentiated she became a totally separate individual. She shared similarities with Adam: a similar body structure, and nervous system; though similar she was nonetheless, separate and different in her hormonal balance, different in her body structure and different in how she would perceive the world. Yet it was the marriage of these two that allowed the world to grow and flourish. Neither was sufficient. Both were needed. It was in the encounter of difference, with distinct perceptions, divergent genetic structures, and variant personalities that the world was able to progress.

The time is at hand for today's heterodox religions, grown in their ability to tolerate otherness, and today's mature psychotherapy to enter into relationship, perhaps even marriage—valuing each other's individuality and uniqueness, maximizing their contact while respecting each other's boundaries.

PSYCHOTHERAPY TODAY

Dominant in psychotherapy today is the recognition that each human being constructs his or her own reality. People experience the same "objective" stimulus "out there" yet each responds differently to that stimulus. Each selects from an overwhelming amount of experience, in known and unknown ways, the parts of "reality" to respond to. Each creates out of the world of experience a separate and distinct reality, and a map of reality, with which one can navigate in the world. Reality refers today to two different orders of reality: *first-order reality* and *second-order reality*. The difference is crucial. First-order reality concerns itself with the properties of things, with agreed definitions, with measurements that we make that establish what something *is*. We have a consensus in the community that something is real. We determine that a red dress is not a blue coat because when we apply our spectroscope we know a certain space is called red, another space blue, and we have agreed that if a garment is cut in one way it is considered to be a dress and if cut in another, it is sold as a coat. We agree that a whale, though it swims in the water like a fish, is nevertheless a mammal. We define what we call a mammal by the way it reproduces, not that it spends its life in the water. We know that gold is a certain color and demonstrates certain properties when subject to analysis. We have created categories, measurements, tests, that define that things are thus and so, and a community has agreed that that is how things are. These things are *first-order reality*. Therefore, one who is in touch with reality knows that a red light is red, a whale is a mammal, and gold is yellow.

Second-order reality concerns itself not with the properties of things, not with what things are (which in itself is a matter of community consensus), but rather with what they *mean*. Both psychotherapy and religion are concerned with the meaning of things, i.e., with second-order reality. We may be absolutely sure that a light is red, but what a red light means is a quite different thing. If the light being red means STOP, we teach that meaning to our children, to save them from harm. A red light may also signify the presence of a house of ill repute. Red may be mandated by the authorities for constructing an EXIT sign. Yet clear-headed, "reality"-oriented individuals may with integrity argue at a zoning meeting that the exit signs should be green because green means moving forward and red means stop. Whether a whale is a fish or a mammal is objectively "verifiable." Whether whales should be protected or what their meaning is in the nature of the world is a question of "second-order reality." Paul Watzlawick[1] gives yet another example of someone who dives into the water to save the life of a drowning man. We can certainly establish, in first-order reality, what has taken place: A body is flailing about in the water, another body has moved toward the first, and one has removed the other from the water. But the question intriguing us in both psychotherapy and religion is, Why did one do it? What meaning does the action have for each of them? What things mean and how we act upon our perception of what they mean is a second-order reality question. As Jews, we specifically think of righteous gentiles who during the Second World War hid and saved Jews from extermination. We wonder, What made them do it? What was their motivation? What was their intention? What meaning did their act have? These questions of meaning are second-order reality.

The "second-order" meaning we attribute to aspects of "first-order reality" helps determine what we are able to do and not do in our world. Knowing that the red of a traffic signal means stop and the green means go

---

1. Paul Watzlawick, ed. *Invented Reality: How Do We Know What We Believe We Know?* (Contributions to Constructivism). New York: W. W. Norton, 1984.

enables us to build larger cities where traffic can move more easily. We have a tinge of guilt and even fear being ticketed and fined for passing a red light in the middle of the night with no traffic around. Yet these same sets of useful meanings have limitations. Anyone who has been involved in a New York City gridlock situation knows that in intensely heavy traffic situations, one needs additional sources of meaning beyond red and green lights. In New York City those sources of meaning wear brown uniforms. The color denotes them as traffic controllers, not police. They supersede the red and green lights and have the authority to give signals which direct traffic in a new way, ignoring the previous meanings.

The sum total of our first- and second-order realities—what things are and what things mean—comprises the internal map we use to get around in the world. Each of us consciously and unconsciously operates in the world out of our own unique internal map. That is a map of how things are and, more importantly, what they mean. All maps are not equal. *Some maps work more adequately.* There are consequences to having one map rather than another. What happens when a map doesn't work? What happens when no matter what solutions a person attempts, things only get worse? Maps that don't work bring people to psychotherapy. Psychotherapy's purpose today might well be described as realigning people's internal maps, so that they might function more effectively.

In pursuit of that goal of realigning maps, psychotherapy today increasingly recognizes that the myths and language we use are powerful forces in governing our lives. Whether those myths and maps are that we are an abused child, or the adult child of an alcoholic, or someone who was dominated by his father, or whose mother was competitive with her—those myths and maps govern and determine our lives. Psychotherapy further recognizes that those myths and maps are selected constructs out of the vast amounts of data that exist. We have learned in psychotherapy that the stories clients tell us are always their particular, unique perceptions and understandings of what may or may not have happened. They are not, nor can they really be for the purposes of psychotherapy, descriptions of what "actually" did happen. They are not "first-order reality" (if there is such a thing). They are rather descriptions of the meaning sequences that our clients have attributed to whatever did happen, edited for meaning and shaped by its perceived significance to them. Clients tell us how they live their lives, think about themselves and others, and act according to those set of meanings. We used to talk about patients' stories as though they were fact. So, of course, we blamed mothers for ruining their children because our patients complained that Mother did thus and so. We ignored the frames that we therapists put around our patients' recounting, influenced by Freud's teachings that mothers were the cause of children's trouble. Therefore we asked questions and led the discussion in that direction. Finding what we knew was there anyway, we said, "Ah-ha, so it was your mother who ruined you." We compiled the evidence and wrote articles and books about mothers' responsibility and helped create a generation in which mothers ended up blaming themselves for how their children turned out. We used to believe that the stories our own presuppositions elicited were "reality." Hopefully we no longer do.

To reiterate: It is the meaning our clients attribute to their stories, the myth that the stories support, the map of reality the stories buttress, that is crucial in bringing a client into our office and crucial in considering how psychotherapy may help that client.

A story out of my own psychotherapy. Though my father and mother were never separated, I was raised almost totally by my father. My mother was very much in the background. (That, in itself, is an interesting statement of framework.) Experiences that most people associate with their mothers, are, for me, associated with my father. My father read bedtime stories to me, sang lullabies, cooked breakfast, took me to school, bought my clothes, was the more physically affectionate parent, etc. During the second year of my psychotherapy (back then it was really serious business, three times a week, and I had friends who were on the couch five times a week, so mine was a bargain), after having talked for a year and a half about my relationship with my father, my therapist one day said, "What about your mother?" I offered that she seemed to be a rather nice lady with whom I had a pleasantly enjoyable relationship. He quickly began to educate me in his particular up-to-date view of the world, influenced I now know by Freud & Co., which embraced the idea that children should be raised by their mothers. We talked about how my father had "kidnapped" me from my mother, and how she surrendered me to him with barely a whimper. I vividly remember (or at least I think I do) him saying that "a lioness fights for her cubs"—letting me draw the inevitable conclusion that my mother was less woman and less mother than she should have been. And so, I "inevitably" developed, or "got in touch with," as my therapist would have put it, a great deal of anger and resentment towards my mother. He had changed my map, the very meaning of my story, and that had "inevitable" consequences. I am aware that he could have framed the "facts" differently, thus changing my story's meaning. He could have wisely offered that my mother recognized that she was more limited than my father in her ability to raise me and therefore she graciously and courageously made the greatest sacrifice a woman can make. She backed away and allowed my father to do the job he could do better than she. That framing of the "reality" would have given a different meaning to the story and might well have produced feelings of gratitude, warmth, kindness, and appreciation for a mother's courage and caring.

Psychotherapy today is intently focused on rearranging the meanings in people's lives, in their maps of second-order reality. If a person becomes depressed, seemingly as the result of losing a job, the depression is linked to the meaning being "laid off" has in that person's map. Persons going through divorce, responding with rage, depression, desperation, worthlessness, all elements of the divorce roller coaster, are acting out the meaning of the partners in their lives. They may perceive their partners as the only ones they will ever have. They may be unaware of other options. They may have learned that a marriage ending marks them a failure. And what a terrible thing it is to fail at something so important. Alternately they could perceive the end of the marriage as a blessing; an end to pain and an entrance to another phase of life. Their response will be determined by the meaning map that guides them, the "second-order reality" they have constructed.

Psychotherapy deals ever more explicitly with the issue of meaning. Meaning may be the core issue in psychotherapy. As psychotherapy has focused more clearly and overtly on meaning, it has inexorably found itself facing issues long dealt with by religion. Spirituality, human worth, the source of our resources, the quest for meaning, symbolic meanings, ritual, and so on, have come to the fore in psychotherapy. Religion, psychotherapy's superannuated antecedent, has been struggling with these for countless eons. Psychotherapy, in its attempts to alter the inner map, has been experimenting with meditation, trance, guided imagery, turning inwards to one's own resources, adopting a style close to prayer, perhaps a first or second cousin once removed. Yet cousins do tend to replicate ancestral behavior. Books on symbols in psychotherapy are now appearing on psychotherapy shelves; workshops on using rituals in therapy are being offered.

Overt spiritual statements, echoes and reiterations of historical religion, are commonplace talk at coffee breaks at therapist conventions. Ten or fifteen years ago these authors would not have ventured to talk about such things, much less publish them. Such talk would have embarrassed a psychotherapist just a few years ago. Psychotherapy and religion have converged, as psychotherapy has become more and more concerned with "second-order reality." Religion, certainly heterodox religion, has long been concerned with "second-order reality," being less concerned with what things are than with what they mean. The danger of fundamentalist orthodoxies is in their taking religion to be a description of first-order reality. In this area an orthodoxy gets stuck when it affirms not only what things mean but what they *really* are, and therefore insists that its way is the only true way.

So psychotherapy has turned back to take a closer look at religion, realizing that religion has always been concerned with the search for meaning in life, and it is of such meanings that psychotherapy is made, and with such meanings that it does its work.

Since each of us comes to the world with distinct sensibilities, perceptions, backgrounds, and training, each person creates his own map of reality. There may be similarities in the pattern of meanings, yet no two maps are identical. Psychotherapy has come full circle to understand the Mishna:

> In the beginning, only one person was created as a demonstration of God's greatness. A human being mints many coins from a single mold and all are duplicates, interchangeable with one another. Yet, God creates everyone in the mold of the first person and there are no duplicates; each human being is unique. Therefore, each and every one of us is obliged to affirm:
>
> For my sake, the world was created. [Sanhedrin 4:5]

It is in our uniqueness that each of us fashions out of creation our map, our myth, our symphony of meanings upon which we act out our lives. These are ultimately our own singular constructs, no matter what may or may not be out there. Paul Watzlawick[2] points out that this inevitably leads to three outcomes crucial in the work of today's psychotherapy.

"First of all . . . if we come to see the world as our own invention, we must apply this insight to the world of our fellow creatures as well. If we know that we do not or cannot know the truth, that our view of the world is only more or less *fitting*, we will find it difficult to ascribe madness or badness to the world views of others and to remain caught in the primitive Manichean conviction that 'whoever is not for me is against me.' The realization that we know nothing as long as we do not know that we shall never know the ultimate truth is the precondition for one's respect for the realities others have invented for themselves." The first outcome therefore is tolerance and an appreciation of difference.

---

2. Watzlawick, *Invented Reality*, p. 326.

"Secondly, such a person [who knows that he has constructed his own world] would feel responsible in a very deep ethical sense, *responsible* not only for conscious decisions and actions, not only for dreams, but in a much wider sense—even for the reality created by self-fulfilling prophecies." The *second* outcome therefore is a sense of responsibility, of ownership, of one's thinking and action.

Thirdly, "This total responsibility would mean total *freedom*. Whoever is conscious of being the architect of his or her own reality would be equally aware of the ever present possibility of constructing it differently. In the truest sense of the word this person would be a heretic; that is one who knows that choice is possible." This third outcome points toward creativity.

The three precious gifts modern psychotherapy brings to its rendezvous with religion today are tolerance and forbearance for the world others have created; responsibility for one's own world as one's own creation; and freedom to move around in it, to re-create it and thereby maximize choice.

HETERODOX JUDAISM/RELIGION

If tolerance, responsibility, and freedom are the gifts psychotherapy brings to this rapprochement, what gifts does Judaism bring?

I refer to heterodox, non-fundamentalist Judaism. The fundamentalist orthodox[3] position assumes that the truth is already known; that the truth they hold is essentially first-order reality and thus *reality is as "they" see it*. Reality has been discovered, largely through revelation, and humanity must be brought to witness and live by "the revealed truth." If we judge a position by its outcome, fundamentalist/orthodoxies of all kinds have throughout history led to a blasphemous aggregate of death and destruction. They have divided people into those who knew the truth and those unfortunates who did not and must therefore be brought to the truth or removed from the scene. Orthodoxies, whether religious or secular, have led to *intolerance* of monumental proportions. Orthodoxies have led to people *not taking responsibility* for their actions, claiming that they were acting in the name of the god, the politics, or the belief in which they trusted unequivocally. Fundamentalists

---

3. Not all who call themselves Orthodox are necessarily fundamentalist. I have Modern Orthodox friends who are in no way fundamentalists.

do not permit themselves the freedom to *create* anew, to be heretics in the best sense of the word. It is also forbidden for others to explore new paths, lest they stray from the "true" way. What is true and real is already known and applicable to all! Orthodoxy is as sure as each football team is, as each army going to war is, as each demagogue is that "God is on our side." The other side, benighted, if not heretic in the worst sense of the word, will be defeated, if not sooner, then later. The outcomes of this have been, to put it mildly, less than benign. My interest therefore is in what non-fundamentalist, heterodox religion brings to the relationship with psychotherapy.

A common objection to non-fundamentalist, heterodox religion is that it is wishy-washy, not really standing for much of anything. Liberal religion, it is said, doesn't give its adherents something solid to hold onto amidst the vicissitudes of the world. Non-orthodox religions are too "subjective," as if there is such a thing as objectivity. How is one to know how to behave, what to believe, what to do, if everyone has their own opinions (and all seem equally valid), if each of us inhabits a different and unique world?

Religion has too often been misunderstood to be a search for certainty. Certainty for how things really are precludes having everyone thinking and behaving differently. If Reform Judaism asserts that each individual is religiously autonomous and Conservative Judaism offers that one can follow either the majority or minority position of its law committee, how does one know what's *really* right? We humans crave certainty. We abhor chaos. We want to see things as others see them. We feel reassured when others experience "reality" as we do. We prefer being "in sync," for it confirms that we are OK and avoids the sense of confusion we mostly detest. When confronted with cognitive dissonance, we wonder, how come "they" don't experience things the way "we" do? "Any right thinking person would see it that way." And as the cognitive dissonance literature demonstrates, we often wonder how come "we" don't see it "their" way. Someone must be *right!* We want to agree, but how can both we and they be right? A monotheistic worldview complicates our accepting multiple "truths" by implicitly postulating that there is only *one* ultimate truth. So we hold to our own (often inculcated) perceptions and reject others' "realities," assuming that they are wrong or, at best, woefully inaccurate. Sometimes, when our maps do not seem to be working, when nothing we try succeeds, when our map fails to get us anyplace worth going, we adopt someone else's map in toto, making a leap into a new way of thinking, seeing, hearing, and feeling. We *convert* and are reborn to a new reality, with an entirely new set of perceptions and meanings, and a new, this time *correct*, understanding of how things *really* are. This is an outcome of our search for certainty and our struggle to avoid the confusion of multiple "realities."

Religion need not be the pursuit of certainty. It can and has been, the search for meaning(fulness)—*not* ultimate meaning, for that is the search for certainty in disguise.

If non-orthodox religion cannot provide absolute certitude nor ultimate meaning, of what use is it anyhow? Non-orthodox religion can be vitally, even crucially, useful in our search. From birth, our reality is significantly molded by the world around us. Our communities' beliefs, our parents' constructions of reality, themselves influenced by their forebears, the very language we inherit help choose what in the environment is attended to, what is ignored, what is important, what is trivial, what the meaning and meaningfulness of "reality" is. All of these help construct our idiosyncratic maps of reality, determining how we will get around in the world. One does not nor can one make the map by oneself. It would take inordinately long, and be terribly limited in its usefulness. We are, of necessity, heirs of those mapmakers who went before. As Watzlawick[4] has put it, "No living being can afford to 'reinvent' the world every day. Most of the time, there is no good reason to abandon a proven solution."

As Jews, we are members of a community that has historically specialized in the search for meaning. We might well describe ourselves as the newest members of the ancient and most honorable guild "Meaning Map Makers." To be sure, ours is not the only guild, nor is our way of working the only way; our plan is not the only useful one, ours is not the only map, but our guild nonetheless has an illustrious history.

Our maps have been in use for countless generations. They have helped our people, and others who chose to make use of parts of our maps, to find their way in the world in meaningful and useful ways.

Parts of our maps show highways that now lead to dead ends. Others lead to quicksand pits in which countless people have been swallowed up. Some show roads that lead to caves containing wondrous treasures, and somehow a new super highway leading from now to nowhere has blocked access to those caves. Other winding roads, difficult to ascend, lead to mountain tops from which the vista is magnificent and awe-inspiring. Some of our maps have useful landmarks that have been eroded with time, encrusted with debris, and they may need to be cleared off or perhaps reconstructed in order to once again be useful. Yet, all in all, our maps have served well.

---

4. Watzlawick, *Invented Reality*, p. 165.

And we, today's guild members, are the inheritors not only of those maps but, even more valuable, of a long tradition of meaning map makers. Their maps are part of that tradition. We cannot be members of the guild without knowing what they did and what they strove to accomplish with their maps. They were adept at finding meanings that work, meanings that fit, that help in getting around in the world. Their ability to find useful sources of meaning in a variety of places and situations is legendary. They were able to adjust their maps to new circumstances, to respond to change in their environment with new, useful structures, which other people were unable to do. As apprentice members of the guild, we do well to study their process and assess their results.

Worshiping one's deity in a foreign land presented a severe problem, not only to the local map our ancestors used, but also to the general map used throughout the ancient world. Though the idea that the God of Israel was creator and ruler of the whole world was struggling for acceptance, the maps of meaning generally in use accepted that a people's god and land were inextricably linked. A god ruled over a specific territory and its inhabitants. II Kings;5 reflects this map. Naaman, Chief of Staff of the King of Aram, is cured of leprosy by Elisha. Impressed by the God Elisha represents, Naaman affirms that "there is no God in the whole world except in Israel!" Naaman, wanting to worship the God of Israel, faces a curious problem. How does he do that, if God's domain is the land of Israel? Using the available map, Naaman solves his problem, by packing a suitcase of holy land dirt, spreading it in its new foreign location and so worships the God of Israel on the soil of Israel— a patchwork solution at best. If a land and its inhabitants were conquered, the god of the land was thereby defeated. If the populace was exiled to a foreign land, they expected to worship the god of that locale, as the Samaritans did when they were exiled from their home *to* the land of Israel, in exchange for the exiled northern tribes. In 586 BCE Judah and Jerusalem were conquered by the Babylonians, the God of the Jews "defeated," God's people exiled to the jurisdiction of a god to whom they were fully expected to pay allegiance. This would have brought a noble experiment to an ignominious end. We would at best have been a footnote in history.

Our good fortune was that the "Meaning Map Maker Guild" was headed up at the time by one Jeremiah son of Hilkiah, of the priests who were in Anatoth in the land of Benjamin.[5] He made some needed adjustments

---

5. Biblical book of Jeremiah; Chapter 1.

to the map. He mapped out a new road, new points on the compass. The *God* of Israel had *not* been defeated. In fact the defeat and exile were all God's plan. God was punishing Israel for lack of covenantal fidelity and nonetheless God was going into exile with Israel. Israel's exile and suffering were evidence of God's *concern*. One day, they would return in triumph to reclaim the land. A new map had been created that fit what was happening. A map that enabled Jewish life to continue in conditions of exile and persecution for over two thousand years. The map worked at least until the emancipation,[6] when new maps pointed in other directions. Auschwitz raises profound questions and doubts about our map's utility. Our long-used map no longer fits our reality. We have since the emancipation been working on a revised map to deal with those awesome events. Whether we will succeed is another question.

Jewish tradition tells[7] of Moses himself standing in the back of Rabbi Akiva's classroom. Moses did not understand a word of what was going on and was astonished when at the end of the lesson, Akiva offered that he was teaching the law according to Moses. The rabbis recognized that changes in the map had made it unrecognizable, even by he who was arguably the greatest meaning map maker of all time.

Our maps *have* changed. The tradition, recognizing that change has happened, is often unaware how it happened, and more often sloughs off responsibility for the change. Change is not easy. The old becomes stiff, rigid, and stuck in place. However, the guild's recognition that the maps *have* changed supports change and a modicum of tolerance. Change also implies the maps' limited utility. And limited utility means that no one person has the final say. No one map covers all the possibilities—horizontally, throughout the world, and vertically, down the generations. The Mishnah, in Sanhedrin, alludes to this sense of tolerance for varieties of meanings when it offers a second reason for the creation of only one person—so that no one might say that "my ancestor was greater, truer, more correct, than yours."[8]

For a relationship to work, commonality, difference, and each partner's awareness of his or her own deficiencies are needed. We heterodox Jews have change and tolerance in our dowry. Yet we have been defi-

---

6. Usually dated from the French Revolution in 1789.

7. Talmud Bavli: Menahot 29b.

8. Ibid. Sanhedrin 4:5.

cient in understanding that others experience and construct the world differently. We know from our own historical behavior towards others and, more painfully, from what has happened to us, how difficult it is for humankind to allow for change and tolerance. We know how hard it is to be tolerant because intolerance is deeply ingrained in our history. It is difficult to be tolerant when one is part of a community that has a particular view that supports a particular map of the territory. So paradoxically a gift we bring to this match is the history of intolerance that we have inflicted on each other and have had inflicted on us. We know the price of intolerance. Among modern psychotherapy's strong points is its tolerance for the varieties and vagaries of human experience. Psychotherapy struggles to accept that someone else's meaning, though different, can be as valid and "true" as ours. Psychologically we are prone to be intolerant; it is in our nature to believe that "they" ought to understand and experience the "world" the way we do. With psychotherapy's striving for open-mindedness, and our religious underpinnings for tolerance, and never forgetting the price of intolerance, together we must zealously *guard tolerance* in every way.

Beyond being heirs to a long line of meaning map makers, with a proven record of creative mapmaking, and beyond our hypersensitivity to intolerance, we bring another priceless gift to this encounter. We bring a sense of *community*, often lacking in today's psychotherapy. We are B'nai B'rit[9] —a community, living in a covenantal relationship with a divine other. It is in and by community that people's maps of reality are shaped and formed. So much of how we think, what we perceive, what we ignore, and what has meaning, the very maps we use are community constructs. Historical Judaism is community oriented. One prays in the plural, shares a common history going back thousands of years; is commanded to think of oneself as present at the Exodus and at Sinai; participates in a common destiny, awaiting the Messianic era when the community will be restored to its glory. In the meantime, each member of the community is responsible for every other member. A religious community provides a rich environment for nurturing tolerance, responsibility, and creativity. In community the guild can do its work of taking responsibility for the reality it authors, creatively changing it where needed, and demonstrating tolerance, not only for the changing, but for those who differ. A community provides a place where fit can be ascertained, where what works can be experienced and evaluated in situ.

---

9. Literally, Children of the Covenant.

Being in community, in a covenantal relationship, we are not only responsible for our own individual map, our own created reality, but also accountable beyond ourselves for what we do with the map we have created. Judaism assumes *accountability* to a divine covenant partner, to those who are our fellows within the covenant, and to those who find themselves outside of its circumscribed parameters. *Individual and community accountability is a profound gift that Judaism brings to the relationship with psychotherapy.* Accountability makes us take responsibility more earnestly. Accountability provides a crucial nuance all too often absent in psychotherapy, whose focus has been on the individual, his or her maps, his or her well-being, with only peripheral attention paid to the usefulness, influence, and importance of community.

The map utilized by this particular community of priests and holy nation obliges each individual to pay exquisite attention to the frame one creates for *the details of daily living.* The meaning is in the details. Our task is to make those details fit into a covenantal frame; to realize them fully in community; and to make their created meaning a part of one's relationship with God, the covenantal partner.

One compass point for Jewish attention to the details has been what we eat. "Kosher" has passed into the English vernacular. Curiously enough, its meaning in the vernacular is similar to what it meant in its original framework. Something kosher was appropriate for use by a member of a covenant community. We well know that kosher has nothing to do with clean—that was a fallacious reading by a cartographer of an altogether different persuasion.

How I introduced my wife who came from another tradition to the vagaries of a kosher kitchen may elucidate this. I had always lived in a kosher home, and wanted that to continue in our forthcoming marriage. I needed to convince her that this was important and to enlist her help in day-to-day maintenance. I started by explaining that foods are divided into those that are kosher and those that are not (*trayf*). This seemed to make some sense because her apperceptive mass included that Jews did not eat pork. True enough, but in a kosher home only certain meats that met specified criteria, and had been processed in a certain way, could be eaten. An eyebrow seemed to lift. I went on to offer that we also distinguished between milk and meat. Her pupils widened a bit. Undaunted, I went on to explain that chicken is defined as meat, while fish (with fins and scales of course) is neither meat nor dairy, but is in a third category called *pareve*. I then proceeded to explain that though chicken is meat, chicken eggs are *pareve*, neither meat nor milk.

That though milk comes from cows, it is nonetheless dairy and not to be eaten with the meat of the animal it comes from. By now, her eyes had glazed over, and she was approaching a deep trance state. I proceeded to explain that dishes and other utensils can only touch either milk or meat, with the notable exception of glass, which, I fearlessly added, was exempt from this prohibition. If silverware violated these prohibitions in any way, the offending utensil can only be reused after being planted in the dirt for twenty-four hours. Her trance deepened! I further explained that there is some question about dishwashers being used for milk and meat, and as a matter of fact, some very traditional families have two dishwashers and even two kitchens to guarantee that no milk products, utensils, items, etc., would come in contact with meat products, utensils, items, etc. Watching her response I was sure she was wondering if she still had time to get out of this relationship with a patently psychotic man. What other craziness might he be hiding from her? She offered as she came out of trance, "Why make life so difficult?" I realized that if someone came into my office and described behavior like this I would immediately start treatment to relieve them of obsessive-compulsive behavior of a most disturbed sort. They might indeed need years of therapy with our goal being to enable them to use the meat silverware with milk products, and further to cure them of this obsessive need of counting the hours between meat and milk.

My future wife's reaction made crystal clear to me that a set of rules I had lived with and accepted since I was a child could also be seen as an obsessive's nightmare. It was only because the map I inherited gave these behaviors a frame of meaning that they made sense to me. My frame had to do with marking our home as a Jewish home and being reminded of that every time we ate. These were important details in a covenantal relationship with the people Israel throughout the world, and with their God, who it is told, had taken the time to command something about what one might eat and might not. It meant taking seriously that the guild of meaning map makers had taken that command and expanded it into the kosher laws. A kosher home was a reminder in conscious and unconscious ways every day, at life's most repetitive acts, that I was accountable and that every small act of eating was meaningful. Since entering the covenant my wife has started to read labels, ensuring that only kosher products enter our kitchen. With the frame the map provides, the behavior has some meaning; without the frame, the behavior is ludicrous.

The sense of accountable responsibility for our own behavior, and that of the community of which we are a part, our burning desire to seek meaning in all of the highways and byways of our maps, thus being zealous members of the guild of meaning map makers, are among our contributions to the new interface. We add to this, as our partner psychotherapy often does not, that *not all meanings are equal*. A danger in the message of psychotherapy is that since all meanings are constructed, none is any better than the others. Our emphasis on accountability in the meanings we create can help psychotherapy not lapse into solipsism.

Both partners know, each from its own history, that people have created new understandings and new meanings and that meanings change over time. Sometimes meanings change more rapidly, sometimes more slowly. And both partners know from historical struggles that have taken place in their own communities, the freedom to create must be guarded, for meaning making comes hard, and people think that when they have meanings that seem to fit, they don't want others to tamper with what they have worked so hard to achieve.

Religion and psychotherapy have come a long way. Of common antecedents, and having individuated sufficiently, they now enter a new alliance, contributing to a life rich with meaning, marked by their similarities and nourished by their differences. They can co-create a community dedicated to meaning making in the details of life, and fashion an experiential framework in which new constructs are tested and evaluated. Their conjoined attributes of tolerance, responsibility, creativity, and accountability can make this a bounteous and blessed relationship. May we live to see the offspring.

3
*Who Become Clergy?**

INTRODUCTION

Monseigneur E. Robert Arthur, the tall, baldish Canon lawyer who was one of Cardinal O'Boyle's closest advisers, put his fingers in the stiff, white collar around his neck and said, "As long as I'm wearing this collar, people will listen to what I say, but without it in two weeks I'm just another guy."†

The idea that clergy are different from the rest of the population is strongly held in Western religion. A clergyman is a different kind of person, "a member of the third sex."[1] Religions affirm this difference by requiring celibacy, or at least a different kind of sexual morality from that of the laity; by ordaining instead of invariably requiring graduation of their trainees; by suggesting that poverty may be a blessing and worldly goods a temptation; by asking them to be prophets; and by affirming that the ministry is basically different from all other callings in that those in it are there because they have heard a divine call. "The medical doctor may have greater status, the attor-

---

*Published as "Who Become Clergymen?" in *The Journal of Religion & Health*, Vol. 10, No. 1, January 1971, pp. 50–76.
†The Rev. Thomas J. Fleming. "Confrontation in Washington—The Cardinal versus the Dissenters." *New York Times Magazine*, November 24, 1968. Copyright 1968 by The New York Times Company. Reprinted by permission.

ney may be more feared, but the clergyman is expected to be more wholly other. His motivations are expected to be more noble, his calling more sacred, his thoughts more pure, his life more dedicated, his sacrifices more generous."[2]

Rubenstein has pointed to this sense of differentness: "Religion abounds in paradoxes not the least of which is the peculiar combination of arrogance and humility which so frequently marks the religious leader. He is in his own eyes privy to secrets unavailable to the multitude. He is also depressed by his own infinite lack of worth for the high charge that rests upon him. Above all, he is lonely and set apart as are no other men. As a Catholic priest he may never know the most important single role available to men, that of father of a family; as a rabbi the clergyman is frequently forced to fulfill expectations of ritual behavior demanded by his community as binding upon him but not upon them. Seldom, if ever, is the clergyman able to relax and feel that he can be himself with his people."[3]

That the clergy are a deviant group in American culture has been suggested by a great many observers.[4] Booth says that "it is a priori unlikely that the psychodynamics of the well-functioning secular population would be the same as those of the well-functioning clerical population."[5] Though there has been a tendency in our society, often on the part of ministers and clergymen themselves, to deny any differentness and to affirm the normality and the undeviant nature of the clergy,[6] the evidence seems to point in the other direction. Bier tried to show the normality and adjustment of the clergy in his well-controlled work with the MMPI, but his conclusions read in the opposite direction. He has since then affirmed that the clergy are "the most deviant portion of an already deviant population [college and graduate school men]."[7] Though clergymen most vociferously object to "being treated as different from other people; being placed on a pedestal; expected to do things not expected of others; or being restricted in behavior; and to the general feeling of being something different . . . of being men of the third sex,"[8] yet the fact remains that they have placed themselves in a situation where they are seen in exactly this way. This sense of differentness and otherness has endless references in the literature. It is a part of the underlying cultural orientation of Western religions toward their clergy. If this is indeed so, the question that we must ask is: Why do men choose such roles, and what is there unique about them that makes them decide to become clergymen?

That vocational choice is to a significant degree determined by personality and may represent a means of conflict resolution is a theory held by both those whose main work has been in the psychology of occupations,[9] those whose emphasis has been in direct work with the clergy,[10] and those who have tried to relate the two.[11] It is hypothesized that there is a relationship between personality and occupational choice. This relationship may be expressed consciously or unconsciously. It may be seen as the implementation of the self-concept[12] or the choice may be made because of the need to resolve certain drives.[13] Booth has pointed out that "what Freud observed about the relationship between infantile trauma and neurosis holds equally true for the relationship between childhood milieu and vocation."[14] No matter whether certain specific types would be attracted by different vocations. Indeed, not only are different personality patterns found among those in various occupational groups, but persons of specific personality types seem to be attracted to certain vocations.

Religion has also been seen as related to personality needs. Since Freud many have seen religion as a phenomenon based on neurotic security needs within the individual. Freud suggested that religion is an attempt to resolve some of the traumata and insecurities experienced in childhood.[15] It does this by recreating man's childhood father on a higher level. The God who is created is thus a fantasy father figure who helps us out with many of the problems of guilt and aggression, sex and ego. Religion is seen as one response to a variety of frustrations. These frustrations may be natural destructive forces from the outer world, decay of the body or the suppression of instinctive desires such as sex, aggression, and ego needs by the civilization. The internalization of these restraints, with the help of the superego, has created problems that man resolves through the medium of religion. Others have picked up on Freud's idea of the conflict between the superego and the instincts and emphasized particularly the sexual and aggressive drives.[16] Flugel pointed out that this conflict is relieved by projection of the superego, which now appears as God.[17] Ranck, Broen, Rokeach, and others have pointed to the relationship of personality and religious positions of various sorts.[18] Whichever theory one adopts, religion and personality seem to be deeply involved. Religion may be seen as one of the most direct expressions of the way in which man resolves many of his ultimate conflicts.

Certainly between them, vocation and religion both would seem to have a great deal to do with personality. One might then hypothesize that the men who become religious professionals, who enter a world of differentness and otherness, do so because of some strong personality determinants that may differentiate them from the rest of the population. If this is so, if this is not a myth, then there is something different about these men.

The purpose of this paper will be to try to review the literature investigating personality dimensions of the clergy. Both the theories and the research done on the personality correlates and other work that may shed light on them will be reviewed to see if there are differential personality characteristics. Such leads may suggest future directions for investigation and hypotheses worth checking out. We may begin to clarify whether this differentness is a myth or has some basis in the personality of the men who become our clergy.

SOME METHODOLOGICAL PROBLEMS AND ASSUMPTIONS

Concern with personality factors of men in the clergy has grown greatly in recent years. McCarthy in 1942 noted that there was no literature to speak of on the subject. "The writer is unable to locate any competent study of the problem of personality testing among Divinity students."[19] Most of the information he obtained came from letters that deans and heads of theological schools all over the country were kind enough to send him. At that time he reports that there was only one personality study of divinity school students that had been made by a large Protestant church group anxious to test its applicants for places in the foreign mission field. Those first results suggested that applicants for mission work tended to be more emotionally unstable than the average person. What there was of the early work seems to have been motivated polemically; it either attacked or defended the clergy. The writing of that genre may be best characterized by two articles that appeared in 1936. Abrams, in an article satirical at best and hostile at worst, pointed to the "sickness" of the clergy on the basis of evidence "compiled from a *Who's Who*." Entitled "Psychic Satisfactions of the Clergy," the article pointed to such satisfactions as "selected by committee of Tennessee preachers to affirm the scripturalness of instrumental music in church worship in a debate lasting five nights" or "gospel singer since the age of 5, preacher since the age of 9."[20] What this proved beyond the author's hostility is questionable. Strange to say, the Abrams article was dignified by appearance in the *Journal of Abnormal and Social Psychology*. The second 1936 article, by Thomas Verner Moore, which achieved only a place in the *American Ecclesiastical Review*, made a serious attempt to investigate the incidence of the rate of insanity and the possibilities of detecting pre-psychotics among priests and religious brothers and sisters.[21] In 1964, the U.S. Department of Health, Education, and Welfare *Bibliography on Religion and Mental Health* reported that during the four years before there were at least sixty-three references to the psychological screening and mental health of the clergy alone.[22] Among the more than 700 articles listed in this bibliography, many of the others dealt in a roundabout way with personality correlates of the clergy.

The field has not been without problems. One of the first of them is the question: Who is a clergyman? It seems self-evident that a clergyman is anyone in religious work. But it is not so simple. "The clergy" includes a rather broad spectrum of people who in truth are doing quite a variety of jobs. A clergyman can be a teaching brother in a high school, a full-time rabbi, a weekend minister in a Revivalist Church, a religious educator, a missionary, a writer of books on prayer, a seminary registrar, a principal in a religious school, a cloistered nun, or a brother in a monastic order. This list includes a much too wide range of people who actually are in rather different professions. A surprisingly large number of works have ignored these rather significant distinctions. Many have merged these groups into one, presenting a single set of data for them all and describing them as one group.[23]

In this paper we shall be interested in the personality correlates of the pulpit clergy. But this too presents a problem. The amount of work done on the pulpit clergy has been too limited to be significant. So, for our purposes we will include work done on the pulpit clergy and those who are in seminaries that directly lead to pulpit work. (In the case of Catholics this means diocesan seminaries.) It is recognized that not all the men who are in the seminaries will end up in the pulpit; nor will they necessarily end up in another form of religious life. It will be the assumption here that for these men in such seminaries the pulpit life is a real option and that there may be personality factors at work causing them to give significant consideration to pulpit work.

Even if we narrow our concern to pulpit clergy and pulpit seminarians, we are not quite out of the woods. A great variety of men fill pulpits. Lenski has pointed out differences between Protestant and Roman Catholic clergymen in terms of their socioeconomic background, class of origin, and their influence on their congregations.[24] Harrower affirms that "one of the conclusions we are able to draw from a comparison of Rorschach test scores for a group of medical students and candidates for the Unitarian Universalist Ministry is that on the basis of these two scores, the Unitarian population contains persons who show . . . greater individuality or less likeness one to the other than do medical students."[25] If this is true within the Unitarian Universalist ministry, we certainly cannot ignore the differences that would obtain between Southern Baptist ministers and Northeastern rabbis. Recognizing that this problem helps confuse the issue, we shall nevertheless try to look for common personality correlates that might apply to most groups of clergy.

What are we looking for? A great deal of the research over the years has been looking for psychopathology or for tendencies leading toward mental health, whatever that may mean. It was hoped that mental health or better adjustment would lead to more effective functioning of the clergy. That better mental health and more effective functioning are not related has been asserted by Woodroofe. "Is it not possible that the most persuasive preachers are those with temperamental, egotistical personalities; that the most helpful pastors are those who have struggled with some moral or spiritual problem of their own; and that the best teachers are those whose intellectual powers have not led them away from the popular mind into the abstractions of clerical culture? Is it not at all unthinkable that God may use cracked and imperfect vessels . . . ?"[26] Argylle has shown that most of this research in terms of adjustment and mental illness has run into a blank wall. He lists a good many of the studies that have been done and says rather hesitantly that "there may be a tendency for Catholic ordinands to be neurotic while the reverse is generally true of the Protestants. . . . All these studies use questionnaire measures of personality some of which are known to be of very low validity, while little is known about some of the other tests. The most valid are probably the MMPI, the California Psychological Inventory, and the Guilford Martin Inventory. However, the three studies using them still give contrary findings."[27] Our concern here will not be with better mental health or more effective functioning. Perhaps the contrary findings that Argylle reports are due to the fact that we are not quite sure what we are looking for when we use on clergy some of the standard tests that apply to general populations. What may, if anything, differentiate the clergy may be something that has not been clearly defined until now.

We shall not be making the assumption that because there are unconscious motivations for one to enter the clergy or that the clergy may represent a resolution of certain intrapsychic conflicts, there is anything wrong or unusual about this. With Booth, we are interested in finding out more about the psychological dynamics that allow an individual to maintain mental health in spite of being a cultural deviant. We assume with him that "the coexistence of private psychopathology and vocational soundness is a practically very important phenomenon"[28] and that as a matter of fact this (psychopathology) would be no bar to an effective ministry.

Dittes pointed out some of the significant methodological problems that have plagued the research in this field. Pointing to the absence of "theoretical concern, conceptual labor," and poor design, he questioned what the research was looking for and what it found, if anything. He pointed out that there are many reports of research that uses clergymen as subjects but that investigates nothing of unique significance concerning clergymen. "The findings in effect prove that what is true for other people is also true for clergymen, namely their academic grades are related to their scores on tests of intellectual ability, or that students with strongly deviant scores on the personality scale are more likely to have emotional difficulties in the ministry."[29] Some research (he was commenting on the research done on ministerial effectiveness) measured what made a successful clergyman without having any clear idea as to what "success" means. Is it salary, prestige, swaying people, increased spirituality, or what? Much of the research may have been answering questions that no one has really asked.

Dittes points to the work of Stern, Stein, and Bloom[30] as a hopeful sign, despite the very small sample of six, because the measures used were well conceptualized and thought through. The attempt there was to predict effectiveness, but personality factors were a by-product. In their work a model of the ideal student clergyman was determined and then an analytic study of the theological students was done. Using the Wechsler-Bellevue, Rorschach, TAT, Sentence Completion Test, and an autobiographical questionnaire, they constructed a model of the successful student clergyman. Following similar procedures with physicists and teachers, they compared the three groups. Some of their findings will be referred to in the coming pages.

A similarly well-thought-out methodology was used by Siegelman and Peck[31] in comparing differential personality patterns of sixteen student ministers, sixteen student chemists, and sixteen career military officers. They constructed a set of predictive personality dimensions based on job role requirements and satisfactions and then tested their hypotheses using the Activities Index of Stern, Stein, and Bloom, a Sentence Completion Test, a personal interview, and a biographical form. From these they constructed a personality model for each career, compared it to their predictions and the groups to one another. Their results are most interesting.

Notwithstanding the difficulties, we shall try to see if the literature, theorizing, and research that have been done shed some light on the personality correlates of the clergy.

MINNESOTA MULTIPHASIC PERSONALITY INVENTORY

No review of the research in this area would be complete without mentioning the MMPI. It has been perhaps the most widely used of all personality inventories with theological students. Some have questioned whether it reveals anything of significant interest about "normal" clergy, yet as Dittes has also pointed out, though "one must be extremely careful not to draw conclusions from it," it may reveal some suggestive leads.[32]

Though one of the best instruments around, it is subject to variables of age, environment, and mood that create problems in drawing conclusions about personality. Bier's work has been devoted to correcting such problems for testing Catholic seminarians by omitting items referring to sex and religious beliefs, and thereby creating his own MMPI. The MMPI is often given to a captive group, which usually means seminary students and as with other research in this field, the number of pulpit clergy who have systematically taken it is limited. Despite these difficulties, profiles are available on populations. Davis, Jalkanen, Kanai, Morse, Kobler, and others have worked in this field.[33] Lucero's and Currens' work has been with a limited sample of psychologically interested Lutheran ministers.[34]

One of the significant lacks in the reporting of some of the data has been the omission of any of the validity scales.[35] These scales L, F, and K are crucial to any interpretation of the profiles. If our concern is with defensiveness, awareness of inner conflict, dissimulation, and the like, then their omission seriously hampers our work.

Seminarian and pulpit profiles tend to peak on Mf. The lack of validity of this scale makes one hesitate to offer any definitive statement, aside from its not being counterindicative of the sensitivity to others, the need to succor and nurture, and the dependency-passivity syndrome to be described later, all of which in our culture are accounted as "feminine" traits. College and graduate school students also tend to have peaks on Mf, but those of clergymen are consistently higher and almost always their highest peak.

Clergy MMPI profiles are consistently higher than profiles of other similarly educated groups,[36] though within what are considered to be normal limits. This may suggest some support for the idea of psychological otherness, which has been mentioned earlier, and for Bier's assertion that "clergy are the most deviant portion of an already deviant population."

High "K" scores as a clergy tradition have been pointed to by many.[37] They have been taken to be indicative of both defensiveness and ego strength. Kanai[38] found that the high K scores of his seminary students correlated positively with defensiveness as measured on Heilbrun's Adjective Check List. Morse[39] found that those who persisted in completing their seminary education were significantly higher on K than were college men. This may suggest defensiveness toward intrapersonal difficulties, a hypothesis that should be further investigated. It may also be due to age, greater maturity, being in graduate school, and consequently having greater ego strength.

Much fruitful work can probably be done with the MMPI in this area, especially if we are not looking for pathology. The relationship of the L, F, and K scale, the Ego Strength scale and the information given by the Dominance and Dependency subscales, and those that measure anxiety should be checked into further to see if any differential information on pulpit clergy is available from them.

"IN, BUT NOT OF"

In a medieval Benedictine monastery . . . a wooden screen was placed between the nave where ordinary Christians sat and the choir with the holy table where the monks sat. This symbolized the double standard of the holy life: that there are two classes of men and only the separated can achieve maximum holiness.[40]

"In, but not of, the world" should be the creed of every Christian, but it is often the peculiar burden of the minister.[41] Set-apartness as a psychological fact appears and reappears in the literature on clergymen. The strongest proponents of this idea have been those who have done extensive work with clergy in analytically oriented psychotherapy and in testing with a variety of projective techniques. Margaretta Bowers, who seems to have coined the word "set-apartness" as a psychological term, has been working for twenty years with "religiously dedicated persons" in psychoanalytically oriented psychotherapy and group therapy. Gotthard Booth has had over thirty years of experience with Episcopal and other Protestant seminarians and clergy, having given (as of 1962) more than 500 psychological examinations and having been involved in therapy with 223 clergymen. He used the Rorschach classically and in light of work done in France, Italy, Hungary, and the USA.[42] This new approach reveals "the basic identification of the individual in meeting other individuals and his collective environment." He and Molly Harrower have also made extensive use of the Szondi Test, which has had a mixed reception in the literature, and the Machover Draw-A-Person. Dr. Harrower has been the chief psychological tester of the Unitarian Universalist denomination and has created a special booklet that includes the Rorschach, the Szondi, the verbal Wechsler-Bellevue, the Miale-Holsopple Sentence Completion Test, several drawing tests including the man-woman, the house-tree, and the most unpleasant concept, and four cards from the

TAT. In addition to these, many others have affirmed this idea of psychological set-apartness of the clergy. Most of these have themselves been clergymen with analytic training and orientation.[43] There is some question whether there is a predisposition among this group to see this kind of set-apartness.

The first words of Bowers' book *Conflicts of the Clergy* are: "The clergy are lonely, set-apart people. Even the healthy, fulfilled, successful ones remember the loneliness of their childhood . . . such lonely, set-apart, often quite gifted children usually become ministers, research scientists, or doctors."[44] Somewhere along the line these children made their basic isolation from the world an integral part of their way of dealing with the environment. It would be this isolation that would involve them later on in work as clergymen. Booth has pointed to the fact that according to his profile of the average ministerial candidate, "the minister's ego is characterized by the repression or tendencies to isolate himself and a conscious or unconscious need to become part of a transcendent relation with the world."[45] Kildahl, a minister and an analyst, has pointed to the ministry as something set apart and different from all other callings. Blizzard quotes ministers saying of themselves that they are set aside by their people to study and to contemplate. Even ministers' wives have been seen to share the symbolic role of their husbands. Denton points out that "the minister's wife shares this symbolic role and, as such, is partly an embodiment of the community conscience. This has the effect of setting her apart and of isolating her."[46] That such set-apartness is not necessarily counterindicative of success has been pointed out by Ham.[47] His work, done with 119 Methodist ministers, was an attempt to measure the aspects of personality that went along with ministerial success. Success was defined in this study as a larger church and a greater income. Using the WAIS, Rorschach protocols with both the Beck and Klopfer scoring methods, and laymen's descriptions of their ministers, he comes to the conclusion that "the high pulpit, formalized ritual, being set apart through ordination and patterns of living, are not chance developments in the church. . . . Conspicuously successful ministers maintain significantly greater emotional distance from people than do ministerial failures." In completing the sentence stem "Nothing makes me more furious," "ministers never mentioned that they were directly provoked by the actions of other people. . . . The ministers did not describe themselves reacting with anger because they themselves were directly mistreated by others. They were 'furious' at others or at general practices or situations but they did not mention that they were personally involved or annoyed by these people."[48] Such an inability to become involved may be indicative of a distance and a kind of defensiveness toward other people that one might well call set-apartness. MMPI research has found that high K scores seem to be a tradition with the clergy. This has been pointed to by Kanai, Jalkanen, and Morse.[49] One of the greatest complaints in terms of job dissatisfaction that Siegelman and Peck found in ministers was the fact that people did not understand them, that somehow people saw them as being different. The man who chooses such a role must in some way feel that the role is appropriate for him.

On the surface, this set-apartness and emotional distance would seem strange in view of the kind of life that the clergyman is expected to live in relation to his congregation. He is to care for people; he seeks involvement in the personal problems of people. Strange that such a man should be described as set-apart. Yet the only "research" that seems to contradict this idea is that by Vinton,[50] in which an attempt was made to measure the perceptual characteristics of those pastors deemed effective by their bishops. Vinton pointed out that they saw themselves as more involved with people than did ineffective pastors. There are some serious questions as to both the approach and the methodology in this work. Vinton used a Pastoral Problem Response blank that he created, a number of cards of the TAT, and three pastoral incidents from the pastor's own experience. Yet even if these pastors saw themselves as more involved, they might have been compensating for the psychological isolation and set-apartness that they have come to feel. That there is a tendency among ministers to be involved with others and a danger that they sometimes get over-involved in others' lives has been pointed to many times. It has been described by Carrigan as a dangerous and inherent tendency among the clergy to merge with people. "One may lose himself in people to the extent that his identity is completely dependent on others. 'Who I am' becomes 'What others say I am; therefore I am not really myself, but the reflection of the image others project on me.'"[51] Indeed, what Booth has described as the repressed need for isolation may be repressed by this tendency to merge, to see one's self as very closely identified with one's congregants and to be a participant in a kind of parafamilial way with their lives. Many clergy become so closely identified with their church or synagogue that the minister or rabbi becomes the institution. They often become needed participants in a family's life cycle celebrations, though whether they are family or friend or something in between is a clouded issue. The clergyman's "own personal need may become so enmeshed with the program he espouses that one cannot determine where one stops and the other starts."[52] That this can happen has been pointed out by Small. In describing the needs for "affiliation and removal" in the job concepts of better-adjusted boys and more disturbed boys, he pointed out that "some" boys attempt to overcome the need to with-draw by selecting an occupation that will force them into contact with people. "You've got to sell yourself, that's what you've got to do." "I'd like to get to know people better; it will help me to get on with them better."[53]

That one may resolve one's set-apartness by "merging and/or over-involvement with others" seems strange, but it is plausible. It is also indi-cated by some of the research that has uncovered personality similarities between ministers and, of all people, research or physical scientists. One is not surprised that there may be a relationship in vocational motivation be-tween ministers and doctors, especially in their role as healers;[54] but cer-tainly a relationship between ministers and scientists would seem to be a bit "much." Yet the similarities are often striking. Schroeder, using a group Rorschach with the Munroe Check List and the Allport-Vernon Study of Values, reported that "both groups [physical science students and theology students] experienced difficulty in establishing warm, interpersonal relation-ships. Theology students were prone to seek refuge in some formalistic way of life or organization. Physical science students may have found this same refuge in the objective and clearly defined rules of scientific procedures."[55] In formulating a personality model common to a group of physics students, Stern et al. pointed out that "most important is the physicist's independence from interpersonal interactions. They are not especially interested in inter-personal affairs and are relatively detached from others in a wide variety of ways. Similarly, emotional stimuli arising out of relations with others do not particularly arouse them."[56] If one is to compare this with the description of theology students in Siegelman and Peck, one is struck by the similarity to the statement: "The ministers never mentioned that they were directly pro-voked by the actions of other people . . . they did not mention that they were personally involved or annoyed by these people."[57] Dittes, pointing to re-search done by Bier and Schroeder, noted that both clergymen and scientists show a kind of "observer and commentator role in society which protects them from getting fully involved in active participation in life. It might be argued that it is this opportunity for a certain degree of disengagement from the actual process of living in society that is a most important attraction in becoming a clergyman, and that whether a man becomes a clergyman or a scientist is due to somewhat minor incidental factors of interest, aptitude, and background experience,"[58] a position strikingly similar to that of Bow-ers. It may be that the scientists have made the decision not to resolve their problem of set-apartness by merging with others, but by retreating into the world of science, and so remaining separate, aloof, and intellectual. The clergyman, on the other hand, tries to resolve the problem by the tendency to merge, to be involved, and as so many clergy put it, to help others.

Whatever the evidence shows, this would seem a fertile area for the creation of hypotheses and the attempt to test these hypotheses about set-apartness. It may indeed be a major determinant for those who choose the vocation of pulpit clergy as a way of being in, but not of, the world.

LOVE

To many, Jew and Christian alike, religion is love. "Love your neighbor as yourself" (Leviticus 19:25) is taken by most men to be the core of their religious faith. The religious person is enjoined to give more love than he gets and to offer it not on the basis of what people do, but just because they are people. The clergyman, when he chooses to be the representative of his faith, is often seen by his constituency as the embodiment of love, and he is expected to give more love than he may get. Indeed, what he gets may often be hostility, disguised and otherwise. That this has its psychological correlates in the ministry and that the desire to love, heal, and succor is a psychological correlate of being a clergyman has been pointed out by many as a strong characteristic of these men. Kagan says that a man who has been denied sufficient love and attention in his childhood may choose to become a clergyman "because in that role he is required to give love and attention generously to other people. Acting out his own childhood frustrations, he sometimes overdoes his attention to his congregation."[59] This need to take care of others and the similarity of this need in doctors has been pointed out by Menninger.[60] A hypothesis presented by Loomis is that the ministry represents a special kind of healing commitment: "The minister has a deep inner need to help others. He is a helper who hurts until he can help others."[61] Loomis has also pointed out that "a few thousand years ago the priest and healer were twin identities of one man who was both, and over the centuries there came to be a differentiation of various functions. . . ."[62] Rabbis Neil Gillman and Israel Silverman, present and past registrars in charge of admission for the Jewish Theological Seminary, have indicated in separate conversations with the author that the overwhelming majority of students, when asked why they wish to become rabbis, respond, "Because I want to help people." This theoretical and personal understanding has been supported by the research. Both Stern et al.[63] and Siegelman and Peck[64] found that theologians tended to be somewhat more openly succorant and nurturant toward others. In addition they tended to be more dependent on them for affection.

Ministers wanted to be sympathetic and to help people when they expressed their troubles, and they expressed the strongest need to support and help others. Bier's data, as interpreted by Dittes, indicated a significant sensitivity toward the world on the part of the clergy. Certainly their continually higher Mf scores would lead one to think in this direction. Among Presbyterian seminarians the same tendency was reported. In responses to the Gough Adjective Check List, the nurturance score was among the very highest scores of those students. As interpreted, it suggested that these men were "helpful, solicitous, attentive to the feelings of others."[65]

To love is noble. For the minister it is also useful. He loves in order to be loved. It is role appropriate, but more than that, the minister's professional advancement depends on it. Ginzberg points out that the rabbi must worry about his popularity since his contracts are subject to renewal and advancement depends on a call from another congregation.[66]

There are men who have a great need to be loved.[67] They also need it shown regularly, for their congregants' love and respect often become the measure of their success. A fine home, a raise, and the success of the Building Fund campaign may rest on how loved the minister is. Siegelman and Peck point out that getting along for future clergymen in high school meant being liked, accepted, and perhaps admired by other students. The minister, as much as he needs to succor, needs succor. His "drive to help others may also be motivated in part by his need to be accepted, liked, and respected." "If am nurturant, I will be liked."[68]

Harrower has suggested that the ministry attracts men with inner conflict about their strong affectionate needs.[69] That this is not the only conflict, we shall see in a moment.

SANCTUARY

That the pulpit or church may be a sanctuary is a thought generally accepted by Western man. It has often been suggested that in religion one can find peace and a resolution of inner conflicts and dilemmas. Even one's inadequacies do not count for as much in a place where God is the overseer and a man is valued for what he is and not for what he accomplishes. Many psychological investigators have suggested that the pulpit is especially attractive to men who have strong inner conflicts to resolve. Wheelis lists the church as "a profession which has the combined characteristics of being truly knowable only from within and offering promise when viewed from without of alleviation of inner conflict, which promise is insidiously retracted by increasing proficiency in the field."[70] He goes on to point out that the church offers particular vicarious gratification of impulse by bringing the minister into contact with evil and the sufferings of parishioners at the same time as it promises to strengthen him against temptation. "The clergy offers an opportunity for satisfying both sides of one or another intrapersonal conflict or ambivalence. The conflict over dependence versus independence, over authority, over the expression or inhibition of hostility would all seem to find particularly successful compromise resolutions in a clergy role where both dependence and independence can be especially well-expressed or in which hostility can be condemned and love extolled—in a hostile, prophetic manner."[71]

That aggression and the feelings surrounding it are a great problem of the clergyman has been suggested by a number of investigators. Dodson, in work done with fifty graduate students from three Southern California universities and compared to fifty seminarians from three interdenominational Protestant seminaries, reported that "seminarians are more guilty and show more discomfort with sexual and hostile feelings and are more intrapunitive in handling hostility and aggression than controls."[72] Schroeder's data indicated that theology students were marked by "deep-seated feelings of hostility and rebellion."[73] Long ago, Menninger pointed to "the need to assuage the unconscious guilt arising from long repressed hostility towards various members of the childhood family by the psychological process of undoing, in addition to the pulpit being a search for a solution to the problem of conflict with authority."[74] Stern's theological students found great difficulty in reconciling impulse expression with the demands of conscience.[75] Indeed, one might suggest that the set-apartness of the clergy referred to previously may result from feelings of guilt about deep-seated hostility and rebellion. One way in which these feelings can be handled is by withdrawal from other people and by over-protestation of passivity, conformity, and kindness, something we shall say more about later.

The profile that we reported before, done by Booth and Harrower, suggested that the average candidate for the ministry was a young man with "inner conflict about his strong affectionate needs, and a tendency to sublimate aggression and to keep it under moral control."[76] One way in which this is done is by keeping "affectionate needs . . . balanced between personal and sublimated objectives, and in the task of maintaining this often difficult balance, he is aided by the tendency to devote his aggressive tendencies to impersonal goals and to subordinate it to the control of conscience and to inhibit the display of personal emotions."[77] Indeed, aggression handled in this way, aggression for the greater glory of God, the church and its ideals, becomes aggression for which one cannot be blamed or punished. One is doing it because one is an idealist, not because one is self-seeking. The clergyman can be as hostile as he wants to. He can express all the aggression he wants to, but he avoids any kind of direct, open retribution. People expect to be castigated by their minister. For their own reasons, they often seem to enjoy it. They may express their hostility more subtly by being glad when he gives a poor sermon, does something foolish, or fails with his Board of Directors. But the clergy's way of expressing aggression leads to another result: The aggression, because it is so role-appropriate, becomes ineffectual in what is essentially a competitive world. It is suggested that the aggression may be so great that some of it cannot be expressed this way and has to be turned inwards; and intrapunitiveness among the clergy is reported by many investigators.[78]

Bowers questions whether many of these men are not isolating themselves within their self-made prison walls in order to protect their loved ones and their communities from the danger of their destructive powers. Rubenstein, in commenting on Bowers, has pointed out: "If she is correct, most clergymen would rather be hurt than inflict hurt; hence they accept roles which contain the never-ending threat of psychic crucifixion."[79] This is a way in which one can resolve one's aggressive feelings, but at a very great price.

The pulpit may be a sanctuary in other ways. As a group, ministers have strong feelings of personal inadequacy. The pulpit may help compensate for this. The Ministry Studies Board of the United Presbyterian Church tells its young ordinands: "You will be taking on in the ministry a very high dignity indeed. The dignity will derive not from you but from your message. Part of it will inevitably affect your own life. In word and gesture you will stand for the most hopeful message it is possible to convey to men."[80]

To the sentence stems "If I only had . . ." and "I suffered most from . . ." ministers overwhelmingly expressed a striving to overcome personal inadequacies. They implied in their comments that they were insecure about certain abilities and personal qualities and were disturbed about this. On the other hand, the officers and chemists involved in the study did not often express this personal insecurity, but saw any lack as due to external circumstances. On the second stem, thirteen out of sixteen ministers noted personal inadequacy as being most distressful to them while the remaining three gave outer circumstances responses.[81] The same phenomenon of personal inadequacy has been pointed to by others including Johnson[82] and Davis.[83]

This phenomenon is heightened by the fact that the clergyman chooses a role that has aspects of vestigial magic and miracle making. The gap between the expectations and the achievements of the clergy is great. The clergyman may see himself as bringing the Kingdom of God to men and therefore reworking the world. He is aware of men's limitations and, deep down, of his own limitations, and he is painfully aware that the gap is immense. He cannot effectively measure what he does since his effect on people is often so nebulous and he perceives the expectations as so overwhelming. Ham has pointed to the relatively weak ego strength of ministers by using the Beck and Klopfer scoring methods of his Rorschach protocols.[84] He maintains that "the more effective ministers display response patterns indicating a relatively weak ego strength in relation to the general population. Ministerial failures, on the other hand, display scores double to three times higher than their more effective fellow ministers." It would be interesting to relate this to the work that is being done with the MMPI and to see what the ego strength subscale would indicate about ministers. If, as has been indicated, it correlates highly with the K scale, then ego strength might not necessarily be low in ministers despite Ham's work.

Eck and La Rere have pointed out that there may be what is called "the super-compensatory vocation in which the psychasthenic, conscious of his inferiority and the inadequacy of his equipment for the battle of life, seeks authority and assurance through the wearing of the uniform for the discharge of some function."[85] These feelings did not begin in adulthood. That they have origins in the childhood feelings of the clergy is strongly suggested. Booth asserts that "the conspicuous social dignity of the [Episcopal] priesthood attracts men who have suffered in their childhood from feelings of inferiority. The church . . . provides security which is by no means of a purely materialistic character. There are many candidates who enjoyed very little parental affection as children and for whom being in church meant, from childhood, the only experience of being 'in my Father's house' or 'being at home'."[86] Ministers seem to be aware of their unhappy childhood. In the work of Siegelman and Peck, the reporting of an unhappy childhood by ministers is a common feature.[87] On a more analytic level, Rubenstein points out that, "Deeply, more deeply than most men, our Rabbi's life was spent seeking the approval and commendation of his dead father. As he neared the end of his own life, he still sought it and was convinced that he would never be worthy of it."[88] That such feelings might lead to a desire to placate the Heavenly Father would, to the analytically oriented mind, be obvious.

The childhood inadequacy felt by the minister may lead to another consequence. He may avoid competing with the world. He may shun the competitive world because he cannot truly compete in it. In the church, as a clergyman, he is safe for he has answered a call far above men's abilities to avoid or to compete with. He is justified by the very fact of having heard the call. He is not representing or advancing his own cause; he is advancing the impersonal cause of God or some ideal. Anna Freud has described the child's tendency to restrict "its ego" as a defense against pain from external sources.[89] She describes this defense as avoidance of activities (e.g., competitive ones) that are likely to produce pain; she describes this as a normal stage in the development of the ego. Apparently with some clergy this is carried beyond that stage. Hostie points out that "there is a group of religious who say 'What would I do in the world; how can I survive all the dangers and difficulties; here at least I am safe; why should I change; in the world I should only go under altogether'?"[90] That seminary students are often shaken by the thought that they cannot stand the competitive world of other men has been described by one who has been in close contact with them for many years.[91] Eck and La Rere pointed out the dangers of what they call "a refuge vocation, when the subject, seized by panic when faced with the responsibilities of life, hurries away from the world because he fears the world, not because he has received a special call to a higher life."[92] And indeed the very higher life that they speak of and the call to that higher life may be a way of avoiding competing with the world. If one has heard the call, one is then in a league by oneself.

How does one remain in a league by oneself and still be involved with others? One tries to be involved in the active modification of reality to conform to a private value system, a dimension or personality that Stern et al. call Exocathection-Intraception and that they found to be exceptionally typical of clergy.[93] A private value system is a way of both rejecting the world's system and avoiding the need to compete with it. One rejects the values of the world and therefore does not have to be involved in the pursuit of those things that those values indicate. And yet one wants to be involved in the world and is caught in this dilemma. One therefore says that one is trying to change the world, yet it is hard to believe this, since one of the dominant features of research in the clergy has also been a greater feeling of dependency and passivity. Schroeder,[94] Roe,[95] Siegelman and Peck[96] have noted this tendency toward passivity and conformity on the part of theology students. In some cases it was described as low dominance. The data that Davis reports for Presbyterian seminary students support the fact that dependency is greater than dominance in the population of Presbyterian seminary students. In 1942,

Johnson, using the Bernreuter (a questionable test), found that salesmen ranked higher on dominance than theology students, which in itself is not surprising.[97] Whitlock, in testing for passivity in the personality of twenty-five candidates for the ministry and using a semi-structured depth interview, a Sentence Completion Test, and the Dominance Scale of the California Psychological Inventory, found that the more passive the person, the higher he scored on the Ministry scale. He suggested that this was related to the popular conception of the ministry as the pulpit ministry. It is likely, he suggests, that a passive individual tends to be easily influenced by such a role concept that may involve a particular idealized self-image. "An idealized self-image is what the subject believes himself to be. It is an unconscious phenomenon but represents the attempts of the person at solving his conflict between what he is and what he wants to be. As long as his idealized image remains real to him, he can feel significantly superior and harmonious in spite of the illusory nature of such feelings."[98] What could be less passive than to be in the pulpit, called by God to change the world?

Passivity, dependency, sensitivity, nurturing, helping others, and a noncompetitive view of life are taken by our society to be feminine attributes. Booth says: "The emotional and aesthetic emphasis of the church services . . . appeals to men who are more interested in the receptive than in the aggressive side of life. In American culture the priesthood represents the only occupation which is socially fully recognized and makes it a man's duty, not an 'escape,' to participate in emotional experiences mediated by aesthetic forms."[99] For some clergy their own sexuality and their attitude to women may be their greatest conflict. Very high Mf scores, a clergy trademark on the MMPI, although not indicative of homosexuality, may make one want to think about conflict in that area. Roe has pointed to the greater feminine interest pattern of the clergy,[100] and Schroeder's data suggested great areas of psychosexual conflict.[101] "Overt homosexuals are sometimes attracted by the fact that celibacy in a dedicated [Episcopal] priest is less likely to be considered suspect as sexual maladjustment than is the case in any other occupation. Unconscious homosexuals sense in the church the possibility of sublimated satisfaction: the aggressive types are made secure in wielding power for the good of the church and of the individual parishioners; the more passive types are able to enjoy affectionate relationships without fear of being exploited by sexually aggressive individuals."[102]

That being a clergyman may be an attempt to resolve this conflict for some Catholics, of whom celibacy is required, has been common knowledge. For some, the problem has become overt. Work with them is described by Bowers[103] and Christensen.[104] Bowers offers some fascinating theories as to the use of religious rituals and roles as ways of resolving these conflicts.

It might be suggested that this unresolved dependency, the need for warmth and love, with an accompanying distrust of warmth and love, the aggression that accompanies this constant search for and inability to accept love may all be part of one conflict. The minister may have learned through his life experience that he cannot be accepted for who he is but for what he does, not what he does for himself, but only insofar as he does for others. The anger that results may so endanger his being accepted and his dependence on others that it must be sublimated in some way. What better way to express the anger so that it cannot hurt, to love and yet at a distance, than by setting oneself apart, becoming an exception, a projection, and a paradigm of what man should be, and by so doing to serve both God and man well?

The pulpit is a paradox. It both is and is not a sanctuary from these conflicts. Yet for many men it offers a way to live, an unspoken deal between what one is and what the environment needs. People need clergy; they need some men to be different, to be "wholly other," to be exceptions. Some men choose to do just that. For some it is a sanctuary in which they can live and be useful. Others find that they have fled into a trap.

REFERENCES

1. Siegelman, M., and Peck, R. F., "Personality Patterns Related to Occupational Roles." *Genetic Psychology Monographs*, Vol. 61, 1960.
2. Kildahl, J. P., "The Hazards of High Callings." In W. E. Oates, ed., *The Minister's Own Mental Health*. Great Neck, NY: Channel Press, 1961.
3. Rubenstein, R. L., "The Clergy and Psychoanalysis." *The Reconstructionist*, Vol. 32, 20–30, 1966.
4. Bier, S.J., W. C., "A Comparative Study of a Seminary Group and Four Other Groups on the MMPI." *Studies in Psychology and Psychiatry*, Vol. 7, No. 3. Washington: Catholic Univ. of America Press, 1948.
   ———. "A Comparative Study of Five Catholic College Groups on the MMPI." In G. S. Welsh and W. D. Dahlstrom, eds., *Basic Readings on the MMPI in Psychology and Medicine*. Minneapolis: Univ. of Minnesota Press, 1956, pp. 586–609.
   Booth, G., "The Psychological Examination of Candidates for the Ministry." In H. Hofmann, ed., *The Ministry and Mental Health*. New York: Association Press, 1960, pp. 101–124.

————. "Unconscious Motivation in the Choice of the Ministry as Vocation." In Oates, ed., *op. cit.*

————. "Tests and Therapy Applied to the Clergy." *J. Religion and Health*, 2, 267–276, 1963.

————. "Selection of Personnel for the Clergy." In *Research in Religion and Health*, p. 59, 1963. New York: Fordham Univ. Press.

Bowers, M. K., *Conflicts of the Clergy*. New York: Thomas Nelson & Sons, 1963.

Dittes, J. E., "Research on Clergymen: Factors Influencing Decisions for Religious Service and Effectiveness in the Vocation." In S. W. Cook, ed., *Review of Recent Research on Religious and Character Formation*. Res. Suppl. to *Religious Education*, 1962, 57, S-141–165.

Blizzard S. W., "The Protestant Parish Minister's Integrating Role." In Oates, ed., *op. cit.*

Kildahl, *op. cit.*

5. Booth, "Unconscious Motivation in the Choice of the Ministry as Vocation," *op. cit.*

6. Cockrum, L. V., "Personality Traits and Interests of Theological Students." *Religious Education*, 1952, 47, 28–32.

7. Bier, "A Comparative Study of a Seminary Group . . ." *op cit.*

8. Siegelman and Peck, *op cit.*

9. Roe, A., *The Psychology of Occupations*. New York: Wiley, 1956.

Super, D. E., "Vocational Adjustment—Implementing a Self Concept." *J. of Occupations*, 1951, 30, 88–92.

Ginzberg, E., Ginsburg, S. W., Axelrod, S., Herman, J. L., *Occupational Choice*. New York: Columbia Univ. Press, 1951.

10. Booth, "Unconscious Motivation in the Choice of the Ministry as Vocation," *op. cit.*

Christensen, C. W., "The Occurrence of Mental Illness in the Ministry: Personality Disorders." *J. Pastoral Care*, 1963, 17, 125–135.

Whitlock, G. E., "Role and Self-Concepts in the Choice of the Ministry as a Vocation." *J. Pastoral Care*, 1963, 17, 208–212.

11. Siegelman and Peck, *op. cit.*

Stern, G. G., Stein, M. I., Bloom, B. S., *Methods in Personality Assessment*. New York: The Free Press, 1956.

12. Super, *op. cit.* (note 9).

13. Murray, H. A., *Explorations in Personality*. New York: Oxford Univ. Press, 1938.

14. Booth, "Unconscious Motivation in the Choice of the Ministry as Vocation," *op. cit.*

15. Freud, S., *The Future of an Illusion*. London: Hogarth Press, 1928.
———. *Civilization and Its Discontents*. London: Hogarth Press, 1930.
16. Fenichel, O., *The Psychoanalytic Theory of Neurosis*. New York: Norton, 1945.
Flugel, J. C., *Man, Morals, and Society*. New York: Viking Press, 1961.
17. Flugel, *op. cit.*
18. Ranck, J. G., "Some Personality Correlates of Religious Attitude and Belief." Ph.D. dissertation, Columbia University, 1955.
Broen, W. E., Jr., "Personality Correlates of Certain Religious Attitudes," *J. Consult. Psychol.*, 1955, 19, 64.
Rokeach, M., *The Open and Closed Mind*. New York: Basic Books, 1960.
19. McCarthy, P. F., "Personality Traits of Seminarians." *Studies in Psychology and Psychiatry*, Vol. 5, No. 4. Washington: Catholic Univ. of America Press, 1942.
20. Abrams, R. H., "Psychic Satisfactions of the Clergy." *J. Abn. & Soc. Psychol.*, 1936:30,423–430.
21. Moore, T. V., "Insanity in Priests and Religious. 1) The Rate of Insanity in Priests and Religious." *Amer. Ecclesiastical Rev.*, 1936, 95:485–498; 2) "Detection of Prepsychotics Applying for Admission to the Priesthood or Religious Communities," *loc. cit.*, 601–613.
22. *Bibliography on Religion and Mental Health 1960–1964*. U. S. Department of Health, Education, and Welfare, Public Health Service, Washington, D.C., 1967.
23. Johnson, E. H., "Personality and Religious Work." *Amer. J. Orthopsychiatry*, 1942, 12:317–324.
Moore, *op. cit.*
Bier, "A Comparative Study of a Seminary Group . . ." *op. cit.* (note 4).
24. Lenski, G. E., *The Religious Factor*. Garden City, NY: Doubleday, 1961.
25. Harrower, M., "Psychological Tests in the Unitarian Universalist Ministry." *J. Religion and Health*, 1963, 2:129–142.
26. Woodroofe, R. W. "The Selection of Candidates for the Ministry." *J. Pastoral Care*, 1951, 5:23–28.
27. Argylle, M., *Religious Behavior*. London: Routledge and Kegan Paul, 1958.
28. Booth, "Tests and Therapy Applied to the Clergy," *op. cit.* (note 4), p. 275.
29. Dittes, *op. cit.* (note 4).
30. Stern, Stein, and Bloom. *op. cit.* (note 11).
31. Siegelman and Peck, *op. cit.*
32. Dittes, *op. cit.*

Kobler, F. J., "Screening Applicants for Religious Life." *J. Religion and Health*, 1964, 3:161–170.

33. Davis, C. E., *Evaluating and Counseling Prospective Church Workers—General Procedures—A Guide for Presbyterians and Seminaries*. Board of Christian Education, United Presbyterian Church of the U.S.A., 1963.

Jalkanen, R. J., "The Personality Structure of Seminarians—The Use of Available MMPI Norms for Diagnosis." Master's dissertation, Roosevelt University, 1955.

Kanai, W., "An Investigation of the K Scale of the MMPI as a Measure of Defensiveness in Protestant Theological Seminary Students." *Dissertation Abstracts*, 1966, 26 (10).

Morse, P. K., "The Strong Vocational Interest Blank and Minnesota Multiphasic Personality Inventory as Measures of Persistence Toward the Ministry as a Vocational Goal." *Dissertation Abstracts*, 1963, 23:3239–3240.

Kobler, *op. cit.*

34. Lucero, R. J., and Currens, W. C., "Effects of Clinical Training on Personality Functioning of the Minister." *J. Clin. Psychol.*, 1964, 20:147.

35. Bier, "A Comparative Study of a Seminary Group . . ." *op. cit.* (note 4).

Kobler, *op. cit.*

Ashbrook, J. B., and Powell, R. K., "Comparison of Graduating and Nongraduating Theological Students on the MMPI. Colgate-Rochester Divinity School." *J. Counseling Psychol.*, 1967, 14:171–174.

36. Morse, *op. cit.* (note 33).

Bier, *op. cit.* (note 35).

Jalkanen, *op. cit.* (note 33).

37. Kanai, *op. cit.*

Jalkanen, *op. cit.*

Morse, *op. cit.* (note 33).

38. Kanai, *op. cit.*

39. Morse, *op. cit.* (note 33).

40. Miller, A., *Christian Faith and My Job*. New York: Association Press, 1946.

41. Carrigan, R. L., "Psychotherapy and the Theological Seminary." *J. Religion and Health*, 1967, 6:91–98.

42. Booth, "The Psychological Examination of Candidates for the Ministry," *op. cit.* (note 4).

43. Kildahl, *op. cit.* (note 2).

Blizzard, *op. cit.* (note 4).

Rubenstein, *op. cit.* (note 3).

44. Bowers, *op. cit.* (note 4).

45. Booth, "The Psychological Examination of Candidates for the Ministry," *op. cit.* (note 4).
46. Denton, W., "Role Attitudes of the Minister's Wife." In Oates, W., ed., *op. cit.*
47. Ham, H. M., "Personality Correlates of Ministerial Success," *Iliff Review*, 1960, 17, 3–9.
48. Siegelman and Peck, *op. cit.*
49. Kanai, *op. cit.* (note 33).
Jalkanen, *op. cit.* (note 33).
Morse, *op. cit.* (note 33).
50. Vinton, J. A., Jr., "Perceptual Characteristics of Episcopal Pastors." Doctoral dissertation, University of Florida, 1964.
51. Carrigan, *op. cit.*
52. Kildahl, *op. cit.*
53. Small, L., "Personality Determinants of Vocational Choice." *Psychological Monographs*, Vol. 67 (1), 1953.
54. Menninger, K., *Love Against Hate.* New York, Harcourt Brace, 1942.
Loomis, E. A., Jr., "The Religion-Psychiatry Program at Union Theological Seminary." In Hofmann, H., ed., *The Ministry and Mental Health.* New York: Association Press, 1960.
55. Schroeder, C. E., "Personality Patterns of Advanced Protestant Theology Students and Physical Science Students," Dissertation, Michigan State University, 1956. *Dissertation Abstracts*, 1958, 18:154–155.
56. Stern, Stein, and Bloom, *op. cit.* (note 11).
57. Siegelman and Peck, *op. cit.*
58. Dittes, *op. cit.* (note 4).
59. Kagan, H. E., and di Cori, F., "The Rabbi, His Family, and the Community." *J Religion and Health*, 1962, 1:350–361.
60. Menninger, *op. cit.*
61. Loomis, Address to the Conference on Motivation for the Ministry, Louisville Southern Baptist Seminary, 1959.
62. Loomis, *op. cit.* (note 54).
63. Stern, Stein, and Bloom, *op. cit.* (note 11).
64. Siegelman and Peck, *op. cit.*
65. Davis, *op. cit.* (note 30).
66. Ginzberg, E., "The Rabbi's Multi-Faceted Role—A Study in Conflict and Resolution." In *On Being a Rabbi.* New York: Herbert H. Lehman Institute of Ethics Conference, 1964.

67. Guthrie, H., and Ashbrook, J. B., "When Ministers Face Themselves," *The Pulpit*, 1960, 31 (6):8–12.

68. Siegelman and Peck, *op. cit.*

69. Harrower, *op. cit.*

70. Wheelis, A., *The Quest for Identity*. New York: Norton, 1958.

71. Dittes, *op. cit.* (note 4).

72. Dodson, F. J., "Personality Factors in the Choice of the Protestant Ministry as a Vocation." Ph.D. dissertation, Univ. of Southern California, 1957.

73. Schroeder, *op. cit.*

74. Menninger, *op. cit.*

75. Stern, Stein, and Bloom, *op. cit.* (note 11).

76. Booth, "The Psychological Examination of Candidates for the Ministry," *op. cit.* (note 4).

77. Booth, "Unconscious Motivation in the Choice of the Ministry as Vocation," *op. cit.*

78. Siegelman and Peck, *op. cit.*

Kanai, *op. cit.* (note 30).

Dodson, *op. cit.*

Schroeder, *op. cit.*

79. Rubenstein, *op. cit.*

80. "The Challenge to Be Presented in the Program of Enlistment." In De Wire, H., ed., *The Guidance of Ministerial Candidates*. Philadelphia: The United Presbyterian Church, U.S.A., 1964. The quotation here cited is from Berger, P. L., "Letter on the Parish Ministry." *Christian Century* 1964, 81:547–550.

81. Siegelman and Peck, *op. cit.*

82. Johnson, *op. cit.* (note 23).

83. Davis, *op. cit.* (note 33).

84. Ham, *op. cit.*

85. Eck, Dr., and La Rere, C., "Psychasthenia and Vocation." In Flood, P., ed., *New Problems in Medical Ethics*, Vol. III. Westminster, MD: The Newman Press, 1956.

86. Booth, "The Psychological Examination of Candidates for the Ministry," *op. cit.* (note 4).

87. Siegelman and Peck, *op. cit.*

88. Rubenstein, R. L., "Death of a Rabbi." Unpublished paper, 1964.

89. Freud, A., *The Ego and the Mechanisms of Defense*. New York: Inter. Univ. Press, 1946.

90. Hostie, S.J., R., *The Discernment of Vocations*. New York: Sheed & Ward, 1963.
91. Southard, S., "Motivation and Mental Health." In Oates, W. E. ed., *The Minister's Own Mental Health*. Great Neck, NY: Channel Press, 1961.
92. Eck and La Rere, *op. cit.*
93. Stern, Stein, and Bloom, *op. cit.* (note 11).
94. Schroeder, *op. cit.*
95. Roe, *op. cit.* (note 9).
96. Siegelman and Peck, *op. cit.*
97. Johnson, *op. cit.* (note 23).
98. Whitlock, *op. cit.* (note 10).
99. Booth, "The Psychological Examination of Candidates for the Ministry," *op. cit.* (note 4).
100. Roe, *op. cit.* (note 9).
101. Schroeder, *op. cit.*
102. Booth, "The Psychological Examination of Candidates for the Ministry," *op. cit.* (note 4).
103. Bowers, Address to the Ministry Studies Board Conference. In De Wire, H., ed., *The Guidance of Ministerial Candidates*, Columbus, OH, May 1965.
104. Christensen, *op. cit.* (note 10).

Symbolic Exemplarhood

4

The Special Tensions of Being "The Rabbi"*

A tired old joke has it that the rabbinate is not a fit job for a Jewish boy.[1] To many rabbis, the joke is not funny at all. Rabbinic burnout has led to a brain drain from the pulpit rabbinate that has serious implications for present and future Jewish life. The burnout comes from the very essence of being a rabbi.

Being a rabbi means being set apart, lonely, and subject to unreasonable expectations and demands from all sides. Being a rabbi means belonging to one's own family, the congregational family, and beyond that, being a parafamilial member of many different families. Being a rabbi means dealing with the inevitable conflict between the rabbi's life cycle and congregants' life cycles; having to decide what to do when an event in the congregational family coincides with one in the rabbi's family. Being a rabbi means not being able to leave a colleague on call—the family is never satisfied with whoever is on call: "After all, Rabbi, he didn't know Mom, so what kind of eulogy could he give?" Being a rabbi means discussing endlessly the conundrum, "Can rabbis have friends in the congregation?" (Younger rabbis

---

*Published as "The Special Tensions of Being 'the Rabbi'," in Sh'ma, A Journal of Jewish Responsibility, Vol. 20, No. 386, January 19, 1990, pp. 41–43.

1. How that applies to Jewish girls remains to be seen. The gender referents here are as originally published. In the author's experience symbolic exemplarhood applies as much to woman rabbis as to their male forebears.

tend to be more sanguine about this than their older, more experienced colleagues.) Being a rabbi means being nurturing and caring—everyone's parent—yet having the kids determine, and then periodically review, how much "Dad" earns. Being a rabbi means that others experience you as being something more than human. It does no good for a rabbi to repeatedly proclaim that he is only human, with human needs, desires, and limitations. A congregant's answer is, "Of course the rabbi is human but after all, he *is* THE RABBI." And, being the rabbi, he is treated as something other than simply human.

Rabbis' spouses complain, saying, "I'm not a rabbi, I only married one, yet I'm treated differently. I'm subject to many of the same experiences that rabbis themselves complain about." And as the kids come of age they too offer the same complaint: "I'm treated differently because I'm the rabbi's child." Protestants have a word for pulpit children—they're called P.K.'s (Preacher's Kids), thus underlining their differentness.

Rabbis and their spouses, especially new ones, hope that if only the congregations would wise up and learn to treat the rabbi and his family reasonably, modulate their demands, and understand the rabbi's humanity, then the rabbinate would be the worthwhile calling they know it can be, and life as a rabbi would be easier. What these rabbis do not realize is that their solution *is* a major problem. For if the congregations were to treat the rabbi as simply human, as the rabbis might sometimes like them to, there would be no need to have a rabbi.

What is the essential fact about the rabbinate that makes all this happen?

> *Being a rabbi means being a Symbolic Exemplar who stands*
> *for something other than one's self.*

It is this symbolic exemplarhood that enables the rabbi to be taken seriously in the first place and the myth that surrounds this symbolic exemplarhood provides much of the rabbinic power to touch individual lives and direct the future of the Jewish community.

It is the symbolic exemplarhood which distinguishes the rabbi from the social worker, psychological counselor, or federation executive. It is the symbolic exemplarhood that makes possible the multiple satisfactions that come from being a rabbi. Yet it is a double-edged sword for it also engenders the isolation, alienation, and aloneness that is endemic in the field, the criticism that comes from all sides, and the experience of living behind a glass wall. Anyone who has been a pulpit rabbi, or a clergyman of any denomination, knows that this is so.

The rabbi's spouse and family are part of the symbolic exemplarhood. The symbolic expectation is that the rabbi be a special, caring, loving Jew who will have a model relationship with his wife and family. This exemplar Jewish couple and family becomes the "proof of the pudding," which demonstrates that the rabbi is special and that his devotion to God and Torah really work.

Thus the symbolic exemplarhood of the rabbi is the hostage of his spouse and family. Their behavior profoundly affects how the rabbi is seen and experienced. There is no way around this! This makes the boundary between the rabbi's public and private life dangerous and vulnerable—especially since he lives in the midst of his flock.

These difficulties cannot be resolved at the congregational level. For the congregation chose to engage a rabbi largely because *they want a Symbolic Exemplar!* They want someone who, beyond his professional roles of preaching, teaching, counseling, administering, and representing them to the community, will, in his very being, be the embodiment of Jewish life, the quintessential Jew. If congregations were to change this about themselves, rabbinic placement lists would be precipitously shortened.

Yet, something needs to be done. It is vitally important that these young people on whom we spend large community resources training and preparing for the pulpit rabbinate, be given all the resources they need to do the job properly and with a modicum of satisfaction. Working out standards for the congregation's expectations of the rabbi will be helpful in a limited way only. Most of what needs doing needs to be done by the seminaries that train our pulpit rabbis and the rabbinic organizations they join.

Those who have knowingly or unknowingly volunteered to be Symbolic Exemplars must, from their first days at rabbinical school, be taught the inevitability of their symbolic exemplarhood. They must be provided with this information so that the existence and consequences of their symbolic exemplarhood will be no surprise when they enter congregational life. They must be taught that symbolic exemplarhood goes with them in *all* their rabbinic functioning and is a tool to be used in the service of the people they are a part of and apart from. They need to know that symbolic exemplarhood grows with each bar mitzvah, each wedding, each funeral, each public experience as a rabbi; that with each of these, another imperceptible layer is added to their symbolic exemplarhood. They need to know that they are never talking only for themselves, that despite what they think or hope, they are experienced as talking for God, for Torah, or for the people Israel. They are expected to be special and different and to act that way. They must further learn that the conflict between their loyalty to their own family and their being members symbolically of the congregational family is a conflict that comes with the territory. It is useless to complain about it or wish it away. Our young rabbis need to realize that rabbis do not belong to their congregations no matter how long their tenure. Being "on" symbolically all the time separates them from their congregations. The rabbi belongs first and foremost to the rabbinic community and it is to that community he must turn for support and nurturing.

How rabbis handle their symbolic role is crucial to their rabbinate. What rabbis need to be taught is how to be exquisite Symbolic Exemplars, strenuous though that be. This strenuous role can be draining and our rabbis need respite from it; they need care and nurturing. They need islands of time and place where their symbolic exemplarhood is put aside and they can be simply human within the larger rabbinic family. In such settings they can have their inner resources replenished, returning to the fray refreshed and renewed.

Recognizing the need, a beginning has been made by The Central Conference of American Rabbis with their Professional Mid-Career Review Program and The Jewish Theological Seminary of America with its Rabbinic Institutes. These two programs, though different in structure and orientation, recognize the need that exists and begin to address it. They are expensive programs which were funded on a temporary basis by two foundations. Recent years have also witnessed the beginnings of rabbinic self-help groups, spouse support groups, hotlines, and the like.

Much more needs to be done. The Jewish community, and especially the rabbinic community, will have to expend greater resources on helping our rabbis. Such programs, though they may be expensive, are worth doing and cost effective when we consider the waste of community resources that the pulpit brain drain engenders. Helping rabbis function more effectively as Symbolic Exemplars is a challenge facing this next generation of rabbinic leadership that dare not be avoided. And that's no joke.

5
Symbolic Exemplarhood
and the Rabbi's Family*

In the sixteenth century, Moses Mintz of Hamburg said that the ideal *Shaliach Tzibbur* (communal representative, especially in prayer) should be

> blameless in character, humble, a general favorite and married; should be able to read easily and understand all the books of the Holy Scriptures; be the first to enter and the last to leave the house of God, and to strive to attain the highest degree of devotion in his prayers. He should dress neatly and wear a long garment and knee breeches. And he should not look about him nor under his mantle. And he shouldn't move his hands restlessly but he should keep them folded neatly. And outside God's house, he should avoid sowing any seeds of anger or hatred against himself by keeping aloof from all communal disputes.

The words of Moses Mintz of Hamburg can easily read as a current description of the ideal pulpit rabbi. My Ph.D. on "The Pulpit Rabbi as Symbolic Exemplar" might have been thrown out as not an original piece of research had the advisors to my Ph.D. been fluent in the Jewish tradition. The tradition does say a great deal about the *Shaliach Tzibbur* from whom the pulpit

---

*Adapted from the Keynote Address of the Central Conference of American Rabbis 1976 Convention, San Francisco, CA.

rabbi is a direct descendant. Almost all the research in the work that I have done on symbolic exemplarhood has been itself exemplified in Moses Mintz of Hamburg's words.

The pulpit rabbi is, most of all, a Symbolic Exemplar. He is the symbol of something other than himself. The pulpit rabbi is a symbolic leader who is set apart to function within the community as a symbol of that community and as an exemplar of their desire for moral perfection. The rabbi is thus a walking, talking, living symbol. He stands for something other than himself and in order to function, he must be seen and perceived that way. And in order to function, the rabbi must act in such a way as not to destroy that symbol.

It is crucial for the rabbi to fill the symbolic aspects of that role. Perhaps the major expectation of the rabbi is that in some crucial way, she is expected to be a different kind of human being. She is the embodiment of what people ought to do, but have no intention of doing.

She is expected to be different in her morality, in her caring for people. She is expected to be different as a wife and as a mother. That, of course, has a lot of implications for the rabbi's spouse and family.

A pulpit rabbi must truly care and must fully believe, or at least must be perceived and experienced as fully believing, in what he is doing. Indeed, who the rabbi is, is more important than what the rabbi does. In my own work, I have quite clearly tested that out. The perception of the rabbi's inner characteristics is the "data" from which the layman determines rabbinic efficacy and importance. Other people are hired or fired or valued in terms of what they do. The rabbi is valued in terms of who he is perceived to be.

For the symbol to exist, a rabbi must have these special attributes. She is expected to be a different kind of person or she must at least be seen that way. That makes functioning as a clergy-technician, to say the least, a very hazardous kind of thing. A doctor may have her bedside manner, a teacher her classroom presence, an executive may be a tiger on the job and a pussycat at home, but a rabbi is expected to be the same person on and off the job. Because if she's not, then how else do you measure really caring and truly believing? A doctor could get by—and I've seen a lot of them—even if she didn't care for people, but was just a darned good surgeon. A rabbi could not. The rabbi could visit the hospital. She could say and do the right thing. But if people discovered that she did not at heart really care, she would be in a very difficult spot. Now that too goes back in our tradition. Speaking about the original *Shaliach Tzibbur*, we discern what one of the measures of the *Shaliach Tzibbur* is. They say of the *Shaliach Tzibbur*:

A *Shaliach Tzibbur* who lengthens his prayers wanting the congregation to hear his beautiful voice—if he does that because of the joy in his heart at thanking the Blessed God in beauty—is to be blessed. If he prays seriously and stands in awe and fear—but—if he merely wants the congregation to hear his voice because he is proud of his voice—he is to be despised.[1]

What must be found out is most difficult and so easy to hide, the purity of the *Shaliach Tzibbur*'s inner heart. That question of authenticity and "Is this person real?" is the basic question down to this day. The symbol is crucial, for it is not what the rabbi does that is crucial, but who she is at the inner level, and, more important, who she is perceived to be. It is the essence of the rabbi. To break the symbol is to lose efficacy. Both rabbi and layman participate in creating and work diligently, though often unaware, at maintaining the symbol.

It is true that rabbis are not the only walking, talking symbols. After all there are celebrities and royalty and presidents of countries. All of these people are public property. That's not an illusion. And the public has adopted the celebrity, or the Queen of England, or the holder of public office as an image of a certain kind and does expect him or her to be that image or that symbol.

A story about a man who played at being one of those symbols. Some of you readers may remember the TV series *Ben Casey*. The lead was played by Vince Edwards. This is how Vince Edwards experienced his life after he had been Ben Casey for a while.

He became uncomfortably aware of the discrepancies of his own life, which happened to include a devotion to betting on horse races, and the God-like image that he had come to represent to the public. "I won't do anything to destroy the image," he said. He tried to keep his private life subdued and separate. For those of you who are pulpit rabbis, this sounds all too familiar.

Yet it was not easy, because magazines published pictures of his horse playing and the public watched him every possible moment. Even his close friends began to be affected. The next quote has a familiar resonance to those clergy who serve in congregations:

Some of my old friends begin to weigh their words when we get together now. They don't see me as plain old Vince Edwards now. What they see

---

1. Shulhan Arukh, Orah Hayyim 53:11.

now is the image. They see Ben Casey. It makes a difference, believe me. Their attitudes change, they stiffen. And I can't say I like that and I'm not sure I like losing a little privacy. I wish it were different in some ways, the whole success thing. But that's how it is; how do you fight it?

That's what happens to a man who only *plays* a role on TV. He is playing at being a doctor. One can easily imagine what happens to the rabbi who is so visible. Whatever private life the rabbi has is extremely vulnerable to that visibility. And in addition, the rabbi is different from the celebrity and different from the politician. He is expected to be a symbol without physical distance and is expected to be a unique and moral person. A celebrity is cushioned from the public. We saw in the book *The Final Days*, about the end of the Nixon administration, what happens when a celebrity is not cushioned from the public. A politician is not expected to be moral. The rabbi is expected to be that as well.

How do rabbi and laity participate in creating and maintaining that symbol while still living in close contact in the midst of the congregation? Like Vince Edwards, a lot of rabbis won't do anything to destroy the symbol. They are careful and circumspect. Some easily accept the exemplarhood of being a rabbi and work hard at it. They try hard to be consistent, fair, sensitive, pious, and moral models. Virtually all rabbis do some editing. They act the role, trying hard to be caring and religious models. They try, as far as they can, to keep the private, private. Rabbis relish every bit of anonymity they can get. They channel their expression of anger only to appropriate places. They try to keep some distance and be circumspect. And indeed prudence, politeness, and restraint do help maintain the symbolic image.

No matter who the rabbi is, each rabbi has the sense that the symbol has limits and rabbis always act in such a way as not to break those limits. What does the congregant do? She does a great deal to create the symbol. First, she attributes to the rabbi special attributes, although not out of malice, and it is important to understand that. When the layperson says of the rabbi, "She's human, but . . ." and attributes special attributes to the rabbi—that the rabbi is supposed to be more moral, more learned, whatever those special attributes may be—that attribution is not being done out of malice. Rabbis need to remember that! Rabbis have presented themselves as rabbis and as being special kinds of people. Rabbis come with ordination, which is quite different from having a graduate degree.

An anecdote from my own life just might be the best way I can show you that kind of special attribute. It is an incident that happened to me and my then wife. It is a true story. Back in 1973, my wife decided that she was going to go to Israel to her best friend's son's Bar Mitzvah. It was the first time she had gone by herself on that kind of long trip. Though coming from a traditional background, she was into Women's Lib. I called the Ritual Chairman of the congregation which was just beginning to give women *aliyot* and said, "Look Mike, Meryl's going to Israel this week, can you give her an *aliyah* tomorrow?" And the next day Meryl got up for her very first *aliyah*. With her knees knocking she went to the Torah, said the blessings, and returned to her seat next to me. At the end of the service, the rabbi,[2] who used to be a camper of mine, didn't say a word. Not one word. Meryl turned to me and said, "For ten years I sat next to you and I slept next to you and I listened to you do all that junk; wishing people well on their trips, blessing them and congratulating them on their twenty-fifth or fiftieth anniversary, and I listened to you and I would laugh at all that stuff. But if he doesn't say something now when I'm nervous about going to Israel, I'm going to be sore as all get out." And she added, "You can't do it for me because you're not *my* rabbi."

That is what happens with the rabbi. Thank God that Laybel found out that she was going on the trip. At the *kiddush*, he made all the proper *Mi-Sheberack*s and everything. Meryl felt better, and I had a lovely weekend.

The other thing is that once a rabbi, you are always a rabbi. Once you have presented yourself in this way, once you've functioned for people in that priestly symbolic role, you are always a rabbi. You can be described as the *goofy, hippie* rabbi, as I've heard a rabbi described. Orthodox people have called a specific rabbi the *Goyisheh* (gentile) rabbi. I've heard of the *tennis-playing* rabbi and the *flying* rabbi and recently, some ten years after I'd been in the rabbinate, I was introduced as the *rabbi who isn't a* rabbi. The adjective leaves the noun untouched. The rabbi is somehow seen and perceived as a different kind of person even if he denies his rabbihood.

In the course of my research, one of the men[3] I interviewed followed another rabbi who had gone into the stock market. In his congregation, he kept on being asked the question "Do you think it's right for a rabbi to go into becoming a stockbroker?" This rabbi says that he asked them what they might have accepted as a legitimate change for a rabbi. And they said,

---

2. Leon Waldman, then (1976) and now my rabbi at Congregation Beth El, Fairfield, Connecticut.

3. At the time of the research (1970–1971) there were no women rabbis.

"Well, a social worker, you know, a nonmercenary kind of enterprise." He asked them why they felt that way, and they said, "Because you fellows are in the rabbinate. That's a lifetime calling, and there's no way out; there's something special about it, and people depend on you." That was his quote.

As long as people know that you are a rabbi, you never lose that kind of specialness. As I mentioned before, laity, of course, say that the rabbi is human, *but* . . . ! I have not found any layperson who does not perceive his/her rabbi as being a different kind of human being in some way. We all know the downshift that happens when a layperson finds out that you are a rabbi. You can hear the gears clank as they start to talk to you about their Talmud Torah education, Sunday school, their religious experiences, or the presence or absence of their belief in God. All of a sudden, you know that an editing and a changing process has taken place in them.

In the research I did, research interviewing rabbis and laymen of those rabbis, a rabbi told me that he was chastised by his congregation for singing dirty songs to the teenagers. And the layman says, "I don't think I would ever tell a dirty joke in front of the rabbi, for some reason, although I'm sure that the rabbi wouldn't object. I don't know. I've never told him one. Now, I would like to be able to have respect for the rabbi both as a human being and as a rabbi. I think that's what I'm trying to do, to find two people in one. And it's not easy."

Every rabbi knows that there are those laypeople who will test the limits of a rabbi. The seductiveness of offering a drink, and another drink, and trying to get the rabbi a little high, and so forth, are all doing the same thing, testing the symbol, seeing whether it is *authentic and really there* under all circumstances.

What are some of the consequences of that perceived gap between being only human and being a Symbolic Exemplar of God and all that is good? Well, for those for whom symbol and self are really one, there's very little problem. They function very, very well in the pulpit for years and years and years. They are some of the great rabbis of America. But I found that what happens with most, increasingly over the years, is a sense of set-apartness that increases with time, a loneliness in the midst of the crowd, a sense of living behind a glass wall separating oneself from the ever-present other.

The other side of that set-apartness becomes a set-apartness from one's own feelings. A story from my own life that you all have shared will exemplify that better than any technical description of research. In Fairfield, Connecticut, where I served and now live, there is a supermarket called Sunshine, which is the Jewish supermarket: They have the bagels and the lox and the kosher style this and that. I remember the experience when I was in the pulpit of going into Sunshine. Walking into Sunshine to buy a container of milk was a work experience for me.

"Hello, how are you? How's Grandma? Grandpa? Your aunt? Your uncle? Everyone?"

And then, God forbid, if I didn't smile wide enough to somebody, if I was perceived as aloof or not caring, I heard about it. It flowed into the network of gossip, which influenced perception and often got back to the board.

I remember after coming back from Israel and no longer being in that pulpit that when I went into Sunshine market for a container of milk and I saw someone whom I really cared about, I was able to smile and say, "Hey, how are you? Long time since I've seen you." And those whom I really didn't feel strongly about, tough! And though it may have gotten around and into the community perception, I didn't have to hear about it or, more importantly, deal with it.

In the words of one of the men at Mohonk,[4] we are "professional lovers." As "professional lovers" who are supposed to be authentic lovers, it is easy to lose touch with a very important differentiation in us. That differentiation is that there are those whom we really love because we really love them, because that is in our guts, and there are those whom we love because we are paid to care for the flock and to love every sheep, the blackest and the whitest, and all the speckled and spotted ones in between. When I discovered that I was smiling because I really cared, and not because it was my job to smile and care, that was taking back something very important for me.

As far as the rabbi's spouse and family are concerned, every rabbi's wife, and in recent years every rabbi's husband, may assert sometimes in a rather loud voice; "I married a man or a woman. *I didn't marry a rabbi!*" Having gone through the literature on this rather extensively, I maintain unequivocally that every rabbi's spouse has married both a real live person and a symbol. Marrying a symbol always has consequences, because the symbolic expectation of the rabbi that she be a special, caring, loving, woman and that she will have a model relationship with husband and family makes the relationship in the home, the relationship with spouse and family, the proof of the pudding. It also makes it terribly lonely. For a Symbolic Exem-

---

4. The first conference the Central Conference of American Rabbis ran for Mid-Career Review took place in 1975, at Mohonk, New York. It was the first of many I conducted in my capacity as Director of Professional Career Review.

plar, the boundary between public and private is potentially a dangerous, risky, vulnerable boundary.

Erving Goffman[5] talks about the "backstage area." I made a mistake yesterday at the St. Francis,[6] and wandered into the backstage area of the hotel. The backstage area of the St. Francis is not elegant. It is not beautiful. I'm sure that is where the waiters let down their hair and feel free to say things they would rather the people outside not hear. That's all backstage, but when they come out, they are smiling and gracious, put the coffee down, inquire if everything is all right, and when finished cordially say, "Have a nice day! It's been nice to serve you!"

For the pulpit rabbi, the backstage area is a *very* vulnerable place and sometimes almost nonexistent. But that's the place where you most measure the rabbi. Is he authentic? Does he do what he says? Is this man really the kind of man that we expect him to be? That makes the rabbi's public image a hostage to his wife's and his family's behavior. This puts a lot more stuff into the marital and family pot that are not items for any other family.

Some examples from my research interviews:

The rabbi keeps kosher, but his wife adores and sneaks cheeseburgers. He agonizes for a long time. How can I be a successful rabbi if I can't even convince my wife to keep kosher? What are we going to do? What flack will I get if a congregant sees? The issue of kashrut ("kosherness") in the rabbinic household is not only an issue between husband and wife, it becomes an issue of the rabbi's relation to the congregation as well as to his wife.

One rabbi reported, "We had a whole big thing in this congregation because my wife wears pantsuits on Shabbat morning, and my Religious Committee had taken a position against it. They printed an article and I had to go print a retraction." In any other family that would not be an issue. I'm not talking here about what a rabbi *should* do. I'm saying that that is additional stuff put into the marital pot that rabbi and spouse have to deal with.

Listen to just one rabbi talk about his kids. He said, "My children ride their bicycles on the Sabbath and I don't mind. I know that from speaking with my colleagues in some communities that children have sometimes been criticized. Or the rabbi has been criticized for having children do something on the Sabbath. I have not been confronted with this although my chil-

---

5. Erving Goffman. *The Presentation of Self in Everyday Life.* Garden City, NY: Doubleday Anchor Books, 1959.

6. The hotel in San Francisco, site of the 1976 CCAR convention.

dren do ride their bicycles on the Sabbath, although if they were teenagers or adults, it would be something where that would cause public comment."

You name me one other person who would even bother to talk about it. The extent to which the rabbi and his wife or the rabbi and her husband take into account how their behavior is seen in public and how it will appear to the world has an effect. It's not a question of what answer we give the teenager who on Friday night wants to go to the basketball game, or wants to play soccer on Saturday morning. The very fact that the issue includes considerations of public exposure becomes a kind of test of a rabbi's symbolic exemplarhood.

Other areas also affect a rabbi's spouse and family. I remember my wife and I having the following conversation in the first six years of my pulpit rabbinate at least twenty times a year. We would come home on a Saturday night and we'd say, "Aren't they a lovely couple? Do you think they could be our friends?" And each time, they were lovely, and loved us and paid their dues and gave to the building fund and said, "Rabbi, you're wonderful!" But they weren't our friends. When I left the pulpit later on, I said to them, "Hey, Lenny and Marcia, what happened during those ten years? How come you never called us? How come you didn't ask us just to go out?" And they said, "Well, you know, we had a party and didn't want you to be a wet blanket." I was no more interested in being a wet blanket at a party than being the man in the moon. But somehow that perception that the rabbi either is busy or that being with the rabbi is going to cause them to have to downshift the gears, or edit what they say or do, leads to that sense of isolation rabbis have, even as we are being among people who love us. Incidentally, congregants generally don't understand this. You try to tell them what this loneliness is and if they really do love you, what they will respond with is, "Rabbi, we love you." And they mean it. They do love you and need to protect that love with some distance.

On the other hand, there are what I call the clergy collectors. Those are the people who will take anyone who has been ordained in any way, call them and invite them and get involved with them. They are often very nice people. They are sometimes the backbone of congregations. They are sweet, nice people, but that's what they are, clergy collectors. And that affects social relationships. Jews often form friendships in the congregation. They often choose congregations on the basis of friendships. For the rabbi, socializing is a work setting. That is where rabbis work, influencing, charming, cajoling, teaching informally, whatever. That kind of thing changes the nature of what Saturday night is, and how many Saturday nights you have available, and what you can do on Saturday night.

The very fact that the rabbi works when others are off, that she is out of sync with the rest of society, that evenings and weekends are major work times, what does that do to a family?

Rabbi's work is other people's recreation. I know it is. I'm a board member of my old shul now. The rabbi, incidentally, is a former camper of mine. I jokingly said to him, "Laybel, I'm going to be on the board. Am I going to give you a hard time!" "So?" he said, "Why should you be different?" But for me, it was different from the old days, when *I* worked evenings and weekends. I don't *have* to go to the board meeting. If I am fatigued from a day's work, I just don't go to the board meeting. It is diversion for me. Though I may care, it's not how I earn my bread. As for him, that is work. And that being out of sync has an effect. The women spoke this morning about spouses having a professional career of their own. What do you do if the rabbi's spouse has a professional career and when the spouse is home with the kids, the rabbi is out? And when the rabbi's around the spouse is at work. What do you do with that?

Or when other fathers or mothers are with their kids, the rabbi is out teaching others' kids. Or, of course, when something in the congregational family interferes with something in the personal family. Each time a decision has to be made, about a funeral or a wedding, and how plans have to be made and what to do when they are interfered with puts another element into the family pot. It is hard to live with the rabbi gone so much of the time, at the beck and call of others, especially when other husbands and wives, fathers and mothers are around.

I know some of you will fight with me on this, but I have the podium so I'm going to say it. I have learned since getting out of the pulpit that the rabbi's family *never really belongs*. No matter how long you've been in the community, you and your family are never really part of that community in the same way that other Jews are. We can kid ourselves about that, but I think that's so. Some of the evidence for that is that, among rabbis whom I know, the best friends of rabbis are other rabbis whom they went to school with fifteen, twenty, twenty-five, and thirty years ago. This is different from the situation with other professionals. I know of very few lawyers who say, "My best friend is the guy I finished law school with, twenty-five or thirty years ago." But for rabbis, those are the people with whom they can really be close. We don't have deep roots in the communities we live in. There's a lot of evidence for that. That is a painful fact, but I think it's so. Rabbis are actually rooted in the community of rabbis, serving nationwide.

There is no doctor's wife who expects to be treated by her husband medically. Even if he's an OB-GYN and she's having a child, she goes to some other OB-GYN. If my family needs psychological treatment, the last one they would come to would be me. But you just try, as the spouse of a rabbi, to go to another shul, to worship there because you find the services more to your liking, or you like being there because you're more "plain folks" than you are as a rabbinic spouse. There would be a lot of explaining to do. The spouse's devotion and the family's devotion and loyalty are always tests of the rabbi's effectiveness and always on view.

The rabbi is supposed to be the spouse's rabbi, not only husband or wife, but minister as well. Only in this career is that so. Again, that puts loyalty to the test. What has the rabbi produced in his marriage?

One rabbi was fired from a congregation because he sent his child to a different synagogue school. His own Talmud Torah wasn't good enough. You can get by with day schools, but his religious school wasn't good enough. He sent him to another religious school down the road and said, "It's my kid. I'm going to do what I want." And he was talking to me from a different congregation.

Symbolic exemplarhood in the moral and religious realm provides the rabbi with a larger-than-life image. There is no way around that. Such an image is at the very core of being a rabbi. The rabbi is designated by others and she volunteers herself to exemplify a caring, nurturing, involved, moral person. She is in a profession in which it is crucial both to appear to be something more than one is while still maintaining ongoing contact with other people. She is the willing helper, the good mother, the para-familial member of many families. And to help her maintain this role, she's given significant protection. She is treated with respect and deference and shielded overtly from others' anger and vulgarity. She is not subjected to many of the stresses that others are subjected to. Without such protection, she could not continue to maintain close contact and still function as an exemplar of those attributes that she is expected to symbolize. The price of this protection for the rabbi is a sense of otherness and difference, of loneliness in the midst of the crowd. The barriers erected by both laity and rabbi that create this insulated and isolated existence are made up of masks put on, words edited, and emotions held in check.

Let me suggest a couple of things. The most exciting thing done recently is the program of Mid-Career Review that the CCAR has begun.[7]

---

7. This was June 1976, prior to the Jewish Theological Seminary picking up on the other ideas and creating the Rabbinic Training Institute for Conservative Rabbis.

This is potentially a rich program for helping rabbis to get to know one another again, to share with one another, to be able to put forth and discuss those things that really share their humanity.

It is our hope that out of this there will be created a myriad of rabbinic support groups. There are a number of those going now, begun after Mohonk, where rabbis can get together and share the fellowship of being human beings in the same kind of profession. One experiences the kind of intimacy that a convention might provide, if it went on for two weeks to a month, and we were able to get by the "My Friday night service is larger, taller, stronger than your Friday night service" kind of syndrome. There is an appropriate place for that at conventions, but to get past that into the whole human dimension and the sharing is the kind of thing that our rabbinic organizations will have to see to.

Creating retreat environments, where rabbis and families can be just regular folks, where they can live outside the purview of their symbolic exemplarhood is essential. Perhaps that would be a rabbinic camp, perhaps some kind of retreat house where rabbis can go to spend vacations together with other rabbis and have a ball, enjoy, and just be persons, without having to shift gears or grow a beard. (A colleague of mine, a Conservative rabbi, grew a beard on vacation to be anonymous. Even so, they discovered him.)

An immense amount of work has to be done towards helping Jewish professionals who are located in the same community support one another rather than being competitive with one another. Rabbi–rabbi relationships, relations between Conservative *and* Reform rabbis, between rabbis of different stripes if they will cooperate, relations between senior rabbis and junior rabbis, relations between rabbis and cantors—all these are people who should be most supportive of one another, especially given their shared isolation. Yet what we find is that they get trapped in their own symbolic exemplarhood. One is Rabbi Rodeph Shalom and the other is Rabbi Beth El and a third, Rabbi Temple. They live existentially at a distance from one another instead of being close and supporting one another. These distancing factors need to be overcome.

There are some other resources. Congregations can, to some extent, be educated as to this symbolic exemplarhood so that they can help to ease the pressure a little bit. Our central organizations can, with the cooperation of individual rabbis, help make the pulpit rabbi less of a prisoner of his/her symbolic image. Salary scales, protection, clearer job definition, crisis intervention, ongoing support, and the like can be done to make the rabbi less subject to the price of his/her symbolic exemplarhood.

One final note and a very important one, for me, before we break. I don't want anything of what I have said to be taken as a denigration of the work of the pulpit rabbi. Let me tell you something. I did more important work during the ten years I was a pulpit rabbi than I will do the rest of my career. Unquestionably! I have no doubt about it. I touched more lives. I affected more people. I made more Jews and I was a much more effective kind of person in terms of my impact on others. I have no question at all about that.

What got to me was the isolation. That's what got to me. And I, in terms of my own life, couldn't live that way. That became the straw that broke my rabbinic back. I could not live that way. For me, it was just personally impossible. There were also a couple of other things which had to do with my megalomania, my own grandiosity. I discovered after the death of one of the great pulpit rabbis of America that neither he nor I was going to be immortalized with great statues or remembered down the generations.

Symbolic exemplarhood is inevitable in the rabbinate. It can be a vitally useful way to live. It is the symbolic exemplarhood that gives each and every rabbi the power and the ability to affect and influence others and, hopefully, to transform the future of the Jewish community. The future of the Jewish community rests on the shoulders of the pulpit rabbis. It is their symbolic exemplarhood that gives them their strength and their power. Know that I don't think you'll ever be free of being a Symbolic Exemplar. But knowing a burden, maybe we can together deal with it.

When the spies explored *Eretz Yisrael*, the question was whether it was a land flowing with milk and honey or a land that devoured its inhabitants. My belief is that the pulpit rabbinate, with our work and with the help of those who care about our work, can at least exist some place in between. Though not the world's easiest task, it need not devour us, and we can, along with Joshua, know God's promise:

> Be strong and resolute; do not be terrified or dismayed, for the Lord your God is with you wherever you go. (Joshua 1:9)[8]

May God strengthen, support, and walk at our side as we go forward unafraid in the work that we have to do.

---

8. From *Tanakh: A New Translation of the Holy Scriptures According to the Traditional Hebrew Text*. Philadelphia: New Jewish Publication Society, 1985.

6

The Inner Life of the Rabbi, or Who's at Home Anyway? And What's All the Commotion About?

A rabbi's inner life is often experienced as a battleground littered with the rubble from decades of inner struggle. Shoulds, oughts, wounded *"selves,"* shards of pyrrhic victories, nagging doubts about one's *Self* and who one is litter the landscape.

A rabbi is a Symbolic Exemplar of the best that is in humankind. This is an essential inescapable component of the rabbinate. Being a living symbol is both the glory of a rabbi's life and a torment of a rabbi's inner being. The awesome ambiguities of rabbinic symbolic exemplarhood make the inner life of a rabbi extraordinarily vulnerable. For life as a pulpit rabbi to be viable, a rabbi must clean up some of the debris in one's inner life, make some order, and engender a greater sense of inner balance.

The awesome ambiguities are that, though "only" human, each rabbi is a Symbolic Exemplar of the divine *and* of a people who encountered the divine. Vertically, rabbis are Symbolic Exemplars of God and are expected to emulate and "stand in" for God. Horizontally, rabbis are Symbolic Exemplars of the Jewish people, enjoined to love and care for every last one. External courage and inner fortitude are demanded in living daily in the world as Symbolic Exemplars and moving forward in that world, with all one's frailties, deficiencies, inadequacies, and wounded *"selves."* The stress and strain of being Symbolic Exemplars, and its weight on their inner life, rabbis know from their everyday "being" in the rabbinate.

Symbolic exemplarhood is a difficult, often irascible, and draining partner, walking with rabbis every place they go, and profoundly affecting their inner life. No matter how hard rabbis struggle, there is no shaking off being seen and treated as fundamentally different from others and, more important, different from one's own perception of *Self*. The expectation of difference implicitly demands that the rabbi exemplify *superlative inner* qualities and inordinately deep-set commitments. A profound sense of inner spiritual being, caring, and commitment is also demanded by those who train and ordain. Their nobly meant attempt to create a "religious personality," a "model Jew" or whatever, only increases the pressure. A rabbi's *private* and *public* life is expected to be a seamless whole marked by the warp of integrity and the woof of caring love. Rabbis know instinctively that their career is always the hostage of others' perception of their inner "soul." A rabbi's sense of oneself as authentic is likewise hostage to the rabbi's perception of and experience living with his/her inner "*self*." Professional achievement and public recognition are never enough. Belief, observance, spirituality, love, caring, devotion, kindness, must all be kept finely tuned and in line with the rabbinic persona presented to the external world. This deep sense of inner religiousness that rabbis are to demonstrate is difficult to sustain and tempting to counterfeit. It is vulnerable to their very humanness. When, inevitably, "negative" thoughts and feelings occur, a top priority becomes freeing one's *Self* of these intrusive "negative others," extirpating unacceptable inner drives and thoughts. This can lead to the attempt to purify, purify, and purify, yet again, one's inner life. This is done to rid oneself of those aspects and characteristics of the inner "*self*" that are perceived as not in keeping with how a rabbi ordained of God and by His people *should* be. Failing in this makes life difficult and leads many to consider leaving the rabbinate, feeling unsuited for this calling.

The stress on the rabbi's inner life may make itself known in the conflict rabbis experience about revealing various aspects of their personality. It may be heard by eavesdropping on rabbinic internal dialogue:

> Am I who I am supposed to be?
> If I'm not, who am I anyhow?
> If I'm not who they think I am, am I a fraud?
> If I keep them believing I am who they think I am, I am a fraud!
> Do I really make a difference?
> Do I really care?
> And if I do care, do I care enough?

What should I do when I don't care?

Do I act as if I do? Fake it?

How do I bless the Bat Mitzvah when I can't stand her or her family?

How do I lead services that I wouldn't attend if I weren't the rabbi?

Is what I'm doing appropriate to my being a rabbi?

Is what I'm doing appropriate to what they think they need?

What are the parameters? How much leeway do I have?

Dare I reveal my doubts, anger, madness, badness, fear, and anxiety?

It would be better if I didn't have such feelings, thoughts, ideas.

What can I do so that these inner conflicts, as persistent as they are, will not be an issue?

Perhaps prayer or greater punctiliousness to ritual and *mitzvot* (God's commands) would purify me?

Am I fit to be a rabbi?

Having worked with a large variety of professions, I have found rabbis and other clergy to be among the most caring and dedicated of people. Yet the level of inner integrity demanded by *Self* and others has no fathomable depth. One can always be more caring, more loving, and more dedicated. The depth of these inner qualities is often deemed inadequate by their possessor.

What resources can rabbis access to heal the inner life? Rabbis would do well to return to the sources which tell us of our creation as humans. Other healing resources come from the work of Gregory Bateson[1] and Stephen Gilligan,[2] which dovetail beautifully with the religious facts our tradition presents.

THE FACTS:

God said: "Let *us* make humankind in *our* image (*tzalmaynu*), according to *our* likeness." . . . God created humankind in *His* image (*tzalmo*), in the image (*tzelem*) of God did *He* create it, male and female did *He* create them. (Genesis 1:26–27)

YHWH, God, formed the human of dust from the soil, He blew into his nostrils the breath of life (*nishmat chayim*); and the human became a living being. (Genesis 2:7)

---

1. G. Bateson. *Steps to an Ecology of Mind.* New York: Chandler Publishing Co., 1972.

2. S. Gilligan. *The Courage to Love.* New York: W.W. Norton & Company, 1997.

This is the record of the begettings of Adam/Humankind! At the time of God's creating humankind, in the likeness of God did He then make it, male and female He created them, and gave blessing to them and named them "Humankind" on the day of their being created. (Genesis 5:1–2)[3]

Each human being is created *b'Tzelem Elohim*. Each is in the image/ likeness of God. That image may be understood to be humankind's cognitive "*self*," since the creating God was and is incorporeal, and any other understanding is or borders on idolatry.[4] The creating God is described in the plural (*Elohim*), and yet singular (God). Humankind is thus in the image of a God who uniquely is both one alone and at the same time more than one.

Our ancestors, frightened of the possible polytheistic implications of Genesis 1:26, offered that it was the imperial "We" in which God spoke, or suggested that this plural language reflected God presiding over and consulting with a heavenly court—in itself a patently non-monotheistic explanation! The idea that God, both unique and many-faceted, might be in consultation with various "parts" of Himself leads to a more authentically monotheistic yet non-fundamentalist position.

Ari Mark Curtin points out that this to us odd mix of singular and plural comes to teach something very important. "By using these first-person plurals, God is revealing something special about God's nature and what it means for humanity to be in the image of God. The . . . divine plural self-references . . . acknowledge . . . paradoxical 'plural' images/likenesses of the God who is nevertheless, overwhelmingly One. Just as humanity's 'God-image' is somehow singular while plural, so is God. God and humankind are to be seen as fundamentally unified while also multiple. God and humankind's nature are each poised between these pluralities: simultaneously singular *and* plural. Human form in the image of God is plural. Human knowledge in the image of God is plural. Fittingly the human ability to conceptualize and communicate is also plural, in the image of God."[5]

---

3. Translations of biblical text by Everett Fox, *The Five Books of Moses* (New York: Schocken Books, 1996), and *Tanakh, a New Translation of the Holy Scriptures According to the Traditional Hebrew Text* (Philadelphia, Jerusalem: Jewish Publication Society, 1985).

4. cf. Maimonides, *Guide of the Perplexed*; Chapter 1 (translation by M. Friedlander, 1881. Hebrew Publishing Co. New York): "In man the 'form' (*tzelem*) is that constituent which gives him human perception: and on account of this intellectual perception the term *tzelem* is employed. . . ."

5. "When God's References Are Plural: A Look at Gen. 1:26,3:22,11:7, in an Overarching Context," *CCAR Journal: A Reform Jewish Quarterly*, Fall 1996. In a personal communication

Each human being is further a symbol of God's presence on earth.[6] Into each the Living God [YHWH][7] has infused the breath of life, saturating each with the precious gift of *Neshamah*.[8] Humankind is [*Neshamah*⟺*Tzelem*]. The *Tzelem* gives thought, form, and direction. The *Neshamah* gives life, energy, and vitality. The [*Tzelem*⟺*Neshamah*][9] is, at one and the same time, both indivisible and in relationship to its other part. Each part sustains and is sustained by the other. Thought, form, and direction alone would lead to a useless spinning of the wheels. Life, energy, and vitality alone would be directionless, and we would be dragged around aimlessly by our feelings. One being removed, the other is incapacitated. Each and both of these occurrences are more than common experiences.

The [*Neshamah*⟺*Tzelem*][10] is of us and with us from our first breath to our last. Though each of us is in the image, with the breath of God enlivening our very being, no two *Tzelem*s are identical; no two *Neshamah*s the same. Thus, no two [*Tzelem*⟺*Neshamah*]s are duplicates. Each is unique.[11]

The [*Tzelem*⟺*Neshamah*] is *not* negotiable. It is a given, ever present in us and in all others. It is *not* contingent on our thinking and feeling correctly, behaving one way or another, on accomplishment or the lack thereof, on perceived goodness or experienced badness. The individual, do what he will, cannot be rid of it. It is one's essence. Though obscured in the murky fog of compromised living, the [*Tzelem*⟺*Neshamah*] is *always* there in us and others, ever present, waiting to be seen, heard, and attended to. When we and/or others turn away from the [*Tzelem*⟺*Neshamah*], neglecting it in ourselves, ignoring and disregarding it in others, harm is done, commitments broken, intimacies violated, children hurt, trusts betrayed, and great evil

---

the author indicated that the full title was supposed to have been "When God's Self-References Are Plural," but the "Self" got lost on the way to the printer.

6. Nahum Sarna. *Genesis Commentary*. Philadelphia: The Jewish Publication Society, 1989, p. 12.

7. This name of God derives from the Hebrew root "to be." Its best meaning is [Was! Is! Will be!]—thus The Eternal. Sarna points out that YHWH "is the . . . immanent, personal God . . . who shows concern for the needs of human beings."

8. From the Hebrew root N<u>SH</u>M—to breathe.

9. The brackets [   ] indicate the interrelated unity of these two elements. The double arrow ⟺ signifies reciprocal relationship.

10. The [*Neshamah*⟺*Tzelem*] and [*Tzelem*⟺*Neshamah*] are considered to be identical.

11. viz. Mishnah Sanhedrin 4:5.

perpetrated. Blame and contempt, anger and condemnation, all too often directed towards ourselves as well as others, increase our sense of alienation and isolation. These turn us ever more away from the [Tzelem⇔Neshamah] in us, and block any chance of experiencing it in others. Perhaps that is why it is written, *"Be loving to your neighbor as yourself. I am YHWH"* (emphasis—JHB).[12]

These *religious facts* greatly impact rabbis' lives with others. The rabbinic charge is to search out, tune in to, stay focused on, respect, nourish, sustain, and sponsor the [Tzelem⇔Neshamah], both one's own and others. That all humans are possessed of the [Tzelem⇔Neshamah] profoundly affects how rabbis think about those with whom they are in relationship. Affirming that all are created [Tzelem⇔Neshamah] affects how rabbis relate to those suffering, those who differ, those who "sin," those who violate Jewish norms; to religious or political opponents, to those whose behavior is outside the expected limits, to those whose intentions are considered malevolent; to those who may even be perceived as inherently evil. Revealing the [Tzelem⇔Neshamah], and returning all of these to it is no small thing. Doing it is wondrous. That rabbis attempt it, though they often fail in achieving it, is certainly audacious.

The more daunting challenge is in attending to and actualizing the meaning of that *fact* in the inner life. It is there that we are most vulnerable to ruptures in our relationship with our own [Tzelem⇔Neshamah]. When we lose contact with our [Tzelem⇔Neshamah], we without fail lose contact with others'. And losing contact with theirs is a sure sign that we have lost contact with ours. That these relationships will break down time and again goes with being human. What do we do when in our inner life thoughts and feelings appear that, despite our best efforts, imply that we are *not* in the "image"? How do we jibe our experience of these "negative selves," which do not seem consonant with the [Tzelem⇔Neshamah], with what our creation proclaims is our core and being? No matter the public persona we present, we consider these "negative selves" to be "persona non grata." "They" distance us from the [Tzelem⇔Neshamah], and leave us feeling diminished. We struggle valiantly that these "negative selves" disappear, or at least have the good sense and common courtesy to stay out of public view.

---

12. Leviticus 19:18. The common understanding is that one cannot love the other if one does not love oneself. Rabbi Akiba in The Sifra is quoted as saying, "This is a great principle of the Torah." It is of interest to note that this often-quoted saying is the second part of a verse which begins, *"You are not to take vengeance, you are not to retain anger against the sons of your kinspeople"* (emphasis—JHB), and ends with the affirmation that there is a greater presence in which both self and other find themselves; thus, *"I am YHWH!"*

Repairing the breach by turning to our [*Tzelem*⇔*Neshamah*] is a supremely important undertaking. It requires establishing a Buberian [I–Thou] dialogue of mutual respect, leading to a loving, personal human relationship between each and all of our *"selves";* those we value and those we distance; the "positive" and the "negative"; the "acceptable" and "non-acceptable." To do this we must value and bless all *"selves,"* and bring each and all back, particularly those *"selves"* previously rejected, into relationship with the [*Tzelem*⇔*Neshamah*].

Building these relationships is no easy task. It is worth the effort because there really is no better choice. The religious *fact* is that *all* of us, not part of us, is created [*Tzelem*⇔*Neshamah*]. Keeping all of our *"selves"* in ongoing relationship with one another and the [*Tzelem*⇔*Neshamah*] present in each of us is what makes it possible to experience the [*Tzelem*⇔*Neshamah*], ours and others', as fully present. When these relationships are flowing back and forth with respect and integrity, we experience the emanation of the quintessential *Self*. It is an experience of the holy.

Dereliction in tending to these relationships inexorably moves us to an [Either/Or] position, a step on the road to fundamentalism. [Either/Or] thinking is a dangerous by-product of our misunderstanding of monotheism, that God is One. It is [Either/Or] thinking which impedes our building these relational bridges. [Either/Or] thinking dominates religious and moral education. The presupposition that underlies this thinking is that we are one, and need to divest ourselves of unacceptable parts in the relentless pursuit of oneness.

From a very young age we are taught to think of our "being" as a singular *Self*. This singular *Self* is to be shaped and molded into a *Self* acceptable to what family, society, and religious community consider to be socially appropriate and desirable, whether that be living by the Boy Scout Oath or the Commandments of the Living God. We are taught that things, ideas, emotions, *"selves"* are either good or bad, are either one way or the other. The *Self* of "To Thine own *Self* be true" means one's good, worthwhile, acceptable *"self,"* the other *"selves"* having been educated out. When inevitably unacceptable *"selves"* show up despite our best efforts to squash them, and take over center stage, people in keeping with [Either/Or] thinking, describe themselves and others in [me/not me] terms.

"It wasn't like *me* to do that."
"That's just *not her*."
"If only you knew the *true me*."
"What I did is just *not me*."

"The *'real him'* is always cheating."

"I just wasn't *'myself'* when I hit her."

[Either/Or] thinking leads to and supports these [me/not me] experiences. The [Either/Or] position lives and thrives in the dichotomies of *Self*/other, me/you, us/them, I/it, good/bad, mind/body, divine/human, strong/weak, love/hate, independence/dependence, inside/outside, masculine/feminine, conscious/unconscious, healthy/sick, this/not this, problem/solution, rabbi/congregant, thinking/feeling, Jew/Gentile, sacred/profane, Symbolic Exemplar/plain folk, and seemingly endless other splits. These [me/not me] relationships, products of [Either/Or] thinking, may be expressed with just about any distinction.

The task [Either/Or] thinking assigns to us is to explore, verify, establish, and purify our oneness. We are to accomplish this mission by converting, conquering, denying, transforming, or using any other means available to be rid of the "negative" unacceptable parts of us and others. We do this for our own benefit and certainly for others' good.

In the inner life this leads to the attempt to convert oneself to a proper way of thinking. Caught in the [Either/Or] position of the fundamentalist, we strive to become more "righteous" and "holy," "observant" and "pious," thus to rid ourselves of the "negative other," the perceived "degrading" thoughts and traits, our badness, selfishness, etc. The inevitable result of the [Either/Or] position is the creation of splits in our own inner life which do not redound to our benefit.

As far as others are concerned, the fundamentalist [Either/Or] position demands that they be converted, or the "problem" of their "otherness" solved by eliminating them in some fashion. That is of course done in the name of a higher truth and without doubt for *their* own "good." When fundamentalism does not have the power in hand, it does it in lesser ways by creating self-isolating enclaves, which serve also to isolate the other. This breaks any ongoing relationship and creates more splits. One need only note the increasing turn towards self-isolation and isolating the other of those who hold our tradition in fundamentalist ways. Those "Torah True" or rigidly Halachic Jews, whose relation is only to the text, not to the ongoing life around and beyond them, try to convert both others and themselves to "a faithful adherence to the text which will overcome some 'outside' badness or evil."[13] [Either/Or] fundamentalism

---

13. S. Gilligan. "The Premises of Fundamentalism." Private correspondence.

shatters the relationship with others so necessary for fully experiencing the [*Tzelem*⟺*Neshamah*] present in each and all of us.

As rabbis, we further bring to that encounter with ourselves and others our relation to the tradition to which we have in some way committed our lives, which has formed us and to which we have given form in our very being. Our relationship with that tradition may take and has taken for us many forms. Our own relationship to the tradition and the tradition's relationship within itself is always unique and different. As each of us is the greater field of which our various "*selves*" are a part, our tradition is the greater field of which we are a part.[14] It too is present in the encounter with our own "*selves*." As rabbis we are ordained to bring it into our work with others. [Either/Or] thinking is a threat to our [*Tzelem*⟺*Neshamah*]'s living [I–Thou] relationship with the tradition. [Either/Or] thinking is an impediment to experiencing the [*Tzelem*⟺*Neshamah*] of the tradition by nudging us towards fundamentalism. Fundamentalism, always inimical to the [*Tzelem*⟺*Neshamah*], ultimately leads to a split between the [*Tzelem*⟺*Neshamah*] of the tradition and our own.

The fundamentalist premise is that there is only one truth and that truth is literally revealed in a special text. Faithful (literal) following of this text will lead to salvation. Such fundamentalism is dangerous to our sense of relatedness,[15] to our "*selves*," to others who differ from us, which actually means everyone, and to our own relation to the tradition we love and tend.

To stay in touch with our [*Tzelem*⟺*Neshamah*] and others requires thinking in a way that affirms our multi-faceted "*selves*" and acknowledges that *all* "*selves*" have a place, can coexist, and enrich our total being. We need to replace our [Either/Or] thinking with [Both/And] thinking. Healthy relationships, whether in a domestic environment or internationally, are always a [Both/And] endeavor.

---

14. The individual mind is immanent but not only in the body. It is immanent also in pathways and messages outside the body; and there is a larger Mind of which the individual mind is only a subsystem. This larger Mind is comparable to God and is perhaps what some people mean by "God," but it is still immanent in the total interconnected social system and planetary ecology. G. Bateson. *Steps to an Ecology of Mind.* New York: Chandler Publishing Co., 1972, p. 461.

15. S. Gilligan, private correspondence.

[Both/And] thinking, to the surprise of many caught in the trap of fundamentalist [Either/Or] thinking, is and has been present in our powerfully monotheistic tradition from the beginning.[16]

[Both/And] relational thinking is the very antithesis of the [Either/Or] position. As presented in the work of Stephen Gilligan, profoundly influenced by Gregory Bateson, it offers a radically different way of experiencing what we have previously thought of as our *Self*. This work can be of great help in healing our inner life and its conflicts.

Gilligan points out that [Both/And] thinking implies:

> There are (at least) two of you:
> You are not a *Self*—You are a relationship.
> Relationship is the basic psychological unit.
> *Self* is a context, not a position.

According to Gilligan,[17] "The relational *Self* is the experience of both '*selves*' simultaneously. The idea is that you are the field that holds and the spirit that connects the differences. Each person is a relationship between '*selves*,' rather than the position of any given '*self*.' *Self* is a pattern of me/not-me connections experienced in a relational field."[18] "*Self* is the experi-

---

16. That God is both singular and paradoxically plural is referred to many times in Jewish tradition; e.g., God said to Moses, "You want to know my name? I am known by what I do. I am called many things. When I judge humanity, I am Elohim. When I war on evildoers, I am Tzevaot. When I suspend judgement, I am El Shaddai. When I am merciful to My world I am Yahweh. (My name is) EHYEH ASHER EHYEH. I will be there howsoever I will be there. I am known by what I do."

[Exodus Rabbah 3:6]

Or noting God's prayer?!

"May it be My will that my compassion overcome my anger and may my mercy prevail over my attributes [of justice and judgement]. May I deal with my children in accordance with My attribute of compassion. May I act towards them beyond the letter of the law."

[Babylonian Talmud, Berachot 7a]

That God is a [Both/And] personality is amply present in Rabbinic tradition; The twelve-hour Divine day is said to include a variety of activities; God spends three hours studying Torah; three hours dispensing justice; three hours providing for the needs of the world's creatures and three hours playing with Leviathan.

[Babylonian Talmud, Avodah Zarah 3b]

17. Gilligan, *The Courage to Love.*

18. Ibid.

ence of a dynamic relatedness between differences. *Self* is neither here nor there, me nor you: it is the conversation that bridges, the spirit that unites, the pattern that connects the differences. This may be described as the principle of relatedness."[19]

Referring to the thought of Gregory Bateson, Gilligan notes, "One of Gregory Bateson's (1955/1972) great insights was that the simultaneous holding of multiple frames or truths underlies the distinctly human experiences, such as intimacy, play, hypnosis, mythology, and psychopathology."[20] (And religion, which Bateson often referred to in other contexts, is one of those great human experiences.—JHB)

"In holding multiple images or descriptions simultaneously, one is freed from the tyranny of what Bateson (1970/1972) described as the pathology of operating from a single position. Life begins to flow through a person's consciousness again, thereby allowing positions, images, and texts to change."

The above profoundly affects how we think about our *Self*, the *Self* of others, and how we relate to the *Self* of our tradition. [Both/And] thinking allows our at least two *"selves,"* and there are more, to be in a loving, respectful relationship. And with others though only one *"self"* may be presented to us, we need to be aware that another, though obscured *"self"* is present and needs to be seen, blessed, and brought into relationship. We and they are not solely one or the other aspect of ourselves. [Both/And] thinking by allowing for the existence of multiple, constantly changing truths also profoundly influences our relation with the tradition. We walk a dangerous precipice when we tilt to one side or the other of any of these relationships. One without the other turns us away from the [*Tzelem*⇔*Neshamah*]. Bateson repeatedly emphasized, "Mind is relationship and difference is the basic unit of mind. Our concern is with the pattern that connects."[21]

The hard question for us is how do we attend to the "pattern that connects"? How do we start to bring the [Both/And] parts of our *"selves"* into a loving relationship with each other, a relationship in which both are blessed and neither needs to be "converted" or gotten rid of. What do we do to be in touch with, accept and love, i.e., to be in a trusting relationship with our various and sundry inner *"selves."* A useful metaphor for staying with and

---

19. Gilligan, *The Courage to Love.*

20. Ibid.

21. G. Bateson. *Mind and Nature: A Necessary Unity.* New York: E.P. Dutton, 1979.

remaining stable as the change goes on, which I am sure appeals to rabbis, is that used by Gregory Bateson: "the acrobat on the high wire maintains his stability by continual correction of his imbalance."[22] Following the example of Bateson's acrobat, rabbis need to move back and forth between these "*selves*" with grace and elegance, appreciating both without trying to obliterate either one in the service of a non-achievable "true *Self*." We are at all times [Both/And]. No part, aspect, or characteristic stands alone—neither the good nor the bad. Each may serve as context for the other. Everything contains its opposite, not over and against, but contains.

To turn back to the [*Tzelem*⇔*Neshamah*], especially our own, requires love, the dedication that flows from love, and skillful acts of sponsorship.

Sponsorship has been described by Gilligan as the "relational connection that engages and awakens the life presence and goodness [of] both '*self*' and other, [so that] . . . 'otherness' may be held, blessed, contained, listened to, etc. such that its human value begins to emerge."[23] "Sponsorship is one of the great practices of mature love. Sponsorship includes the relational skills of deep listening, naming and blessing, challenging and protecting, containing and encouraging, connecting and being with [religious-N.B.—JHB] and communal ritual."[24] In the inner life, sponsorship means honoring and giving human presence to our "persona non grata," all the thoughts, feelings, and emotions that we have difficulty living with. This means sponsoring and honoring what we have formerly considered the unacceptable parts of ourselves that we have striven to eradicate. Sponsorship gives them a safe place, a home in the inner life, bringing them back into the world and into relationship with the [*Tzelem*⇔*Neshamah*]. The envy, greed, cruelty, badness, in essence what the tradition has referred to as the *yetzer hara* (evil impulse)[25] must be given, as the tradition has, a place in the *Self* equation.[26]

---

22. Bateson, *Mind and Nature: A Necessary Unity.*

23. S. Gilligan, private correspondence.

24. Ibid.

25. viz. Rabbi Samuel ben Nachman observes, "Now God saw all that he had made, and here: it was exceedingly good!" (Gen. 1:31). This includes the Evil Impulse. Can the Evil Impulse be called good? Yes; were it not for the Evil Impulse, no man would build a house, nor marry a wife, nor have children, nor engage in commerce. King Solomon said, "All labor and skillful work comes of a man's rivalry with his neighbor" (Genesis Rabbah 9:7).

26. viz. Man is bound to bless God for the evil, even as he blesses God for the good, for it is written: "*Now you are to love YHWH your God with all your heart, with all your being, with all*

Sponsorship, starting with our own "*selves*," is a crucial skill no rabbi can be without. We start with our own "*selves*" because there is no sponsoring others until we have lovingly sponsored our own previously rejected "*selves*," our "negative otherness." It is an act of love toward ourselves and toward the [Tzelem⇔Neshamah] which God has made of us. Sponsorship is likewise crucial in all relationships with others, be it a spousal relationship, parenting, teaching, praying, and life itself. Not choosing sponsorship or not being skilled in doing it makes being a rabbi incredibly difficult.

Gilligan points out that sponsorship is vulnerable to "a few distinct challenges . . . in maintaining . . . connection to the field. One is where you come to believe that your tradition is the only correct one. You then move from being a sponsor (one who awakens the goodness and gifts of life) to a recruit for an ideological position. You're no longer living in the field, you're locked into a mental concentration camp. It's an easy slip to make, one I think each of us falls into many times a day. That's why we need to be communing with the spirits who have walked the path before us: so we can continually find our humility, our awe, our connection to 'before and after' in the 'here and now'."[27]

Once that is done and the formerly unacceptable has been given a human place, love and sponsorship can be an effective means of honoring and renewing the tradition we are in. Again, according to Gilligan, "a sponsor does not operate in a vacuum . . . [sponsorship] requires that the sponsor surrender to a larger field than him or her *Self*. [The sponsor] is a part of a beautiful tradition of awakening the human spirit. . . . [The tradition—JHB] is the real "sponsor." There are many streams in this river of consciousness . . . [The sponsor] must walk and swim in at least one to be a good sponsor. Thus, being a good sponsor requires that [the sponsor] connect with those that have gone before . . . and those who have started a little bit after . . . [on that particular path]."[28]

A few helpful hints for checking on who is "at home" so one can welcome and bless them and so return to the [Tzelem⇔Neshamah]. Doing this can start the process of becoming the relationship you really are. Relatedness and love between differences starting with your own "negative others" is required.

---

your substance" (Deut. 6:5) (emphasis—JHB). "*With all your heart*—with both your impulses, your good impulse and your evil impulse" (Mishnah Berachot 9:5).

27. S. Gilligan, private correspondence.

28. S. Gilligan, private correspondence, February 1998.

A useful question in establishing who is causing the commotion and needs to be sponsored is,

"If only I didn't do or experience (or could get rid of) X, then this really wouldn't be a problem."

X marks the spot of the neglected *"self."*[29]

For example:

"If only I didn't feel so *inhibited*, I would be successful."
"If only I didn't get so *angry*, I could get on with my life."
"If only I didn't lack *devotion*, I could be a good rabbi."
"If only I didn't *dislike* people, I would be a better pastor."
"If only my congregation *listened*, I could be happy."
"If only I did not feel *set-apart*, I would know I'm OK."
"If only I didn't feel inadequate, I would enjoy the rabbinate."

As Gilligan puts it, "The idea is that when this unacceptable experience or behavior arises, the person . . . cannot hold the 'tension of opposites' between this experience and his regular sense of *Self. This is where the break in relatedness occurs . . . and symptomatic behavior is likely to arise.* Returning the neglected *"self"* into the relational *Self* is thus the crucial step in healing."[30] Welcoming one's "inhibitions," "anger," "lack of devotion," "dislike," "not being heard," "loneliness," "inadequacy," and on and on, initiating a dialogue/relationship with them and with the [*Tzelem*⟺*Neshamah*], means establishing a respectful loving conversation between different positions of identity.

Having been created [*Tzelem*⟺*Neshamah*], we are clearly not without resources. A number of questions can help access these [*Tzelem*⟺*Neshamah*] resources:

When do I feel most myself?
After a period of stress, how do I get back to feeling myself?
When/what are those times when the commotion inside quiets down?
When am I so absorbed that time and boundaries are not issues?

---

29. Gilligan, *The Courage to Love.*

30. Ibid.

These, what might be called [Tzelem⇔Neshamah] states, are often marked by an absence of the internal dialogue mentioned earlier and by a comfortable breathing pattern. A rabbi may find these quintessentially [Tzelem⇔Neshamah] resources in study, in prayer, in doing a mitzvah, in walking in the woods, painting, writing, talking with a friend, playing or listening to music, or a myriad of other experiences. The answers to these questions are benchmarks of the [Tzelem⇔Neshamah] in us. Bringing the experience a rabbi has while doing them into relationship with oneself, others, and the tradition itself is a crucial undertaking. Shuttling back and forth between what is going on and those resources is a skill to be carefully honed.

In situations where the [Tzelem⇔Neshamah] resources are honored and used appropriately, relational differences can operate in a [Both/And] setting with a tone of conversational connectedness—the sort of [I–Thou] relationship described by Martin Buber. In this kind of intimacy, there is an experience of a "me," a "you," and the relational *Self* of "us" that is felt when both the "I" and "Thou" are respected and treasured.

It's tough work, but somebody's got to do it. And who better than us? And if not now, when?

7
The Silenced Modim—
Modim d'Rabanan:
Tending Our Wounded Selves*

Note to the reader

There are numerous *Modims*. When the cantor, during the public recitation of the Amidah (the eighteen benedictions, a central feature of every service), chants the regular "*Modim*" the individual worshipper is instructed to read the "*Modim d'Rabanan*" silently. The two texts vary to some degree. What follows is the English text of the "*Modim d'Rabanan*."

We are grateful to You Adonai our God and God of our ancestors, God of life, who creates us, and all that lives. Blessing and gratitude are due your ineffable name for giving us life and sustaining us. Continue to enliven and sustain us; gather our *exiled* to Your Holy place, there to consummate your commandments, do your will, and serve you with a whole heart. For all this we are grateful to You. Blessed is the God of gratefulness.

MODIM ANACHNU LAKH
(WE ARE GRATEFUL TO YOU)

Gratefulness is appreciation for blessings received. Cast in God's image, each starts life blessed and grateful. In the exuberant chorus of *Modim*, there is one *Modim* that lives in silence. A *Modim* virtually hidden, almost driven underground, tucked away in the siddur (prayer book). A *Modim whose* destiny it

---

*Published as "Reflections on the Silenced Modim: Modim de-Rabanan." Reprinted with permission from *Conservative Judaism*, Vol. 52, No. 1, Fall 1999, pp. 61–63. Copyright the Rabbinical Assembly.

is *never* to be recited publicly. A *Modim* snubbed by omission even in private prayer. A *Modim relegated* to silence in the wings, while some other *Modim* is given center stage. Yet this silent *Modim* so constrained in public prayer *and* private prayer, wounded in its eloquence, resolutely, though often in small print, hangs on tenaciously in the siddur, to be read without sound.

Who then are the grateful "we" who having no voice mutely mouth the words:

> *MODIM ANACHNU LAKH*
> (*WE* ARE GRATEFUL TO *YOU*)

"*We*" is all of "me." Accounted for, are all our diverse "*selves*," Some of our "*selves*" are blessed, and valued. Other of our "*selves*" cursed, and rejected. Some of our "*selves*" we display. Other "*selves*" we hide. To some of our "*selves*" we give voice publicly and privately. To others we turn a deaf ear. Some of our "*selves*" we curse as worthless. These wounded and exiled "*selves*" especially are included.

The cursed, wounded "*selves*" result when "violence" (some unintended) tears at the fragile, vulnerable "Divine Image" in which we are cast. In childhood, the "Image" being tender, this happens all too easily. For too many others, trauma happens later on. A particular "*self*" is wounded even as other "*selves*" continue to grow. Life being what it is, few escape whole, unscathed. We give names to these wounded "*selves*": anxiety, depression, low self-esteem, insecurity, fear, and so on. We experience "*them*," these cursed "*selves*," as symptoms and we label "*them*" problematical. We struggle to rid ourselves of "*them*," try to stifle "*them*," hoping, that at least "*they*" stay hidden, at best silent, ignored by us, unseen and unheard by others. At times when "*they*" do show up, we are so mortified and appalled that we relinquish the field to "*them*" and "*they*" seem to be all we are. For that time, "*they*" are us. And we have the experience of saying, "That just wasn't me," "*I* would never do that!" "I just wasn't my*self*."

Where do these wounded "*selves*" reside? "They" languish in the rifts that mark our [Either/Or] dichotomies; our splitting of our world into [me/not me]; [good/bad]; [rational/irrational]; [independent/dependent]; [sacred/profane]; [mind/body]; [conscious/unconscious]; [strong/weak]; and on and on. When we say that a certain thought we have, an impulse we entertain, some act we do, falls into one or the other of our [Either/Or] dichotomies, and determines who we are, we create these rifts. We hold tightly to the notion that our true *Self* is *either* one *or* the other side of these splits.

We struggle to opt for what we "should" be and condemn and curse our un-blessed other. We have learned from childhood that who we are is a choice between one or the other of these splits. We have been painstakingly taught to overlook that we *are* [Both/And] rather than [Either/Or].

This thoroughly mastered notion of *Self* is not useful. Each of us, no matter how solitary, is not a *Self*. Each of us is a Relationship. *Self* occurs in the relationship between our various "*selves*" (and between our resulting *Self* and other "*selves*"). When both/all "*selves*" *are* simultaneously blessed and val-ued, acknowledged and appreciated, and in I–Thou respectful contact, *Self* comes to be.

So the silenced *Modim* hangs in there, and says "read me," in silence as you must. And know that the silence also is a blessing, because it is in the silence that all "*selves*"*selves* can be heard. "I" the silenced *Modim* give mute voice to the gratefulness of the wounded, often cursed "*selves*." Their grate-fulness is testimony to their appreciation for having been created, blessed, and sustained by God. With "my" expression of gratefulness, voiced on be-half of all our "*selves*," those that have no voice, those tucked away, those condemned to silence, at best unacknowledged, mostly cursed, "I" the si-lenced "*Modim*," "myself" an almost unrecognized "*self*," in stillness give voice and place and blessing to the "*selves*" that have been exiled, cursed, and re-buffed. On behalf of all exiled "*selves*," the silenced *Modim* affirms that each "*self*" is blessed and valued and has a place. This *Modim*'s gratefulness pro-claims that all "*selves*" are God's creation, and thereby share God's blessing and provenance.

So, "We" thank God for creating, nourishing, and sustaining all our "*selves*." Embracing those we have struggled against, who we have strained to stifle. "*We* " pray that God bless all our "*selves*" bringing those "*selves*" we have exiled back to God's holy place. When that happens, the "I-Thou" con-versation between "*selves*" can commence. And it is in that conversation that *Self* happens. With all "*selves*" blessed, present and accounted for, in relation-ship and discourse with one another, then, and only then, can God's will be done with a full and whole heart. For that promise "We" are "all of us" grateful.

Educating About Symbolic Exemplarhood

8
By the Power Vested in Me: What Rabbis Need to Know and Do*

Being a rabbi means serving as a Symbolic Exemplar of the best that is in humankind. Being a walking, talking, living symbol is extraordinarily difficult. Though a component of the rabbinate that provides a major source of efficacy, influence, potency, and power, it has over the years been a drain on many rabbis. Initially seductive, and often denied by "new" rabbis who say things like, "I'm just going to be a regular guy/gal; I'm sure I can have good friends in the congregation; I'll have them call me by my first name"; only to discover that their first name turns out to be "Rabbi." Rabbis find as they move toward mid-career that their symbolic exemplarhood is at the root of their discontent. They complain about living in a "glass house," loneliness in the midst of the crowd, always having to be "on," and being treated differently than anyone else. Having picked one of the most public of callings, rabbis yearn for anonymity. Rabbis want to hold their husbands' hands, and not have congregants offer, "Oh, what a cute couple they are; look at how they kiss each other." They are relieved when going to the movies to find that no congregants are present. Yet no matter how hard rabbis try, there is no shaking off being Symbolic Exemplars. It clings to them, an irrevocable component of each rabbinate.

*Published as "'By the Power Vested in Me': Symbolic Exemplarhood and the Pulpit Rabbi," in *Conservative Judaism*, Vol. L, No. 4, Summer 1998, pp. 59–66.

What makes rabbinic symbolic exemplarhood doubly difficult is its attribution to the rabbi of superlative inner qualities and inordinately deep-set commitments which the rabbi must exemplify in a relatively unprotected private and public arena. The Queen of England has layer upon layer of insulation from her public. A political leader's inner motivations are not expected to be pure and holy. A star quality entertainer is measured by some verifiable talent. The rabbi's private and public life, though uninsulated, is expected to be a seamless whole marked by the warp of integrity and the woof of caring love. Rabbis know instinctively that their career is always the hostage of others' perception of the inner "soul" of the man/woman doing the job. Pulpit skills, whether preaching, pastoral, administrative, or others, are subordinate to others' perception of one's inner qualities. This also makes the rabbi hostage to his/her own spouse and family. What happens in those ordinarily private arenas is perceived when opened to public scrutiny as an indication of what the rabbi's inner being is "really" like. Over the years, in working with a large variety of professions, I have found rabbis and other pulpit clergy to be among *the* most caring and dedicated of people. Yet a level of inner integrity is demanded that has no fathomable depth. One can always be more caring and more dedicated. And the depth of one's caring, integrity, and other inner qualities is often too exposed for comfort. Being a Symbolic Exemplar has been until now perhaps the greatest source of rabbinic alienation, leading rabbis to rebel against the exemplarhood. Rabbis protest, "I don't bar/bat mitzvah them; it happens when they become thirteen"; "I don't bless them, I'm at best a conduit"; "I don't marry them, halachically they do so by . . ." The rabbi's protest is an elegant statement of "*I just want to be me, I just want to be human.*" As long as they have presented themselves as rabbis they are more than just "me," more than just human. Rabbis are Symbolic Exemplars. There is no choice!

The late Len Hirsch *z"l* offered that: "Understanding power is understanding that courage is needed to act in the face of awesome ambiguities and pressures."[1] For rabbis the awesome ambiguities include the fact that though "only" human they are Symbolic Exemplars of the divine and of a people who encountered the divine. The pressures that come from being Symbolic Exemplars, rabbis know from their everyday "being" in the rabbinate.

---

1. "Parables from Politicians: Lessons for OD from the Political Realm." Speech to OD Network 1980 Spring Conference, May 1980.

To use the rabbinic power implicit in their being Symbolic Exemplars, rabbis must *accept* and be *comfortable* with being walking talking symbols, and need to be *skilled* in using their symbolic exemplarhood as a major source of their rabbinic power. Congregations will lose much if they do not attend to the price symbolic exemplarhood can exact, and they need to help rabbis sustain and use their exemplarhood while avoiding the enervating price that can often result.

There follows a partial, limited, albeit important list of the rabbinic powers that symbolic exemplarhood aids, abets, and indeed makes possible.

It is their symbolic exemplarhood that, among other things, enables rabbis:

1. *To bless people.* All of us recall someone in our past who "blessed" us, and how important that was. Rabbis need to believe that when they bless someone, they are doing something important. Establishing what blessings are needed and how they are to be given so that they "take" is a crucial part of rabbinic work. Symbolic exemplarhood helps blessings happen.

2. *To name and by naming create new entities.* When rabbis say, "I now pronounce you husband and wife," they, by saying those words, create a new status. Rabbis are vested with the power to marry, to name a baby, to give a convert a new identity. As Symbolic Exemplars, they have great power to label, to characterize; you are a *loving* man, a *courageous* woman, a *proud* Jew or whatever. Rabbis need to recognize and believe in their power to create new realities with words, a power to be used carefully, with discretion and respect for its potency.

3. *To help people heal.* Rabbis can make a positive difference in a person's physical health and well-being by what they do in contact with the ill, in hospital and home. As Symbolic Exemplars of the God who heals beyond what the physician is capable of, and of the people Israel whose love, caring, and responsibility extends to its member who is ill, they have great power to heal spiritually and, yes, even physically.

4. *To pray for others.* If praying for others makes a difference, rabbis need to believe that when they pray for others they do something that makes a difference. Symbolic exemplarhood helps make that difference.

5. *To confer significance by symbolic presence and acts.* The rabbi by his/her presence is at least the Jewish People's minister plenipotentiary, and

at most God's ambassador. Rabbis need to believe that in their symbolic role *they* bar/bat mitzvah a child, *they* consecrate a marriage, *they* make an event holy. Congregants stand ready to affirm that what the rabbi is doing has a meaning beyond his/her own necessarily limited self. It is symbolic exemplarhood that makes this meaning possible.

6. *To absolve guilt on behalf of a higher power.* Rabbis need to know that symbolically they speak for God in letting people know that they are forgiven, that the God of us all is humane and understands their humanity.

Symbolic exemplarhood is not a substitute for competence, or for personal integrity. Used competently, and with integrity, it is a primary source of rabbinic power. These symbolic acts, coming from and appealing to an experiential non-rational part of our being, are potentially the most powerful tools a rabbi has.

Yet, symbolic exemplarhood stresses the rabbi intrapersonally as well as interpersonally. Intrapersonally this may show in the conflict rabbis experience about revealing various aspects of their personality. The conflict may result in internal dialogue and self-alienating questions such as: Am I who I am *supposed* to be? If I'm not, *who am I* anyhow? If I'm not who they think I am, *am I a fraud?* If I keep them believing I am who they think I am, *I am a fraud.*

Interpersonally it means the rabbi must always weigh, Is what I'm doing appropriate to my being their rabbi and their perception of that? What are the parameters? How much leeway do I have? How much leeway does my spouse have? The sense of vulnerability is always there. It exists in the web and context of rabbinic–lay interaction. It is created both by what the layperson does to maintain the symbolic exemplarhood of the rabbi, and by what the rabbi does to maintain and protect that same exemplarhood.[2]

What can be done to ease the burden? What can we do to ameliorate the intrapersonal havoc and ease the stress and distress of the interpersonal dance that goes on between rabbi and congregant?

Rabbis, the seminaries that train them, and the rabbinic organizations that sustain them would do well to concern themselves with keeping

---

2. Jack H Bloom. The Pulpit Rabbi as Symbolic Exemplar. New York: Columbia University, Ph.D. dissertation, 1972.

rabbinic symbolic exemplarhood effective, while still protecting rabbis from the seemingly inexorable downside. This is no small task, for during the time these "rabbis to be" are in the care of our seminaries, their experience is the very opposite of what it will be in the congregation. At the seminary they are on the inside of a tight-knit group. It is a daunting challenge to make them understand that they are in for a shock and will soon be outsiders, seen as Symbolic Exemplars and "holy" folk, and their ability to be *themselves* will be constrained. Once in pulpits, rabbis get little enough chance to "be" outside of their symbolic role. They are caught in the symbolic dynamic from the very beginning of their pulpit work. The dynamic increases *each* time they function as a symbol. Each bar mitzvah, wedding, funeral, invocation, etc. adds to the rabbi being something other than simply human. Even rabbinic conventions provide little respite. Rabbis appear there in symbolic role as "Mr. B'nai Israel" or "Ms. Beth El," comparing the magnitude of their services, the size of their budget, the scope of their programming, and where they are in their career.

Though more needs to be done, some beginning has been made by rabbinic groups. The Professional (Mid-Career) Review Program and the Chesky Institute of the Central Conference of American Rabbis, as well as the Rabbinic Training Institutes, pioneered by Rabbi Steve Shaw, and sponsored by the Jewish Theological Seminary of America have made attempts to at least partially deal with this difficult problem.

Congregations composed increasingly of intelligent, sophisticated and hopefully, sensitive people, who recognize the symbolic role power of those who choose and are chosen to lead us, need to do more to stem the loss of effective leadership that results from symbolic exemplarhood.

For both rabbinic and lay groups it will take no less than a revolutionary shift in our thinking to support symbolic exemplarhood and to prevent the depletion of resources it causes. A shift in our thinking so central that though it will be crucial, it will not be easy.

[EITHER/OR]

[Either/Or] thinking has dominated our internal and external maps for a long time. The move from polytheism to monotheism has not been without its costs and dangers. The belief that there is only One True God has sometimes led to the blessed affirmation that all humankind is equal. It has with less benign consequences also led to rejecting that there is more than one way to know the one God, especially if that way is different from what we are told that God has commanded. Monotheism can be taken to imply an essential oneness in us and the world. Our thinking has been dominated by the pursuit of that unity, and the ultimate meaning seemingly implicit in it. It is a dangerous yet understandable inference drawn from monotheism that as there is only one God, there is only one way to the divine and that just happens to be the way *I* or *my tradition* or *my people* have discovered. *You either* acknowledge that "truth" *or you* are in some way benighted, and must be set right. Monotheism, and the quest for *ultimate* meaning, for all its truth and benefits, unfortunately has produced a dangerous by-product: [Either/Or] thinking. [Either/Or] thinking is found throughout our own and other traditions. Things, ideas, etc., are either one way or another. It is in the dichotomies of sacred/profane, good/evil, rational/irrational, secular/religious, kosher/treif, clean/unclean (*Tameh/Tahor*), [this/not this] and seemingly endless other splits. [Either/Or] thinking is at its core a fundamentalist position. There is *one* way. Both intrapersonally and with others, an attribute, idea, person, or whatever that is not that *one* way needs either to be converted to the "true" thinking or gotten rid of. We are obliged to bring both ourselves and others into line both for the wayward's benefit. [Either/Or] thinking allows no other way.

     [Either/Or] thinking has spilled over from religion into many other areas, one of which is psychology/psychotherapy, where the quest for oneness has had a profound effect. It lies at the base of much psychological theorizing, and of struggles between the various schools of therapy. The psychological and spiritual pursuit of what our singular identity is, and just precisely who we are, has been a dominant theme in a whole garden variety of psychotherapies. The presupposition that underlies this thinking is that we are *one*, and need to integrate the disparate aspects of ourselves, and the task of psychology has been to explore, verify, and bring us to *oneness*. In psychology this has led to much [either/or] thinking as when people describe themselves in [me/not me] terms. It wasn't like *him* to do that. That's just not *her*. There is a TRUE YOU. Anything else is NOT YOU. And you are to aim at always being the TRUE YOU!

     In thinking of symbolic exemplarhood, [Either/Or] inexorably leads to the fundamentalist conclusion that you (the rabbi) are either a Symbolic Exemplar of the *Divine* or you are *nobody*. Your task therefore, should you decide and have the ability and commitment to undertake it, is to convert your unacceptable part, or get rid of it. Maybe the reason Orthodoxies become ever more scrupulous, ever more stringent, is their relentless attempt to convert this "unacceptable" part. Perhaps more stringency, more regulations, observing more minutiae will finally succeed in doing it.

In an [Either/Or] situation, distance is an advantage. It would not do to see the Queen of England in her morning toilette. What you don't see you can more easily overlook in the [Either/Or] equation, which only has room for one view. The offending part must be hidden from sight. "What will it look like to the congregants if what they see is a part not in keeping with who I am as a symbol?" That question is a result of [Either/Or] thinking. We cannot afford [Either/Or] thinking which makes an issue of conquering, transforming, or getting rid of the other parts of us. We need to think differently. We have to learn to think in a way that affirms our multifaceted selves and know that they can coexist and enrich our total being. They can even greatly enrich our rabbinic beings and our loving contact with those we serve. The "unacceptable" parts are an advantage and not a disadvantage.

[BOTH/AND]

We have increasingly been realizing that there is overwhelming evidence "that people apprehend reality in at least two fundamentally different ways; one, variously labeled intuitive, automatic, natural, non-verbal, narrative and experiential, and the other analytical, deliberative, verbal, and rational."[3] Recently, the *New York Times*[4] reported on the discovery of another brain, located in the gut, which produces a variety of experiences independent of the brain in the head. We have long known about our conscious and unconscious "minds." All of this implies a new way of thinking about ourselves (and others), a way that involves [Both/And] thinking. We are not solely one or the other aspect of ourselves. We are at all times [Both/And]. *No* part, aspect or characteristic, stands alone. Each may serve as context for the other. Our concern is with the pattern that connects.[5] And our task as [rabbi/person] is how to have the [Both/And] parts (and there may be more) of ourselves be in a loving relationship with each other. A relationship in which

---

3. S. Epstein. "Integration of the Cognitive and the Psychodynamic Unconscious." *American Psychologist*, August 1994.

4. Sandra Blakeslee. "Complex and Hidden Brain in the Gut Makes Cramps, Butterflies and Valium." *The New York Times*, January 23, 1996.

5. Gregory Bateson. *Mind and Nature: A Necessary Unity*. New York: E.P. Dutton, 1979.

both are blessed and neither needs to be "converted" or gotten rid of, in a futile quest for oneness. When that relationship is going on satisfactorily, head and heart, rational and emotional, etc., are experienced as "just there." In Stephen Gilligan's[6] words, the elevator between heart and head moves easily back and forth. That is when we are just going about our regular business with little or no awareness of life being a problem. Whatever happens takes place in the context of relationship, and not because of any individual characteristic in our selves and in the others we deal with. In [Both/And] thinking, these at least two selves are in relationship. [Both/And] thinking allows for the existence of multiple, constantly changing truths. The rabbi is in a [Both/And] relationship, both within him/herself and in the rabbi–congregation relationship. [Both/And] thinking allows for the pulpit rabbi to be *both* Symbolic Exemplar of the divine and just "plain folks." The skill rabbis need to learn is deftness in shifting back and forth between the two, knowing that one need not interfere with or preclude the other. They need to avoid being short-circuited by [Either/Or] thinking which seems so ingrained in us.

Rabbis need to learn how to be in touch with, accept, and *love* their other selves. They need to move back and forth between their symbolic self and their "regular" self with grace and elegance appreciating both without trying to obliterate either one in the service of a non-achievable "true self." Rabbis need to recognize the fullness and richness [Both/And] thinking provides, and to shuttle back and forth without feeling duplicitous or hypocritical. A metaphor for this, which I am sure appeals to rabbis, is that used by Gregory Bateson[7]; "the acrobat on the high wire maintains his stability by continual correction of his imbalance." For rabbis, the moving back and forth may not need to be as rapid as those of the acrobat, but rabbis need to be able to make the needed adjustments in order to maintain rabbinic stability and effectiveness. To do this means acting as God's Symbolic Exemplar when *that* is appropriate, and being other than that when *that* is appropriate. "While I'm acting as that symbol, I *truly* am that. When I'm not, *I'm not.*" Rabbis need to know clearly how not to get the two roles inappropriately combined, how not to do one when the other is needed, how to take each seriously and neither so seriously as to interfere with the other. Seminaries and rabbinic organizations need to help rabbis learn [Both/And] thinking, despite the

---

6. Stephen Gilligan. Personal communication.

7. Bateson, *Mind and Nature.*

pressures of youth,[8] and of congregational life,[9] both of which foster [Either/Or] thinking.

Congregations can do much that will make rabbis' lives easier. They provide a context for symbolic exemplarhood. When they engage a rabbi, congregations need to make sure that they *know* that they are entering a [Both/And] relationship. It is not enough just to say, "the rabbi is human." That is often taken to mean that the rabbi makes mistakes which take away from his/her true self. The implication is that if he or she cleans up their act, that one true self will shine through. If he/she can't "clean up their act," their true self is shining through but they are not cut out to be a rabbi. That is an inheritance of [Either/Or] thinking. Such thinking which attributes to the rabbi some "inner/innate" characteristic undercuts the power and efficacy of the rabbi's symbolic exemplarhood, which takes place in context. It is not sustainable under that mode of thinking. The rabbi is not one or the other, he/she is [Both/And]. In a [Both/And] sense being truly human means having more than one self. The task is for these selves to be in loving relationship with each other. Only when the rabbi is in such an I–Thou relationship with him/herself is an I–Thou relationship with the congregant/congregation possible.

Presuppositions need to be changed about who the rabbi is and what the rabbi–congregational relationship is. The rabbi's self will be more richly experienced by congregants as a [Both/And] relationship, a relationship that's wonderful to behold. Human beings, rabbis and congregants included, are often astonished when they become aware that one can manifest one characteristic and its opposite and *can fully enjoy both.*[10] Didactic and experiential instruction, workshops and lectures, whatever is needed must be used to teach [Both/And] thinking and to detect and deflect [Either/Or] thinking wherever it appears in congregational life. Such thinking can also inform congregants' relations with fellow congregants, with non-Jews, and with congregants'

---

8. Late adolescence and young adulthood are wonderful mediums for [Either/Or] thinking.

9. The congregational context in which the rabbi is experienced is another medium that supplies a superb nutrient for [Either/Or] thinking.

10. I have seen more eyes glaze over and trances begin (the confusion that opens the way to new learning) when workshop participants responding to the question "Who are you?" have presented an aspect of themselves, and then had the diametric opposite said about them, and were then told, "Isn't it nice that you can enjoy both at the same time?" Exercise courtesy of Stephen Gilligan, Ph.D.

inner selves. It can also immeasurably enrich rabbi–congregation relationships by recognizing that they too are in a [Both/And] relationship.

[Both/And] thinking may at least stem the loss of Jewish leadership that the difficulty of being a Symbolic Exemplar has entailed. Rabbis and laypeople must work together so that rabbis are able to know, believe, and say, "*I may not be much, and yet I'm a symbol of the divine and I'm here with you— by the power vested in me.*"

9

The Seasons of a Rabbi*: Dilemmas and Suggestions for Training

Being a rabbi means being set apart in the Jewish community to serve as Symbolic Exemplar. Symbolic exemplarhood is crucial for all clergy and no less so for the rabbi. Jewish tradition exerts much effort not to portray the rabbi as a person set apart. Pulpit rabbis, struggling to deal with their symbolic exemplarhood, spend much time and energy pointing out to their congregations that they are "only human." Yet, the fact remains that rabbis, having set themselves apart, are most certainly set apart by those they serve.

Rabbis are set apart to serve as Symbolic Exemplars of religious and moral rectitude. The resulting symbolic exemplarhood in the moral and religious realm provides the rabbi with a larger-than-life image. Such an image is at the very core of being a rabbi and is unavoidable. The rabbi is both designated by others and has knowingly or unknowingly volunteered to exemplify a religious, caring, nurturing, involved moral person, a paradigmatic model of what a Jewish human being should be. Choosing a profession in which it is crucial to be perceived by others to be something more than one is, while still maintaining ongoing contact with other people, the rabbi takes on being the fulfilled Jew, the spiritual savant, the willing helper, the good parent, the knowing older sibling, the parafamilial member of many fami-

---

*Presented at a joint conference of the Placement Commissions of the Central Conference of American Rabbis and the Rabbinical Assembly, December 16, 1998.

lies. To help rabbis maintain their symbolic exemplarhood, they are given significant protection. They are treated with deference and formal respect, shielded at least overtly from others' anger and vulgarity, and are not subjected to many of the stresses others face. They are treated as other than.

Without such an encompassing wall of protection, a rabbi cannot continue to maintain close, almost intimate contact and still function as an Exemplar of those attributes she is expected to symbolize. Symbolic exemplarhood, endemic to the rabbinate and a major source of rabbinic power and effectiveness, is not without cost. The price of this protection for the rabbi is a sense of otherness and difference, of loneliness in the midst of the crowd. The barriers, erected by both laity and rabbi, made up of masks put on, words edited, and emotions held in check, create an insulated and isolated existence.

Those who become rabbis come to this calling wanting to help, support, and nurture others, but for most being a helpful supportive nurturer is not sufficient. If it had been, they might well have gone into one of the other, and, let it be said, easier helping professions. Being a professional lover/helper is not enough. Beyond wanting to help and nurture, rabbis want to transform others. Changing others' inner beings, their core reality, in a most radical way, is where they perceive the action to be. Such change is often in the direction of an external transcendent reality that is experienced as both benign and demanding. That reality may be God, Jewish tradition, faith, Halachah, commitment, ultimate meaning, or communal destiny. It is almost always a "reality" which both supports and challenges. This combination of nurturing, supportive helper and one who changes others' inner reality leads to the rabbi's manifestation as a person both benign and demanding and is endemic to being a rabbi.

This rabbinic desire to radically transform others from who they are into someone new may be linked to the rabbi's awareness of his own psychic wounds, pain, and limitations. This may lead to feelings that he needs to transcend his own finite humanity to be healed. One can help oneself by becoming more than one experiences oneself to be. A not ignoble solution, though fraught with problems. The rabbi hopes to self-transform by embodying abstract attributes and qualities, by fulfilling the "oughts and shoulds" of life, by becoming an exemplar of the good, moral, and true. At his best, the rabbi identifies and empathizes with the pain and shortcomings of other people. Others' limitations compounded by the rabbi's own, rouses the desire to help oneself and others by converting both self and others. Converting others as a way to support and affirm one's own transformation is a phenomenon we have seen in the religious arena, with reformed smokers, self-help groups,

Alcoholics Anonymous, and on and on. Working with others in that way supports the hope that one day the rabbi might not be a person who only appears to be more than he is, but might truly *be* more than he is at present. If the rabbi can nurture, help, challenge, and change others, the rabbi will be nurtured, appreciated, valued, and transformed.

What might be the self-experience that could make a person seek support and nurturance by meeting the needs of others, striving to appear to be more than one is, and dedicating oneself to persuading others to do the same? Let us suppose a family in which a child's perceived experience is that her own needs for nurturance, care, and affection are not met. Perhaps the child's understanding is that they are not met because the significant others are themselves in need of such nurturance and affection. The child (with cause or without, since cause is a sometime thing) concludes that there is a role as family healer and/or exemplar of family expectations she should fill. The unspoken hope is that by filling that role, servicing others, appearing to meet their needs, being the nurturing, caring person the family seeks, she will be rewarded with nurturance, care, and affection. That this entails carrying a burden that in reality a child can only appear to carry is not computed by the child. To do it, she will have to be in some radical way transformed, or invested with some transcendent power. Until such transformation happens she, only by mutual agreement of herself and her family, can be a symbol of that role, which it is hoped may heal the family's pain. The developing child has to act as if the expectations of others are really her own. The hope is that one day they will be her own. Though feeling herself unable to meet those demands, refusing to do so is impossible. She may at some level feel that there is no way to say no without increasing others' pain, their demands on her to help, and, consequently, her own pain and inadequacy. To appear to be more than one can be, to nurture, is a way, imperfect at best, of getting some nurturance. The child learns to act the role, to try to make it her own, to be sensitive to others' expectations, symbolize the good and thus help maintain and sustain the family, and also get some satisfaction for herself.

For those rabbis who grew up in rabbinic families, this way of dealing with the world might well have been imbibed with mother's milk. The model presented in such a family was that of the helping and often suffering servant. The rabbinic father was often giving so much to others that his family did not get the nurturance it needed. The father *was* supported for helping others. The child in such a family could easily have learned that it was the same for him. One must get what one wants by giving it to others. To be helped one has to help. To support one's own way of being, one must change others. One can imagine other non-rabbi families where the same lesson was in some way taught.

However that may be, a young person chooses to be a rabbi, sensing at some level that her personality and the pulpit are a good fit. That is often true. The world wants people who will serve as an example of a more loving, caring, and "religious" person.

Yet the pulpit experience often turns out differently than anticipated. After an initial honeymoon period, disenchantment often sets in. The rabbinate supports only part of her feelings, that part which demands that the rabbi be a Symbolic Exemplar. The other, more human part, which demands nurturance and care, recognition and appreciation for who one is rather than for who one seems to be, goes unsatisfied and unfulfilled. Even working very hard at being a Symbolic Exemplar does not elicit the response wanted. To understand why the pulpit often turns sour, we must consider how the pulpit rabbi's training and subsequent career interrelate.

Before entering the pulpit, the young person attends rabbinical school pursuing the transformation that they hope will come with being "Rabbi." The very fact that rabbinical school offers *semicha* (literally laying on of hands, symbolically passing inner attributes to another generation), ordination rather than graduation, implicitly promises that incorporating yet another system of expectations, a specific "religious system," will finally result in being transformed. Enough study, enough piety, enough devotion, more sacrifice, and greater commitment, really living by the rules will lead to "the appearance of things" finally being exchanged for an authentic new reality. One will no longer be just plain folk. One will be a rabbi.

That our seminaries collude with the young candidates in their pursuit of this transformation is not surprising. They can hardly do otherwise. Seminaries in their rabbinical training capacities are not simply academic institutions, providing knowledge and tools for their graduates to use as they will. They are there to make rabbis out of regular people. In the words of one seminary's stated purpose, to transform students into "Jewish religious personalities." They present, inevitably, a rabbinic ideal, a Jewish paradigm for their students to emulate. This model, no matter how benignly administered, dovetails with the students' innate sense that they must transform themselves and the seminaries' implicit/explicit promise that they will help them achieve that transformation. In the past the model, from another time and place, was that of the lifetime student and pious scholar using study as the gateway to being a different kind of person. Seminaries' updated models affirm the hope that somehow the young ordainee will have been transformed into a "model" religious Jew. The ordained rabbi will be the embodiment and symbol of the whole Jewish tradition, a qualitatively different person from the beginning student.

Given the Divinely endowed uniqueness of each human being and the vagaries of human experience, many students find that they once again are unsuccessful in achieving transformation. The classic model, noble as it is, though woefully inappropriate for our time, only accentuated feelings of guilt and inadequacy, unworthiness, and personal inauthenticity. The newer programs, though well-intentioned, always run the risk of creating a gauntlet beyond academic achievement that students must successfully negotiate to fulfill the seminary's specific model for what a rabbi ought to be. No matter how benign the model or how much the young rabbi may stretch to fit it, the neophyte rabbi's perception of self is often that he does not measure up to the model. The inside "being" and the one presented to the seminary in order to be ordained and to the world are not lined up, not in sync, not in tune. Striving to incorporate the model, twisting and turning to make it fit, it often is not in keeping with who they are and therefore impossible for most of them to fulfill. So the hope for transformation recedes into the future even as ordination is granted. Perhaps transformation will happen in service to God's people.

In the pulpit, the rabbi is in a well-reinforced role. It is a role as nurturer and healer and change agent, which has always promised a source of nurturance and affection, and provides a sense of safety, familiarity, and protection. The new rabbi finds instant status, respect, and deference. She works hard at meeting laity's expectations and the expectations her seminary education has pointed to. The evanescent hope remains that transformation is just over the horizon if she meets these expectations. But integrating others' expectations and making them experientially truly part of self (no simple task) is beyond the reach of most new rabbis. The expectations remain in a real way external to the rabbinic self-perception. As the rabbi goes on in role, she becomes aware that the goal of transformation recedes even as it is pursued. The young rabbi is not transformed any more by her later incorporation of a religious position than by the earlier incorporation of family expectations or the seminary's hopes for her. The rabbi becomes increasingly aware that one is loved for being what one appears to be and not for what one experiences oneself to be. The more the rabbi is rewarded for how she appears to be, the more inadequate the rabbi feels in her ability to authentically fulfill the expectations.

Rabbis may constrict themselves even more than others expect of them. Having presented himself to the community as a more moral, caring, and religious person by the very fact of being a rabbi, and thereby a Symbolic Exemplar, the rabbi proceeds to persuade, cajole, and sometimes demand of his laity to do the same. Demanding good behavior from others is also a way in which the young rabbi can try to deal with inner feelings that are not experienced as exemplary. He may project these onto congregants, berating the congregants for having them. Urgently urging others to change their behavior may release pent-up feelings about the burden the rabbi feels that others have put on him. Anger often surfaces with those who will not do what the rabbi is trying to do and wants them to do. But the fact is that rabbis have taken this burden upon themselves. Not being clear that this is something they have taken on themselves, and castigating others for not being all that they might be, may vent anger, but it also tightens the screws of symbolic exemplarhood.

The rabbi, knowing no acceptable way of dealing with those feelings, attempts to solve the "problem" with more of the same, striving to be a still better exemplar and demanding of others that they follow her example. If they did, the hope is, that the gap between them would narrow, yet in reality it only expands and extends the exemplarhood further. Since most others do not demand of themselves above human behavior, they most often do not follow the rabbinic example. This leads to greater disenchantment and an increase in the pressure on the rabbi. For the rabbi, demanding of others that they change only means that the rabbi must be that much more of an exemplar. The rabbi, caught in her own words, must be consistent and practice what she preaches. What the rabbi has demanded of others, the rabbi must do. Preaching against materialism limits the rabbi in the next salary negotiations. Having preached repeatedly about caring for all God's creatures, the rabbi must at least appear to care for all, few exceptions allowed. And so it goes. The rabbi gets ever more locked into her exemplarhood. The attempted solution becomes the problem. That leads to an increase in the pressure experienced, and the cycle ratchets up another notch.

The laity join the rabbi in structuring and maintaining the rabbi's exemplar status. Ordinary people know that symbolic exemplarhood, despite being very real, is a fabrication. The rabbi after all is human, possessing all the physical and emotional vagaries to which humankind is subject. Yet the myth is vitally important. Laity want Symbolic Exemplars living among them—rabbis who fulfill the "ought" of their own lives. Such persons are a portent that people *can* be what people *ought* to be. The laity want a helper, a nurturer, an understanding ear, but someone who would change their inner being is not number one on their list of priorities except in a very hypothetical way. So the laity set the rabbi apart, "protecting" the rabbi in role with distancing maneuvers, keeping rabbinic humanity partially out of awareness. This keeping the rabbi in a symbolic role also isolates him. Doing this is not a problem for the laity. The laity are with the rabbi on a very part-time basis. The laity easily avoid the intrusion of the rabbi's symbolic role by not inviting the rabbi to situations where that role would be a complication. The rabbi, on the other hand, is most often with laity. They observe the rabbi's behavior or will hear about it soon enough since gossip about the rabbi is a safe and popular community bond. To them, the rabbi is always the Exemplar and, aware or not, behaving appropriately or not, is always experienced in the prism of exemplarhood. The essence of a symbol is that it stands for something beyond itself. If it stands only for itself, it no longer functions as a symbol. A living, breathing Symbolic Exemplar of the good represents the good and does not stand only for oneself. Being seen as "only" human and therefore sometimes less than a model of love, caring, and general probity is hazardous to the rabbi's symbolic status. It is a danger that the laity strive to prevent, instinctively and effectively protecting the symbolic status by treating the rabbi as other and different, in essence, from other people.

The rabbi thus becomes increasingly set-apart. The young rabbi has placed herself in a situation in which she must move away from her human side in the direction of a symbolic existence. Contact with others, especially congregants, is increasingly in the symbolic role. One's own feelings must be guarded and contact with others is in an increasingly circumscribed area. As experiences pile up, the laity increasingly view the rabbi as a symbol. If the rabbi could *become* the symbol, there would be no gap between one's symbolic role and one's humanity. One's contact with others would be authentic and complete. That does not often happen and so the rabbi grows increasingly set-apart *both* from her own feelings and from others.

The rabbi, like all clergy, will always be a symbol. There is *no way* around the symbolic demands of the rabbinate. Being a set-apart person, a nurturing, caring, ministering figure, can be a creative and useful way to live. Being a symbol of more than one is can also constantly reiterate to those who choose to do that, that they are less than they appear to be and certainly not what others have hired them to be. Some rabbis live with this reasonably comfortably. For some it becomes an enervating burden.

Among rabbis there is a good deal of tension around being a symbol and remaining a person. Symbolic exemplarhood is a full-time occupation for them. Rabbis often become preoccupied with how to be symbols and yet remain human. Pushed in the direction of exemplarhood, rabbis have trouble separating out and dealing with their humanity and its relation to their symbolic role. They are in a situation in which each move towards symbolhood seems to diminish their humanity, and a move expressing the vagaries of one's humanity often seems a threat to the symbolhood. This often results in the rabbis being at some distance from both their symbolic role and their human selfhood.

The struggle to maintain their human selfhood leads many rabbis to being uncomfortable with and sometimes just plain out of touch with their symbolic role and its crucial importance. The symbolic role is often belittled by rabbis, who all too often diminish what they mean to others in this way. The rabbi is at his most symbolic when officiating as "priest" at a life cycle event. It is at such times that laity most profoundly experience the rabbi as what he appears to be rather than what he is. The rabbi is invested with the aura of an entire tradition and bears a message and meaning that comes not from himself, but from that for which he stands, be that God, Israel, Torah, or whatever. The rabbi, whether accepting a teenager into Jewish responsibility, blessing a marriage, or eulogizing a dead loved one, does those things as a symbol. It is as a walking, talking, living symbol that the rabbi gives meaning to these life transition events. Perhaps such symbolic roles pull too much to one end of the continuum. Moving too much in the symbolic direction risks losing totally the "humanity" of the rabbi. To maintain some balance between his personhood and his symbolhood, the rabbi denies the latter.

Too much movement in the direction of her own humanity is also dangerous for the rabbi. Partially because it is this very humanity and its limitations that the rabbi has been dedicated to transcending. But also because being a rabbi means the distinction between one's public role and one's private life is whittled down to virtual non-existence. "Human deviations," even in private, run the risk of discovery and consequent danger to the symbolic role. Because what the rabbi "is" is more crucial than what the rabbi "does on-the-job," the rabbi's humanity and symbolhood reflect on each other and each is the benchmark of the other. It is how the rabbi acts when seemingly out of public view and how that fits with the rabbi's public image that is an ultimate test of the rabbi's exemplarhood. Even the rabbinic family's behavior has to be considered in terms of its effect on the public image. Thus, conflicts between the spouses, where the spouse attends synagogue and how often, whether the children go to basketball games on Shabbat, or their behavior in or outside of the synagogue, all evoke a level of concern not present in other families. That level of concern has to do with how the behavior affects the symbolic image. Rabbis often find that friends are hard to come by. Those he has will most often be "clergy collectors," who gravitate to anything ordained. But an intimate relationship in which one can say and do what one wants, where one can drop the mask of symbolhood, where one can share one's own intimacies and vulnerabilities, grows increasingly difficult. Not having what Erving Goffman[1] refers to as a backstage area in which he can relax and be himself, the rabbi is always "on" with congregants or local laypeople to whom he has presented himself in role. Some who were childhood friends, camp mates, or fellow students who predated the decision to become a rabbi will allow a certain amount of openness with him, but such "treasures" are not frequently found in the rabbi's congregational life. It is no accident that rabbis maintain long friendships with their rabbinical school friends. Years after ordination, though separated by time and space, they are still the rabbis' closest friends, with whom they can be most open. Once having appeared in a symbolic role, the editing, distancing, and setting apart process has begun. A beloved friend of the author, a rabbi who had also been beloved in the pulpit and who had worked hard to cultivate friends, pointed out that it was at best a trade-off. For those who were his friends, he functioned less as rabbi, and those for whom he was rabbi, there was a tacit distance in the relationship. Many successful rabbis note with sadness after fifteen or twenty years in a pulpit that if they were to leave that pulpit tomorrow, they would leave town without a single close intimate friend.

Given these stresses, it is not surprising that rabbis, even as they act symbolically, will deny their symbolic exemplarhood. They accept their humanity, deny it by trying to transcend it, and then find it essential to reassert their own humanity. "Don't forget, I'm human" is a plaintive attempt to reclaim a status that seems in danger of extinction. The pressures of the rabbinate gravitate towards the symbolic role and away from being just a person.

This combination of acceptance and denial is an attempt to deal with a situation which can be quite painful in that it alienates one from both self and others, and in which one perceives few options. Total acceptance or denial of either one's human limitations or one's symbolic life is perceived of as a

---

1. Erving Goffman. *The Presentation of Self in Everyday Life.* Garden City, NY: Doubleday Anchor Books, 1959.

danger to either one's life as a rabbi or one's life as a person. So the rabbi remains in the center pulled from both directions. But it is at the *ends* of the continuum that one must go to experience both the richness of one's symbolhood and the fullness of one's humanity.

The young person who wants to use Jewish tradition to transform both oneself and others, who wants to be an interpersonal helper, who chooses to do that with Jews, who cares enough to dance at many weddings and grieve at many funerals, who wants to be a helping and changing part of many families is a good candidate for the pulpit. The fact that the novice rabbi has drives and motivations of which she may not be fully aware, which have brought her to seek the pulpit, is not a negative factor. Such motivations can support being a good pulpit rabbi, allow her to contribute much and gain much. Such a candidate may well be attracted to the pulpit by its implicit promise to help her appear to be more than she is. The pulpit *can* deliver on that promise. It *cannot* help its occupant transcend herself. Appearing to be more than one is, is for the young candidate only an intermediary step towards becoming more than one is. That transformation, difficult at best to actualize, leads as time goes on to the distance between symbol, *what one appears to be*, and person, *what one is*, growing greater and greater. The symbolic life can become difficult to bear.

It is *not* inevitable that a field so long prepared for, one that can provide great satisfaction, one whose personnel come to it highly motivated, must of necessity turn sour. More must be done to train rabbis to deal with their symbolhood, to live more comfortably and creatively with it.

They must be helped to know that their humanity and their symbolhood do not have to contradict and destroy each other. These two aspects ("*selves*"; see Chapter 7) of their *Self* need to be in loving relationship. One "*self*" can serve to create the symbol laity want and that the rabbi, by background and training, can be. The other "*self*" can be comfortable in its "human" dimension, knowing its own basic non-negotiable worthwhileness despite being less than perfect. Knowing and accepting these two "*selves*," the rabbi can focus more clearly on what he wants and distinguish that from what others project onto him. The rabbi thus needs to simultaneously know and value the importance and usefulness of the symbol the rabbi is and his own humanity. The rabbi's *Self* emanates from the ongoing relationship and dialogue between these inner parts. Helping the rabbi accept these two "*selves*" would paradoxically allow the rabbi to be both more symbolic and more human. It will make the rabbi better at his work and more satisfied with life, professional and personal.

The transition from rabbinical school to one's first position in the community as a Symbolic Exemplar, though filled with excitement and hope, is a drastic change. Students in seminary are in a radically different existential situation than when they enter a pulpit. In rabbinical school the student is a part of a close-knit community, striving to define itself with common purposes and with a goal one day to make the world safe for Judaism. It is a community in which being Jewish, no matter how understood, is a top priority, touching everyone. It is a community demarcated by its relationship over and against or with the faculty.

When students move to a pulpit, they go from being insiders to being outsiders to the community, no matter how successful they are or how long their stay. They are hired and expected to be Symbolic Exemplars and are in a very different situation from the seminary life they have just left. They are no longer in a peer group. The community they serve has powerful, if often unenunciated, symbolic expectations of them.

How to teach the reality of symbolic exemplarhood and its effects to students still in seminary is one of the great conundrums of our time. They can in no way fathom what will happen. When presented with the experience, they engage in the same denial I engaged in when I first showed up in Bridgeport, Connecticut, eons ago. *It will not happen to me. I won't live behind a glass wall!* I did not then, and they cannot now, understand that it is not their choice. Their choice is how they respond to this tremendous change and how they deal with it.

Having been invited regularly to speak to the graduating class of one of our seminaries, I found talking to students about future symbolic exemplarhood was like whistling in a hurricane. Three to five years later the same students, now rabbis, greet me saying, "Now I know what you were talking about back then. I wish they would just treat me normally."

Even attempts to provide students with rabbinic experience do not do the job. Internships and bi-weeklies, forays into the congregational world, as crucial as they are to teaching the student rabbinic skills, have the student return to home base, there to recount successes and failures in these skirmishes. Later on when pulpit and community are one and the same, the experience is radically different. The gap cannot be closed.

What to do? Reality may have opened doors for us. Our seminaries are already educating more than pulpit rabbis. The rabbi as chaplain, pastoral counselor, interpersonal helper, individual change agent, community organizer, adult educator, youth educator, moral exemplar, scholar, and on and on. Implicit in this new reality is not only that there are a lot of different jobs for rabbis, but there are a *wide variety of ways in which a rabbi can be a Symbolic Exemplar.*

In training pulpit rabbis specifically, our seminaries must create and encourage a more open and varied pulpit rabbi model to present to the student looking for transformation. That there are a *wide variety of ways in which a rabbi can be a Symbolic Exemplar* should be among the prime lessons of rabbinical school religious formation. Our seminaries will have to establish a multi-model system of exemplars. The seminary's task becomes producing many different kinds of rabbis. Not one model of religious personality, but a wide variety of models. Inscribed on the gateposts of our seminaries should be *Eliu v'eilu divrei Elohim Chayim*—God's words are spoken and heard in multiple ways. Thus recognizing that the meaning of the Mishnah in Sanhedrin 4:5 is that God's will for us is pluralism. Student rabbis may, nonetheless, tend to incorporate what they perceive as the seminary's model of what a rabbi should be. This might seem to make the seminary's work easier. Our rabbinical schools must help them resist that tendency. The seminary must be especially wary of the student who incorporates the institution's "party-line," or who may reverentially model oneself after a charismatic faculty figure. The student must be challenged and encouraged to evolve his or her own personal "party-line." This presumes a multi-model, open system in which the student can explore and challenge, be challenged and respond, struggle and change. If the student is not able to struggle and change while in school and does not know that their stance at ordination is temporary at best, the rabbi produced will be more "brittle." The young ordainee may have incorporated an image of a rabbi, but when the struggle to change inexorably bursts forth she will be constrained by the model taken in and will feel that to change that model is to risk the limits of one's rabbihood. After those hopefully exciting and collegial student years, the rabbi will be exposed to the congregation's projected expectations, added to those of her seminary. The rabbi will find it hard to carve out an area for her selfhood, unless she has had training in doing that from the first day of rabbinical school. If one can test the limits while in seminary, bend them without fear of loss of status, be explicitly heretical, in the best sense of that word, one will less fear such loss of rabbinical status while pursuing later growth.

The multifaceted single image of the rabbi, which currently exists, can be split. The young rabbi can be encouraged to explore and take on himself one kind of symbolic role among the many different ones available. More important still is that these tasks can be done by a wide variety of "rabbinic" or Jewish "religious personalities." The student can in this way explore and tentatively select which expectations of seminary and/or laity he will choose to meet. Such choosing may seem to imply rejecting others. That is only so if we take an [Either/Or] position. Students may choose a way, while not denying the validity of other ways, while affirming which are appropriate for themselves and which are not currently appropriate. This choosing happens anyway, but making it part of the educational framework can bless it, accomplish it better, and save much pain and waste. This is a first step in helping students differentiate themselves from colleagues and from others generally. Learning that there are a wide variety of ways one can "be" will not prevent laity from projecting their expectations onto the rabbi in later years. It will help the rabbi respond more authentically to those expectations.

A new skill will have to be added to the curriculum of the rabbinical schools. Every pulpit rabbi must be thoroughly trained in what it means to be a symbol; how to do that exquisitely well; how to be flexible in doing that; and how to shuttle back and forth between being a symbol and being plain folk. This will take teaching a [Both/And], rather than an [Either/Or] position, about which I have written elsewhere (see Chapter 8). The student will have to know that being a rabbi means being a Symbolic Exemplar (it's inevitable) and must learn how to do that and still know where one's symbolic role and one's self begins and ends. Because the psychological ramifications of being a symbol are so many and because being a symbol is such a crucial function of the pulpit rabbi, this task cannot be avoided.

A great deal remains to be done. Those who have chosen to serve as rabbis, to become Symbolic Exemplars, carry our hopes for a vibrant Jewish future. We can do no less than help them carry that burden lightly, with grace and elegance, that they may do their holy work.

Using the Power of
Symbolic Exemplarhood

10
Witnessing, Naming, and Blessing

A<small>s</small> Symbolic Exemplars of both the Divine and those human icons of God, infused with the Divine breath,[1] rabbis have among their major tasks alertness to, witnessing of, providing ongoing testimony for, advocating on behalf of, and naming and blessing[2] the often obscured and sometimes rejected [*Tzelem*⟺*Neshamah*][3] in themselves, in others, and in the world at large. That which is unwitnessed, unnamed, and unblessed can never be fully human. And that which is not fully human detracts from God's presence in the world, thus, as it were, diminishing God. Locating, witnessing, naming, and blessing the often elusive, hidden, "turned away from" [*Tzelem*⟺*Neshamah*] is crucial to rabbinic work.

---

1. Genesis 2:7.

2. Stephen Gilligan includes all of these under the rubric of "Sponsorship." viz. *The Courage to Love*. New York: Guilford Press, 1997. "These various skills of transforming the relationship are called 'sponsorship' in self-relations. Sponsorship is a relational connection that engages and awakens the life presence and goodness both self and the other . . . this is where sponsorship is so crucial: as a relational space where an 'otherness' may be held, blessed, contained, listened to, etc. such that its human value begins to emerge."

3. The brackets [ ] indicate the interrelated unity of these two elements. The double arrow ⟺ signifies reciprocal relationship. See Chapter 6.

Witnessing requires that the rabbi at all times and in every encounter bring full awareness to the [*Tzelem*⟺*Neshamah*] always present and, especially in stress, almost always obscured. The rabbi, hopefully centered, aware of his own [*Tzelem*⟺*Neshamah*] evidenced by a felt sense in his body, infinitely more than the simple affirmation of an intellectual truth, becomes a sort of satellite dish, an antenna to pick up the distant, often scrambled transmissions and emanations coming from one's own and others' [*Tzelem*⟺*Neshamah*]. This tuning device picks up that behind others' anger, there may be loving concern. Underneath the rigid unyielding exterior, there may be a big heart, and hidden from view in the suffering may be courage. All these and a multitude of other hidden parts are evidence of the ongoing, never ceasing presence of each human's idiosyncratic and thus unique [*Tzelem*⟺*Neshamah*].

To paraphrase Gilligan:[4] The main ingredient in witnessing the [*Tzelem*⟺*Neshamah*] is intentionality. A rabbi has made a decision to support and become interested in the [*Tzelem*⟺*Neshamah*] of her self, the other, and the greater community. She has taken a "solemn pledge" to witness, behold/ take interest in/ be delighted by/ become attentive to/ become curious about/ support/ acknowledge/ protect/ honor/ etc., the [*Tzelem*⟺*Neshamah*] always present and hopefully awakening in each person or community. But intentionality is not sufficient. Practices/traditions/disciplines must be invoked implicitly or explicitly. The great thing about witnessing and sponsoring is that it requires that the rabbi surrender to a larger field than herself. The rabbi is part of a long and beautiful tradition of pursuing and realizing the [*Tzelem*⟺*Neshamah*].

Another primary tool available to the rabbi in the endeavor of naming, beyond his own "being" and his symbolic exemplarhood, is language. Language is *the* one tool that pervades the entire rabbinic enterprise. How

---

4. Gilligan's own words from a personal communication, February 1998: "The main ingredient in good sponsorship is intentionality. A person consciously makes a decision to support and become interested in the awakening process of a person or community. He or she makes a commitment or 'solemn pledge' (as indicated in the dictionary meaning) to behold/take interest in/be delighted by/become attentive to/become curious about/support/acknowledge/protect/ honor/etc., the natural awakening process that is already occurring in that person or community . . . but intentionality is not sufficient . . . practices/ traditions/ disciplines must be invoked implicitly or explicitly . . . the great thing about sponsorship is that it requires that the sponsor surrender to a larger field than him/herself . . . that is, you are part of a beautiful tradition of awakening the human spirit."

language is used influences virtually everything that goes on in the rabbinic day, and everyone the rabbi has contact with. Much has been learned about how language creates, molds, sustains, and changes "reality."

Using language to "name" is one way of touching and creating new "realities." A name may be thought of as an alias, as on my Macintosh computer, that enables me to access a programmatic reality hidden somewhere in my computer, and bring it to view so it can be of use. Rabbinic symbolic exemplarhood gives the rabbi a special, unique ability to use language to name, to create new aliases, and, by naming, to bring forth hidden attributes, and to change experience by bringing new realities into being.

Technically, a name is a word or words by which an entity is designated and distinguished from others.[5] Language used this way is of course descriptive. But as J. L. Austin points out,[6] language can be used to make things happen, to create what has not been there before, such as new statuses, obligations, and expectations. Austin calls these Performative Utterances. A Performative Utterance is where "the issuing of the utterance is the performing of an action."[7]

Using language this way is very different from saying, "The weather is changing," or "John is tall." Those words do not make anything new happen. They do not create new realities. Naming when done as a Performative Utterance makes something happen. It creates new realities. A new reality replaces what has either not seemed to have been present before (a sort of *creatio ex nihilo*) or brings to the fore, in a new way, what was hidden, obscure, disorganized, or rejected (as if from the primeval chaos).

Austin offers an example of a Performative Utterance: "I name this ship *Queen Elizabeth*,"[8] said under the right conditions with the proper vintage champagne in a shipyard with a designated person doing it, etc. By this Performative Utterance—what we shall call an act of naming—the ship goes from being a hulk of steel, wire, plastic, and whatever, to being the *Queen Elizabeth*. The ship now begins to have a history and might be said even to develop a "personality" of "her" own with which many have a "relationship."

---

5. *American Heritage Dictionary*, Standard Edition.

6. J. L. Austin. *How to Do Things with Words*, Second Edition. J. O. Urmson and Mariana Sbisa, eds. Cambridge, MA: Harvard University Press, 1975. An indispensable little book; required reading for any who function as Symbolic Exemplars.

7. Ibid., p. 6.

8. Ibid., p. 5.

The foregoing statement is very different from saying, upon seeing the ship dock, "That's the *Queen Elizabeth*." Saying that makes nothing happen. It is a descriptive not a Performative Utterance.

Scripture early on makes naming crucial. Genesis understands that witnessing, naming, and blessing are essential.

> God said, "Let there be light!" And there was light. God saw the light that it was good. God separated the light from the darkness. God called the light: Day! and the darkness He called Night![9]

God not only creates the world but, by witnessing what has been created and naming it, moves the primeval chaos into a new reality. The light was light, but day is a new reality one can relate to. This makes possible for his future creation, humankind, to be in relationship with it. And that makes it *good*.

Man himself is given the task of naming the animals, giving order and meaning and relationship. The implication follows that though the creatures exist, relationship with them can only take place when they are properly named.

Bradley Shavit Artson points out that

> Adam is unique in creation by virtue of the ability to know an animal's true nature. In finding each animal's appropriate name, Adam demonstrates deep empathy and wisdom—perhaps this is the evidence that he is made in God's image.[10]

That words change realities and relationships is indicated in the Mishnah of *Nedarim* (Vows).

Alyssa Gray points out that "should a man have taken a vow that his wife should derive no benefit . . . from him . . . he has effectively divorced her . . . divorce could be effected by vow."[11]

---

9. Genesis 1:3–5. Translations of biblical text by Everett Fox. *The Five Books of Moses*. New York: Schocken Books, 1995.

10. Bradley Shavit Artson. "What's in a Name? Power or Empathy." *CCAR Journal: A Reform Jewish Quarterly*, Fall 1997.

11. Alyssa M. Gray. "Making Central the Peripheral." *Conservative Judaism*, Vol. LI, No. 1, Fall 1998.

At the funeral of the man each of them had been married to, I witnessed the first wife "naming" the widowed second wife, by publicly saying to her at the funeral, "You are a most gracious woman." That act of naming created a new reality and identity that can change and sustain a new and different relationship.

It was common knowledge that around age forty many people felt a sense of discontent. Life was not living up to the possibilities so fervently hoped for. The very work they had dreamed of and been educated for now increasingly grew empty of meaning. The marriage partners they had only a few years back pledged eternal love to now seemed unexciting and even boring. The name "seven-year itch" had already found its way into common parlance, describing the dangers facing such marriages. Behavior would often become erratic and inappropriate. "Burnout,"[12] itself only recently "named," was declared to be a cause of the soon to be named syndrome. All this existed prior to "Mid-Life Crisis" being named. Naming created a new entity. "Mid-Life Crisis" now became a new entity, a pseudo illness, par for the course, and an almost inescapable part of the life cycle. It was now less pathological. Everyone was subject to it. It was thought of in a new way. It could be treated. Programs were formulated to deal with it.[13] At the very least, having been named, the name offered an explanation for the person going through "it" and gave those around a way of accounting for the person's weird behavior. Naming can create something new. And proper naming makes a new relationship possible.

Rabbis, as Symbolic Exemplars, have great power to label, to characterize, and in a word to name. "You are a *loving* man. "I sense the presence of a *courageous* woman." "Your sacrifice demonstrates what a *proud* Jew you are." "You truly are a *big-hearted* person," etc. If the naming is successful, and becomes part of the person's self-identity, something truly important has been brought to be. Not all labeling or relabeling becomes naming. Sometimes repetition is needed, or naming needs to take place in another way, and in another context.

---

12. "Burnout" was given a "name" by the late Herbert Freudenberger in his 1974 book, *Burnout: The High Cost of High Achievement*. He defined burnout as "the extinction of motivation or incentive, especially where one's devotion to a cause or relationship fails to produce the desired results" (*New York Times* Obituary, December 5, 1999).

13. The Professional Career Review Program of the Central Conference of American Rabbis, conducted by me since 1976, came out of a discussion about Rabbis and Mid-Life Crisis, and a subsequent grant to the CCAR by the Merrill Foundation, to deal with this now "named" and thus well-established condition.

Beyond characterological naming, rabbis have the power, by careful and judicious witnessing and naming, to do special work with the suffering, ill, and dying. This involves accessing, witnessing, and naming parts of one's personhood that illness has paradoxically either hidden or revealed. The rabbi needs to be witness to the other side of what is being presented by the sick. Outward courage may mask inner fear, and the fearful may have reserves of courage not immediately on view. Accessing those hidden attributes and resources, witnessing the ever-present [*Tzelem⇔Neshamah*] and naming it appropriately is a most important part of rabbinic work.

Life cycle changes are a fertile field for naming. Rabbis are vested with the power to name a baby; to change something fundamental in a convert; to "Bar Mitzvah" a thirteen-year-old; to "marry" two single adults. The new "names" experientially create new realities, legal entities, statuses, and identities. Those so "named" are vested with new and different obligations, expectations, responsibilities, and hopefully new ways of perceiving themselves. It is one of those things that a rabbi makes happen with words. Naming a child is paradigmatic of this power. The child, as was the original creation in Genesis, is an inchoate blob of protoplasm barely distinguished from the parents from whom it comes. With the words "Let her name in Israel be So-and-So, the daughter of So-and-So and So-and-So"[14] the child becomes a separate person with an identity differentiated from the parents. A new status has been created with words. Rabbis create a new reality and confer a new status when they say after the proper formalities have been observed, "Therefore, by the power vested in me, I now pronounce you husband and wife." With these new "names," something new has been created. It makes a profound difference! To know that profound difference, one need only attend to what happens to couples who live together unmarried, and the eruptions and disruptions that happen when they get around to marrying. Experientially rabbi's pronouncements change a man into a husband and a woman into a wife.

Naming creates new realities by witnessing what is implicit in the universe; constellations ever present though long hidden; patterns in others' behavior that we as [*Tzelem⇔Neshamah*] seekers are looking for and by proper naming, bringing them into human "being," perception, experience, and discourse. Naming can give a new meaning to those already existing realities that are present, but unacceptable, kept from human "being." Naming that which had no name makes relationship possible. And it is only in

---

14. The Jewish liturgy's formula for naming a new baby.

relationship that "things" attain human "being." We witness and name and by naming open up the possibility of relationship with and among all the parts in a human being. And thereby bringing forth and creating what seem like new entities.

Neil Gillman writes:

> To the question, "Did Freud (or whoever first talked about egos) discover the ego or invent it?" the answer is clearly both. Freud discovered the pattern, at least partially because he was looking for it and knew what to look for. But then he identified it, gave it a name, and fitted it into his broader psychodynamic theory (or myth). But Freud discovered the ego because it was out there to be discovered. The ego itself, in distinction to its name, is not a fiction, not a pure invention out of the blue.
>
> . . . Of course, a psychologist whose interpretive structure (i.e., his psychodynamic theory) does not include the myth of the ego will not see an ego. Again, we use metaphors to characterize the ego that we see: strong, weak, shaky, flimsy, solid, etc. . . .
>
> To elaborate: to see an ego is to see a pattern that is, in a sense, invisible. What we do objectively see is the way the child plays with blocks and interacts with teachers. But the psychologist "sees through" the overt behavior and then "sees" a solid or flimsy ego. Where is the ego? "In" the child, or "in" the behavior, or, more precisely "in" the activity that the child performs.
>
> . . . Does the physicist invent the quark or discover it? Again the answer is both: he discovers the pattern, but because his theory provides him with a name and a way to identify it when it is there, he can then see the quark. But the quark-pattern is out there to be discovered; it is not a fictitious creation of the physicist.[15]

Here I take the liberty of paraphrasing Gillman:

> Witnessing the presence of the [*Tzelem*⇔*Neshamah*] is like witnessing any of these, probably most like witnessing an ego, in the sense that the [*Tzelem*⇔*Neshamah*] is a pattern of activity that is always present in humankind, as an ego is "in" the person. . . . Again, the experience is a relationship experience: The witness brings his interpretive structure (the Torah's religious myth) to his witnessing, and sees the pattern that we call the

15. Neil Gillman. "On Knowing God." *Conservative Judaism*, Vol. LI, No. 2, Winter 1999.

[*Tzelem*⟺*Neshamah*]. Do we discover the [*Tzelem*⟺*Neshamah*] or do we invent it? Both. We discover and are witness to the [*Tzelem*⟺*Neshamah*] patterns no matter how hidden. And then our task is to name, bless, and generally sponsor them so as to bring them to "human being."

What is the [*Tzelem*⟺*Neshamah*]? Why bother to witness it in the most unlikely places? . . . No one can claim that we invent egos and quarks, unless, again, we don't believe that the [*Tzelem*⟺*Neshamah*] is religious fact, there in the first place, or that it is worth bothering about. What we must do is to identify certain patterns and then give them a name, which gives them a human/divine presence. Or we have the name, and then identify the patterns as, in fact, present in our experience . . . the [*Tzelem*⟺*Neshamah*] is not invented. It is both out there and in us waiting to be witnessed.[16]

The rabbi as witness to the pattern, names it, and invites it into human "being." Rabbis need to believe that whatever the state's legal procedures (for example, birth certificates or marriage licenses) or the requirements of Jewish law, the experiential "fact" is that rabbis name infants, Bar Mitzvah teenagers, confirm confirmands, marry couples, convert Jews by choice, consecrate houses, and assist the departed on their journey.

Rabbis uncomfortable with this power retreat into halachic minutiae, saying that all children become Bar Mitzvah by attaining age thirteen (JHB—true, but irrelevant to the experience); that the marriage takes place when the groom gives the bride the ring or they sign the *Ketubah*[17] (JHB—again true,

---

16. Ibid. Gillman's original words: "Seeing God is like seeing any of these, probably most like seeing an ego, in the sense that God is a pattern of activity that is 'in' history and nature, as an ego is 'in' the person. Here, the frame of reference is immense, the broadest possible canvas: all of nature, history, and human experience. Again the experience is interactional: the believer brings his interpretive structure (the Torah's religious myth) to his seeing, and sees the pattern that we call God. Do we discover God or do we invent God? Both. We discover the patterns and then identify them, name them, and the names are our inventions, just as we invent the names ego and quark. But if the patterns are discoverable, they are out there to be discovered.

What are these God-patterns? . . . No one can claim that we invent egos and quarks, unless, again, we don't believe that such realities are there in the first place, or that they are worth noting. What we do is identify certain patterns and then give them a name. Or we have the name, and then identify the patterns as, in fact, present in our experience . . . the various patterns that we uncover . . . are not invented. They are out there to be discovered."

17. The marriage contract read at Jewish weddings, outlining the bride's and the groom's responsibilities to each other.

but irrelevant to the experience) or, politically correct, say, "Shouldn't we be encouraging a less hierarchical understanding?" Anyone can lead, pray, officiate, or whatever. Or other legalisms . . . it happens when certain state forms are filled out. It is true that clergy, vested with power by the state, help rabbinic words create and confirm a new entity. Far beyond what the state vests in us, rabbis are the Symbolic Exemplars of God with a much greater power than the power of the state and indeed of Jewish Law, the Halachah.

If we would pay closer attention, beyond what we have been taught in our seminaries, to our own mind/body experience, to occasions when we were "named" in some way, "Bar Mitzvahed," "married," described as possessing some special attribute, we would easily acknowledge this "fact." Knowing that in reality nothing changes and yet everything changes, we could stop fighting against and bemoaning our power. We would feel OK using it in the service of those we love.

Rabbis are encouraged to have a sense of awe toward the naming experience. They should not underestimate their power to create new entities with words. It is a power rabbis can use beneficially in many ways by properly "naming" and blessing people and events. Rabbis need to recognize, accept, and believe in that power to use it with discretion and respect for its potency. Internally, the rabbi, witness to a hidden attribute, about to name would do well to envision a door opening before him with an opportunity to make a difference in the other's experience. "I am about to create something new. I am about to bring forth something that did not exist in the world of human 'being' before. This is serious business. I need intention, ability, and confidence. This child will go through life with the name I intone. These two will now be husband and wife, a couple, different from what they were just minutes before. This convert will be a part of a new people. This person can see her *self* differently. New expectations and behavior will be built around the new reality I am about to create with my act of naming. The person(s) I am naming will become a more human 'being'. The [*Tzelem⇔Neshamah*] will be more present."

Rabbis, who take this role seriously, will not just "rattle off" eulogies, invocations, benedictions, but will even take chance personal encounters as an opportunity to witness and "name" evidence of the hidden [*Tzelem⇔Neshamah*]. All of the above will be seen as opportunities to "name" and create new realities. Rabbis, knowing that they are invested with and trained in the use of this power, will do it with a seriousness and intentionality appropriate to a sense that they are doing something very powerful and important.

BEING A BLESSING AND BLESSING OTHERS

As ordained Symbolic Exemplars of God, standing for the best attributes of humankind, rabbis carry a precious yet burdensome blessing. Our calling is to bless God for this blessing and help others to do likewise. Beyond that we shoulder the more complex responsibility of blessing others. We have as our task exemplifying the blessing in ourselves and evoking and blessing in others the gift of being created [*Tzelem*⇔*Neshamah*].

At the primary level we affirm God's blessing and other gifts to us by thanking and blessing God for them. Elliot N. Dorff explicates this traditional meaning of "blessing":

> "Bless" is not a word we use much in everyday speech. When we do say "bless you" to other people, we usually mean something like "thank you" with a tinge of "praise you." That is actually not far from the meaning of the Hebrew root *barekh*, possibly coming from the word *berekh*, "knee," for then "bless" would mean to bend the knee in recognition of a boon and in thanks to the benefactor . . . taking note of an important aspect of life and expressing appreciation to God for making that phenomenon part of our lives.[18]

Dvorah Simon, a psychologist, offers:

> The traditional Hebrew blessings also come in the form of blessing God—essentially thanking God for giving us bread, light, etc. by blessing God—*Baruch Atah Adonay* = Blessed are you, our Lord, who has (fill in the blank, e.g., created fruit, commanded us to do this ritual act, etc.). We are sanctifying the objects and acts in question, making holy our relationship with a piece of fruit . . . a kind of mindfulness, bringing the simple act into a relational context with the universe of creation. I don't know how this relates to therapy but I think it's in the thread of "*it ain't me doing it.*"[19]

Joshua Gutoff points to the relational context:

---

18. Elliot Dorff. "Knowing God Through Prayer." *Conservative Judaism,* Vol. LI, No. 2, Winter 1999.

19. Personal correspondence with the author, writing about blessing in a therapy context.

And so: God created everything, and we are to love God with everything we are and have; . . . For those who see that the heavens are really God's heavens, the gift of the earth must be responded to. *Shalom aleichem*,[20] says God through the scent of the herb, the taste of the fruit. *Aleichem shalom*, we say through the *bracha* (*blessing*) . . . the functional meaning of "Baruch Ata" is "You are Present"; the blessing—when said mindfully—helps establish a relationship with God in the phenomenon at hand . . . the second person form of the opening of the *bracha* is . . . crucial to the real work of the *bracha*.[21]

As important as the above is, giving thanks for God's gifts by saying the one hundred blessings we are obliged to say every day, or pronouncing *Yevarechecha*[22] (the priestly blessing), wherein we transmit an ancient blessing formulated by others that all need and can use, are the *easy* parts of blessing.

Blessing others on God's behalf is the more audacious act, occurring at a level far beyond the above. Such blessing of others is crucial to being a rabbi. Blessing others with one's personal presence and words is one of the ultimate acts of love a rabbi can do. It is a primary way of attending to the [*Tzelem*⟺*Neshamah*] that is in others and in us.

Gilligan, coming from a psychotherapy context, emphasizes the importance of blessing and being blessed:

The point is, you really do exist as a human being. Your beingness is blessed. To forget or to ignore this leads to great suffering. . . . The experience of beingness is first known via blessings from influential others.[23] Most people can remember someone in their lives—a family member,

---

20. Literally, "Peace unto you." Colloquially, "How do you do" or "Howdy."

21. Joshua Gutoff. "Blessings and Ethics: The Spiritual Life of Justice." *Conservative Judaism*, Vol. XLIX, No. 4, Summer 1997.

22. Numbers 6:22–26. "YHWH spoke to Moshe saying: Speak to Aharon and to his sons, saying: Thus are you to bless the Children of Israel; say to them: 'May YHWH bless you and keep you! May YHWH shine His face upon you and favor you! May YHWH lift up His face toward you and grant you *shalom!*'" Present in virtually every service, it is the most widely used blessing by any who bless.

23. See Chapter 1, p. 81, for the totally inadvertent blessing of Cindy Dimenstein whose birthday occurred the day after her rabbi's birthday.

teacher, friend—who really saw them as special and unique. This is not a cognitive event; It is about [witnessing—JHB] seeing and calling forth the spirit of life that infuses each person. Blessings are crucial acts in the emergence of each person into the world; without them, love and other skillful human acts are not possible.[24]

Michael Paley affirms the importance and the effects of having been blessed in a crucial way by Zalman Schachter:

> May the One who blessed our ancestors also bless this one as he struggles with his adolescence. May he have the energy to finish his college applications and may those admission officers have the clarity to understand his special gifts.

Paley writes:

> I had never been blessed like this before. I thought at the time that blessings were reserved for God, to receive and to give. But at that moment, being so involved with the issues that Zalman mentioned, it made sense to me that if God could bless our ancestors, then why not me in a moment of need?
>
> Many years have passed since Zalman blessed me, but his charge still rings in my ears. His blessing helped me to feel part of something greater than myself and to realize that there were worlds beyond the ones that I could see. His blessing gave me a certain sense of much-needed harmony with myself, my community, and maybe with the universe at an unexpected moment.[25]

What enables us to bless another? In Jewish tradition God is described as the "King of all Kings, the Holy and Blessed One."[26] Earthly royalty[27] is

---

24. S. Gilligan. "The Relational Self: The Expanding of Love Beyond Desire." In M. Hoyt, ed. *Constructive Therapies*, Volume 2. New York: Guilford Press, 1996, pp. 216–217.

25. Michael Paley. *Shma, A Journal of Jewish Responsibility*, Vol. 26, No. 507, February 2, 1996.

26. viz. The Aleynu, which concludes virtually every service.

27. We shall use royalty where not directly quoting. Beyond being politically correct, it is arguably more accurate. Historically the royal archetype was almost always, but not inevitably, male. viz. Elizabeth I, among many others.

esteemed by the biblical author to the extent that their behavior is consonant with the Supreme Ruler of All. These archetypal demands dovetail with
rabbinic Symbolic Exemplars, who are archetypes of the God who created
us. That this is important is affirmed by John W. Perry, who asserts that
the King is "the central archetype, around which the rest of the psyche is
organized."[28]

Moore and Gillette in discussing the archetypal functions of the King
point out:

> The first of these is ordering. [It is for this Divine ordering of the world
> that we give blessing, a la Dorff, Simon, and Gutoff—JHB] . . . "the sec-
> ond function of the King . . . was . . . blessing. Blessing is a psychologi-
> cal, or spiritual event. The good king always mirrored and affirmed oth-
> ers who deserved it. He did this by seeing them—in a literal sense, in his
> audiences at the palace, and in the psychological sense of noticing them,
> knowing them in their true worth. The good king delighted in noticing and
> promoting good men to positions of responsibility in his kingdom. He held
> audience, primarily not to be seen . . . but to see, admire, and delight in his
> subjects, to reward them and to bestow honors upon them. . . . He recog-
> nizes them and he is generative toward them. He bestows upon them his
> blessing. Being blessed has tremendous psychological consequences for us.
> There are even studies that show that our bodies actually change chemically
> when we feel valued, praised and blessed.
>
> . . . They need to be blessed. They need to be seen by the King, because
> if they are, something inside will come together for them. That is the ef-
> fect of blessing; it heals and makes whole. That's what happens when we
> are seen and valued and concretely rewarded . . . for our legitimate tal-
> ents and abilities.[29]
>
> It [blessing] stabilizes chaotic emotion and out-of-control behaviors. It gives
> stability and centeredness. It brings calm. And in its "fertilizing" and
> centeredness, it mediates vitality, life-force, and joy. It brings maintenance
> and balance. It defends our own sense of inner order, our own integrity

---

28. John Weir Perry. *Roots of Renewal in Myth and Madness: The Meaning of Psychotic Episodes.*
San Francisco: Jossey-Bass, 1976, p. 51.

29. Ibid., p. 63. In this context "young men," in our context all humankind.

of being and of purpose, our own central calmness about who we are, and our essential unassailability and certainty. . . . It looks upon the world with a firm but kindly eye. It sees others in all their weakness and in all their talent and worth. It honors them and promotes them. It guides them and nurtures them toward their own fullness of being. It is not envious, because it is secure, as the King, in its own worth. It rewards and encourages creativity in us and in others.[30]

Bradley Shavit Artson points us in this direction with an understanding of blessing that is especially relevant to what we can do as rabbis:

> The earliest hint of a different understanding of *Baruch* comes from the Midrash, where the Rabbis explain the verse "and you shall be a blessing" (Genesis 12:2) to mean "you shall be a spring (*Berecha*): . . . This *midrash* diverges markedly from the tradition of *Baruch* as praised/blessed. Here the term doesn't imply praise or thanks. Instead, being blessed means that *one in turn can bestow fullness and well-being on others*. . . . [emphasis—JHB] God blesses Abraham . . . means that Abraham will become a source of blessing, a fount of abundance for all whose lives he touches. [This] reveals an understanding of *Beracha* (Blessing) as causative.
>
> Why is God The Blessed One? Because everything belongs to God and God generously shares it with creation . . . it tells us that God can afford to be generous, since God is the Creator and owner of all there is.[31]

Following Albo[32] Artson offers, "The word Blessed [*Baruch*] is an attribute descriptive of the One who bestows an abundance of goodness. . . . Blessed [*Barach*] indicates that God is the source of all blessings, and that all benefits and good fortune of every kind come from God.

"If Blessed [*Baruch*] is understood as an adjective, then it reveals that God is a steady source of blessing."[33]

---

30. Robert Moore and Douglas Gillette. *King, Warrior, Magician, Lover: Rediscovering the Archetypes of the Mature Masculine.* New York: HarperCollins, 1990.

31. Bradley Shavit Artson. "Baruch ha-Shem: God Is Bountiful." *Conservative Judaism,* Vol. XLVI, No. 2, Winter 1994.

32. Artson points to Joseph Albo's medieval classic, *Sefer Ha-Ikkarim,* Book 2, Chapter 26. Albo understands Blessed as an adjective, like "merciful" or "compassionate" (implying that it is descriptive of God's nature, or that it is a quality that God bestows on everything else).

33. Artson, "Baruch ha-Shem: God Is Bountiful."

Because rabbis are blessed with being God's Exemplars, blessing others, thus sharing this bounty, is incumbent upon us. Though a truly crucial, inviolable part of being a rabbi, it is often experienced as an embarrassment. The discomfort may have a variety of sources. It may emanate from a sense of personal inadequacy or a sense of our own limitations, or overtly or covertly feeling that as a Symbolic Exemplar, one is an "impostor," or from our very human "being," in which our own [*Tzelem*⇔*Neshamah*] is all too often hidden from our purview. More generously and less pathologically, it may involve noble thoughts about human equality, the divinity of all humankind, and fear of the potential hubris involved in blessing those already blessed. Our trepidation is that we, who are unaware of our blessing, dare not bless others likewise afflicted. We may be even more frightened of taking ourselves too seriously and evolving into one of those pompous, grandiose, overstuffed caricatures of what a rabbi can be. That all too real danger is acknowledged by Moore and Gillette:

> The Shadow King as Tyrant . . . arises . . . when the Ego is identified with the King energy itself, (and) has no transpersonal commitment. *He* is his own priority. . . . The whole psyche destabilizes. The planet pretends to be a star. The true Center of the system is lost.[34]

Relationship is the powerful centering antidote to that danger. *Blessing of the other must be grounded in relationship.* Blessing starts in the blesser's I–Thou, loving relationship with her other "selves," those very "selves" we struggle to define as "not me." Blessing continues in the blesser's awareness of her own relationship with God, whose bounty and being has made room in the world for us and our unique "being." Blessing others is in the relationship of who we are with those others who are also blessed, but whose blessing is as it were in hiding. God both is the source of and calls forth from us our own bounty. A break in these loving I–Thou relationships impedes blessing. Gilligan points out, "Problems arise when a single identity is isolated from the family of identities. Solutions occur when relatedness between multiple identities is brought into play."[35]

These multiple identities are present within our "selves" and our own multiple "selves'" relationship with others, who are also multiple identities.

---

34. Moore and Gillette, *King, Warrior, Magician, Lover: Rediscovering the Archetypes of the Mature Masculine*, p. 71.

35. S. Gilligan, *The Courage to Love*.

It means holding at one and the same time that "*it ain't me doing it*" (Dvorah Simon), and beyond that, when both parts are in relationship "*it is me doing it.*" We are at one and the same time, the recipient of blessing, the conduit of blessing, and the source of blessing. Holding all these in relationship simultaneously is imperative, so that our [the "*me doing it*" and the "*ain't me doing it*"] now in a respectful [I–Thou] relationship may enter a similar relationship with those we are called on to bless. This enables us to call forth from them and audaciously bless the often hidden bounty of their "being"— of *their* unique [*Tzelem⟺Neshamah*]. We who bless are a relationship and a part of a much greater relationship. Blessing is only possible in relationship.

Feeling impaired in blessing others diminishes our rabbinate significantly. We avoid blessing others at our peril. We do well to get comfortable with that part of our work. Discomfort with a skill that is so crucial is merely a sign that we need to live and accept the blessing of our symbolic exemplarhood, who we are as rabbis. Uneasiness with blessing others points to a relationship with the "not me" parts of us that needs to be made whole. We need more practice and comfort in doing our crucial work. We dare not turn away from the [*Tzelem⟺Neshamah*] in us and in others. It is a crucial part of being a rabbi, and is to be blessed in all we meet.

Paley learned a lot from being blessed:

> Years later when I was a rabbi, I would prepare for Bar and Bat Mitzvahs with families by asking them about each person that would be called to the Torah. For each *aliyah*, I was able to "bring down" a blessing tailored to that individual. I would focus on the special contributions of the friend or relative, include the person's professional skill and conclude with a hope that the person would continue contributing to their relationship with the Bar or Bat Mitzvah. Blessings for lawyers might praise their ability to use language precisely and charge them to help the growing adolescent during a time when language loses its clarity. With grandparents, I would mention an unusual moment that they had shared with their grandchild and encourage them to *shepp* the well-deserved *naches*.[36]

---

36. Paley, *Shma, A Journal of Jewish Responsibility. Shepping naches* is deriving pleasure from others, mostly loved ones. The feeling a grandparent has when a grandchild does some wondrous act is *naches*.

That *is* a giant step beyond the reciting of formal ritual blessings and beyond being a conduit for ancient blessings. Blessing and encouraging the presented, positive aspects in others is very important.

The *more* crucial and difficult task is blessing the part not presented, the part being struggled with, the part which has no human existence and is experienced as the "not me." Realizing what it is in others, which is often unexpressed, witnessing the struggle and essence that begs inarticulately for naming and blessing, and blessing both struggle and essence with words of one's own, words not received and not encoded in the text, is a rabbinic skill of the first magnitude. It was this very part that Zalman Schachter touched when he blessed the young Michael. Sensing a young Bar Mitzvah's turbulent energy, a student's sense of inadequacy, the conflict in a mother's heart, the fear behind the brave face a hospital patient puts on, or conversely the courage hiding behind the fear, all the "not me's" that, though always present in the encounter, are so often hidden in the shadows, is a prerequisite to blessing. Yet it is those "hidden" parts that not only are unsettling to their "owners," but also throw us potential blessers off center as we struggle to deal only with what is being presented. To bless those wounded, hidden parts is a great art and skill.

Blessing those parts, as we mentioned earlier, requires first of all that we be centered, in touch with our own [*Tzelem*⇔*Neshamah*]. When knocked off center, which will happen all too often, have ways of getting centered. Being centered is experienced as a calm alertness of one's own mind/body as one returns to and sustains contact with one's own [*Tzelem*⇔*Neshamah*]. This makes room for one's own center and allows an act of *Tzimtzum*[37] that makes room for the other's presence with neither being compromised. It is from this centered place that a rabbi as a symbol can bless the other.

Moore and Gillette point out the blessed and blessing state that can be achieved when we succeed in staying centered:

> But when we are accessing the King energy correctly, as servants of our own inner King, we will manifest in our own lives the qualities, of the good and rightful King, the King in his fullness. . . . We will feel our anxi-

---

37. Literally, contraction. Taken from the kabbalistic idea of God withdrawing to make room for the creation of the world.

ety level drop, we will feel centered, and calm, and hear ourselves speak from an inner authority. We will have the capacity to mirror and to bless ourselves and others. We will have the capacity to care for others deeply and genuinely. We will "recognize" others. We will behold them as the full persons they really are. We will have a sense of being a centered participant in creating a more just, calm, and creative world. We will have a transpersonal devotion not only to our families, our friends, our companies, our causes, our religion, but also to the world. We will have some kind of spirituality, and we will know the truth of the central commandment around which all of human life seems to be based: Thou shalt love the Lord thy God [read, "the King"] with all thy heart and with all thy soul, and with all thy might. And thy neighbor as thyself.[38]

How do we go about achieving that centered place, that ongoing contact with our [*Tzelem*⇔*Neshamah*]?

Useful resources[39] for witnessing, naming, and blessing which need to be accessed with training and discipline include:

1. Acknowledging that you have the authority as Symbolic Exemplar, ordained of God, to bless others.
2. Taking blessing others seriously and attending to it carefully.
3. Accepting as a given *the* major organizing principle: The [*Tzelem*⇔*Neshamah*] in you and the other is *always* present.
4. Learning to hold multiple truths simultaneously.
5. Increasing your awareness of the ever-present [*Tzelem*⇔*Neshamah*]. Nourishing boundless curiosity, amazement, and admiration about its many faces, especially those hidden. Awe as to how it is awakening.
6. Maintaining a calm alertness of mind/body, while connecting with one's own center and the others. Know that in order to have a problem you have to let go of your center.
7. Shifting focus away from what is being presented by the other and is foreground. Thus opening the view to searching behind and seeing beyond, while making room for and honoring what is being pre-

---

38. Moore and Gillette, *King, Warrior, Magician, Lover: Rediscovering the Archetypes of the Mature Masculine*, p. 73.

39. These resources evolved from ongoing discussion and correspondence between the author and S. Gilligan.

sented. Once one is witness to and senses the presence of the [*Tzelem*⇔*Neshamah*], naming can begin with blessing not far behind.

8. Asking yourself, "What unspoken/wounded part of this person, currently inchoate, needs to be named?"

9. Or alternately, "What blessing does this person need?"

10. Being aware of the bounty you wish to share.

11. Knowing the signs of being stuck. We all get stuck, and "fall off the horse." Common signs include body locking, feeling stressed, wanting to be elsewhere, bored, getting a headache, etc. Remembering that in order to have a problem you have to let go of your center.

12. Returning to your own center, your [*Tzelem*⇔*Neshamah*]. Breathing, listening to your own heartbeat, doing an activity that you know from experience clears your head, e.g., praying, walking, painting, talking with a friend, reciting a *kavanah*[40] or an intention that you need.

13. Maintaining constant curiosity.

14. Treating your "naming" or "blessing" as a performative action., i.e., the words delivered appropriately in the proper setting will bring something "new" into existence.

15. Knowing some of the signs of proper naming and blessing. Noting how the other resonates with what you are doing, slows down, becomes absorbed, appears quiescent and touched. Knowing your own body/mind experience when you have been properly named/blessed and that I–Thou texture of connection that fills the space between you and the other. Extrapolating that to those others you name and bless.

Blessing is most effective delivered straight on with intense yet relaxed intention, with words meaningfully intoned and expressed, not rattled off, with eye contact maintained, with touch if appropriate, and with a demeanor of body and senses that absorbs the self and other.

Blessing may also be done by other indirect methods including metaphor or ricochet methods, such as talking to a third party about the person you want to bless with the blessee present, or even more indirectly with the blessee not present, but knowing it will get back to the blessee. Save and utilize these when "straight on" is for some reason not available to you.

---

40. A special prayer, often made up on the spot, focused on one's special intention.

EPILOGUE

And you shall bless me also.

(Ex. 12:33)

It is the middle of the night. He who will be known down the ages for his hardened heart is now heartbroken. His heir who had been the guarantor of his, Pharaoh's, own divine status is now dead in his arms.[41] The supreme ruler of the upper and lower kingdom, embodiment of Ra and of Horus, the gods of Egypt, his divine dynasty brought to its knees, defeated in the battle as to who the living God really is, is abjectly doing what he must do. Having summoned Moses and Aaron, he is sending them and their people on their way. Letting go of a workforce, he frets for his failure in failing to guarantee Egypt's future, a solemn duty with which he has been charged. And as he presses them to leave with no further delay, in an act that is either chutzpah, stupidity, pitiful, or all of these, asks to be blessed. Bless me also, Pharaoh asks of Moses, guardian of the teaching and of Aaron, master of the cult, the plenipotentiaries of the living God, the very people who have brought this dreadful night to be.

If Bless, as we have seen, is an attribute descriptive of the God who shares His bounty and goodness with all His creation, of whom does Pharoah ask this blessing? What is the bounty/blessing Pharaoh seeks?

The careful reader will duly note what follows:

The children of Israel had done according to Moshe's words; they had asked of the Egyptians objects of silver and objects of gold, and clothing.

God had given the people favor in the eyes of the Egyptians, and they let themselves be asked of (Ex. 12:35–36).

And the selfsame astute reader will note the careful use of the words:

So did they *exploit* the Egyptians (Ex. 12:36).

The Egyptians, despite their great anguish that night, are able to see beyond the Israelites as enemy. They respond to what they are asked for. They share their bounty.

From Moses and Aaron, no blessing is forthcoming. Pharaoh's plea goes unheard and unheeded. No blessing/bounty is forthcoming. There is no salve for his wound. There is no blessing that Egypt will survive. He is not promised that his torn heart will heal. He is not reassured that there is a future worth having for the humbled representative of Ra and Horus.

---

41. Charles David Isbell. "YHWH and the Gods of Egypt." *CCAR Journal*, Winter 1999.

Perhaps the silence came from anger over centuries of slavery; perhaps from an understandable feeling of wanting the whole thing over with; perhaps from the haste duly recorded in scripture of getting out; or perhaps more crucially from not being aware that it was in their power and even perhaps their duty as representatives of the living God to bless even Pharoah.

What was the overflowing bounty Moses and Aaron, God's plenipotentiaries, and indeed all Israel had in full measure that wondrous/appalling night. It was in the reality of the contact with the living God, who had heard their cry and come to redeem them. That God, whose bounty could include even Egypt, as it indeed had in the days of Joseph. The *Baal HaRachamim* (master of mercy) whose compassion is over all. Now Pharaoh and his people are those who suffer and are deeply wounded. But even though we understand the feelings of Moses and Aaron, nonetheless there is no bounty of the living God shared with Pharaoh.

And so we note (Ex. 14:5) that, inevitably, the unblessed suffering heart flips back, hardens this time with no record of divine intervention. Dare we say because it was not witnessed or blessed at the propitious moment? And so pursuit and enmity, the desire to subjugate, resume. Without blessing of the suffering and pain, and that which is noble in Pharaoh, the hardened heart reasserts itself. And though the story inexorably leading to the covenant at Sinai must include the redemption of God's people, nonetheless a mighty horde is destroyed. And it is told that God's joy in His own triumph could not be complete.[42]

Because rabbis are God's Exemplars, blessing others is incumbent upon us.

Blessing others, sharing God's bounty, is a truly crucial and inviolable part of being a rabbi. As Symbolic Exemplars of God, we can do no less.

Our people and the world call out to us in their pain.

---

42. Megillah 10b and Sanhedrin 39b.

11
Curing and Healing

When I was a newly minted pulpit rabbi, visiting the hospital was a chore that I seriously disliked. It was in my youthful perception an import from other religions more concerned with the world to come than was the Judaism of my youth. I was envious of those rabbis who had gotten out of doing it. Some avoided pastoral care by serving congregations in large metropolitan areas with a surfeit of hospitals that made just getting to them a full-time job. Others trained their congregants not to expect their rabbi to visit the hospital. And in the pecking order of the rabbinate in my day, "He's a good pastor" often meant that he didn't especially preach or teach very well. I *had* little choice. It went with the rabbinate in Bridgeport, Connecticut. Part of my job description was visiting congregants in the hospital. Rabbi Harry Nelson *z"l*, one of America's great rabbis, a superb educator and administrator whose assistant I was, had impressed upon me that he had built his 1200-member congregation in Bridgeport Hospital. That at least seemed a plausibly good reason to do hospital visits. Besides, if I didn't do it, I heard about it. I knew at some level that our tradition expected all Jews to visit the sick. Yet, besides pleasing the relatives, I didn't think that beyond congregation building, it really made much of a difference. I did not believe in or value what I was doing. I was less than aware that it might remotely have anything to do with healing. A successful hospital visit collected "brownie points" from the family for having done or attempted to do my pastoral duty. I was especially pleased to visit empty beds where I left my card. I would check the name off my "to visit" list so that when I got back to the office I could say that I visited "Aunt Sarah" and *unfortunately* she wasn't there. She was out being x-rayed or sleeping peacefully. Far be it from me to disturb her healing sleep! It was a boring chore. What I wasted during those years, unaware of and perhaps frightened by what I could have done, was using the potent power I had as a rabbi to help heal the ill.

It is only now that we increasingly recognize that spiritual, emotional, and physical well-being are all indissolubly linked. Given this, rabbis' work in this area has become crucial in our time. In recent years, greater emphasis has been placed on rabbis making a positive difference in a person's physical health and well-being. What rabbis do in contact with the ill, in hospital and home, *can* help people heal and assist in curing.

I hope that rabbis today do not have the sense of relief that I had, but rather feel disappointed and frustrated that they missed a great opportunity, when the person is out having some hospital procedure done. The opportunity missed is the chance of having a powerful effect by their very presence, by what and how they communicate with that ill human being. Rabbis need see *bikur cholim*[1] as a chance to change the direction of the illness by seeding ideas about healing, repairing the relational breach in the patient's human integrity, and in the patient's relationship to the world beyond. These have an actual impact in changing the actions of the immune system and can move towards healing. Rabbinic symbolic exemplarhood puts rabbis in a very special position and reinforces the impact of their work.

A CAVEAT

Recently clergy dealing with the ill have drawn a distinction between healing and curing. Growing up respecting "science" and witnessing numerous medical "miracles" has led to paying obeisance to the often awesome power of modern medicine. We have deferred to the medical world with God gaining access only as a last resort. We assume that we are impotent in the realm of cure. God cures, and then not always, only when all else fails. We are led to this conclusion because our use of curative language (of which more anon), our prayers with and for those who are ill,[2] and other methods, such as laying on hands, don't always result in the melting of a tumor or a continuation of a

---

1. Visiting the ill.

2. In the synagogue liturgy these are referred to as *misheberakhs*. "May the God of our Ancestors bless and heal So-and-So, the child of So-and-So."

life. To protect our dignity and our usefulness, we turn to a minor though not unimportant semantic difference between two virtual synonyms, healing and curing. Though healing and curing are overwhelmingly interchangeable, perhaps for reasons of turf, healing has been assigned the meaning of restoring "spiritual" wholeness. Curing (physical) is the domain of the physician and healing (spiritual) the province of the clergy. Though this does carve out a limited, though nonetheless critical, area for the clergy, it also perpetuates a remnant of Greek dualism which has dominated our thinking for too long. The evidence is plain that the two are intertwined. The healing I am writing about in this chapter is both physical healing/curing and spiritual healing/curing. Rabbis and all clergy are directly involved in curing. We need not be apologetic about that, though we definitely need to be better trained.

We have come full circle. Originally all healing was in the hands of the religious functionary. "Primitive" people understood that what one thought and believed was irrevocably linked to healing. There is immense evidence today that the "primitives" were on to something big. Though from the day we are born we are dying, the evidence shows that a person's belief system, mood, etc., are crucial determinants in deciding that day.

Some of the things we know[3] about the interrelationship of [mind⇔body], [cognitive⇔somatic], etc.:

> Stress has a major effect on physical health, affecting everything from back pain to cancer.[4,5,6]
> Psychological depression reduces the immune system's capabilities.
> Heart patients with religious leanings live longer than those without such faith.[7]

---

3. *The American Psychological Association Monitor*, Vol. 26, No. 12, December 1999.

4. Ohio State University psychologist Janice Keicolt-Glaser, Ph.D., and her husband, immunologist Ronald Glaser, M.D., leading PNI researchers, found that medical students, during the stressful exam time, show a decline in the activity of the cells that fight off tumors and viral infections. They have also found that people who are caring for a spouse with Alzheimer's disease show decreases in immune activity.

5. In a study published in 1991, psychologist Sheldon Cohen, Ph.D., of Carnegie Mellon University, injected nearly 400 healthy subjects with a cold virus, and found that those who reported more stress in their lives were more likely to develop colds.

6. John Sarno, M.D. *Mind Over Back Pain*. New York: William Morrow & Co., 1984.

7. *Mental Medicine Update*, Vol. 4, No. 2, 1995. "The study involved 232 patients over 55 years of age, all of whom had elective open-heart surgery for coronary artery or aortic valve

Women who undergo group therapy as part of their treatment for breast cancer live longer than those who receive no such treatment.[8]

Men with HIV infection who receive guidance in relaxation or other therapeutic techniques show a delayed onset of AIDS-related symptoms.[9]

Expectation, as seen in what follows, is a powerful force in keeping people alive.

Mr. Wright had a generalized far-advanced malignancy involving the lymph nodes, lymphosarcoma. Eventually the day came when he developed resistance to all known palliative treatments. Huge tumor masses the size of oranges were in the neck, axillas, groin, chest, and abdomen. The spleen and liver were enormous. Our impression was that he was in a terminal state, untreatable, other than to give sedatives to ease him on his way.

In spite of all this, Mr. Wright was not without hope, even though his doctors most certainly were. The reason for this was that the new drug that he had expected to come along and save the day had already been reported in the newspapers! Its name was "Krebiozen" (subsequently shown to be a useless, inert preparation). Then he heard in some way that our clinic was to be one of a hundred places chosen by the Medical Association for evaluation of this treatment. We were allotted supplies of the drug sufficient for treating 12 selected cases. Mr. Wright was not considered eligible, since one stipulation was that the patient must not only be beyond the point where standard therapies could benefit, but also must have

---

disease. . . .Those who found at least some strength and comfort from their religious feelings were *three times* more likely to survive than those who had no comfort from religious faith. Also, those who participated in social and community groups . . . had three times the survival rate of those who didn't take part in any organized activity. Those seniors who had both protective factors—religious and social support—enjoyed a *ten-fold* increase in survival."

8. One of the most important examples of the link between psychological factors and health outcomes came from Stanford University psychiatrist David Spiegel, who, along with renowned group psychotherapist Irvin Yalom, M.D., led support groups in the 1970s for women with advanced stages of breast cancer.

9. Researchers such as Michael Anioni, Ph.D., associate professor of psychology and psychiatry at the University of Miami, have found that asymptomatic HIV-infected men who undergo stress management training show a slower rate of decline in the immunological cells that the AIDS virus attacks than did men who received no such treatment.

a life expectancy of at least three, and preferably six, months. He certainly didn't qualify on the latter point, and to give him a prognosis of more than two weeks seemed to be stretching things.

However, a few days later, the drug arrived, and we began setting up our testing program which, of course, did not include Mr. Wright. When he heard we were going to begin treatment with Krebiozen, his enthusiasm knew no bounds, and as much as I tried to dissuade him, he begged so hard for this "golden opportunity," that against my better judgment, and against the rules of the Krebiozen committee, I decided I would have to include him.

Injections were to be given three times weekly, and I remember he received his first one on a Friday. I didn't see him again until Monday and thought as I came to the hospital he might be moribund or dead by that time, and his supply of the drug could then be transferred to another case.

What a surprise was in store for me! I had left him febrile, gasping for air, completely bedridden. Now, here he was, walking around the ward, chatting happily with the nurses, and spreading his message of good cheer to any who would listen. Immediately I hastened to see the others who had received their first injection at the same time. No change, or change for the worse, was noted. Only in Mr. Wright was there brilliant improvement. The tumor masses had melted like snowballs on a hot stove, and in only these few days, they were half their original size! This is, of course, far more rapid regression than the most radio-sensitive tumor could display under heavy X-ray given every day.

Within ten days Mr. Wright was able to be discharged from his "deathbed" practically all signs of his disease having vanished in this short time. Incredible as it sounds, this "terminal" patient, gasping his last breath through an oxygen mask, was not only breathing normally, and fully active, he took off in his plane and flew at 12,000 feet with no discomfort!

This unbelievable situation occurred at the beginning of the "Krebiozen" evaluation, but within two months, conflicting reports began to appear in the news, all of the testing clinics reporting no results. At the same time, the originators of the treatment were still blindly contradicting the discouraging facts that were beginning to emerge.

This disturbed our Mr. Wright considerable as the weeks wore on. Although he had no special training, he was, at times, reasonably logical and scientific in his thinking. He began to lose faith in his last hope which so far had been life-saving and left nothing to be desired. As the reported results became increasingly dismal, his faith waned, and after two months of practically perfect health, he relapsed to his original state, and became very gloomy and miserable.

When Mr. Wright had all but given up in despair with the recrudescence of his disease, in spite of the "wonder drug" which had worked so well at first, I decided to take the chance and play the quack. So deliberately lying, I told him not to believe what he read in the papers, the drug was really most promising after all. "What then," he asked, "was the reason for his relapse?" "Just because the substance deteriorated on standing," I replied, "a new superrefined, double-strength product is due to arrive tomorrow which can more than reproduce the great benefits derived from the original injections."

The news came as a great revelation to him, and Mr. Wright, as ill as he was, became his optimistic self again, eager to start over. By delaying a couple of days before the "shipment" arrived, his anticipation of salvation had reached a tremendous pitch. When I announced that the new series of injections was about to begin, he was almost ecstatic and his faith was very strong.

With much fanfare, and putting on quite an act (which I deemed permissible under the circumstances), I administered the first injection of the doubly potent, fresh preparation—consisting of fresh water and nothing more. The results of this experiment were quite unbelievable to us at the time, although we must have had some suspicion of the remotely possible outcome to have even attempted it at all.

Recovery from his second near-terminal state was even more dramatic than the first. Tumor masses melted, chest fluid vanished, he became ambulatory, and even went back to flying again. At this time he is certainly the picture of health. The water injections were continued, since they worked such wonders. He then remained symptom-free for over two months. At this time the final AMA announcement appeared in the press—"nationwide tests show Krebiozen to be a worthless drug in treatment of cancer."

Within a few days of this report, Mr. Wright was readmitted to the hospital in extremis. His faith was now gone, his last hope vanished, and he succumbed in less than two days.[10]

---

10. From Ernest Rossi. *The Psychobiology of Mind-Body Healing*. New York: W. W. Norton, 1993, pp. 4–6. The original report on Mr. Wright was written by one of his personal physicians, Dr. Philip West, a reliable observer who played an important part in the story (B. Klopfer. "Psychological Variables in Human Cancer." *Journal of Projective Techniques*, Vol. 21, 1957, pp. 331–340).

How we think affects our expectations and our immune system.[11,12] Our beliefs make up our thinking and our thinking shapes our beliefs.

SOURCES OF RABBINIC CURING
AND HEALING[13] POWER

Rabbis *are* Symbolic Exemplars of the best that is in humankind. Rabbis are invested with and I shall suggest do have special powers of curing and healing. Being a walking, talking, living symbol is extraordinarily difficult, yet it is an essential component of the rabbinate. Though a weighty burden, it is a component of the rabbinate that provides a major source of efficacy, influence, potency, and power.

As Symbolic Exemplars (and there is little or no choice about that), rabbis are perceived as ordained of God and emissaries of the Jewish people with special powers that provide opportunities to affect those systems that govern health and well-being.

To use the rabbinic power implicit in being Symbolic Exemplars in their work of healing, rabbis must accept and be comfortable with being walking, talking symbols. Rabbis need to believe that they can make a positive difference in people's physical health and well-being by what they do in contact with the ill, in hospital, synagogue, and home. They also need to be skilled in using their symbolic exemplarhood wisely and with courage.

Symbolic exemplarhood is not a substitute for competence or for personal integrity. Used competently and with integrity, it is a primary source of rabbinic power in their work healing the ill. Symbolic acts, coming from and appealing to an experiential non-rational part of our being, are potentially among the most powerful tools a rabbi has.

To use symbolic exemplarhood maximally, rabbis need to adopt a mode of thinking that is [Both/And]. (See Chapter 7.) Recognizing the fullness and richness [Both/And] thinking provides allows the rabbi to shuttle back and forth without feeling duplicitous or hypocritical. A metaphor for

---

11. See note 5.

12. UCLA psychiatrist Fawzy I. Fawzy, M.D., for example, conducted a study involving a six-week structured group therapy for newly diagnosed patients with good prognoses. The subjects maintained greater numbers and activity of tumor-killing cells compared to a control group.

13. From this point on, healing and curing will be used interchangeably.

this, which I am sure appeals to rabbis, is that used by Gregory Bateson: "the acrobat on the high wire maintains his stability by continual correction of his imbalance."[14] For rabbis, the moving back and forth between being an exemplar and being just "regular folk" may not need to be as rapid as those of the acrobat, but rabbis need to be able to make the needed adjustments in order to maintain rabbinic stability and effectiveness. To do this means acting as God's Symbolic Exemplar when that is appropriate, being other than that when that is appropriate, and knowing that she is both at the same time. "While I'm acting as that symbol, I truly am that. When I'm not, I'm not." How to take each seriously and neither so seriously as to interfere with the other is what we are going for.

For the pulpit rabbi, work in ministering to and healing the ill is only part of his work. The pulpit rabbi has multiple opportunities to be experienced as a Symbolic Exemplar. Bar/Bat Mitzvahs, weddings, namings, and funerals all contribute to that. He is for the ill a major link to the community beyond the sickbed. This multiplicity of roles is a distinct advantage. For those rabbis/chaplains whose full-time work is with the ill and the dying, the aged and the infirm, the Alzheimer's sufferer and the stroke paralyzed, symbolic exemplarhood is of even greater importance, but more difficult to achieve than it is for pulpit rabbis. In the hospital setting, where all others are valued for their perceptible skills, whether the surgeon's hands, the accountant's audit, the nurse's ability to take blood, rabbinic/pastoral skills seem ephemeral in nature, nebulous, and hard to evaluate. In such a setting, where people are in crisis, the appearance of God's symbolic emissary may be even a more potent factor, though one more difficult to attain. In the hospital/institutional setting the rabbi's symbolic exemplarhood may be even a greater hostage to others' perception of the rabbi/chaplain's inner qualities. The hospital chaplain has chosen to work with the ill and their loved ones almost exclusively and may be thought of as a one-dimensional paid employee. The deep spiritual caring he is to demonstrate is both difficult to sustain and easy to automate, as any nurse or physician will attest to.

Nevertheless, for both pulpit rabbi and hospital/institutional chaplain, symbolic exemplarhood, though difficult and often irascible, is a powerful partner, walking with her every place she goes, and affecting everything she does with those ill and those healing. It is symbolic exemplarhood that gives the rabbi special efficacy. It is crucial that rabbis under-

---

14. Gregory Bateson. *Mind and Nature: A Necessary Unity*. New York: E.P. Dutton, 1979.

stand that they stand for something far beyond themselves. Rabbis need to enter the encounter with BY THE POWER VESTED IN ME emblazoned on their banner.

And while doing all he can, and doing it unapologetically and as expertly as he can, each rabbi needs to know that he cannot know the effect of everything he does. And when he fails, which will be often, he needs to fail lightly, knowing that even God has not done much better in this business of healing/curing. Maybe that is why God has subcontracted some of this holy and difficult work to his anointed servants.

When people are ill, rabbinic symbolic exemplarhood grows. What rabbis say and do becomes ever more vitally important. What people believe of rabbis, whether rabbis are comfortable with that or not, gives rabbis influence, potency, and power. People under stress and confusion are looking for and will attend to anything that will diminish that stress and confusion. Being ill and vulnerable, suffering fright and isolation provides heightened need, shakes up belief systems, and opens one to new dimensions of thinking. It opens for the rabbi a pathway to start to change belief systems. What people believe has a great deal to do with their resources for healing, from pumping up their immune system to strengthening the state of the body their physician is working on. The rabbi's task is to make benign and maximum use of that mental and emotional opening and to search out and sponsor anything within the person that will move him/her toward health. What people think about their health, changes their health.

Symbolic exemplarhood can be an ally in helping rabbis change others' beliefs, and helping their beliefs help their healing/curing.

The human being the rabbi is dealing with is not a *Self*, as we have hitherto understood that word. She is a relationship. The patient, like each of us, is a relationship between different "*selves*." Our concern as rabbis is noting and mentoring that relationship between different "*selves*." The rabbi with the ill has to have the unusual (until it has been experienced many times) experience of being in relationship with a relationship. It cannot be emphasized enough that the patient is a relationship, rather than a *Self* as we have heretofore defined it. The rabbi is looking for and trying to ascertain by observation, talking, and being, which part of the patient's relationship is being presented, and which part is hidden or neglected. The patient's sense of relationship is impaired, quite likely very out of kilter. It may have been impaired before she became ill. It is, since she is human, seriously affected by what has happened to her. The trauma, the violence done to her *Self* (her relationship[s]) by her illness, has more than likely wreaked havoc. The rabbi is the rescue squad—the 911 team to get her back in relationship as best as that can be accomplished. The rabbi's task is to create/re-create a spirit of connectedness between, at the least, her two "*selves*," somatic and cognitive, that both may be felt and fostered. In illness the odds are great that her relationship with herself, what we will call her sense of *being* is threatened. Her relationship with that which is beyond her "*selves*," with the rabbi, with God, with significant others in her life (her sense of *belonging*), is also threatened and her ability to relate, to conduct the conversation, i.e., her *relating*, is impaired. The special task undertaken by rabbis in healing is to help others retrieve under conditions of trauma and violence or achieve for the first time a sense of relatedness, a sense of [Both/And]. The question of identity is central to our work as chaplains and healers.

When the ill are in crisis, when symptoms present a severe threat, when the scar tissue covering an old emotional wound is torn away under the stress, a state of severe threat to one's very integrity is evoked or reevoked. In that situation a person's felt sense, his everyday cognitive sense of *Self*, all too easily disappears, contracts, dissociates, or is otherwise nullified. He is no longer who he was and is often petrified of who and what he will be. Some people in pain will talk about just wanting to get back to their "normal '*self*.'" The "*self*" one lives with day by day and presents to others. This "*self*" is typically predominant, *except* when self-identity is at risk as it is in trauma and illness. At such times, the deep feelings and processes of the somatic "*self*" emerge more powerfully, even to the point of taking over. One is as it were dragged around by one's emotions, evoked by the danger and the threat.

To support and foster [Both/And] thinking our concern as rabbis must remain focused on the pattern that connects.[15]

[Both/And] implies;
There are (at least) two of you:[16]
You are not a self—You are a relationship.
Relationship is the basic psychological [and religious—JHB] unit.

The overall message a rabbi needs to get across is that she is an advocate for all "*selves*." A rabbi's work is to help the patient know, "You really do exist as a human being. You have a center, a core of being that is blessed,

---

15. Bateson, *Mind and Nature: A Necessary Unity*.

16. This and the following three paragraphs are paraphrased from S. Gilligan. *The Courage to Love*. New York: W.W. Norton & Co., 1997.

that goes beyond your illness, that is beyond the part that you present for the world to see." This will take more than just repeating the words. It will take reestablishing the feeling of beingness which comes out of the relational *Self* and dealing with the other side, whichever it might be and wherever it may be hiding.

A third aspect of the relational field may be described as influential others. These others may include social individuals such as parents, friends, teachers, enemies, children, and spouses. They may also include God, spiritual beings such as angels, or one's sense of a Higher Power, as well as one's ancestors. That is where a rabbi's symbolic exemplarhood provides an edge if used wisely. These influential others are sponsors that guide and define one's life, especially when a person's identity is in flux, both early in life, but even more so when illness strikes. A person has emotional connections to an influential other. The rabbi as Symbolic Exemplar stands for the God who has placed the [*Tzelem*⟺*Neshamah*] (see Chapter 6), the non-negotiable core, in each of us. That [*Tzelem*⟺*Neshamah*] is open, touched, and, though vulnerable, remains accessible in such relationships.

An influential other may bless or curse one's beingness.[17] Blessings and curses are not cognitive events. They are spiritual or identity events. Most people can identify presences in their lives who really saw and blessed their essence. This is what makes the rabbinic role in naming, sponsoring, and blessing so important.[18,19]

People think of the rabbi as a special emissary of God. Even the lifelong atheist, with a bad Hebrew-school experience, gets aroused when the

---

17. In a perhaps apocryphal story, Golda Meir (the former Prime Minister of Israel) and a rabbi were once talking. The rabbi noted that he was able to consult with fellow rabbis about very important decisions, and wondered whether Golda's position as leader of the country allowed her to have confidants. She replied that she consulted with two people on every important decision: her grandmother (who was no longer alive) and her granddaughter (who had not yet been born).

18. Rabbi Amy Eilberg, Director of *Kol Haneshama*, JHC's hospice care program in San Francisco, offered the notion of "holy *chutzpah*," the nerve to believe that "perhaps I can convey God's blessing." She suggested that even when physical healing is not possible, it is possible to pray for *refuat ha-nefesh*, healing of the spirit. The rabbi must attempt to be the conduit between community and individual, bringing the community with her every time she enters the hospital room.

19. See Chapter 10.

emissary of the "non-existent" shows up. The rabbi may have to alter what he does with the non-affiliated and the non-believer and the denier. It may be something as simple as casting some doubt into their negative certainty.[20] And, if *they* are correct and there is no God, there will be no one to recognize the important work you have done and you can work that out in therapy. What people believe offers rabbis the capability and the power, which rabbis need not hesitate to use. Most, however, do experience their congregational rabbi as a link from the outside world, a link to the Jewish people. If you know that you can have an influence on someone, and there is virtually no one you cannot influence if you're flexible enough, use it, use it, use it.

Within the hospital framework rabbis are a major link between systems. A rabbi symbolizes that there is something beyond the medical attending and organizational community. Even the full-time chaplain, paid by the hospital, does well to present herself as being outside the regular hospital system. Whether congregational or chaplain, she is the minister plenipotentiary of the Jewish people, of the world outside the illness and of course vertically God's employee ordained of God, vested with special power. Virtually no one else has this combination. The rabbi embodies these all in one. Rabbis need to be strongly encouraged and trained to use the power.

Rabbinic efficacy not only comes from what people believe of the rabbi, it more crucially emanates from what rabbis believe of themselves.[21] What the rabbi believes in and of herself will influence what the patient believes, and those beliefs have, as we have said, a profound influence on health.

GETTING TO "I'M HERE"

Human beings have a natural innate ability to take on the coloring and feelings of the environment.[22] Maybe it started with our ancestors Adam and Eve, both created of the same raw material. Maybe it evolved from the early

---

20. Thanks to Bill O'Hanlon.

21. *American Journal of Clinical Hypnosis*, Vol. 25, Nos. 2–3, October 1982–January 1983. "When one person attempts to help another . . . the success of that venture lies in the skill with which that help is given . . . we must inquire into the belief system of the therapist, the beliefs of the patient, the capacity of each to relate to himself and to the other, the sensitivity to respond: and *the ability to communicate*."

22. Ainslie Meares. *American Journal of Clinical Hypnosis*, Vol. 25, Nos. 2–3, October 1982– January 1983. "We have within us a protective biological mechanism by which we tend to take on the emotion of those around us. In primitive times we would take on the fear of

campfires, where those sensitive to the emotions and feelings of others survived and passed on their genes. However that is, when people are feeling anxious, the anxiety will pass into those in contact with the anxiety. People unawares pick up the unspoken behavior of other people. Sitting in a restaurant, watching any two people, especially a couple in love, you will notice how they start to mirror each other's behavior. Watch how without a word, the actions of one influence the other. Be in a group where everyone is depressed and notice how you feel. Be in your office and notice how when you change your body position after a while, the others present will change theirs.

The visiting Symbolic Exemplar needs to develop some immunity to that very human tendency, while not becoming so closed off, distant, and removed that he cannot be of use to God or humankind. He needs to be centered, balanced, safe in the storm, not buffeted to and fro by it. The rabbi at best needs to be the one who imparts the atmosphere, one to whom the environment responds and not the other way around. A Symbolic Exemplar needs to be balanced in relationship to himself, the person he is in contact with, and the God who has ordained him.

The rabbi's *Self* needs taking care of first. Knowing that her *Self* is a relationship and attending to any wounded parts is primary. Nothing can happen without that. The rabbi's own feelings of fright, inadequacy, helplessness, vulnerability, or whatever need to be attended to. This visit may be a reminder of her parent's illness, her husband's diagnosis, her loss of a child. She must be open to her at least two "*selves*," the relation between them, and the relation between "them" and the context. Getting centered and grounded in any way she can, whether that be by prayer, meditation, or simply attending to her own breathing and heartbeat, each and both of which are unconditionally hers, from birth to death.

Getting himself into a mental state of calmness and reassurance before getting to the hospital is crucial. When he is on his way to the hospital or when he enters the hospital, he needs to take a few minutes for himself to get centered and balanced and therefore into a state of calmness. This means returning to his own core, to his own [*Tzelem*⟺*Neshamah*] (see Chapter 6) in a way that works for him.

Each of us has our own special way of returning to our core, our own special way of becoming absorbed. Often these are variations of self-

---

others around us and so be alerted to danger although we did not know what was threatening. Likewise if the others were relaxed and at ease, we ourselves would be free to let ourselves go off guard as there was no danger about."

hypnosis. We know how something like hypnosis works. It's a regular part of our experience. Nothing unusual, except that we don't use it in a systematic way and don't know that we can do it. When a person thinks about something, muscle groupings react, blood flow changes happen. If that thing is exciting, frightening, or erotic, certain changes will happen. If it's calming and soothing, other changes take place. This has the fancy name ideomotor activity. It is something "Granny" could have told us. It is something we have all experienced. When you see a certain picture, hear a certain song, you will notice that things happen in your body. Self-hypnosis gives you some control over what you get absorbed into and, therefore, how you feel physically and emotionally. There are hypnosis' close cousins, meditative procedures. Perhaps it is a special prayer, a *Yehi Ratzon*[23] that is yours and helps you to get back to yourself. Perhaps it is thinking of a place you love, and transporting yourself there in your mind's eye. All, or any of these or any that are specifically yours, help move you to a state of calmness and personal reassurance before you go in. Spend five minutes praying for the ability to help others heal, for the ability to stay calm and in a comfortable place with the person(s) you are about to visit. Pray that you will not go through the hospital simply as a chore to be done, but as a healing contact with another human being that can really do much that can help turn the illness around. The very fact of your presence, calm and centered, even without your saying a word, can be an influence on the environment, and so on them. Keep what you are doing to prepare light, so that you will not trance out and be stuck in the outer room, engaged in a deep somnambulistic trance long after visiting hours are over.

One aspect of getting and staying calm is knowing who your employer is and that you are there to do a job. A participant/observer given the power as Symbolic Exemplar of God, source of health and resources, creator of the immune system, of humankind's talent for thinking and healing. Invoke God as your backup helper, active not passive. Think of yourself as God's ally in the work that has to be done. You are on the side of God, who is walking next to you as you go in and may give you the ability to heal and perhaps to cure.

In that relationship you need also to know that you are enough. It is important to feel calm, secure, centered in an OK place so that you can really be useful. Remember that in order to have a problem, you have had to let go

---

23. A common beginning in Jewish prayer. "May it be Your will Oh God that . . ."

of your center, the [*Tzelem*⟺*Neshamah*] which is your core.[24] Centered, you can say about yourself, "I can move people. I can touch people. Sometimes I will fail with people, yet I like the God who created me can say, 'I am who I am,' and that's more than enough." We take our own power away. We give it away. You have the power to be powerfully influential with the sick.

Going into the hospital room she is, at one and the same time, aware of her own power, her own presence, willing and available to do whatever she can. While at the very same time she knows that *not* having to achieve, *not* having to accomplish is equally important. All of this is not a matter of technique, though her learning what the realities of communication are is vital. It is a matter of her presence as a Symbolic Exemplar which makes the significant difference. It is not one or the other. It is, as always, [Both / And].

It is told of Milton Erickson, one of America's truly great therapists, that when patients came into his office and saw its rather humble surroundings, he would fix his gaze on them and say, "But *I'm here*." Each rabbi needs to affirm that. Your presence is more than enough.

GETTING TO WHO'S THERE

Having achieved being centered, grounded, and, therefore, calm, you need to take some time before you go in for the visit to switch gears to think about what it is that this person needs. Ask yourself, "What am I 'going for' with this person today?"

The FRAGILE[25] inventory is a good general scale to guide your search. Your patients will be dealing with **F**ear, **R**esentment, **A**nger, **G**uilt, **I**ndecision, **L**ove (relationship) problems, and **E**nvy. All and any of these, plus the diagnosis or possible diagnosis, will lead to a diminution of self-worth.

What is your goal with this person today? What do you want to accomplish? What is your target? What are the various ways you will attempt to attain that target? What will be the evidence that you have achieved it? What other ways will you try if what you do doesn't seem to work?

The goal may be as simple and obvious as finding out what this person needs from you at a future time. Or it may be an end of life issue, helping this person deal with oncoming death. It may be anything in between such as a change in expectations and beliefs. It may be reestablishing contact

---

24. S. Gilligan. Personal conversation.

25. This is not original. I saw it someplace but do not recall where.

with family members so that the ill person is not being cut off from loved ones. Establishing what they need and how you are going to communicate in a way that is going to lead toward what they need is very important. What can I (the rabbi) do that will help this person heal, deal with pain, cope with permanent life changes, and even oncoming death? The rabbi needs to be clear about what outcome he is going for, and what will be even a shred of evidence that it is being achieved. Much of this will often revolve around seeding ideas. How you talk when paying a hospital call will depend on the goal you want and ways ideas can be planted.

To do this, rabbis need to learn as much as they can about the world their patients live in and how they structure reality. This is the "language" of those they are dealing with. How the people they are dealing with are organized; what maps they use to get around in life; how they think; how their belief systems work. To do this means knowing their "language," values, concerns, and resources. This means knowing their "history" as they perceive it and as others interpret it, and as much as rabbis can know about another person. Each and all of your patients and congregants are uniquely different. In this area, a fundamentalistic position, affirming that "one way fits all" is extremely counterproductive. No two people respond the same way. Using many of the skills you learn may work with one person and not another. Touching might be powerful in increasing one person's coping skills, and just too "touchy-feely" with another. A *misheberakh* with an entire congregation holding hands might raise one person's sense of worth and thereby increase the immune system's capacity to heal, and do nothing for another. You need to learn about the world they live in. We hope you already know about your world.

Perhaps you have been asked to visit Mr. Cohen, a relative of a congregant whom you do not know well. The doctor has informed Mr. Cohen that his tumor is quite aggressive and that he has, at most, four to six months to live. You have gotten calm and centered and are ready to go in. You need to stop and think, "What outcome do I want to go for in this visit? Do I want to establish what resources Mr. Cohen has, and if so, resources to do what? Is he a fighter? Has the time frame paralyzed him? Does he need forgiveness, or does he need to forgive? Who is he, anyway? Maybe this first visit, I need just to get to know him and build some trust. Maybe I need just to evaluate what his model of the world and of illness is." Knowing that what you want is at best tentative, that you may not get what you want, that you may have to adjust what you want when you are in his presence, and he lets you know one way or another that his needs are different from what you thought they were when you prepared in the hospital chapel. Given that you may have to make great changes on the spot, you nevertheless need to go in prepared. How you are and what you say when you pay a hospital call are going to depend on what the patient needs, the goal that you want, and the ideas you want to convey and those that can be planted in a person.

Learning others' *languages* means learning to talk their talk, learning to use the words they use, to speak in their manner. Think of the lack of rapport you experience with someone who speaks a foreign tongue, and the answer to your requests for directions is just gibberish. Rapport may begin when with hand language or pointing they seem to understand and you understand them. You need to consider what your patients' background is, how they came to think as they do, talk as they do, act as they do. You need to imagine how in different circumstances you might have gotten to think, feel, and experience the world as they do. In sum you need to know your patients. Some simple examples: Words and talk generally mean something quite different to men and women. Men and women will talk differently about sex and power, work and children. People, depending on their background, ethnicity, or their family history and the rules (overt and covert) they grew up with, and even their genetic endowment, are different. Another difference is how they process experience inside their heads, how long it takes them to process information, and how they express what they have processed. Part of their *language* is the tone, pace, and volume of their voice. Attend to these also. The important thing to remember is that they are certainly different from you. Their experience is not yours. Both of you are unique. That you can even communicate with them is a miracle.

As a pulpit clergyman you hopefully have a much richer experience than most people in your congregation. If you are a hospital chaplain, you have witnessed a great deal of pain and suffering. Both have experienced a lot, and each can respond out of his own wealth of experience.

What else might you do if you wanted to change Mr. Cohen's perspective on what is going on? You might have decided that the doctor planted a non-useful idea and your aim is to shake up the time frame. A very direct way might be to say, "The doctor doesn't know what she's talking about." This is unlikely to work. How might you do it more indirectly? (We will be talking about indirect communication more later.) You might want to take a shot in the dark by talking about the times other authority figures were wrong about how long things would take. In World War I, the authorities all said the troops would be home by Christmas 1914. The war lasted four more years. You might talk about people who lived much longer than their medically allotted time. If you don't go the direct route you might say, "Oh, I had a friend[26] whose father just died at ninety-six. Thirty-five years ago they opened him up in Bridgeport Hospital and told my friend that his father had six months to live. That was thirty-five years ago." If that works, fine. Let's assume that you don't want to be that direct. You may want to explore times when time played tricks on Mr. Cohen, when time waiting for something to happen seemed longer, when things lasted longer then he thought they would.

You might talk about another set of expectations that people had that did not get met. For someone who is a sports fan you might talk about a player or a team that was expected to be out of the game early, who hung in there against all odds and survived to play another day. You might talk about a player who had no home runs last year. Nobody expected him to do anything and to everyone's surprise he had eight home runs in April. You might tell a mother about someone else's kid who was "doomed" but found unexpected resources and turned out just fine. You can talk about expectations that someone didn't meet, and who went his own way. That is more indirect.

I watched a truly sensitive doctor interrupt a time frame and plant useful hope in my father who got sick in September 1959. Wanting only the best treatment, he flew to the Mayo Clinic. My father had cancer of the pancreas and was operated on. The doctor told me over the phone that in three months my father would feel a little better, in six months he would be worse, and that 99 percent of the people with his diagnosis were dead within a year. What to do? What to tell him? My first cousin was like a sister to him, having been raised in the same house in Romania. Her policy with her husband who had just died of cancer was, "Never say!" She admonished me in the strongest of terms not to tell him. I (and my therapist) thought he had a right to know, but I was scared of his knowing the "whole truth." The doctor said to me, "I want you to accompany me, but I want you to let me do the telling." He reassured me that he would tell my father in a way that would optimize things. I flew to the Mayo clinic and in my presence that doctor said to my father, "Mr. Bloom, we did everything we could do. We've removed as much of the malignancy as we could, but we could not get it all. Some people have lived with this for fifteen years." My father, who was sixty-five at the time, gladly included himself in the category of "some people," those pancreatic cancer patients the doctor referred to, though they were a very

---

26. I do have such a friend. This is a true story.

small percentage. He would gladly settle for the possibility of living fifteen years. The original projections, statistically based, turned out to be untrue. He lived another two and a half years. He danced at my wedding, outliving the phone prediction by a full year and a half.

Had he said to my father what the statistics indicated, he would have done my father a disservice. What he provided my father with were the facts. The truth is, that though we may classify someone as terminally ill, we don't know that for a fact. People have remissions. People for whom funeral arrangements have been made keep the undertaker waiting for twenty-five years. In a certain sense, all of us are terminally ill. That's true. What we need to do, without making any kind of absurd predictions, is to let the person know what the "facts" are in such a way as to indicate that the "facts" are not all there is and are not immutable.

What happens for a lot of dying people is that they are surrounded by denial. Because of the anxiety of the people around them they are treated as dead prematurely while still very much alive. Dying is not dead. Dying is a part of living. When we start to treat the person who is dying as a non-person, who shouldn't have feelings, who shouldn't be scared, who shouldn't be going through what he is going through, we collude in having him not live to his very last breath. If you do anything that can be important as a pastor and as a caring person, you can let the person know that you will not collude in that. I am not suggesting that you go in with a bulldozer and breach a patient's own denial. But it is your job with the dying to keep the door open for talking. It is important that you indicate your own continued openness to talking about *anything*. When those around the dying person want to keep the secret, it's for *their* own comfort. Isolating the critically or terminally ill so that they cannot talk about the most important experience in their lives makes them dead before their time. Your availability as clergy, your accessibility, your place as God's representative, your role in prayer give you added ability for those people to be able to share whatever they need to share with you.

It is of course important to respect the person's boundaries. You don't become more frank than is reasonable for a patient to accept at first blush. Nor do you simply go with your own curiosity.

A most egregious example of letting one's own needs and curiosity ride roughshod is one that happened to my good friend Reverend Richard Rush.[27] Thank God for his resources. He recalls:

---

27. Personal communication from a beloved friend, now a retired minister, who is one of the world's least self-righteous and most righteous people.

Late evening on a night in May 1999, I have just survived the second of two heart attacks, treated in different hospitals, less than a week apart (I had been discharged from the first hospital having successfully passed a low stress test and shown good results on ultra sound, standard EKG, and blood tests prior to discharge). The second MI (much more serious than the first) occurred within six hours of coming home. Frantic efforts on the part of the ambulance crew and the E.R. staff of the second (and nearer) hospital have stabilized me; I am inserted into a fleece-lined "body bag" preparatory to being transferred by emergency helicopter to Mary Hitchcock Hospital in Lebanon, NH (near Dartmouth College). There is a lull in the activity in the E.R. People are tidying up, congratulating each other on having stopped the MI, engaging in conversations in twos and threes around the room. I close my eyes to rest and am immediately aware of a female voice at my right ear saying, "Reverend Rush . . . may I ask you a question?" I look up and into a surprisingly young face of a uniformed nurse or nurses' aide. "Yes," say I.

"I just have to know . . . I'm terribly interested in this topic. . . . Are you having a 'Near Death Experience' right now?," she asks. "WWHHAATT?!," I retort. "Yes," she continues, and repeats the question. I am stunned and instantly offended. "You mean. . . . Am I seeing a bright light at the end of a long tunnel, and hearing heavenly music, and feeling the brush of angels' wings nearby and seeing figures of dead relatives coming toward me beckoning me forward . . . that kind of thing?" I ask incredulously.

"Yes! Yes!" she eagerly responds. I am thunderstruck. Then I am aware that I am angry. I want to find some snappy retort to put this creature in her place. "Let me take another look," I suggest, pausing to find the right retort. Aha! Got it. "Wait . . . wait . . . I see a kind of choir, wearing robes . . . standing in a single line facing me . . . swaying, chanting, clapping their hands in rhythm . . . they're saying something I think I can make out . . . it's . . . it's . . . 'We don't want him . . . we don't want him . . . we don't want him. . . .'"

She gasps, retreats. I chuckle inwardly and reclose my eyes. The sounds of a descending helicopter can be heard out in the parking lot of the hospital.

You don't do that or anything remotely approaching that. You allow for the limits of what the person is able to handle. But if your ears are open, and if you are listening carefully, attending to what *is not* being expressed as well as what *is* being expressed, you will know what that person is willing to share with you. You have to be secure in yourself, too, to know that you are willing to open up and talk about dying despite your own fear of your own death, which is where we are all coming from, because it is where we are all going to.

What that doctor back in the Mayo Clinic did was give my father the facts. My father was then able to deal with the facts as best he could, either to put them aside, or not to put them aside, to do what he could do in terms of his life. It was no longer a secret. No one had to go around pretending that he was going to get well tomorrow. No one had to treat him as already dead.

There was a woman in my congregation in her forties who had her breast removed, was assumed to be cured, and later had the cancer metastasize to her spine. Her husband and their two adult children, both in their early twenties, decided to keep this a secret from Mom in order to "protect" her. I walked into the hospital one day and around Mom's bed stood an assortment of sisters-in-law and brothers-in-law, all joking and laughing. "Don't worry, Mildred. You'll be fine. Everything will be OK. Just don't worry about it." There was a feigned and forced optimism. Mildred was going home the next day. There was nothing else that could be done in the hospital.

I said to her, "How are you, Millie?" She responded, "Are you going to tell me stories, Rabbi?" "No stories, Millie, but if you want to talk, I'm available." That was all I said. Those words opened the door to her sharing her thoughts and feelings with me and being able to have the family resume "live" contact with her in her remaining days.[28]

There were few other things in my ten years in the pulpit that were as important as that. Certainly, to that family there was nothing as important as that one statement that made being alive until the end possible. The statement was simple: "No stories, but if you want to talk, I'm available."

TALKING THE TALK

Beyond availability and presence, language is *the* one tool that pervades the rabbinic enterprise. How language is used influences virtually everything that goes on in the rabbinic day, and everyone the rabbi has contact with. Much has been learned about how language creates, molds, sustains, and changes "reality." Wise use of language in the context of symbolic exemplarhood is a powerful tool in curing and healing the ill and suffering.

---

28. A slightly fuller version of that episode is in Chapter 1.

For rabbis to have a profound effect, expertise in using language is crucial. Language is the ultimate symbolic tool in the hands of the ultimate symbolic people. Beyond believing that what they say and how they say it can make a positive difference in a person's physical health and well-being, rabbis need to use language (written as well as verbal) wisely. Language is to be used with rabbinic integrity and with respect for the integrity of those they are influencing. Rabbis need to learn to use language in a way so as to achieve specific goals. The ability to use language to seed ideas about healing, break non-useful expectancies and create useful ones, challenge deleterious belief systems, access alternate mental states to diminish pain, evoke and bring to the fore resources, strengthen the immune system, mobilize community support, and use prayer potently are all among the effective tools that involve using one's mouth with one's head. All or any of these can have a powerful influence on people's belief systems, and belief systems can cure and heal.

TOOLS FOR USING YOUR MOUTH WITH YOUR HEAD

Using language direct and indirect to normalize people's experience, to seed ideas and change frames by the elegant use of presupposition, linking, accessing resources, relabeling, playing with time frames, and using stories, each and all can impact on people's healing.

Given that the main means of communication the rabbi has available is language, and a main tool for using language, one's mouth, is with the rabbi at all times, rabbis need to use their mouth with their head.

What follows are a number of language tools which combined with rabbinic symbolic power can make a positive difference.

Normalize

We start with a don't: Don't tell people that they shouldn't think or feel the way they think or feel. Don't tell people not to feel something. Your success rate, if you are lucky, may approach 2 percent, not more. Telling people that they shouldn't feel or think something is a way of implying that something is wrong with them. It only serves to reduce their confidence. *People think and feel the way they think or feel.* To achieve rapport, which is indispensable, the rabbi needs to normalize other people's experience. People don't like to be told that their experience isn't appropriate to what is going on, that they shouldn't experience whatever they are experiencing. The unconscious mind does not and cannot process negatives. Telling a child,

"Don't spill the milk," or a lover, "Don't feel jealous," or a friend, "Don't eat dessert," or the classic example, "Don't under any circumstances think of the color green" will only help spill the milk, arouse jealousy, incite salivation, and get someone to think of green. The unconscious, being unable to process the absence of something, "a negative," will by dropping the negative hear what remains.

Normalize whatever it is they express. Let them know that they are not bad or foolish to think and feel the way they do. It is after all their experience. It is thereby human. Your response should normalize the thought/feeling and so bless it and welcome it into a human presence in some way. Normalizing reduces stress and makes them feel less vulnerable. "Me too" is a simple and very good way to normalize. "I felt that way when I . . ." "I understand that a lot of people have felt just what you feel." "It's natural to think that." "Some people deal with that by . . ." "Sarah told me the same thing and she came through OK." "I've had that feeling also." *Don't tell anyone what they should feel, instead of what they are feeling.*

Beware of pep talks. Though well meant, they are an elegant way of shutting off feelings. "You'll be fine." "Keep your chin up." "There's nothing to be upset about." "Count your blessings, other people are worse off than you are." Or, "How can you feel that way . . . when you have (fill in the blank) a lovely spouse, good children, live in such a nice place" or whatever. Be careful with, "You have so much to be thankful for." I recall telling a depressed young man in his thirties, complaining about his lack of female companionship, that after all he was a good-looking, sensitive person to whom women would naturally be attracted. He responded by saying, "That is exactly why I'm depressed. Telling me that only depresses me more."

Utilize Both Direct and Indirect Communication of Ideas Your Patient Needs

Being direct is terrific and is recommended as the first resort. Jack Riemer,[29] a rabbinic colleague at a seminar, gave a wonderful example of direct communication from a Symbolic Exemplar:

A widow came back from her husband's funeral and people had food set out and encouraged her to eat. In her grief she stubbornly refused. "I don't

---

29. One of America's great rabbis, in a personal communication.

want to eat ever again." The rabbi said, "You have to eat because the Torah said you have to eat." She would not have heard that from anybody
else but the rabbi, who clearly was authorized to speak the words of Torah. He was using his symbolic exemplarhood—the words that come from
his mouth are the words that come from on High.

Sometimes direct communication simply doesn't work because it
evokes too much conscious mind interference. "That may be what you think,
Rabbi, but I know otherwise," said overtly or in the interests of politeness
more often covertly. There are a multitude of ways of giving messages in the
presence of others that are indirect. All of us are always communicating both
directly and indirectly, whether we are aware of that or not. If you have to
use indirectness, do it in a sophisticated way and with integrity.

Be Willing to Experiment—Try Out Alternate Ways of Communicating

In December 1982, my cousin Srul, who was then eighty-two, had
just had a leg amputated due to diabetes. The medical staff discovered that
they hadn't done it right so they decided to do it again until they got it right.
They amputated again and charged him for two amputations while noting
that he still had one leg! My cousin Lenny, his son, called and said that Dad
was in a very bad way, suffering from some major infections and there was
some question as to whether he would live much longer. Lenny suggested
that I should go see cousin Srul. Perhaps I could do something. I drove the
hour and a half trip to Mt. Sinai Hospital, wondering all the way what I
might be able to do that would be of some use. Upon my arrival Srul greets
me with, "Oh my favorite cousin!" and promptly passes out. What was I
to do? Leaving and telling Lenny that I had been there crossed my mind
more than once. What also crossed my mind was that Srul was a regular at
my family's *Seder*[30] every year. I had also just read that when all other systems are gone, the auditory system is the last to go. "Well go for it," I said
in my head. Let's see what happens. I started to talk to the unconscious
body lying there about the last *Seder* he had attended, how he had sung
loudly, and had so much fun. For an hour and a half I described in detail
my plans for the first *Seder* following my divorce, which relatives would

---

30   The family festive meal, the first night of Passover.

be present, how I would enjoy his singing, what we would do, what I would do, what Lenny would do, at this Passover *Seder*. I repeated myself endlessly and to me what seemed boringly.

I never spoke to him about healing because, even if he were conscious, he would have doubted that he would heal because he felt so lousy. I never once mentioned that he would feel better. I never once mentioned that he would get well. I relentlessly kept talking about the *Seder*.

The *Seder* came three and a half months later, and Lenny told me that they couldn't keep him away. They pleaded with him that he was fresh out of the hospital, still ill, in a wheelchair and didn't need to take the sixty-mile trip. They didn't understand what was going on. He was adamant: "I've got to go to Jackie's *Seder*." My endless talking about the *Seder* not only had apparently motivated Srul, but had also *presupposed* that he was going to be healthy enough to be there.

It was an interesting experiment. Rabbis need to experiment. It will not only prevent boredom, but something new may be learned. Mistakes and seeming failures will happen. They are steps on the way to knowledge.

Some Indirect Ways

My Friend John[31]

People are often guarded when being talked to directly. As you talk they are processing internally, often fending off much of what is being said. This puts some limits on the effectiveness of direct communication. Listening to stories about others, they are often less guarded, and the message can be gotten through indirectly. So telling them about "my friend John," who went through something similar to what they are going through, and how "John" resolved his difficulties can be very powerful. The "story" is after all about someone else. It makes no overt demands on the listener, though it probably is of great interest as it in some ways parallels her experience. The expert communicator can take this a step further by marking the important part of his message out for the patient. This may be done by casually pointing at the patient, or with changes in voice or pace quite out of her conscious experience, as the "My friend John" story is told. Let us say that he wants

---

31. To the best of my knowledge, first described as a specific technique by the late Milton Erickson, one of the greatest therapist communicators of our time.

Jane to focus on learning something about the quality of her life from the medical procedure she is about to undergo. He can talk about someone he saw last year who had been through major surgery, and was amazed by how much she had learned that changed her life. As he is telling the "My friend John" tale, he can strengthen his message in the above ways, or mark it out for Jane by saying something like, "This is what she told me, *Jane.* Take good care of yourself!" He is directing an important message at his patient, avoiding conscious interference. He can well increase the chances of being heard.

Quotes

This brings us to delivering messages in quotes. When you use quotes, you are not delivering your message in a direct way to the person for whom it is intended. You may have noticed clear signs, like a vigorous negative shaking of the head, that the direct route is closed. Instead you tell them a story about something or someone else. Your way of delivering the message is by embedding it in the story and putting it into quotes. Let us say you want to tell Arthur to enjoy his life. You might say, "There was a guy who came to my office. I told him a lot of stories. The name of the guy was Fred. What I told him, Arthur, was 'enjoy your life'." The quote comes out of the story about Fred. It is not about Arthur and, therefore, Arthur is hopefully more open. It is delivered to Arthur in quotes. If she wants to suggest more rapid healing for Arthur, she can without using his name say, "And I said to him (not the intended messagee Arthur), you can really heal more quickly than you imagine."

Ricochet Shots

There are implicit rules of behavior in our society. One strong rule is that if you are not being spoken to you can't object. So if you want to pay your spouse a compliment, and you know that he has trouble hearing compliments, you can do it by talking to a third person in his hearing. "You know my husband is really an excellent cook and caregiver." You do it with a richochet shot. You are in the hospital room and you want to access the patient's resources, courage, ability to tolerate pain, or whatever. You find yourself with more than one person in the room. And there's a message you want to get to person X. You turn to Y and say something, overtly or covertly, about X. "It's astonishing what X has been able to overcome in her life. She handled her divorce in a way that showed great courage. She is a woman of fantastic strength." You are not talking to X. You are talking to Y. The message is not blocked as easily, and has a better chance of getting through.

Going Inside

The recipient of any communication has to go inside to make sense of what is being said. That that happens in a flash is true, yet there is no other way. Getting the other to do an internal (transderivational) search is a way of getting a message across without requiring that the other respond overtly to it. If you want your patient to think about something without asking her to do so, you can tell her about that "something" in your experience. If you want to find out about whether or not she has sibling support, you can talk about your own brother or sister and how he or she responded to you when you needed it. If you want her to start thinking about her relationship with her husband, you can start to talk about your spouse. You may want to explore something, see if she's ready to deal with it without committing yourself fully. You can explore whether she wants a fully straight report by talking about your own honesty, and times you didn't want to hear what people said to you, even if it was true. You don't have to ask overtly. You can get her to respond internally without being overt. The other will start to process it in her own head. There is little choice. Thus you can get the process started without invading her privacy.

If you make a statement like, "Modern women know how to ask doctors intelligent questions," that evokes an internal transderivational search to establish whether or not she falls into the category of "modern woman." If she does, and few would deny that they do, it becomes an implicit suggestion to ask intelligent questions. If you say in passing, "Jews really know how to make maximum use of the health care system," the first inner response is a search to make sense of the communication. "Who is being talked about?" Am I in that category? Since she is a Jew, it applies to her.

Stories

Stories are a powerful way of getting a message across. They have been, since our childhood, a way in which powerful messages about life, behavior, and interpersonal relationships were taught to us without our being told these things directly. We are trained to listen. We love to be absorbed by them. They are not directly about the patient, so he need not object directly. They are processed internally as in some way applicable. Yet they are "just stories," which means that the conscious mechanisms are not analyzing them as tightly.

Working with a local group of Protestant clergy in Fairfield, Connecticut, I suggested that using stories gets useful thinking processes going inside their congregants, without being direct. One of their aims was to increase Sunday attendance without saying some variant of, "You have to come to church every Sunday." One can tell a story about "my friend John" who after five years of churchgoing really found his life transformed. One may want to pace the receiving person a bit more than that. The receiver may think that churchgoing is medieval, irrelevant junk. The receiver may be paced by saying, "My friend John strongly objected to church and after five years of struggle, dragged there by his wife, he started to find, to his surprise and astonishment, occasional moments that touched him deeply. Eventually in search of more such moments, he came more regularly." One might choose not to talk directly about church attendance. One can start to talk about a subject more "distant." I chose as a teaching example one from my own life, though I used it in the third person. Using it in the third person was a way of making it more indirect. If it was first person, it would have been experienced quite differently. It was a "story" about a kid who loved basketball. It was very important for him to make his high school team. He would go out and practice in the winter with rain or even ice on the pavement with two pairs of gloves on. He cajoled his father to erect a pole with a regulation backboard and basket. He had his father make and put a smaller metal ring in the basket, which just fit the ball. He would shoot and shoot and shoot until he could finally, when he stepped to the foul line, sink three out of five shots with ease. At times he would remove the ring, which made shooting seem incredibly easier and satisfying. Periodically he would reinstall the "basket inside the basket" so he could hone his skills shooting at the tougher, smaller target and on and on. That may just be telling a story from one's own past, but that's a story about practice, commitment, skill, and satisfaction. It has seemingly nothing to do with church attendance. Yet it does. The preacher may have to tell fifteen of those before she achieves any results, but she needs to plant those seeds. We all come from traditions rich with those kinds of stories. We often ruin them and their effect by explaining them and their purpose. "I'm telling you this story because . . ." often serves to kill what we want to accomplish. We all too often do that in our sermons. We tell the story and then kill the unconscious message by explaining it or "the moral of the story is . . ." That's what we were taught to do! We were taught to take a text, make a proposition for a sermon, and then explain how this text applies to their lives today. That's probably why most of our sermonizing is ineffective. It is important to learn to play with stories. On the way to visiting someone who is ill, while you are driving in your car, think about what kind of story you can tell. Have some fun with it. Stories are great.

Seeding

John Chapman single-handedly changed the face of the Ohio River valley. Around 1800, carrying a cargo of apples brought from the orchards of the eastern states, he drifted down the Ohio River, stopping wherever he saw a likely spot to plant a few apple seeds. He planted those seeds in anyplace where there was a chance they might take. From his legendary efforts, multitudes of apple trees grew, and in American legend he became known as Johnny Appleseed.[32]

As a rabbi, think of yourself as a Johnny Appleseed of communication. As you talk you seed ideas all around you. Hopefully, you do that in "soil" you have already prepared verbally, increasing the chance the seeds will root and grow. Remember! Johnny Appleseed is known for those seeds that flourished, not for those that did not take. And it took a lot of seeding to get his celebrated results. The seemingly simple act of conversation can help prepare and affect the future you want for yourself and others. And remember further: Apple trees and their fruit did not happen all at once. Seeding takes time. Full-grown results are not instantaneous. Some seeds don't take, and one planting often is not enough. You have to spread a lot of seeds for some of them to take. And, for a seed to grow and bloom takes time. Your constant seeding shows your trust and expectation that some *will* take and your *expectation* is a powerful resource. Seeding ideas helps you and your patient get what you want, if it is worth having. Seeding, with the flexibility and trust of Johnny Appleseed, can increase the odds that what you want is going to happen in the future. Seeding is the planting of what you want to grow in that future. You change the future by seeding ideas, wherever and whenever you can. You affirm that your goal is going to happen and often is happening and that your conversational partner will eventually, when it has bloomed sufficiently, notice it. If you have seen still interval pictures of a seed developing into a plant you will know what I mean. It seems it all happened instantly. Yet it happened bit by bit and when you look after an interval—there it is!

There are a number of tools that will help you spread and seed ideas to maximize their effect. It will take practice to use them wisely and fluently.

Presuppositions, Wisely Used, a Powerful Tool

A presupposition is a statement which depends on something else being true for the statement to be true.

---

32. John Chapman, *Grolier Multimedia Encyclopedia*, 1995.

The something else is often not overtly referred to in what you say, but it must be or have happened for what you are saying to be true.

Some simple *presuppositions:*

If you say, "*I am driving to work,*" *presupposed* is that there is a car or other vehicle which you can drive, roads to drive on, and that you work.

If you say, "*I am going food shopping,*" *presupposed* is that there is something known as food, a place where food can be bought, and that you have money or a credit card or food stamps with which to buy food.

If a friend says, "*This book will improve your competency as a rabbi,*" she *presupposes* that you read English, and that you already have some degree of competency.

By implication something *else* has to be true for you to be able to drive or shop or read this. This *seems* absurdly simple. Using presuppositions is after all just the way we talk. We naturally use presuppositions without much thought. If we didn't, we would talk in such long sentences that we would never get to the point. "Let's get a cup of coffee," would turn into a sentence exploring the existence of coffee, of countries that produce it, the means of making it, how to brew it, and so on and so forth. If we didn't *presuppose* that there is coffee, the coffee would be cold by the time we got it.

The problem with the run-of-the-mill *presuppositions* we use all the time is that we use them randomly. They are seldom well aimed and timed so that we can effect systematic and useful change. Used artistically, well-honed, top-quality *presuppositions* can be extremely powerful engines of change.

Remember: By using statements that imply that something you *want* to be so is *already* there, you start to create a new reality. That reality need not be good or positive. *Presuppositions* are neutral and can be used to produce bad results as well as good ones. The difference is in your integrity, intention, goodwill, and training.

Presuppositions can be used in many useful settings.

If you say to a patient, "When we play tennis next year," you presuppose that your currently ill partner will be well enough to play and enjoy tennis. You are talking about a healed time *without* talking about the process of healing.

You are seeding an idea by presupposition.

If you tell your communication partner who is bedridden with the flu about going dancing next weekend, you have presupposed that he or she will be well. You are talking about the time he or she is well *without* talking about *getting* well. Dancing only makes sense if the person is well. So, getting well is presupposed. *You are seeding an idea* by presupposition.

When a friend is in the hospital and you talk about going on vacation with him, specifying all the wonderful experiences you'll have together, you are not only seeding a future pleasant idea but also presupposing that he will be healed from surgery. You are talking about a time when he is *well and not talking about getting well. You are seeding an idea* by presupposition.

Presuppositions often bypass the conscious mind and seed ideas at an unconscious level. In the above examples you are seeding ideas about health and bypassing conscious doubts. You may thereby be assisting their immune system in helping them get well. It is crucial to remember, *language evokes experience*. Experience can be pleasant or unpleasant. Seeding with a presupposition can be good or bad. What you say and how you say it can start the change even as you're talking.

Presuppositions That Avoid an Argument

These are presuppositions that enable you to avoid arguments about whether something is so or not. Let's say you want to attribute to and encourage in your patients something they would do well to focus on and access. That might be smartness, initiative, courage, pain tolerance, hope for the future, faith in their own immune system, their ability to make good choices, recognizing that those around them really care, etc. And you want to *avoid* discussion of or arguing about whether "that" is really so. You want it to be the case. You want it presupposed. To accomplish this the presuppositional use of *aware* or *realize* is useful. You might say to them, "Are you *aware* of how smart you are or how much initiative you demonstrated in asking the doctor that question? Do you *realize* the courage you showed by going through that procedure?" By focusing the discussion on their being *aware* of, or *realizing*, what you want to be the case, you are presupposing that your patients *are smart or courageous* or whatever. What is up for grabs and being talked about is whether they are *aware* of that "fact." You presuppose what you want to seed. If you say, "Are you aware of how much your spouse (family, hospital staff) love you?", their love is not the question, only the patient's awareness of how much. If I ask you, "Are you *aware* of how much you are learning about your resources for healing?", the resources for healing are presupposed. What is up for discussion is how much is being learned. The word *aware* is a very useful word. Other words useful in this way are *know, sense, perceive, comprehend, appreciate*.

Do you *realize* what you mean to your family?
I hope you *appreciate* how competent your caregivers are.

Do you *know* the wonderful reputation this hospital has for curing exactly your problem?

Do you *sense* how much you mean to our congregation?

Do you *really comprehend* how much she cares about you?

You'll be *surprised* at the good feelings you'll have sooner than you expect when you go home.

The important thing in this use is to take for granted a "reality" you want to seed, about healing, resources, etc. You use a word that focuses attention on something else so that the "reality" becomes presupposed. While you are talking about whether your communication partner *knows* or *realizes* or *senses* some "given," the reality of the "given" becomes presupposed.

More Presuppositions That Implant and Access Resources

If you say, "How would the old you have handled that loss, that illness, that change in life's abilities?", you are presupposing that there is a new you with resources and different characteristics, who behaves in a new and hopefully more useful way. *You are seeding an idea* by presupposition.

Many seriously ill people do not think that they have the resources to get better. Such beliefs only further degrade the immune system. As an elegant communicator you are trying to bypass conscious mind interference. One of the ideas you want to get across is that they have the resources to get better. Presuppositions are a way of talking to their unconscious mind. You can talk about a time in detail that presupposes a healed state, that they got to by courage, or an ability to heal quickly.

Presuppositions That Play with Time Frames

Some words help access resources by playing with time frames. They are simple words like *before, after, new, old, when, thus far,* and that short, powerful word *yet*.[33] All presuppose by setting a time limit on the perceived absence of resources, and imply a blossoming of resources.

Threatened by illness, patients will often focus on experiences of times they had difficulty coping. Those bad experiences, exacerbated by current fear, become current events. And useful resources that have been present in other circumstances in their lives are obscured. The rabbi needs to counteract that.

Yet is a powerful, instant tool.

---

33. Thanks to Bill O'Hanlon for much that is here.

For example, your patient says, "I can't stop being so frightened." You quickly respond, "I see you haven't been able to stop being frightened *yet*."

"So you haven't had any help *yet* . . ." presupposes that help is on the way.

If you say, "Well, you haven't been able to deal with your loss *yet*," you are presupposing that the patient *will* be able to deal with the loss. It just hasn't happened *yet*.

If you say, "So you haven't gotten the knack of lowering your anxiety *yet*," you are interrupting the thought/feeling that the patient will never be able to feel calm. You are presupposing that the patient will be able to be calmer. It will happen, only it has not happened *yet*.

"So you are not feeling better *yet*" presupposes and seeds feeling better.

Before and *after* are no slouches either. *Before* you do X presupposes that you will be doing X. "Before your healing gets underway you'll have to go through some discomfort" presupposes, paces, and seeds healing.

If you say to your patients, "Have you ever exercised before?" you are presupposing their exercising now. That is quite different from "Have you ever exercised?" Say the sentence again both ways and you will understand what I mean. One implies that they are exercising. The other does not. Just tacking on *before* makes a difference.

After you do X reflects a time when X has been accomplished. What is presupposed is that you or they *will* be doing item X. The only question is the timing. Remember, language evokes experience. Someone describes an exciting experience and you feel a tingle in your body. What you say and how you say it starts the change even as you're talking. By presupposing you create the expectancy that what you want will happen.

If you say, "*After* you have come out of surgery," you are presupposing that they have the resources and will survive the surgery.

When is useful, as in, "*When* you are feeling better," and presupposes that they will have a change in feelings.

If you hear, "I haven't ever been able to face difficult situations," the words "*thus far*" flash on your radar screen and you insert them into the conversation. "Thus far you haven't . . ."

"I always do X (a negative attribute)—*up to now*." "You've always done X" is your immediate response.

"I don't know what to do." You reply, "*So far* you haven't known what to do." "I'm very angry with all my doctors" leads to "You've been very angry with them *till now*."

When your patient says, "I can't stop doing it," or complains that "I don't know how," you *sort for tense* and put a time frame limit on it: *yet, up to now*, or, for a little variety, *thus far* or *till now*.

These are simple, yet powerful blocking tools where negative attributes need to be blocked and kept out of the present and the future. *Yet* and its relatives are exceptionally useful when the past is putting limitations on the present and the future. Use them to cultivate resources.

Questions That Presuppose and Open Possibilities

Wanting to create new realities, you do *not* ask questions that can be answered with a simple "yes" or "no." "No" answers especially can leave you stuck in the same old place. To avoid "yes" or "no," you think of what you presume and ask based on that presumption.

Asking patients, "Is there anything I can do for you?" risks their saying no, and together you have established conclusively that there is nothing you can do for them.

Rather, ask, "In what way can I help?" which means choosing among the different ways.

You do not ask, "Are you going to cooperate?"

You do ask, "How are you going to cooperate?"

You do not ask, "Do you want me to be of help?"

You do ask, "How do you want me to be of help?" *or* "In what way can I assist you?" *or* "What are you aware of that I can do for you?"

You do not ask, "Were there any times in the past that your faith helped you?" A "no" answer leaves you and the patient at a dead end. You do ask, "What were those times that your faith helped you get through times you didn't think you could get through? There must have been some! Let's search for them." Instead of asking, "Did you ever succeed in overcoming tough situations?" you ask, "What have you done that succeeded?"

In this mode you find ways of phrasing questions that *presuppose* something that you want to be there and, if there, can help your patients. Yes, you can help. Yes, faith made a difference. Yes, they have experienced success. Yes, there *is* something you can do for them. You do not ask a question that allows a straight "yes" or "no" answer, unless what you want *is* a yes or no answer. You use questioning to presuppose something you want that is worth having.

Presupposition is a very powerful tool. You, the intelligent reader reading this book and having read thus far (*your intelligence is presupposed*), can discern the similarity among the wide variety of things you can accomplish with presupposition.

Linking Whatever to Whatever

Linking is a simple to use, yet very powerful language tool. We use linkages all the time. The *mezuzah*[34] on the door, the *tzizit* on the *tallit*,[35] reminding us of all the commandments of God, are examples of linking. When you tie a string around your finger to remind yourself to call your aunt or to pick up something on the way home, you have, whether you realize it or not, resorted to the human capacity to link. Things that intrinsically have no relationship are tied together. Our parents used linking to educate us and to get us to do one thing or another. "When you finish your homework you will feel good" is a typical parental linkage, though not an elegant use since it is a bit chancy, if you didn't finish your homework.

What you are using is a language form known as an implied causative. Being more human than otherwise, implied causatives are deeply ingrained in us. We were all trained and raised with them, and indeed they seem hardwired into us. When someone suggests an outcome and links it to something inevitable in our experience, our awareness is pointed to the outcome that has been linked. The receptivity is there, built in. Linking's power is that *anything can be linked to anything.* You can create linkages between things that have *nothing* to do with each other. Linking works by implying that one thing will "cause" another. If X happens, then Y will inexorably follow.

You tie an outcome you want to something that is inevitable and/or verifiable in the experience of the person you are talking to. You make that which is inevitable the *cause* of what you want to seed (happen). There is no "real" relationship, only the one you say exists. Looking at the string around your finger does not *actually* remind you of anything, any more than finishing your homework actually *caused* you to feel good. You are making one thing contingent on another that is going to happen anyway. Linking is a superb tool for seeding ideas you want to get across.

Some examples of linking with the ill or those in crisis follow. Remember, you pick what you want to *seed* and link it to something *inevitable* in your partner's experience. (The *inevitable* is *italicized*. What you want to <u>seed</u> is <u>underlined</u>.)

As *you go in for procedure X* you'll be aware of your own <u>resources for healing</u>.

---

34. Parchment with scripture affixed to the doorpost of a Jewish home, a reminder of God's presence.

35. The prayer shawl's fringes are a reminder of God's commandments.

Sometime after I leave you'll become aware of the profound <u>courage</u> you have.

Your being so frightened is the first step your body is taking to <u>deal with this threat</u>.

When *springtime comes* you will feel <u>more energetic</u>.

As *you celebrate your next birthday* you will be aware of how much <u>healing has taken place</u>.

When *you wake up* you'll be aware that <u>the worst is behind you</u>.

When *you wake up* you'll be surprised at how <u>comfortable parts of you feel</u>.

No <u>gain</u> without *pain*.

Passing through the hospital you'll know <u>how much they can help you</u>.

You'll be surprised as *you wake up* how <u>well rested you'll feel</u>.

Getting through the surgery will <u>make you proud</u>.

You'll be <u>delightfully surprised</u> by how soon *after the treatment* you'll have some feelings of hunger.

Getting out of the house will make you know how well you've <u>tolerated</u> the *chemo*.

You know, Sarah, *when you go for that MRI tomorrow,* you'll find yourself <u>smiling</u> about the really bad jokes I told you.

As *you pass through the hospital on the gurney tomorrow morning* you'll be aware of <u>how funny things look from that angle</u>.

As *you see each member of your family visiting* you'll be aware of <u>how much they love you (or you love them)</u>.

As you can appreciate, *each visit to the hospital* will get you to <u>use linking</u>, an extraordinarily powerful and versatile tool to seed ideas your patients need.

Accessing Coping Skills

There are few more helpless feelings than being in the hospital. I had an experience when having a relatively minor procedure done. I was lying on the stretcher wearing a Johnny-coat that barely covered my wonderful legs and heard someone say, "Who is going to take this one over?" This one. "That's me she's talking about." It doesn't take much to imagine how vulnerable and depersonalized a patient feels when the diagnosis is serious and major procedures need to be done. Hospitals seem to be a conspiracy to deprive a patient of self-respect, any sense of one's ultimate worth, dignity, and especially coping skills. We know that lack of coping skills leads to depression. And depression leads to many bad things, including negatively affecting our immune system. We know that what we think directly impacts our health. Our beliefs make up our thinking and our thinking shapes our beliefs; all this touches our coping skills and our awareness of them, and our language and how we talk shapes all of the above.

We know that people who feel that they can *cope* do a lot better. One of the rabbi/chaplain's jobs in healing is to help access inner resources that have to do with coping. You want to bring the conversation around to coping mechanisms the patient has used before in coping with prior challenges successfully. Resources the person has used in the past are resources he needs now and needs to have cast into a future time frame. When you talk about the past you are talking about it in the present. The pulpit rabbi has a tremendous advantage over the medical community because the rabbi can know the person well, knowing the history and perhaps having witnessed examples of coping skills in the person's life. Even a hospital chaplain can spend some time getting history and getting to know her patient.

Among the questions the rabbi needs to ask are, What coping skills does the patient need now? How has the patient demonstrated these coping skills in the past? The task is to know about such skills, or in the absence of such knowledge hypothesize about them, by generalizing from shared human experience the coping skills patients must have demonstrated just to get to where they are today. There are always coping skills for them to access, including those they may not acknowledge or even recognize because the content or context in which they were demonstrated was different. By accessing resources that have to do with *coping*, we can help convert the negative stress of threat into a positive coping experience of challenge.

A coping skill might be something as simple and as seemingly complex as knowing that this situation is survivable, will end, and that there will be a time after surgery. Virtually all people have in their portfolio of experiences life events that seemed insurmountable, were endured, overcome, and became part of their past. That might be preparing for their Bar Mitzvah, military basic training, taking comprehensive exams, giving birth, learning how to read from the Torah as an adult, or preparation for some great event. The more you know about their history, the more you know about their coping. You can, by talking about those times, put them indirectly in touch with their coping skills. You access a time when *they* never thought they would get through but they did. If they did a great job of it, so much the better. But just getting through is enough. You don't *sabotage* your work "explaining" what you are doing and saying something such as "And the moral of the story is . . ." You just retell the story and you keep telling stories of situations when they got through. If you know virtually nothing about them, there are still universal experiences that they coped with. They learned to walk, to read, to ride a bike, to drive, to earn a living. All of these "universal" experiences needed coping skills. You can access resources more directly. You can say to someone you know, "You are a courageous guy. In all the twenty-five years that I've known you, I've been astonished by the courage you have shown and the challenges you've met, the obstacles you've overcome." When I was going through my divorce, my trusted good friend Rabbi Arnie Sher looked at me intently over the lunch we were sharing and said, "Bloom, you're a survivor." I was not at that moment feeling like I would make it, but he accessed that survivor part of me. What he planted and I started to access and focus on were other difficulties that I came through. You can be more indirect. If they are sports fans you can talk about how your and, even better, their favorite team was doing so badly and how they got through that bad spell. In your conversation you access parallels in their experience that have to do with coping. We have a tradition that is rich with stories about coping, everything from Isaac surviving his father's behavior to it taking forty years in the desert to get to the promised land.

To help their coping they may need to know that people love them. You can bring evidence from the present, their family's support, or from their past history. If such history is sparse you can tell stories about people you know who felt unloved, but there *were* people who loved them but they couldn't get through because the phone was busy. The coping skills a patient needs are many. Your task is to help access them.

Relabeling

What we call things makes a difference. As a rabbi you have special powers in this area. Relabeling is a relatively simple and most useful tool.

You can change experience by assigning things and processes new names. Relabeling an unpleasant process "growing pains" is a time-tested method and indeed can change the experience for both those going through the "pain" and those witnessing it. You can truthfully but unwisely say to a hurting friend, "Your healing will be long and difficult," in which case you will have labeled his healing and prepared him to experience a long and difficult time. Such is human nature! With a slight change you can still be truthful and by relabeling say, "Your healing will not be too easy." You have respected his felt experience, only what you have seeded is the "easy" label. Since the unconscious mind does not process negatives, what will be processed is the degree of easiness in the healing. "Your healing will be long and difficult" and "Your healing will not be too easy," though thought of as interchangeable, are two radically different communications. Hopefully, by choosing one over the other you can shift your patient's perception and consequently his experience.

A woman reports pain. How do you respond? Some of the classic useful ways are by distraction, relaxation, or medication. Language can assist in relieving pain by labeling it something else. She talks about pain and you respond by talking about discomfort. Discomfort is *different* from pain. It is more tolerable. If she responds by saying, "This is not discomfort, this is pain. You can't imagine how much it hurts!" you do not self-destruct. You accept her experience while not abandoning your efforts to change her experience. Perhaps you start to talk about those moments when she is not aware of the pain, or it is lessened and has moved in the direction of discomfort, and she feels just a bit better. You move by inches when you need to. You constantly, at a subtle level, and while respecting her experience, *never telling her that she shouldn't feel that way,* relabel and rename as you go. Use different nuanced words to shift the experience. You move pain into discomfort, discomfort into uncomfortable, and uncomfortable into not too pleasant. You can change slowly into gradual and gradual into not too quickly. Though that may not be too easy to do initially, with practice, you will gradually find yourself more adept at doing it.

Visiting my wife after surgery, I noticed that the nurse had put up on the wall opposite the bed a "pain" chart which was a face asking, "How is your pain today?" on a scale from one to ten. I suggested to her that the chart was a great idea but to change its name to a "discomfort" chart. I offered that people experience discomfort differently than pain. If the renaming takes, and it is worth a try, discomfort is a lot better than pain. We are talking about perception. And in pain as in pleasure and so much of life, perception is a very important factor. Any relabeling should be within the listener's experience and possiblities. That means that you cannot get sold on selling your name for their experience as the correct one. If you even were to succeed in doing that you will inevitably get the equivalent of buyer's remorse. Naming and relabeling should be in sync with both where you want things to go and your communication partner's realities.

Accessing Resources by Shifting Tenses

I used to feel bad.
I feel bad.
I am going to feel bad.
I will always feel bad.

Say each of the above out loud to yourself. You will notice a change in felt experience.

You used to do X is different experientially from *you are doing X*, which is experienced as different from *you will do X*, or *you always do X*, which merges past, present, and future.

Talking today about the past *makes the past present*. An example of that would be when my wife Ingrid and I went to the revival of Rodgers and Hammerstein's musical *Carousel* in the mid-1990s. My last association with *Carousel* was in 1958 when I saw *Carousel* with a woman whom I was dating. We broke up and I was depressed about the breakup. I used to play the recording in my dorm room over and over, feeling indescribably sad. I told Ingrid that *Carousel* reminded me of that old relationship. Ingrid asked, a tinge concerned, "Does it remind you of her now?" It clearly reminded me of her *now*. I did experience a tinge of melancholic feelings. In some ways that sadness long past became current events. When we talk *about* the past, we are talking *in* the present. And the more vivid and the more present tense you use the more current you make it. This part of being human can be turned into a useful tool. You start to access past *coping* and if your patient is willing to hear it, you start to shift to present tense. "You used to show courage" becomes "You show courage." Starting from the perspective of some past event you move it into the present and move the present into the future by seeding. "Down the line you will be doing this and that." You suggest to them that they are able to do what they did in the past both in the present and in the future. You can also access past happy and coping events, thus bringing them into the present and casting them into the future.

Past for Future Use Locker

The coping resources shown in the past are useful to note and employ as a resource to build on. You should know about such resources in your patient and they should be available to you at all times. If your patient's history has had good and positive aspects—and what person's past is totally absent of such—move those good memories, those positive resources from the past, into the present and seed them for the future.

When you overcame that life-threatening situation . . .
That time you were so strong, calm, and gentle . . .
When things were going smoothly and easily . . .
When we had fun doing X or Y . . .

These are the kinds of statements you store up for use.

If you are going for good stuff in the future, it is important to remember the good stuff in the past. Sometimes when we are in the midst of trouble, when we are hurt or angry, frightened or vulnerable, violated or weak in the *now*, we act as if good things never happened. Good things *did* happen, powerful resources were demonstrated by your patient, and you need to keep these elements of the *Past for Future Use* on your radar screen. You will have to change the tense to use it well, but at least you know it is there for your use now.

"When I am thinking about how years ago, I went to my first job interview, I always think about how encouraging you are." This is an example of shifting an attribute demonstrated in the past into the present. By using present (thinking) about past (encouraging) one starts gently to move a resource that was good in the past and to bring it forward. "I see in my mind's eye your shining face when I first told you I loved you." "I recall what a terrific person you are." These are a couple of examples of moving the past into the present.

You want the good parts of the past to be available to your patients as resources now and for seeding and planting them in the future, so when the future becomes the present, they will once again be there for those in your care. The good parts of the past are a terrific resource. Put hope from the good that did happen in the Past for Future Use Locker.

You can get really sophisticated with this, and learn to use language in inventive and resourceful ways. You can move into the future and put things in the past so that they become more "real" and "solid."

"When we call you to the Torah, what name will we have used?"

In our daily experience we feel most sure about what we perceive as having already happened, regardless of our tendency to distort the past. The future, even if vivid and specified, is experienced as more indefinite. After all, the future has *not* happened yet. You can't tell exactly what will happen. It can go a lot of different ways. So to make it more firm and clear you plant your feet firmly in the future and talk about what from the future present is the past. The past as we recall is what *really* happened. Try experimenting with that by using both the past and the future tenses. By shifting tenses in mid-sentence, you have talked about the future as if it is in the present tense, and you are talking about the past. You have mixed and shifted time frames to ensure that your presupposed message gets through. What have you not touched at all? You have not touched getting better. When things are in the past tense they take on greater reality because they *have* happened. You don't want to get into fights with people about their healing. You want to plant seeds. When you jump to the future, make sure you add a multitude of details whether using present or past tense. "After services as we went over to the kiddush table, the same old kiddush, you told me in detail that Joe was . . ." You appeal to all of the senses in exquisite detail. Details make things real.

"When you celebrate your twentieth anniversary [*first tense shift coming*], you will be looking back on this time and saying [*second tense shift coming*], those were tough years, but your loving each other got you through them so you can enjoy your life today."

Embedding

Embedding enables you to package the message you want to get across inside another, seemingly different message. It is a help in avoiding conscious mind confrontation. Confrontation, though highly valued, is often less than useful. Embedding helps you get a message across indirectly. You can embed messages in many different ways.

The Embedded Question

If you don't want no for an answer, you don't ask a question that can be answered by no. We have dealt with that earlier, but it's nice to have multiple ways to do things. You can *embed* the question. Though you will be delivering a statement without a question mark at the end of it, it will function as a question, but will *not* require a verbal answer from the other.

Some examples:

I wonder how much your faith will help you through this.
I ask myself in what way you will access resources for healing that
    are uniquely yours.
There are a variety of ways to get through this experience. I wonder
    what yours will be.
I wonder how long it will take for you to realize that I am good for
    you.
I wonder how much your spouse means to you.
I am curious whether you know how much the congregation misses
    you.
I ask myself just how you are going to meet this challenge.
I don't know how much of your courage you'll use to face this.
I don't know how much pleasure you'll have from going on Sunday.

I wonder just how much your love for your spouse this coming year
will help in how quickly you heal.
I wonder how you will heal in your own ways, unnoticeable as you
heal to others or even to yourself.

You may wonder as you read the above sentences whether you are
asking a question or are not asking a question. Remember that questions
are often experienced as "attacks" and we often feel immediately defensive. "Where did you get that dress?" or "Did you see my glasses?" will often
immediately evoke uncertainty in us as to whether we will give the "right"
answer. The embedded question helps you avoid that, while still asking a
question. Certainly, what you have said does not *require* an external answer by the other. It is only a statement about what you are wondering or
are curious about or have asked yourself. But it *will* be experienced by your
communication partner as a question, pondered internally and given at the
very least an internal answer. And internal answers provoke thought and
often lead to external statements which are not experienced as answering
someone else's question.

The Embedded Command/Suggestion

This is a way of putting a command or suggestion into a communication without the recipient experiencing it as a command or suggestion. Most
of us from childhood on do not like to be ordered to do something and many
of us get defensive when others suggest something to us. The embedded com-
mand/suggestion is a way of getting around that. A way to do that is to embed
the command/suggestion in a larger linguistic structure. You use a general
term that covers the group a person is a member of, while not referring to
them specifically, and describe authoritatively something that the group does,
is good at, etc.

Jews know how to ask doctors intelligent questions.
People can heal quickly.
Women find resources that men don't know about.

Or you can use it as part of a longer communication in which you
are telling a "story": . . . And I told him, "Jews know how to stand up to
doctors and get what they need."

The intonation, the look you give, the tone of voice you use, how you mark out the non-verbal components as applying to them will determine how much of a command this is.

Some examples (the *command* is in *italics*):

Speaking to a person scared of a procedure—"People *feel a surprising degree of calm* when they go through this."

Speaking to a group of senior citizens—"Mature people are able to *learn a great deal*."

Speaking to someone who is ill—"People can *heal quickly*."

Speaking to a female—"Women can *be sensitive* to what men need."

Speaking to a newly married man—"Men who care for their wives *do the dishes* without being asked."

To someone going to see the doctor—"Intelligent patients know how to *ask the right questions, and stand up for their rights*."

Since each of us must figure out when we hear a communication, who and what is being talked about and when we are included in the category of people referred to, the message with its included suggestion or command is directed at us, even though we are not specifically referred to. Am I included among Americans, mature people, women, men who care, intelligent patients? If so, the message is for me. And though not formally commanded, at least a powerful suggestion, perhaps even a command, has been made as to what I should do.

Using Your Own Experience to Embed Messages

This is another way of using a transderivational search.

My wife Ingrid during the early days of our relationship would use her own experience as a seeding embedder. Without telling me that I should not be feeling the way I was feeling, which was being enraged with my ex-wife, without telling me that I would feel better in a few years, she described her own experience. "What happens down the road is that I don't feel the way about my ex that I used to. Somehow I am able to talk to him about the kids and I'm not angry with him anymore." She kept seeding the idea that, with time, change in a specific direction would happen. I could not object because she wasn't talking about me. Yet she was also talking about my experience. Enough of it was the same. And the presupposition was that, with time, things change. This works well if you've been through the same experience and have come out OK.

These are only a few of the things a rabbi can do in pursuing curing and healing. Symbolic Exemplar of God who heals the ailing and frees the fettered,[36] author of both physical and spiritual restoring to health, who heals far beyond what the physician is capable of, and as Symbolic Exemplar of the people Israel, whose fervent prayer is רפאנו יי ונרפא,[37] heal us both physically and spiritually, and whose love, caring, and devotion provide support and community to the member who is ill. The rabbi has great power to heal people in all ways.

---

36. From the daily service.

37. From the daily service: Heal us Lord and we shall be healed.

12
*The Eulogy as a Tool in Grief Work**

Attitudes to which the bereaved are especially susceptible—denial, guilt, anger, and a sense of meaninglessness—can be dealt with through the sensitive and skillful use of the eulogy.

The eulogy is a duty no rabbi can escape. Sometimes it is an onerous one; sometimes it is a personally painful one. All too often in the busy pressure of our lives it becomes one of those things that we just must do, and that we take for granted. Yet it is one of the most significant things that we do. All too often we handle eulogies rather mechanically. We have a stock framework and sort of build from it, and wonder whether in those cases we do really help the family as much as we might.

If the eulogy can be significantly important, how then shall we write one to have the greatest effect? In a recent issue of *The American Rabbi*, Rabbi Robert Kahn[1] suggests that

> . . . a funeral sermon ought to begin with a text or parable. The wise preacher will begin his funeral discourse by seeking and selecting a text, whether from the Bible, Rabbinic literature or other sources on which to tie his thoughts.

---

*Published in *Pastoral Psychology*, Vol. 21, No. 209, December 1970, pp. 38–45.

1. Robert Kahn. "The Funeral Sermon." *The American Rabbi*, April 1967.

The author then goes on to point out that "there are a group of them [texts] which almost preach themselves."

Others, in writing about eulogies, point out how one must be scrupulous, be honest, how one must make sure to praise the dead, and other such words to the wise. Linn and Schwarz[2] note "that the function of the eulogy is to do honor to the dead and to comfort the bereaved." Perhaps here we might consider in what areas the bereaved need comforting and how the eulogy can help do this. Perhaps it might be better to know what the immediate needs are at the time of bereavement and how we can help meet them.

Lindemann,[3] Bowers,[4] Jackson,[5] and many other authors[6,7] point to a number of problems that the grieving person is faced with, problems with which we should be able to help the bereaved deal. First, there is reality—the fact that he who was, is no more; that dead is dead. There are great tendencies to deny the reality; to hope somehow that the deceased will walk into the room, that he will reappear. Lindemann points out that "there is in the early stages of mourning preoccupation with the image of the deceased." The feeling is present that if only one does not rearrange the world in which the deceased lived, does not move his clothes, or change his room, that somehow he will reappear.

The problem of guilt is one which every mourner must face. There is always a feeling of guilt toward the deceased. The mourner asks himself, "What is there that I could have done that might have changed all this; is there something more that I could have done; could I have been different?"

With guilt walks guilt's partner—anger. Anger is always present in bereavement. There is a feeling of hostility toward the dead, toward others in the environment, and often enough toward oneself. The widow may be angry with the husband who has "gone and left her." She may be angry with the doctor whom she may consider responsible for the death, and hostility may be directed in a great many areas. Linn and Schwarz[8] point out that:

---

2. L. Linn and L. W. Schwarz. *Psychiatry and Religious Experience*. New York: Random House, 1958.

3. Erich Lindemann. *Beyond Grief: Studies in Crisis Intervention*. Northvale, NJ: Jason Aronson, 1979.

4. Margaretta Bowers et al. *Counseling the Dying*. Nashville, TN: Thomas Nelson & Sons, 1964.

5. Edgar N. Jackson. *You and Your Grief*. Great Neck, NY: Channel Press, 1966.

6. H. Feifel. *The Meaning of Death*. New York: McGraw-Hill Book Co., 1959.

7. R. L. Fulton et al. *Death and Identity*. New York: John Wiley & Sons, Inc., 1965.

8. Linn and Schwarz, *Psychiatry and Religious Experience*.

A grieving person is always an angry person. Love is mingled with hate and the note of anger is unmistakable in the widow's weeping complaint about her husband—"Why did he do this to me?"

Another of the problems that the mourner must face is that there has occurred a loss in the meaningful patterns of his life. We might say a loss in what Lindemann calls "the patterns of conduct," which leads to a loss in patterns of meaning. The mourner questions whether life has a meaning, especially in the case of a sudden and tragic death. Anger and rage combine to make the question a more pointed one. Jackson[9] points out:

> When a man or woman in full vigor is stricken, we cannot accept it as natural or well-ordered. . . . Our grief is made more poignant by a lack of understanding; it is made sharper by the fact that it was unexpected. It seems more cruel because when death is sudden or untimely it always finds us in the midst of plans and hopes and dreams that must now be forever unfulfilled.

In many tragic deaths, finding the meaning is not easy, and yet somehow we know that humankind can only live, as Viktor Frankl has pointed out, by "looking to the future, sub-specie, *aeternatis aeternitatis*." We can only live with the sense that things have fallen into some kind of meaningful pattern. Meaning is also lost because people establish patterns of conduct around the lives of others—a wife gets used to her husband calling at lunchtime, or a husband gets used to a wife having dinner on the table. One gets accustomed to certain noises and movements associated with the dead partner, and these are now no longer into the ordered pattern of life. This loss of meaning and the very sudden adjustment of the pattern must be dealt with by the mourner if he is to pass through the mourning successfully.

All of these feelings must not only be recognized, but must be released. One of the great dangers is keeping a stiff upper lip, being overly poised, and thereby not coming to grips with these feelings, some of which are difficult for a person to face up to in our society. One does not wish to be on the verge of hallucinations in denying the death of someone; one does not enjoy being burdened with guilt. One feels uncomfortable with anger and rage directed against God or man, and one wants to find some kind of mean-

---

9. Jackson, *You and Your Grief.*

ing and not to admit that there is no meaning; and so, their feelings must be gotten out. The literature in so many places has pointed out that such feelings must not be denied and no matter how they come pouring forth, they must be given that opportunity.

One last word about the needs of the grief-stricken, tied indeed to a good deal that has just been said, and that is that there must be some hope for the future, that this is not the end. Freud[10] has been quoted as saying:

> Our conscious behavior . . . relates to the problem of death almost exactly as primitive man. In this respect, as many others, primitive man lives unchanged and unconscious. Our unconscious does not believe in its own death; it behaves as if it were immortal.

And here, too, the rabbi must meet an important need—the need that man feels that this cannot be the end, that in both the life of his beloved and in his own life, there is something beyond or indeed implicit in the death of anyone else—his own mortality. This is often one of the most difficult things for many rabbis to do, and yet it is the very basic assumption of our calling that life is something beyond the processes that go on here on earth.

These are some of the things involved in the psychodynamics of mourning, and some in which the eulogy can be of great help to the mourner. I believe the eulogy can and should be built to help meet these various needs which are both general in that they apply to most mourners, and specific in that each case experiences this individuality. As a teacher of mine at Seminary pointed out: "For you it may be funeral number 893; for them it is number one." Jackson[11] points to this obliquely when he lists the things a funeral must do:

> It must face the reality of death and (must) help free you from guilt and self-condemnation; it must help you express your feelings and direct you beyond the death of the loved one to the responsibilities of life. It must in a personal way help you to face a crisis with dignity and courage and provide an environment where loving friends and relatives can give you the help you need to face the future with strength and courage, and the fu-

---

10. Sigmund Freud. "Thoughts on War and Death." Standard Edition, Volume XIV, 1957, p. 296. Quoted in Linn and Schwarz, *Psychiatry and Religious Experience*, p. 187.

11. Jackson, *You and Your Grief.*

neral also gives testimony that there is a tomorrow; others have faced and lived through it with grief, and they point the way for you.

The part of the funeral that can most do this is the eulogy. It can be structured in such a way as to directly help the bereaved find significant comfort and to make a beginning of grief work.

Morris went into the hospital for minor surgery. I received a call the next day that he had died on the operating table. He had been a vice-president of the Synagogue, quite active, a small, wiry, very healthy young man who everyone thought would live to be a very old age. His wife was shocked, as were all who knew him. She went through almost all of the stages of mourning. She experienced real hostility and anger about which she felt quite guilty and had to be assured again and again that the rabbi did not blame her for her anger; that he understood that she would be angry with everyone including God himself. She had been deeply dependent on her husband during the thirteen years of their marriage. During that time, they had grown closer and closer in a very affectionate way. She tended strongly to deny his death and indeed, any time she heard the sound of a truck near the window, she would open the curtain, expecting to see him at the wheel. She refused utterly to remove any of his clothing, and brought herself only with great difficulty to dispose of some of those things—his tools and other effects—which represented him to her. She had some guilt feelings toward her husband, mingled with anger. The guilt was transferred onto others and she would say, "I didn't drive him the way the other women drive their husbands. I never asked for what they all asked of their husbands." And she would come back to that theme again and again. "What do they want from their husbands; don't they realize how lucky they are; why do they push them so hard?"

And yet, she was terribly embarrassed to admit that she was a bit angry also with her husband for leaving her. "Rabbi, I guess it's all right that I'm sometimes angry with Morris"—and she shared her children's feeling when they questioned why he died so suddenly—"We could have arranged one day when we would have treated him like a king." Or she would ask me again and again, "You know I always loved him, didn't you, Rabbi? And he was always sure of my love. He told you that, didn't he?" The anger that went along with the guilt was directed in fairly healthy ways, though she was a bit uncomfortable with it. She would question why she had this bitterness toward others and whether she was always going to have it. Was it all right to be angry with her husband? Why was she so bitter toward the doctor who operated and toward other women who didn't appreciate their husbands?

Morris had always prided himself on being a European husband who made all of the important decisions in the home. She had focused her life around him and in over-solicitous care of their children. Suddenly having him dead tore this pattern apart and took a great portion of the meaning out of her life. The one reality that she turned to again and again to restore some meaning was the children. "If I didn't have the children, I don't know what I'd do."

Though she grasped at this, she still had a sense of great emptiness about any meaning in life, especially with the sudden death. She searched first for an answer from the doctors on why it had happened; there was none; the loss of meaning was more poignant, since during the last few years they had grown closer, understanding each other more and more, and as she put it, "Morris himself had really achieved a certain degree of equanimity these last two years. He used to tell me that he now knows what it was he wanted in life, and now this had to happen." Among the problems that the eulogy had to face was that a life so suddenly cut off at its peak still had a meaning.

In this situation, I knew the deceased well; yet in most situations the same can be done. Sometimes careful listening to what the family has to say can point the way for us to give specific validation to these general needs. Even when one comes in "cold," one can assume that the overwhelming majority of these needs must be handled, and that handling them, and understanding the guilt and rage and the other factors involved, would be the preferred way to help the family, rather than using or weaving a framework out of a text.

In this eulogy, the beginning dealt with the reality and the suddenness of the death by not mincing words as to what had happened, but indicating that he who was so alive was now just so dead; that he was dead and that he would not be back. This was experienced with great shock by all of those assembled, including the rabbi, who was a friend of his, and if the rabbi could express his own brokenheartedness, it might be permissible for others to express their feelings. The guilt was dealt with by pointing out to the widow that all that he had become would have been impossible without her love and affection; that indeed, their relationship and how much they meant to each other, and what she gave him, was something he could have found nowhere else. The attempt was made also to give some meaning to this and to discern a meaningful pattern in his life, and indeed it was phrased just in that way: "To give some meaning to the years that you shared." The pattern that dominated was the pattern of growth. This young man who had little in the way of a propitious background had accomplished a great deal and had grown all along the way. The institution from which he was being buried—the Synagogue—had been the format for that growth, and the people who were there for the funeral in droves had all been touched by his life. His life had not just passed through this world meaninglessly—there was indeed a pattern of growth and significance to it. One also had the obligation to point out that there was a pattern of meaning that had to be picked up now; a pattern to which the wife was going to respond—and that was, of course, the children. This had to be done obliquely because there was another child involved from a previous marriage who was a source of some embarrassment in this situation. The very fact that so many had come to the funeral, so many were able to cry, was not unimportant. The inclusion in the eulogy of a personal mention by one person who would never have come to the widow's mind as being a mourner—the maintenance man at the synagogue—helped to comfort and sustain her and made her sensitive to some of the meaning in her husband's life. The maintenance man had depended on her husband and considered him to be an indispensable part of the synagogue life. I also wanted to touch on the eternal, and this was done by picking up a reference that the deceased had made to a prayer that he had not said since wartime, one that is used in Judaism as the confessional.

By using that allusion and indicating that we prayed that the God of Israel walks with him today was a recognition of one of the basic needs we all have. We want to know that our life does not just end with the grave. It is not always easy for clergymen who have a liberal bent in religion to affirm with the same simplistic faith what generations before have affirmed, but some reference to it must be made, and it can be said in good conscience and in a way that is helpful to the bereaved.

THE EULOGY

Morris was so young, so vigorous, so full of the future, and now he's dead. He had plans and hopes, and now they are not to be, for his life was cut short so suddenly and so meaninglessly. How shall we speak today of a sorrow beyond words. Yet speak we must, though the words be but a pale reflection of the reality that was his life, and the depth of our sorrow.

I was his rabbi. More than that, he and I were friends. It was a friendship that grew over the years. He built the house my wife and I lived in, and if it was once, it was a hundred times that he was there to check something, fix something, or add something, and share a cup of coffee and some conversation with us. We used to sit on Friday evenings in my study or stand in the night air when it was warm, and talk of all those things friends talk of. We talked of our families and friends, our jobs and frustrations, of the synagogue, its people, its problems, and its prospects; we talked of little things and big ones; we talked of all the things that make a friendship. There was in our relationship a clarity and an honesty that makes friends of people. He got to know me and I got to know him; he taught me and I taught him. Our paths crossed in a thousand ways these past seven years—and now he is gone. What shall I say, more than that I am brokenhearted.

He loved this synagogue and he gave to it unstintingly. He gave of himself and his resources. This pulpit, the one there which the cantor uses, the ark behind us—are all the work of his hands. You could always call on Morris to bring, to fix, to set up, and to do, all with no fuss and a genuine cheerfulness. We can count on the fingers of our hands the times he was not here on a Friday night these past seven years. We can count on the fingers of our hands the times the Kiddush[12] cup was not filled by him, the synagogue not opened and closed by him, a mourner not escorted into the service by him. He touched the lives of many of you here this day. He called you to see if you had a High Holyday[13] ticket, and he made sure that there was a place for you to sit when you came here. He called asking you to do the *mitzvah*[14] of making a *minyan*[15] at a house of mourning. It will indeed seem strange this coming week not having Morris organize and guarantee that the *minyan* and prayerbooks will be there. He met with those of you who had young people preparing for Bar Mitzvah,[16] explaining before the Bar Mitzvah what had to be done and what you could expect. He gave of his own money; he sold raffle tickets, whatever there was in the synagogue that needed doing—Morris could be turned to, to help do it. It might be the planting of the front lawn or in the last note that was in his box, getting Molly some bolts for the Memorial Board. Things big or little, all of these he did without complaining,

---

12. Kiddush, the prayer that sanctifies the holy day, is traditionally recited over a cup of wine.

13. The High Holydays occurring in the fall include Rosh Hashanah (New Year) and Yom Kippur (Day of Atonement).

14. Fulfilling God's command.

15. The quorum of ten needed for a service.

16. At age thirteen, a young person is obligated for the fulfillment of God's commands. This occasion is marked by being called to the reading of the Torah, and participating as an "adult" in the service.

with cheerfulness and without the need of great recognition, for as he used to say, he got his wages in other ways. It was as if he had taken as his life's motto the words of Rabbi Tarfon, who used to say:

> The day is short and there is much work to be done. The laborers are sluggish, the reward is great, and the Master is insistent. You are not obliged to complete the task, but neither are you free to desist from it.[17]

Indeed, his day was too short, but he did much with it and it is our task to complete the work. In this synagogue he will be missed. His place will not be easily filled.

And it must be said that this synagogue did something for him. It gave him something unique and he knew it and treasured it. It helped him to grow and to realize so much of the man that he was. He became Ritual Chairman almost by mistake and he would be the first to tell you that he knew nothing of ritual when he started. What he did have was a truck that could be used to move chairs at a time when we were at the Masonic Temple and needed chairs moved, and so he would tell you he was chosen. Had you told him that he would one day be a pillar of the synagogue, he would have chuckled; and yet he was to become that. He grew into the role. He developed tact and confidence, the ability to overcome his innate nervousness and to speak before the Board and others—and gradually he had the awareness that something indeed had happened to him, and that this congregation had grown to love and respect him. He and I spoke of it just two weeks ago in one of our Friday evening chats. He told me of the wages he got from all his work here and what it meant to be an officer and a vice-president of the congregation. He spoke of his happiness and how he sensed that people felt positive and good towards him, and how much this meant to him. It meant a great deal to him. And it didn't happen in a day; but it did happen; and it happened here. In recent months—just in the last few weeks—he was moving into new areas, concerned with the congregation's future and trying to guarantee that future. For him indeed, this was Beth El, the House of God, in the most meaningful sense; for here the Almighty helped him discover the person within, the Morris we came to cherish.

The boy who came from Austria bore the name of Israel, and like his namesake of biblical times, he was destined to struggle and to be scared,

---

17. Teaching of the Sages 2:20–21.

but like him, he was destined to grow. Perhaps the great pattern of his life was the pattern of growth. He grew, he was defeated, but he dusted off his pants and got up and plunged ahead to more growth. Circumstance dictated that his education be limited, but he became a voracious reader. The bookshelf of his home is packed with books which he had read—history was a favorite. Morris grew. In his personal and business life, when he was down, he got up and moved on. There was a restlessness and a searching in him which did not guarantee that growth would be easy, but made it happen, and over the years he found himself. The boy who came from Austria grew over the years into a man—a man of whom one might say, in the words of Shakespeare: ". . . the elements so mixed in him, that nature might stand up and say to all the world: This was a man." His life was cut short just when things were best. Part of our great pain is that this growth was so suddenly and abruptly stopped, just when it seemed in fullest bloom.

> The pine hath a thousand years,
> The rose but a day
> But the pine with its thousand years
> Glories not o'er the rose with its day,
> If each but serves its purpose
> Ere it passes away.

Susan, I know what Morris meant to you. I know also what you and the children meant to him. We know that though we share your pain, there is no pain like yours, and we know of his concern and of his love for you. But I think you should know this—you gave a great deal to him. Your love and devotion were priceless to him. You gave him stability and understanding. Perhaps the greatest thing of all was the ever-growing sense of communication that was taking place between you and that bode so well for the future. A good marriage is one in which life gets better and fuller, and together, you and he were discovering that. That knowledge will not lessen your pain, but it will give meaning to the years you shared. We pray that you might be able to take up the strands that are left in a garment so abruptly torn, and weave them into a pattern of meaning.

I loved him and many of us here loved him. We want you to know that. Many have become aware of the myriad ways in which he touched their lives; and he touched many lives in many ways that we don't know. Many of us can only echo the words of Mr. Dave Greaves who said: "I have lost a good friend, for he was a man who cared."

I saw him at the hospital Thursday night. He was chipper and looking ahead, though underneath no doubt not a little nervous about the routine surgery. He told me that he had said the *Shema*[18] the night before, for
the first time since his Air Force service. And I'm sure he said it Thursday
night as well. I hope and pray that the God of Israel walks with him today,
and that he will find a just reward for all that he was and some recompense
for all that he might have been; and I pray that the God of Israel and all men—
who is the *Baal Nechamot*[19] —may comfort us in our sorrow; help us to en-
dure our pain and move on in testimony to all that was good in his life.

This eulogy is not an unusual or an outstanding one, but it does show
how the eulogy can be a means of providing the framework for the grief work
that must be done. That work is a major task for anyone who has suffered
loss. To base the eulogy on a text and then weave it into something that fits
the text more than the situation may be clever, but not helpful. The religious leader has a unique chance to bring the insights and meanings of his
position and his knowledge to the task of comforting the mourner; that is,
he can do it if he knows what the needs are and how he can build the eulogy
to meet those needs.

The eulogy can be a vital tool. It is a public expression, one in which
others concur by their very presence, and one which can provide a framework for dealing with the reality, as well as the guilt, anger, rage involved,
and the ultimate meaning of life and death. It can be a source of hope and
courage to the family and to the mourners who must go on. It is not a task
that can be taken too lightly. It is not one that can only be learned in a homiletics course. What we need is a deeper understanding of the psychodynamics of mourning and how the eulogy can meet those needs to perform one of
the most important jobs that we are called upon to do.

---

18. "Hear, O Israel: The Lord is Our God, the Lord Alone," watchword of the faith and
the traditional bedtime prayer.

19. God is known as the master of dispensing comfort.

13
Ten Commandments for Rabbis

Rabbi Arnold Sher, Placement Director of the Central Conference of American Rabbis, invited the author to conduct a workshop for rabbis who were in transition, taking on new congregations. These ten commandments differ somewhat from the original which appeared at Sinai instantaneously amidst thunder and lightning. They were heard for the first time in 1999 in Pittsburgh, Pennsylvania. With apologies to the original Author, they had been gestating in the author's mind for a while. They bear repeating as do the original. They are intended for rabbi communicators both in transition and those settled in their job. The Oral Torah is available by contacting the earthly author. We will do and we will listen is clearly the order of the day. Following these commandments can make life as a Symbolic Exemplar easier.

I   You are unique. Each congregant is unique. Your congregation is unique. True and certain this is. Each and All of you operate from distinct maps of reality, none of which is real. Know for sure that you have been redeemed from the serfdom of old certainties and brought to the possibilities of a land flowing with milk and honey.

II Do not worship your idols of the past or denigrate theirs. Honor others' "reality." Meet others, congregant or congregation, at their model of the world, not yours. Difference is a challenge that will help you learn and grow. Grasp and enter their "reality." Use their reality in moving to new outcomes worth having.

III   Respect *all* messages from your congregation. They are making the best choice available to them at the moment. Remember that the iniquity of their ancestors is upon them and upon you to the third and fourth generations.

IV   You shall believe that your congregation wants to be Jewish, understanding, cooperative, generous, and helpful. They *are there!* They have all the resources needed to live a full Jewish life. Observing this commandment will assist you in accessing their presently hidden attributes.

V   Remember to *separate* their *intention* from their *behavior*—
        THAT YOU MAY BE LONG IN THE RABBINATE.

VI   You shall be clear, positive, and specific in your desired outcomes: That you may know where you are going and if you get there. That you may not wander in the desert for forty years.

VII   You shall dovetail your desired outcomes with your congregants' desired outcomes, though this may mean taking small steps. You shall honor small steps, remembering how far YOU have come in the desert with small steps.

VIII   You shall not kill or diminish My Image in yourself or others by blaming. You shall always remember: *The meaning of your communication is in the outcome and <u>not</u> in your intention.* This tool is given to you that you may enhance, and not destroy.

IX   You shall maximize your flexibility. You shall not mistake rigidity for truth, nor obstinacy for integrity. You shall have multiple ways and great patience to communicate with and so influence your congregation.

X   You shall not covet being anyone else! You shall not covet your neighbor's talent, abilities, personality, or any attribute that is theirs.
        YOU ARE ALL YOU NEED TO BE
    and that is more than enough. You know more than you think you know. Besides, you can't be them anyhow! You and they, each of you and both of you, all are blessed by God, being created [*Tzelem*⇔*Neshamah*]. Keep your and their [*Tzelem*⇔*Neshamah*] in view, at hand, and attended to at all times. So may you live long and prosper in the vineyard of the Lord.

III

The Rabbi as Symbol
in the Public Arena

14
*Journey to Understanding**

In May, 1963, nineteen members of The Rabbinical Assembly were sent by the Assembly's convention as its delegation to Birmingham, Alabama, during the racial crisis in that city. (For a description of that delegation's experiences, see "To Birmingham, and Back," by Andre Ungar, Conservative Judaism, Volume XVIII, No. 1, Fall 1963.) Jack H Bloom, Rabbi of Congregation Beth El, Fairfield, Connecticut, was a member of that delegation. His article was adapted from the paper he presented to the Conference on the Moral Implications of the Rabbinate, held under the auspices of the Herbert H. Lehman Institute of Ethics in the Fall of 1963.

Why did I go? I am not by nature a hero or a martyr. And it would have been easy not to go, simply by not volunteering. I was frightened. I wasn't convinced that going was the best course of action. No impelling ethical urge or impassioned oratory moved me. I had no history of standing up for Negro rights. I had never before publicly committed myself that way. I don't like to stick my neck out. But something within me made it impossible for me not to go.

When other northern clergymen had gone south, I had privately and publicly questioned the wisdom of their act. I remember thinking such thoughts as: They don't understand the southern situation. They can't solve

*Published in *Conservative Judaism*, Vol. XIX, No. 4, Summer 1965, pp. 11–16.

the problem. When they return, the local people will be left to pick up the pieces. Is it just a publicity stunt? And what about the situation in the North? What were they doing in their own communities? On the other hand, I think, I envied the fact that they stood by their convictions on this issue. One week before the Rabbinical Assembly Convention sent the delegation, Rabbi Richard Israel of Yale, who had been in an Albany, Georgia jail, asked me if he could add me to the list of people making themselves available in the event that the Southern Christian Leadership Conference needed volunteers for Birmingham. He must have sensed my ambivalence, for he told me that I didn't have to commit myself on the spot. I could decide when and if I was called.

At the convention, when the critical situation in Birmingham was being discussed, I finally felt that I should put up or shut up. I had often preached that, "There comes a time when a man must take a stand." Here was a chance for me to take a clear-cut stand, to get off the fence we all so diplomatically sit on propped up by many "ifs" and "buts." History was being made. Why shouldn't I be part of it? There was some ego satisfaction involved in this chance to do something significant. And there was a desire to see what the fuss was all about, to savor the experience as an experience. My studies and my religious training made my going possible, but that was just a part of my motivation. I went for a variety of reasons, and for no one's sake but my own.

I suspect that most of those who went shared my ambivalence on the racial issue. To a large extent, we had the same background. I was raised in a northern, "lily-white," Jewish middle-class home. I had been taught that all men are brothers, that America is the land of the free. But the only Negroes I knew were the maid who came to our house on Friday, and the men who washed my father's car. These were real to some extent; the others were abstractions. I could not conceive of the Negro as a brother, certainly not these Negroes. The verbal commitment of the environment demanded racial equality, but on the hidden agenda the Negro remained a *schvartzer*.[1] And there was in my life little occasion to test the verbal commitment. Like the environment, I was ambivalent. The Negro was equal, of course, but. . . . Is he ready for equality? And what about the high crime rate? Will the value of my property go down if a Negro moves in? Would you want your daughter to marry a Negro? I shared the image and stereotypes of the Negro com-

---

1. Yiddish slang for a black person.

mon to the liberal white community. I did not experience the Negro as a living brother. At best, he was an abstraction.

At one point in the trip our group's ambivalence came to the surface. One hour away from the convention we wondered what we were doing anyway. And if Everett Gendler (one of the group's leaders) couldn't tell us exactly why we were going, we would really let him have it! At this point laughter broke the inner tension we all felt. Something had driven us all. Something made us want to act. Everett, of course, couldn't tell us. The problem was ours. We were ambivalent, and we would have to resolve our feelings in Birmingham. After two days there, we knew why we had come and why we could go again.

The two days in Birmingham were the most significant religious experience of my life. The act of going was to have an effect on my inner ethical and emotional structure almost like that of a conversion. In one area of my life, an ethical position became real. Much that happened to me cannot be communicated, because I cannot verbalize it. Part of what I can verbalize may help to clarify how the change came about. During two days in Birmingham, the Negro became real, his problem became real, and religion generally and Judaism specifically assumed a great contemporary role.

I had been in Birmingham for half an hour when I experienced an infinitesimal part of what it means to be a Negro in America today. As a Jew, it had not happened to me. I was denied entry to hotels and motels. And not because they were full.

Arriving in Birmingham at 3:30 A.M., we were taken to the A. O. Gaston Motel (a Negro motel), where there was room for fifteen men. Four of us would have to go elsewhere. The four of us from Connecticut volunteered, and we were taken by our Negro hosts to a new motel whose parking lot was one-quarter full. Rabbi Harry Zwelling walked in to ask the clerk if he had room for four men. The clerk noted who had brought us and asked if we had reservations. When he told him that we didn't, he stated that he was filled to capacity. This happened a second time. We then decided that we really needed a night's sleep. We parked at some distance from another hotel and sent Rabbi Stanley Kessler to get rooms for us. He returned saying that all was arranged. Then the clerk ran out of the front door. He had either been called by one of the motels that had turned us down, or somehow had heard that we had been brought by Negroes. "I'm terribly sorry, but I've made a mistake. The rooms have been reserved for a late flight that's coming in in a little while. I won't be able to have you tonight." He was polite, but we still didn't have a place to sleep. Our hosts then told us that there was no point looking any further because "every place in Birmingham knows you're looking for a place to sleep. You'd do just as well to come back to our motel and we'll see what we can do." It was only a sample, but it made quite a difference to me.

I don't think I'll ever get over what happened when we entered a Negro church that first sweltering evening. A rally was in progress as the nineteen of us filed in with our *kippot* (skullcaps) on. Everyone stood up for "our rabbis," applauding, shouting, reaching out to touch us, calling out, "God bless you," "Thank you for coming," asking for our autographs. There wasn't a dry eye among us when the packed church improvised a new verse for the freedom song, "We Shall Overcome." It began, "The rabbis are with us." We spoke to the rally. We heard others speak. We found ourselves participants in a religious movement, a movement in which our own experience meant a great deal. We knew what freedom meant; we knew what it was to stand alone; we knew what it meant to be an outsider, to be alienated, and that night this knowledge was real. The fact that the lineal descendants of the people of the Exodus were there meant a great deal. We heard others say that non-violence is the way, that one must understand the man behind the hose. We heard hope, not anger, and we heard that one must witness with the body when other avenues are closed. Much became real that night. Religion became a vital force. And especially did the lessons of my own tradition come alive. Responsibility, conquering one's impulses, loving one's neighbor, the *Seder*[2] lesson, caring for one's fellow, all became alive. Through religion, the tragedy of the American Negro could be translated into an opportunity. And Judaism had something to say to them and to me. My history was theirs, for now they were marching to freedom and somehow they would negotiate a miraculous passage through a sea of hate and indifference, to a new future.

During those days the Negro became real, he became an individual. In part this resulted from the fact that we were living within a Negro community. We met all kinds of people: a bright youngster whose life ambition was to be a secretary because her sense of reality told her that a Negro could hope for nothing higher; a Negro dentist telling us about the problems of voter registration; a college student involved in the demonstrations who remembered seeing a neighbor lynched outside her window; a youngster asking, "Are all Jews rabbis?"; a Negro out of work, living in the most segregated community of the South, telling us that he stayed in Birmingham be-

---

2. The family festival meal, the first night of Passover.

cause it was "home." Human contacts played a part, but the clincher was that for the first time I was led by Negroes. They were in charge, they gave the orders and the leadership. These were not maids and car washers who formed my subconscious image of the Negro. They included Martin Luther King, who explained to us that segregation changes an I–Thou relationship into an I–It relationship, and a young graduate of the College of the City of New York, who sensitively and brilliantly explained the situation to us that first morning during *minyan*[3] as we sat around the table in *tallis*[4] and *tefillin*,[5] and a young minister, himself not far out of his teens, leading a meeting of teenagers with a *kippah* on his head, and a young man from Detroit who in a tense situation patiently explored with us what might be the most dignified and effective way to demonstrate, and a weekend minister who led a group of his people through a barricade of police fire hoses. These men brought about a change in me. They radically and for all time altered my image of the Negro. Negroes were no longer an abstraction. They were no longer a sociological problem. They were real.

I really knew that this had happened only after my return to Connecticut. I was watching a baseball game on TV. For the first time, Al Jackson, a Negro pitcher, was a person, not a Negro; a pitcher, not an oddity. I had become a bit more color-blind. I saw a Negro couple walking with their child and they looked different to me than they had before Birmingham. I bought some recording tape at a store in Harlem and the clerk was just a clerk to me. Suddenly missing were my self-pleased condescending tone of voice, the feeling of being so nice to treat a Negro as an equal, the over-solicitousness that often creeps into the behavior of liberal whites when dealing with Negroes.

The act of going to Birmingham changed me. To some extent I empathized with the Negro; my religious commitment was really relevant and the Negro was my brother.

Because I am a rabbi, when I went, my congregation went with me— some willingly, some not willingly, but everyone went. People ask, "What about the North?" I am convinced that the effect at home was as significant as the effect down South. Some of my congregants were proud. Some wished they could have gone. A few volunteered for next time. One said, "Rabbi,

---

3. The quorum of ten needed for a service.

4. A prayer shawl.

5. Phylacteries with which traditional Jews wrap head and arm at morning services.

you not only pray for our country, you're doing something about it." I can't say that wasn't nice to hear. Some were glad it was Jews who went. Some thought it was brave. Many hedged. They wondered if it was wise. Would it really help, and after all, what about the North? But it made many face up to their feelings about Negroes. My going had forced the issue on them. "Rabbi, I like Negroes but . . ." was a reaction I heard many times in the weeks that followed. Sometimes it had to do with a man who had hired a Negro TV repair man whom no one would allow into their home even though he was an expert repairman. What should his employer do? Sometimes it had to do with housing or intelligence or crime, and once it was our synagogue maintenance man whose children had been beaten up and robbed by four Negro thugs. The fact of my going had forced the issue on many people. It had to be discussed. The results of the discussions varied, but a problem which could all too easily be ignored in a white suburban community had to be recognized. As one congregant put it when I asked him what effect my trip had on the congregation, "It woke everyone up to the problem."

As a unit the congregation itself woke up to the problem for the first time. It asked the head of the local intergroup council to speak about the problems that might be coming in our own community. In arranging the program, the chairman told me, "Rabbi, we know where you stand." Knowing where the rabbi stands makes a difference in a congregation, and a thousand sermons could not communicate what one act did. The teenagers responded with a typical "What can we do to help?"

In the general community my going made a difference. The battle is in the North as well as in the South, and in any battle an evaluation must be made of who is on which side. By going, I publicly committed myself to one side. As a result, the forces for open housing and intergroup cooperation have felt free to count me on that side and to call on me for help. And by implication I have no doubt committed my congregation.

The fact that I went as part of a delegation meant a great deal within and without my congregation. Many of my congregants felt this was a responsible act because it was sponsored by a national group. These included many who felt that the previous actions had been little more than publicity stunts. A Negro porter approached one of my congregants and told him how glad he was that the Jews had now publicly taken sides in this issue by sending their rabbis down to Birmingham. He was glad that the Jews had done this, for they understood what it meant to be persecuted as a minority.

If my trip had no effect other than that shown in the following incident I think it would have been worth it. One of my congregants is a contractor who employs day labor. He is a devoted, hard-working congregant who in four years has missed one Friday evening service. He has heard me speak about a multitude of topics, including Little Rock, Arkansas and Jackson, Mississippi. About a week after I came back from Birmingham and had spoken about the trip in the synagogue, he came to me and said, "You know, Rabbi, this is kind of hard to admit . . . this week, as a result of what you did, I employed some Negroes on the job, and you know something, for the first time in my life I didn't see them as monkeys."

Like it or not, the rabbi is a symbol of what ought to be important. When he succeeds in resolving his own ambivalence on an issue of crucial importance, the "ought" implicit in his communal existence becomes that much clearer. The act of going to Birmingham was not insignificant. It can be disagreed with, but not discounted. Our people are told that they ought to do many things. One ought to do something about civil rights. One ought to live more Jewishly. One ought to realize that the two are the same. The fact that these "oughts" came from a rabbi's Jewish background was not lost on the congregation. As a result of this experience the "ought" became a little more imperative.

In describing Moses' role in bringing the Jews out of Egypt, the Reverend Ralph Abernathy, at a rally held in a church, told of Moses' call to lead his people to freedom. Homiletically he described Moses' encounter with a bush that could not be consumed, and he told how Moses avoided looking at the bush. God finally forced Moses to look at the bush, and Moses looked at it until the fire of that bush burned within him. With that fire within, Moses took the first steps towards redeeming his people. I think that many of us felt that way about our "Birmingham" experience. Something about those days transformed our brothers' burning desire for freedom and equality into a flame burning within us.

15
A Refusenik Odyssey[1]

After signing our wills in Steve Saft's[2] office, we proceeded to
Kennedy airport to catch Swissair. Arriving in Zurich, we found a day room
where we could take a nap. We arrived in Moscow at a quarter to four in the
afternoon. The border guard in his little booth looked at me very carefully.
After much looking at me and the photograph, he asked me to take my hat
off, checked me, double-checked me (I twirled my mustache to indicate that
I was the same person as in the picture), and then allowed me through. We
had some trouble getting luggage carts. Ingrid and I decided to go through
customs individually with separate bags to maximize the chance of everything being OK and minimize their perception of the amount of stuff we were
bringing in. In going through customs, I noted who was doing the inspect-
ing, and chose the inspector who, due to his sparse hair, seemed to be the
oldest and who was indeed in charge. I got on the end of his line hoping he
would want to finish with me quickly to go for "tea" break. He checked my
small green carry-on bag which had in it more camera supplies than one can

---

1. Written with the gracious assistance of my wife, Ingrid, upon our return from the USSR
in 1988. Ingrid's words, taken from a tape she helped make, are indicated in the text. It
obviously could not be published at the time. It is presented here as it was written then.

2. Our lawyer for this purpose.

imagine. It contained Dick Rush's[3] two cameras with extra zoom lenses, a Polaroid camera, my own camera and another extra zoom, and a walkman. It was jam-packed. He double x-rayed it, but never asked me to open it. He did ask me to open one suitcase, took out a number of the children's books by Isaac Bashevis Singer that the Conference[4] had asked me to take, picked up Chaim Potok's book *Wanderings—History of the Jews*, and said to me, pointing to the cover, "This is the wall of Christ?!" I pleaded total non-understanding of what he was saying. He finally put the books back after some further inspection, and did *not* mark the back of our visa with anything that had to be taken out of the country. Luckily, he did not come upon the oranges from Israel that I had stashed in another suitcase. Ingrid had already passed through without any problem and without having any bag opened at all, although I wasn't sure of that. I had a fantasy of her being interrogated by the KGB,[5] all the contents of her suitcases strewn on the floor, explaining who Sean Bloom in Dublin[6] was and why he was getting twenty-five Superdance USA T-shirts, lipsticks, jeans, and eyeshadow for his Bar Mitzvah.

> INGRID: Since I acted totally incompetent in not knowing what I was doing they might have let me through without too many problems.

I changed some money at the bank as per instructions, $100 and got the almost ludicrous sum of sixty rubles for it. At the black market rate, which we did not trade at all, we would have gotten three to four hundred rubles.

We then proceeded to the Intourist desk and they whisked us quickly in a rather old, black Volga sedan right in to Moscow to the Intourist Hotel. We went in along very, very wide roads, the car just cruising along. We realized only later that the pedestrians had all been put underground. They were in underpasses. Our car seemed just to move along with virtually no red lights until we arrived at the hotel. Ingrid, on the way in, made the first

---

3. The Reverend Richard Rush, a Protestant minister and beloved personal friend, and friend of our people, who contributed many items for us to take into the Soviet Union. He appears in this book in another context in Chapter 11.

4. The Conference on Soviet Jewry, under whose auspices and direction we were going.

5. The Soviet secret police.

6. "Sean" was Ingrid's creation, and had he existed, he would have had one swell Bar Mitzvah.

use of our cigarette lighters. We had picked up a couple of packs of disposable cigarette lighters in our last couple of days in the States that cost $2.99 for five. They had a two-dollar rebate on them so each one ended up costing twenty cents. I suppose we chose giving lighters instead of cigarettes as tips to put the burden of guilt on the person lighting up. To watch the car driver's face light up when he was given this "souvenir" of America was an incredible experience that was repeated each time we dispensed a lighter. Lipstick, eyeshadow, and pantyhose served the same purpose for the women. At the Intourist, we were assigned to room 1830 which luckily turned out to have a tired, old Toshiba air conditioner. 1830 was a two-room suite, one front room and one room for the bedroom since we had deluxe accommodations by Russian standards. There was a little refrigerator in the suite. We discovered just how lucky we were to have the Toshiba when we learned from sweltering tourists that most of the rooms in the hotel were not air conditioned and we were in the middle of a heat wave with temperatures in the nineties. It also served as a noise cover for us when we inadvertently blurted out something that we should not have said. Throughout the entire stay in Moscow and Leningrad, the temperature varied in the ninety- to the 100-degree range. A day or two in Leningrad the temperature was over 100 degrees.

After settling in a bit I went out of the hotel to make my first call as instructed. Of course in looking for a phone booth, I turned right and had to walk about three blocks. A left turn (no doubt appropriate in the USSR) would have revealed a booth thirty yards away. I thought a one-kopec piece, given to me by Steve and Marilyn Kushner[7] at our Stateside briefing, would do the job. Sometimes it did. Sometimes not. Only later did I realize that it took two kopecs at least to do the job and the fact that one sometimes worked was a comment on the vagaries of the telephone system. Valery Engel, the historian, was to be my first contact. I did know his number, 281–1772, by heart (secret agent 0018). I had with me a credit card–sized, secret coded computer address list which broke down completely a couple of days later. I was reduced to using Ingrid's tiny white address book in which we had coded the phone numbers. I called and a woman answered who did not speak English very well, and said that Valery would be back at 9 P.M. I then tried to reach Yuri Sokol and some others but got no answer. To pass the time and

---

7. My colleague, Rabbi Steven Kushner, and his wife, Marilyn, had briefed us extensively on what we needed and how to behave while inside the USSR. Their advice was extremely competent and useful.

do our tourist thing, we walked into Red Square, viewed the Kremlin, saw those onion churches—St. Basil's—all of which were just across the street. It turns out that Lenin's tomb and the Kremlin were closed because of the nineteenth party congress. We have no recollection of eating supper that day or, for that matter, other days as well. Bringing food stuff into Russia was very, very useful. We laughed when we packed peanut butter, Triscuits, granola bars, dried fruit, etc., yet those items turned out to be invaluable. It's very hard to find places to eat in this large metropolis. I went back to call Engel again, did reach him, and he said that he could see me Sunday night at 9 o'clock. I got a bit nervous because, though it was only two days later, it seemed an eon away. I decided to call someone else and tried Chelenov[8]— no answer—tried Gutman—no answer—and then tried Sergey Vainshtein. I reached Sergey, but he was leaving for Leningrad the next day for vacation. It seemed everyone, even Refuseniks, were on vacation. In some desperation, I asked him if there was someone he would suggest that I might contact. He then suggested that I call Lev Gorodetsky.[9] I called and his wife answered. She arranged for us to meet at metro station "Aeroport" the next morning at 9:30 A.M. in the center of the platform. I asked how we would recognize him. She assured me that he would recognize us. At 9:30 the next morning we went to the center of that specific platform, when a man in a rather beaten-up shirt and old Levi corduroy pants approached with a big button on his chest that said "כשר".[10] He introduced himself and we proceeded to walk with him to his apartment. On the way Lev told us that his father had not agreed to his leaving for Israel so he was not technically a "Refusenik," but he was hopeful that his father would eventually do that and he could then apply to leave. He told us that he was the president of the *Igud Hamorim*, a group of fifty Hebrew teachers in the Soviet Union, who had organized themselves to improve the teaching of Hebrew and history, and fight *Neshirah* (going to America instead of Israel). I thought that although he was not on my list, he was a lucky find, what with my own background in Jewish education and being Chairman of the Bureau of Jewish Education in Bridgeport. When we entered his rather modest apartment, we met his wife, Katya, also

---

8. Chelenov, Gutman, and Vainsthein were all active in the Refusenik movement, and were on my list to contact.

9. Lev, though not on my list, was a truly lucky find. We have remained friends to this day.

10. Hebrew for kosher.

a Hebrew teacher, who was nine plus months pregnant. We talked about Hebrew teaching, their hope for legalization, their teaching needs, the fact that Eugene Voronov had been given a license as a Hebrew teacher but that it was then withdrawn illegally. Lev is forty-one and this is his second marriage. Katya has two children, a four-year-old with Lev and a ten-year-old from a previous marriage. The hope is that this new baby will be a boy. (A boy, Ariel, was born on July 5, 1988.) They served us something that looked like orange drink. We started to distribute Dick Rush's Pentax camera, one of the Superdance USA T-shirts, one of Irwin Peck's[11] gold necklaces, some cosmetics, some pantyhose, and a tape player, though it became quite clear that the tape player was the least useful of things because what they needed were tape recorders (more about that later), a couple of tapes, a blouse, magic markers, and so on. Lev asked the camera's worth so that he could know how much it would bring to forward the work. Lev's single-minded thrust was to forward the work of the *Igud Hamorim*. He was concerned that the National Conference start to deal with the *Igud Hamorim* in a coherent way to get supplies, lectures, and equipment to them. Lev had been a computer engineer before he got into Hebrew teaching a number of years back. The copy of *Byte* magazine that was originally for someone else was given to him and he was thrilled. Lev was also thrilled when I gave him a picture of my daughter Rachel and myself in front of an armored personnel carrier.[12] He said he wanted the picture to reassure parents about their kids being in the army in Israel. He found it very important and inspiring that Rachel had such a wonderful experience in the Israel Defense Forces. He was also especially pleased that, as it worked out, the copy of the *Jerusalem Post* I gave him had a long article about Natan Sharansky, who had been a personal friend of Lev years earlier. As far as my lecturing and teaching were concerned, it turned out that the clandestine Hebrew schools, like the Refuseniks who went to their dachas, also broke for the summer so teaching was not possible.

Ingrid had indicated some interest in an artist that Pat O'Reagan from her school knew. Lev called and we were on our way to an artist's studio to

---

11. Irwin, a jeweler, generously supplied Stars of David and *Chais*, חי.

12. Rachel went to Israel to escape the divorce her mother and I were going through. She joined the army and had a distinguished career being chosen Outstanding Recruit and, later, Outstanding Soldier. She was given a prime assignment teaching young men to drive and handle armored personnel carriers.

see some magnificent work. One print Lev actually ended up buying as a gift for us by paying what turned out to be the awesome sum of seventy-five rubles. We found that these Refuseniks and activists were very, very generous. The artist inscribed his work for us. It was an interesting studio in that there was some wonderful primitive work that the artist refused to sell and some work that was a gross satire on Stalin, which we thought was dangerous but they did not. He put in our package a picture of one of the satires of Stalin and Lev wanted that picture for himself. It had, as matter of fact, been printed in *Der Spiegel*, a German magazine.

Lev asked us to meet again at 4:00 P.M. at a different subway station, Mayakovskaya, and said he would take us to something special.

We returned to our hotel after noon and ate at the buffet. Ingrid then inquired at the desk as to the location of the nearest Marriage Palace. The information clerk was stunned that any foreign tourist would be interested in that, but did locate where the nearest Marriage Palace was and told us how to get there by metro.

> INGRID: About the Marriage Palace. A wedding takes place in a designated area every ten or fifteen minutes. We had a bit of difficulty finding the Marriage Palace at first, but we just followed brides and that's how we got there. They had several rooms that had nice upholstered furniture and somebody would stand there and ask for the couple's vows and they would get their official stamp and a short lecture. We asked a young couple if they wanted us to take their Polaroid picture. They were really rather frightened and didn't want to do it until Jack took a picture of me and handed it to me rather ostentatiously. They then said OK and we took Polaroid pictures of one of the couples. They were absolutely excited to get them, gathering around the developing picture and chatting rapidly about it. It may have been the most exciting thing that had happened to them on that day besides getting married. We also gave the bride lipstick and the groom a lighter. Their faces lit up and they felt that they were really great presents. In return, the bride's family gave me a rose, which I am seen with in the picture that Jack took in front of the Marriage Palace.

We met Lev at four o'clock that afternoon in the center of Mayakovskaya metro station. The metro is an absolutely fantastic underground achievment. Ingrid noted that it does have the feeling of the old movie *Metropolis*. Moving hordes of blank-faced workers to and fro. It is filled with polished marble statuary and runs very efficiently. We met Lev there and went to what was going to be a demonstration at Pushkin Square. I asked Lev how he knew there was going to be a demonstration. "Word of mouth" was his reply. As it was described by some of our new friends, Pushkin Square is now Moscow's Hyde Park. There were people there with banners asking for new political parties to be formed and hordes and hordes of police controlling the crowds in a more benign way than ever before. The police showed no weapons of any kind, but they did sometimes carry people away into vans and moved them with some force. There were a lot of loudspeakers interrupting the orators, drowning them out, saying, "You have to clear out . . . time has elapsed." These demonstrations would not have been possible a year or two ago. It was in Pushkin Square that we met Victor, who was an important part of our experience in Russia. He is a stocky, heavy-bearded, Georgian fellow who looked like he could have ridden out of the Cuban hills with Castro. He wore a blue hat imprinted with "Sun Country" on it. He had studied English for only two months. He was sometimes hard to understand. He sometimes had to search for words, but he was going to speak English no matter what. He made himself remarkably well understood.

> INGRID: As a foreign language teacher I learned something very important. Victor said that he has no passive knowledge of English, he uses everything, every word and that I think is a wonderful statement.

We did not know just how important Victor would be to us. He was apparently Lev's protégé. He indicated to us that although he was from Teblisi in Georgia, he was going to Leningrad where his wife, whom he had married a short time ago, lived. Victor is twenty-eight and his wife, Elena, whom we met later, is twenty-one. Now, you would not want to meet Victor in a dark alley. He is very husky, very strong, and afraid of no one. Like Nachman of Bratslav, he says, "It is crucial to not be afraid."

At Pushkin Square, we had our first contact with *Pamyat* (Memory), which is an anti-Semitic Russian group devoted to purging Russia of the Jews, claiming that all that is bad in Russia has happened because of the Jews. Glasnost has given them free speech as well. We watched Victor and a young man from Baku, who had already received permission to leave, get into discussions with these people. Some had small tape recorders to tape the ongoing argument. The demonstration overall was really very impressive. The Jews at Pushkin Square with us, some of them identified by the Mogen Davids around their necks, were all astonished at how much arguing and discussing was going on.

INGRID: Unfortunately, I found the need to go to a bathroom at that point
and it was almost impossible to find such luxury. Lev took me through
I don't know how many streets to find a public bathroom that was closed
for the day or week . . . who knows. We then continued quite a distance to come to a hotel. Natives of Russia are not allowed to go into
these hotels. We had a confrontation there so that I could go in and
use the facilities. Life is very difficult in Russia.

After being with Victor and this other young man from Baku for some
time, we became concerned that Lev and Ingrid had been blocked off by the
police and could not get back to us. The police would systematically block
off a part of the crowd, letting people out, but not back in at a specific point.
They finally did return from their jaunt through the city of Moscow in search
of sanitary facilities.

INGRID: Lev pretended that he was my Intourist guide, and I screamed
that my husband was in there and we were able then to return.

You can imagine an Intourist guide with a big button on his chest
saying Kosher in Hebrew letters!

We then went to a park to relax a bit. We had one of the endless,
endless, endless glasses of apple juice which we had in Moscow. Lev treated
us to that apple juice followed by some ice cream. We sat in the park observing busloads of blue-shirted police. Lev said that he would make contact
with Ilana Marmostein,[13] whom I had called the night before unsuccessfully,
and that Victor would take us to Ilana's house since Lev couldn't be away
from his nine plus months pregnant wife very often. We started off on a fifty-
minute trip to Ilana's. First by metro, then by tram, and then walking. Ilana's
apartment, actually her mother's, was in the poorest condition of any that
we saw. Her own apartment she said was across town, but she lived with her
mother who had not given her permission to emigrate. Her mother had retired only this last month and was now considering giving the precious OK.
We met Ilana, a chubby, vivacious thirty-two-year-old woman who works
as an editor. Her life and love is Hebrew and teaching it. She learned Hebrew from a teacher who already emigrated. She is, from what we could see,
a consummate Hebrew teacher. She showed us, over tea and a table full of

---

13. A devoted early childhood Hebrew teacher.

cheese and cookies and such which hardly anybody touched, some of her work: poems in Hebrew and translations into English, songs she had written, and photos of Purimspiels[14] in her apartment. She sang us a little song about teaching an in-utero child to be quiet in this difficult land.

> INGRID: She was also saying that her salary as an editor was very minimal, and as a Hebrew teacher she said that you don't get the same fees that other teachers get for tutoring. It is more like an almost voluntary position for voluntary payment.

It was Ilana who made what seemed to be a totally absurd request, which was to get a machine for dubbing tapes at the Beriozka, the hard currency store. I was getting increasingly concerned that the kind of stuff we had brought in for Hebrew teaching was not as useful as it might have been. The same way that I had dubbed my tapes at home, they could have dubbed their tapes. If we had brought in a small tape recorder, a little larger than a walkman, a pair of them, one for Ingrid, one for me, with headphones and some patch cords, and an AC converter/transformer, we would have had a usable tape-dubbing unit with no problem.

> INGRID: She also wanted an invitation to Israel sent to her official address.

We then returned with Victor to our hotel. It was a long trip on the bus on this late summer night in Moscow. Victor said as we rode the bus that he was not very Shabbat and I wondered what it meant to him to be Shabbat. We later discovered the depth of his commitment. He talked about his library in Leningrad and how they lent Haggadahs for Passover and hoped that they would be returned. I told him that I had brought a Haggadah along to add to his storehouse. We talked about Teblisi Jewish life, his affection for Lev, his thoughts about Jewish life in Russia, and were soon back at the Intourist, having passed Pushkin Square, where the demonstration begun seven hours earlier was still under way. We shared some Pepsi with him and he was off to Leningrad. He gave us his number which we could reach when we arrived there. We asked him to contact Mikhail Blank[15] so that they could set up some teaching sessions which was, after all, what I had come for. We

---

14. Light plays and farces presented for the holiday of Purim.

15. A Refusenik who was on my Leningrad list.

shook hands, hugged each other—*Shalom*, till Wednesday. Ingrid and I trudged upstairs to the tenth-floor tea room to get a bite to eat. We had had no supper. So ended one of the longest and fullest days I can imagine.

Sunday morning we started out to walk past the Kremlin and down to where the Intourist desk had showed us the synagogue was. It was even starred on their map, a six-pointed star no less. We started out the wrong way and ended up walking past the Kremlin and along the Moscow River, which looked polluted. It was hot and dusty. We came to the synagogue and went inside, where we were met by a little old man. We had been told that any donations to the synagogue were pointless since they "go directly to Gorbachev." We saw a man who was fairly young and vigorous, apparently the Chief Rabbi of Moscow, but he too is a KGB informant. We went into the main synagogue, tried to take a couple pictures of the inside, when a young man by the name of Roman Barulin came over to us wearing, of all things, a Eugene O'Neill Theater Center (located in Connecticut) T-shirt . He started to tell us about his own status. He was beginning to learn some Torah. His father did not live with his mother, and refused to give him permission to emigrate, but he was still trying to get out. He also wanted a letter of invitation. He was a short, rather charming young man making his way in English. I wondered about the presence of informers and such in the synagogue, but it turned out that Roman knew Lev, and Lev did indeed vouch for him the next time we saw him. We pulled out of our bag of supplies another Superdance USA T-shirt. It is useful to understand that the T-shirts apparently go for between fifty and sixty rubles there, so it's quite a significant gift. We also gave him one of the little silver Mogen Davids that Irwin Peck had given us. His face absolutely lit up. We took pictures with him and he gave us a big hug and kiss at the end of our visit.

> INGRID: He also told us about anti-Semitism in Moscow; that the Jewish cemetery had been vandalized and that very few policemen came to do anything about it. In fact, they suspect that the police may have been helping in the matter. We heard a lot about anti-Semitism.

He also mentioned that people had come to throw stones at the synagogue and that they had to organize an informal patrol there.

We spent the rest of the time Sunday afternoon walking around, looking at the Bolshoi theater, going under underpasses, up from underpasses, down into underpasses, walking around the Kremlin, and that kind of thing. Much of anything of interest was blocked off because of the nineteenth party congress.

Then came one of the fun experiences in our Russian odyssey, the kind of experience couples tell each other in the presence of the grandchildren. Ingrid had found the Operetta Theatre which was a significant "turn on" for her. We were looking at the billboard of the Operetta Theatre, trying to figure out what was playing. A woman with a minimal knowledge of English said she could not translate the whole thing, but the last word was mouse. Ingrid convincingly said, "I don't know any operetta that has the word mouse in it."

> INGRID: Later on I went back to the Intourist office at the hotel and had them translate to me what was playing. I found out that it was *Die Fledermaus* by Johann Strauss. That is my favorite operetta of all and I got very excited about the whole thing. They had first given me a different date for the *Die schoen Galathee* by Franz von Suppe, which played that night and I went to that too. I love opera and operetta.

But she's *never* heard of any operetta with the word mouse in it!

> INGRID: Plus, the Intourist office does not push this because usually tourists are not interested in it. Theater is very cheap there and if you go by yourself to the theater you can manage to get tickets in all kinds of different ways. Intourist would rather sell you the Bolshoi theater where you can see an opera for forty or fifty bucks. Actually, the best tickets are somewhere around three or four rubles apiece if you go there personally, if you can get the tickets. We figured out that there are little pavilions where you can buy theater tickets. They actually post them on the window. They hang them facing outside so you can see what kind of tickets are available. I did get tickets to the *Die schoen Galathee* that night. Of course I also tried hard to find tickets to *Die Fledermaus*. We went from ticket booth to ticket booth and all they had were some for seventy kopecs each which would have put us in the peanut gallery, right under the roof. We bought two of the seventy-kopec tickets and continued to search. They were sold out on Sunday for Monday night's performance.

Sunday night I went to meet Valery Engel, as per my first phone call. (I had also tried the first night to reach Sokol, but had been hung up on a couple of times. Apparently he is a very difficult man according to the others. Though to this moment, I'm not sure if it was he who yelled at me. His books were given to Lev for transmission to him.) Someone had given me incorrect instructions on the metro and I was half an hour late. It turns out that I was also half an hour late at the wrong stop. I phoned Engel. He asked where I was and said I was at the wrong stop, but he would come to meet me. I imagined that the head of the Jewish History seminar, who conducted learned historical seminars every week in Moscow, was a man in his forties or fifties. I was stunned to see a twenty-seven-year-old young man walking up to me. He took me to the apartment of his wife whom he had recently married. The apartment was up to date, clean, pleasant, though the public entrance ("if it belongs to everyone, it belongs to no one") was on its way to decrepitude. Engel is trying to incorporate Jewish studies legally into the system. He needs historical periodicals, books, etc. To my surprise, he showed me that sometimes materials, even books, could come through the mail. He showed me a book which I had at the last minute left home, for fear that I would look like a bookmobile going through customs. We speculated that perhaps they'd let it through because it didn't say anything Jewish on the cover. He also had a letter from Jonathan Sarna of the American Jewish Archives in Cincinnati. I never did meet his wife who apparently is quite shy. According to what Lev told me later on, she is not an activist. Engel avoided army service, which would have given him "access" to secrets and would have prevented him from leaving the country later on, by faking a depression, being admitted to a psychiatric hospital, and given anti-depressants which did indeed depress him. He said that since he has come out of the hospital, he is much less fearful of what will happen to him. He even thinks that he can get a sponsor for his work at the University. For his dissertation he wants to work on the Jewish Factor in Russian Foreign Relations, immigration, and the like. He is a rather stiff pedantic type, with whom one has to work very hard to get a laugh. I could imagine him as a stern professorial type in his forties. He runs the history seminars every Thursday night although now, of course, it was "on break" so nothing could be done as far as my teaching. I gave him the encyclopedia in Russian and some of the tapes that I had. I also carefully placed one Jaffa orange on his desk. He smiled! He also indicated that a tape dubbing machine would be very, very useful and wanted an English/Cyrillic typewriter. I returned to the hotel close to 1 A.M., a metro veteran by now, trudging through underground passes, and arriving at the Intourist in a pouring, heat-relieving rain. On Monday we went to the GUM department store.

INGRID: I don't know why I get to contribute when it comes to shopping, but it is a huge place, very impressive. It's like a mall and every hall-

way is a different color. It's glassed to the sky with iron work in different colors in different hallways and fountains at intersections. There
were hundreds of shops. There were people standing in lines. In fact,
people were standing in line wherever you went. You ended up standing in line wherever there was a line because you were wondering
whether something could be had. Finding anything worth having was
lucky. We had learned that in our constant "hot" pursuit of mineral
water or anything to drink or eat. The GUM department store was very
interesting, but you would never want to buy anything there.

On Monday evening I was supposed to have an appointment at 6 P.M.
with Lev to transfer a letter from the *Igud Hamorim* to the National Conference on Soviet Jewry. Lev had told me about wanting to do that, but wanted
to consult with his associates first. Someone had said that there was a good
French meal at the International Hotel. We were looking for a meal, would
do anything for a meal, but we ended up at the wrong metro stop and walked
to the wrong hotel, The Ukraine, a Stalinist behemoth with spires reaching
to the sky. We went in, sat down in the dining room, and promptly got
thrown out. Outside again, with one of our take-along meals, bread and
cheese from breakfast, we found a pineapple drink stand and ate a 3 o'clock
lunch. Then came one of the lucky events for the activists and not so lucky
for my pocketbook. We were walking across the street toward the metro
when we saw a window display. It was a *Beriozka*, a hard currency store. We
walked in to look around and to perhaps get a fur hat for Ingrid or something
and there they were—tape dubbing machines! I was ready to buy one at that
point, but they would not take a credit card for the Sharp which was small
enough to put in my green bag. There was a Sanyo which was bigger. Actually it was a large "ghetto blaster." I was nervous about schlepping it into and
out of the Intourist Hotel past the inspector at the door, so I decided to wait
and talk to Lev about it. I met him at 6 P.M. in front of the Intourist, and
walked with him around the corner to a park bench. He showed up with an
immense, empty, rather moth-eaten leather carrying bag. He handed me the
letter, wrapped in a Russian newspaper. Lev indicated to me that the letter
should really be destroyed before I left the Soviet Union since, if it was discovered at the border, it could get him and his co-signers into significant
difficulty. I exchanged things with him for his wife, Katya, including the lovely
houserobe from Joan Rosenbaum,[16] dungarees for Lev's child, some T-shirts,

---

16. Another contributor to my smuggling cache.

a whole bunch of stuff that would be useful to sell, and many books. We didn't know which books to leave for Leningrad. We also gave him a package for Ilana of Hebrew teaching texts, magic markers, and pantyhose, and gave both Lev and Ilana a Jaffa orange. First Lev turned it down, but when I told him where it was from, his face lit up. We were sure that Ilana, in passionate love with anything Israeli, would be ecstatic over a Jaffa orange. They turned out to be really significant gifts. I told Lev that the *Beriozka* had a dubbing machine and he suggested that we meet once more the next day at a metro stop and go to the *Beriozka*.

That night it was time for *Die Fledermaus*. All we had were those seventy-kopec tickets which might have been nowhere, but then Ingrid moved into action.

INGRID: I again went to the box office checking for better tickets. This was about fifteen minutes before the start of the show. The box office lady said, "*Nyet*," no way, there were absolutely no tickets available. I pulled out a pair of pantyhose and pushed the seventy-kopec tickets over to her with the pantyhose and, all of a sudden, the best tickets in the house appeared, which we happily took and the lady happily took the pantyhose. We were sitting in third-row orchestra. It seems that a whole bunch of tickets were kept there just in case somebody from the Congress might be stopping by to see an operetta. *Die Fledermaus* was of course great fun since we know it very well, but they added a lot of talking and took out two of the most important songs. I can't really tell why, but one of them was Prince Orlofsky, the Russian Count's song where he says that he loves to invite guests and he likes to drink and he likes to throw glasses around and he'll throw the guests out in case they are not having a good time. I wonder if taking out the song has something to do with their alcohol problem. They should not be drinking all the time. Maybe it had to do with the line "*Chacun a son goût*" (Each to his own taste)—not appropriate in the workers' paradise.

Gorbachev seems to have done something about the alcohol situation in Russia. Apparently there has been a lot of alcohol abuse. As Victor pointed out, there were a lot of alcoholics and children of alcoholics who didn't seem to fare well. There were a large number of birth defects as a result of the alcohol problems in the country. There was one child who was armless, apparently, Victor said, the result of the mother being an alcoholic. We saw many intoxicated people throughout our stay in Russia. Gorbachev has taken much alcohol out of circulation by rationing beer (and you couldn't find beer anywhere). Even the hotel only seemed to serve it at certain times. I remember a little old English lady standing in line in front of me trying to get beer and the man told her there was no beer. She responded with "Oh darn!"

Later that night, back in our room, I took some pictures of Lev's letter to the National Conference from the *Igud Hamorim*. So at this point I had both the letter and the film. We had in addition been warned not to talk about our trip since the rooms were presumed bugged, and not to put anything down the toilet such as notes, because there was someone at the other end sifting through such incriminating evidence.

We met the next morning, went to the *Beriozka*, and bought this immense ghetto blaster for 171 rubles, close to $300, which I put on my credit card. The clerks refused in any way to wrap the big box. The box said Sanyo on the outside and showed a full, lifesize picture of the "ghetto blaster." We had a number of Russians come over to us while we were waiting for a cab, asking, "Where did you get that? Where did you get that?" They were not, as I feared, KGB. Lev said it's a standard question in Russia whenever scarce goods are seen. The Russians, always prepared with some kind of bag in which to carry goods home, wanted to know where you got it so they can run and get it themselves. Lev asked me, "What do you call that machine?" When I told him it was a "ghetto blaster," he laughed and said, "That is what we will do with it here." He preferred that the "loot" be taken back in a cab. When I had given him books the day before and other supplies, he also took a cab home. We got into the cab. He took us to the Pushkin Museum where we were to visit and do our tourist thing. We got out at the museum. He stayed in the cab with the "ghetto blaster." Now the *Igud Hamorim* in Moscow has a tape dubber, a true ghetto blaster, and I have a lot of good feelings of having done something very worthwhile.

Upon entering the Pushkin, I faced a dilemma. They wanted me to check my green shoulder bag. Everyplace I went, I kept all of my papers, all the addresses people had given me, requests for letters of invitation, tickets, and all the stuff for the National Conference and any valuables with me in my green shoulder bag. I moved *nowhere* without it. When they insisted on my checking it, I left my camera in it, but took all of the valuable papers out and put them into my shirt, next to my body, only returning them to their accustomed place in my green carry-on bag when we left the Pushkin. I don't know where I would have been without my green shoulder bag.

We then decided that since we were on the kind of mission we were on, we should visit Gorky Park, scene of the novel. It turned out to be a rather grungy amusement park, not very well taken care of. We went there, took a boat back to Red Square, met some East Germans from Dresden, Ingrid's birthplace, and went back for what we had hoped would be a delightful meal at the hotel. We had had no civilized meal since we arrived except for the buffet at the Intourist. Monday night, we made arrangements that meant our going in to eat at 7 P.M. on Tuesday to a restaurant in our hotel that accepted rubles for payment. We were absolutely sure that we would be finished by 10 o'clock when we had to leave the hotel to go to the railroad station. We were seated promptly at a table with an American Pakistani businessman and two Russian prostitutes. We were told by another single tourist that the particular prostitutes, who congregated around the Moscow Intourist and the Hotel Leningrad as well, were not considered to be on a low level in terms of Russian society, and that most of them were KGB agents anyway. At our table the American Pakistani and the two young prostitutes were sitting eating caviar and sturgeon and indeed seemed to be enjoying themselves despite their not knowing English and him not knowing Russian. This was followed by other entertainment, but no meal. Our meal was served at about two minutes of ten as we were leaving. We walked out in a huff and had to pay about thirty rubles ($50) for that non-meal. We were feeling hungry and furious about being ripped off. At 10 P.M., the transfer to the Leningrad station was prompt. While waiting to get on the train, whom should we meet, but our next-door neighbors from Fairfield. The porter who had moved our bags was to get thirty or sixty kopecs, but the lighter I gave him was so exciting that he did not bother about his fee.

> INGRID: As usual Jack was hungry and was searching around for something to eat and was tired of granola bars. He went into the station to find something to drink and came out with a whole big cake that he bought and we had for breakfast the next morning on the train. He saw a line, got on it, and what should there be at the beginning of it but a cake!

It is interesting to note that we were in what is referred to in Russian as "soft class," the Russian version of first class (it reflects the class struggle). Soft class was an overnight sleeper, a train from the 1930s or 1940s, with a stewardess who served tea twice.

We arrived in Leningrad Wednesday morning. Again, Intourist was efficient. They took our stuff and moved us quickly, although Ingrid almost got lost talking to a couple of Germans. We arrived at the Hotel Leningrad at 7:30 A.M. Another lighter went to the driver who smiled profusely. We were shown our room at the Leningrad, which was sumptuous. A large living room with a bedroom attached, a view of the river with the destroyer *Aurora*, a hero of the Revolution, and a view of all of eighteenth- and nineteenth-century Leningrad. As soon as we got in, we had breakfast and then went to find a telephone. As usual, we took a right turn instead of a left where there was a phone about twenty yards away. We ended up walking across a bridge into another part of Leningrad to make the first contact. Victor had promised to call Blank ahead of time to organize a teaching session. I had been unable to organize any groups in Moscow to teach anything because all of the underground schools were on vacation as well as the regular schools. I called Blank, but got no answer, called Victor and did get an answer. He said that he had been trying to call Blank, without any luck, but he would meet us. We arranged to meet at a metro station around 2 o'clock. We spent the morning walking around a bit, lost and feeling irritable in the oppressive heat. We went back to the hotel, got a map of Leningrad, walked to the closest metro, the Lenin Square Station, which is the Finland station of Revolution fame. We went a couple of stops and met Victor again, easily identifiable by his "Sun Country" cap. He took us to his home at the far end of the metro line. The apartment was quite clean although the public areas had that low-income housing look. The apartment itself had a double door. One door opened out and the inside door, upholstered, opened in. This was Elena's parents' apartment where Victor had been living with his wife, Leah (Elena Dynina), without really having permission to live in Leningrad. As soon as Victor got into the apartment, he put on his own *kippah* (skull cap). It had been hard to tell from his behavior the previous Shabbat, when he rode with us, how observant he really was. He had said then that it did not feel like Shabbat and his "Sun Country" hat was, at best, ambiguous, perhaps only protection against the relentless sun and not there to honor the living God of Israel.

Leah had started to learn Hebrew at sixteen and now, her Hebrew being reasonably accomplished, is one of the leading Hebrew teachers in Leningrad. Leah is also a graduate of a culinary institute in Leningrad. She is planning to open a cooperative where Jewish dishes will be served. We were told that Leah's parents objected to her leaving. Leah described her father as a very simple working man. It was not clear what her mother did, but she too objected to Leah's applying to leave. The walls of their apartment were decorated with posters of Israel, anything that could be gotten in: art post-

ers, tourist posters, maps, a potpourri of books, parts of book sets, orthodox prayer books, conservative Haggadahs, a potpourri library. Anything that
anyone had brought in. We gave them the large *mezuzah*[17] we had brought,
tapes, and the ever-present Superdance T-shirt (one of the twenty-five we
distributed). Leah opened a cabinet to put the cassettes away and revealed a
mass of Jewish material. We gave Victor Carole Rubin's[18] "We Are One"
Am Echad pin. Victor was absolutely thrilled and put it on immediately. Lev's
protege now had his own button.

Victor's story is rather interesting. He is being groomed by Lev to
be sent to Teblisi in Georgia to organize Jewish life. He sees himself as a "Jewish Life Organizer." He is not a Refusenik and has not applied as yet, although
he seems strongly Zionistic, and will only support those who are strongly
Zionistic. He organizes sending things to different parts of the Soviet Union.
Lev is his mentor whom he respects immensely. He put on the button as a
kind of homage to Lev whom we never saw without his Kosher button. To
the best of my knowledge and understanding, Victor has only one Jewish
parent, but he identifies so clearly that it is awesome. He is astonishingly
knowledgeable in a wide variety of fields. A most unintellectual-looking guy,
he is clearly very, very bright. He and Leah had been married about a year.
They talk from time to time about having to be in different places for a while
to do their work. Victor earns some money by doing some very simple con-
struction work, which the government cannot trace. His father from Teblisi,
who is apparently well-to-do, assists in supporting him. Victor's description
of Teblisi is of a very different kind of place than Moscow or Leningrad. He,
of course, doesn't consider himself a Russian. None of the Jews do, but he
even more so, being a Georgian. He describes Teblisi as a place with 7,000
Jews having three synagogues that are full, a community with *mikvehs*,[19]
shochets,[20] kosher meat supply, and a generally active Jewish life.

We were not Victor's only visitors. While he was taking us around,
his wife was meeting some people from Los Angeles. Even our next- door
neighbors from Fairfield had indicated that a number of the people in their
group had broken off from the tour to visit some Refuseniks, visits that mean
an immense amount.

---

17. Encased biblical verses marking the doorpost of Jewish homes.

18. Another contributor to the cache.

19. Ritual baths.

20. Slaughterers whose specialty is kosher slaughtering.

INGRID: Victor apparently came from a very interesting, very cultured family because his grandmother's uncle was a famous artist whose pictures hang in the Louvre of all places. I think his grandmother played the piano, which was very unusual for Teblisi and that area of the world.

If there is anything that I remember best about Russia, it's probably spending half of the time in Russia on the subway, changing trains one way or another in a drafty but not too hot environment while on top it was really very hot and dusty.

As we were sitting there drinking tea, which helped quench our persistent Leningrad thirst, Victor and Leah said that they would try to organize a meeting for the next night so that I could do some teaching. I gave them some of the names I had on my list. They indicated that one had left for Israel. Some others were out of town, but they would do their best to put together a meeting. We then made arrangements for Thursday for Victor to take us to the Hermitage.

On Thursday morning we visited the Leningrad Choral Synagogue. The little lady, who spoke little English and to whom Ingrid gave some cosmetics and pantyhose, was most appreciative. We also saw a morning service going on at about lunchtime in the little synagogue in the back of the main synagogue.

We went to the Hermitage and saw a line seemingly a mile long. A lighter, a lipstick, and word that we were foreigners got us in immediately, no waiting, nor did anyone on the line object. The Russians are used to more privileged folk getting preferential treatment. Inside we visited Ingrid's beloved Impressionists, were awed by the endless galleries, noting how poorly the paintings were kept. Yet this was truly one of the world's great museums. It was at the Hermitage that I was again struck by Victor's level of observance. We had become quite used to taking bread and cheese from breakfast and making sandwiches so that there would be something we could have at lunch. We offered him a cheese sandwich. He indicated that he could not eat it because he would have to say a blessing over it, which required the washing of hands. Nonetheless, he did enjoy the granola bar that we had and the dried California fruit we had been told to bring.

INGRID: The Hermitage must be one of the largest museums in the world. It was certainly very impressive. The rooms are gorgeous, but I was struck by how little care has been taken of some of the paintings. I have great affection for Impressionism and they do have some lovely Im-

pressionist paintings; however, they are placed so that you can barely
see them. Some have glass in front of them and the reflection ruins the
viewing. Because of the heat they keep the windows open for ventila-
tion, but the humidity is very bad for the paintings. Some of the oils
seemed to be cracking and not in very good shape.

Upon returning from the Hermitage, Victor waited outside our hotel
and I filled two large shopping bags he had with books. We were waiting for
a taxi outside the hotel and I said something to Victor in Hebrew where someone behind us said, in Hebrew, "Oh, you speak Hebrew." He turned out to
be a Palestinian Arab, one of a group of six. They proceeded to hassle Victor
about his *Am Echad* button, about his desire to go to Israel, about where he
belonged and where they belonged. Victor, who gives no "quarter" in any
fight, started to get involved with them and I started to get concerned that
they could easily see the titles of the books in the shopping bags and what
might happen if this went too far. Victor wisely decided to withdraw from
the confrontation. He came over to me and said, "I think that we have to go
to a different taxi stand." I was relieved as we walked past the front of the
hotel, hoping we would not be followed, not by the KGB this time, but by
the Palestinians. Victor proceeded to the taxi. I was to come to his apartment two hours later in order to meet the group that he and Leah had
assembled.

On Thursday night Ingrid went to the Kirov opera to see *The Be-
trothal in the Monastery* by Pushkin, with music by Prokofiev. I went to the
meeting that Victor and Leah had set up at 7 p.m. for a large group. On the
way there with a satchel full enough to give anyone a double hernia, we passed
some police cars that had pulled up outside Victor's apartment block. I had
another fantasy of the KGB in the apartment, being interrogated, asked what
the T-shirts, lenses, and cameras were for when Victor interrupted my dark
fantasy telling me that the cops were there probably because some guy, with
too much vodka in him, had hit his wife—so we trudged on. I schlepped the
suitcase out there vowing that I would bring it back empty.

Victor and Leah were quite apologetic that people were late. But
gradually a group assembled. I started by meeting Alexander Blinov, who
has been in refusal since 1979, and I thought was the longest Refusenik I was
to meet, which turned out not to be so. Blinov, who has sparkling eyes, was
there when I came. He used to be an engineer, who is now working as a
foreman in a laundry boiler room, along with former criminals, drug addicts,
and the like. His wife, daughter, and mother-in-law have emigrated to Is-

rael. He was living alone with his cat "Chatul."[21] In order for his wife and daughter to get out of the country, they had to go through a divorce. So Blinov is formally divorced from his wife who now has another name. His wife and daughter are now in Israel, his wife living in Haifa, and the daughter in Jerusalem attending the preparatory program of the Hebrew University. Blinov is a charming, delightful man just waiting to leave. I promised to call his wife in Israel and to do anything possible to assist him in leaving. He wonders what he's doing in Russia. He's hoping that by the time the next human rights delegation comes perhaps he'll be released at that point. He wonders, the way the other Refuseniks do, what possible use can he possibly be in Russia and why would they want to keep him anyway.

Victor and Leah had invited a rather mixed assortment of guests, one of whom called himself Jim Weiss. His father, a leading architectural designer in Leningrad, had had a stroke. He didn't say what his mother did, but he spoke to me in broken English, indicating that anything that I could do to help him get out of the country by himself, so that he could then help his parents get out, would be appreciated. He wasn't clear as to where he wanted to go, to the United States or to Israel. Victor drew sharp distinctions between people who wanted to go to Israel and people who wanted to go to the States. A young man, Vladmir, wanted to go to New York and was adamant about it. He wanted a letter of invitation, but Victor would not even allow me to take his name. A young guy who came with his wife and daughter is, rather unbelievably, a vegetarian in Russia. What he eats in the land of no vegetables is beyond me, yet he must be doing something right. His iron grip almost broke my hand. He was the most controversial of all the assemblage, recommending resettlement for the Arabs, fulminating against Gorbachev, Russia, etc. Victor loved him very much. He took the small *mezuzah* I gave him with much appreciation. You would not call him Orthodox in any shape, manner, or form, yet he puts on *tefillin* every day as a kind of demonstration of his own Jewishness in the Russian environment. A twenty-one-year-old young woman, Olga, a close friend of Leah's, had been in Leah's Hebrew class but missed class too often to learn any Hebrew. She is a very pretty young thing, who spoke only German. I could have used Ingrid's help talking with her. A young woman physician of twenty-five wanted to know what things were like in the United States for young women physicians of twenty-five.

---

21. A rather generic name since *Chatul* in Hebrew means cat.

A while later, Zachary Levin came in, a Refusenik from 1978 and an outstanding Hebrew teacher. He has a lot of his extended family, brothers and sisters, already in Israel. He reported that he was able to get some teaching materials more easily from Israel now than in the past. Glasnost is apparently making that easier.

We noticed during our trip that there were a number of different groups among the Russian Jews we met. Some were straight Refuseniks who have not been allowed to emigrate. Others were activists who had not applied for emigration and were interested in creating Jewish life in the Soviet Union. Still others wanted to emigrate anyplace outside of Russia, not necessarily Israel or the United States.

The group was then organized to listen to a talk. It was hard to know what to tell them. My mandate from the National Conference was to push Zionism. A rather difficult one, since I am settled in Fairfield, Connecticut. I decided to tell the story of my own Jewish life in America and then to answer any questions. Speaking in Hebrew, translated by Zachary Levin and Leah into Russian, I told them how my father had left Romania in 1914 with the border guard saying, "That's one less goddamned Jew in Romania." I told of my father's ambivalence about having chosen to go to America when his best friend went to Palestine. I told of my father's encouraging my brother Sol's going to Palestine in 1947, and my own history as a Zionist. I spoke of my day school education, having learned Hebrew at Camp Massad, six months in Israel in 1953–1954 as a Hebrew teaching student, becoming a rabbi as a result of those six months, a year in Jerusalem in 1969–1970, doing a clinical psychology internship at Haddassah, regular visits thereafter, my daughter Rachel's spending her two years in *Tzahal*, Israel Defense Forces, resulting in her becoming *Chayelet Mitztayenet* (Outstanding Soldier), my daughter Rebecca's time in high school in Israel and her pre-army training, up to today. They asked me, "What was the most important thing about living in Israel?" I offered that it was the feeling of being at home, of having Purim and Passover in the streets and in the schools. I told them about our non-Jewish American friend, back in 1970, complaining about how left out she felt at Passover time and that our response was that that's how left out we feel at Christmas time. I offered that those over the years who settled in Israel did not do so because there was a pot of gold at the end of the rainbow, but, rather, because they wished to help the Jewish people live and survive creatively. There were different questions at the end of the short talk. Many were about what should be done about the Arabs. Serge was adamant and demanded transfer. I noted how easy it was for the oppressed to become the oppressors. I stayed, guzzling tea and cookies until 11:30 P.M., not realizing that these were the white nights of Leningrad, so it was like afternoon out. Indeed the night before, Ingrid and I awoke at 2:30 A.M. and saw something that we had only heard about. Looking out over the Neva River, we saw the midnight sun sitting there in the sky in the middle of the night. By 11:30 P.M., I had totally emptied my satchel of everything that I had brought. Leah handled it all very well, putting everything in another room and having people go in and pick out what they wanted. I took the Carole Rubin Jewish jewelry and distributed it among the people in the room. Leah fell in love with a blue sparkling spangled blouse that had been Ingrid's and was now hers. A pair of jeans went that night though I know not to whom. I had brought some sugar substitute for Boguslavsky, but he had apparently left for Israel. So, Victor took some for his own father. I had also brought my last seven Jaffa oranges, which after numerous oohs and aahs were appreciatively and quickly devoured. So back I went to the hotel with a mercifully empty suitcase. I had kept my vow.

On Friday we went to see the Green Belt of Glory, which is a huge cemetery outside of Leningrad that dates from the siege of Leningrad. There are 500,000 people buried in these mass communal graves. Victor told us that in the Leningrad defending army there were many Jews, since Leningrad had a large Jewish population, but there is no mention of Jews specifically in either of the small museums there. In Vilna, according to Victor, the regimental orders were given in Yiddish and of the ten or so medal of honor winners, six were Jews. That, too, is not mentioned anyplace. The only way to check that is to go to the museum in Vilna to see the actual copies of regimental orders in Yiddish. Victor noted that there is a systematic attempt to wipe out anything that is noted as Jewish in the Soviet Union.

Both Misha and Victor on separate occasions noted that Stalin truly hated Leningrad and wanted to have it destroyed, which is why he did not simply surrender it to the Germans. He preferred that the people be exterminated. Walking back from the great statue of Mother Russia, which dominates the Green Belt of Glory, we noticed a number of couples making a pilgrimage there immediately following their wedding ceremony, apparently a result of the Russian people's desire not to forget what happened.

We then returned to the center of Leningrad and Victor took us around Nevsky Prospekt, Leningrad's large, grand boulevard. Leningrad had an additional problem for us, in that we could not touch the water. Gross warnings from the State Department suggested that Montezuma's revenge would look like nothing compared to what would happen if we drank Leningrad's water. We were sufficiently frightened so that all that we would drink was bottled. Of course during the heat, our hotel ran out of mineral water, so all that was left was a sickly sweet soda pop, unless we used dollars at the hard currency bar, in which case we could get sickly sweet Coke or Sprite.

> INGRID: The other half of our trip, we spent tracking down mineral water. It was a real "yucky" kind of water. We went all over town, once about forty minutes out of our way to try to find some mineral water and ended up in a fine hotel, the Hotel Europeskya, and sat somewhere in a corner and found some mineral water on the second floor. You were just thirsty all the time and not a drop to drink.

It was on Friday that we ventured into the Europeskya in pursuit of that warm mineral water and managed to get Victor into a hotel he was not allowed to go into. During the day Victor was carrying around a magazine and he showed me a copy of an article written by the head of the Arab Communist Party in Israel, who is a member of the Knesset. The article was a negative one about Israel's arms sales to various countries in the world. Victor told me that he always read these articles "inside out," so that he would discover something about Israel by reading them from the opposite perspective as the author, since only negative articles were allowed to be printed in the Soviet Union about Israel. The arms sale article thus was read by Victor from the point of view of showing him how strong Israel is.

Victor had to go away on Shabbat to visit with his in-laws at their dacha. It is interesting to note that Shabbat begins at 1:00 A.M. on Saturday morning and ends at 2:00 A.M. on Sunday morning. Victor suggested that I contact Misha Kazanevich, who is the longest (fifteen years) Refusenik in Leningrad and tied for the longest in Russia. Although already quite tired, I called Misha at 8 o'clock that night. I did the "I'm a friend from America" routine.[22] He responded, "Oh Jack, Victor has told me all about you." He wanted to know if I could meet him at 9 o'clock, one metro stop short of Victor's place. Filling my green traveling bag again with T-shirts, tapes, etc., and my zoom lens, which for some reason I had not taken to Victor's the night before, I set out. I was tired and saw an available cab after trudging to

---

22. It was indeed a routine taught us by the Kushners on behalf of the National Conference.

the Lenin Square station. The cab took me to the appointed metro stop. It ended up costing five rubles, not marked on the meter. After waiting a few minutes, I saw someone approach cautiously. We looked at each other and then looked away from each other. Then Misha approached and introduced himself. We started on the way to his apartment. He told me about his Refusenik status. Upon applying for emigration fifteen years ago, he was thrown out of his job as an electronic engineer, became a porter, then a gate keeper at a pedagogical institute. The boss of the institute, a kindly man, said that he was too intelligent to be doing that kind of work. He took him inside to become a kind of night watchman/foreman. He told of employment papers being provided by friends to prevent his being arraigned on charges of parasitism. He told of destroying those papers immediately after using them so that those friends would not get into trouble. He told of his company's executives threatening him because he was the first of their numerous Jewish workers who applied to leave. They would see to it that he would never get out. Until now, they have apparently succeeded. He told how he finally became a professional photographer, individually, without any government sanction, and having to give 71 percent of all his earnings to the state and was currently making about 150 rubles a month. He was being refused for secrecy and he said that the secrets for which he was being refused now appear in children's magazines. One of Misha's perplexities is, "What do they want with me after fifteen years of being a Refusenik? Are they keeping me for hostage?" Upon repeated inquiry, he has received a number of letters back saying that his secret standing is still in effect. Maybe, he offered, the secret they are trying to hide is just how far behind the West they are. With a forlorn look on his face, he says, "What do they want me for, of what use am I to them in this society?" He received a letter from a Colorado congressman wishing him well and hoping that he would get out. Misha would appreciate more letters from congressmen from all over the United States. He thinks that it would be helpful. He also received an invitation to the Fourth of July party at the American Embassy. They seem to be eager to help.

I had given away virtually all my camera equipment, except for my own camera and its zoom lens. I told him that I had a zoom with me and I hoped it would fit his camera. He asked what kind of camera I had and I said a Canon AE1. He indicated that he had a Canon body on which the zoom would fit perfectly. He was thrilled by the gift. We entered his apartment which was quite nice. It was an apartment that he had gotten with his wife and mother the year before he went into refusal. I met his eighteen-year-old daughter Janna who had lived since she was three years old in a state of refusal, a lovely young woman. The camera that he had had been repaired numerous times. He said that he had taken over 400,000 pictures with it. He indicated that he would really appreciate it if a mechanical Canon camera could be gotten to him. Victor had told me that Misha produces books that the movement needs by taking photographs of the books and developing the negatives. He has his own darkroom so has some control over what he can do. I told him of my problem with Lev's letter. He said he would take care of the letter and all the other written and printed material, all of the addresses, and letters of invitation I had in my possession. He said that he would meet me the next morning and give it all back to me.

I was at his house for two hours and was quite tired, but was kept awake by a lot of tea. I met his daughter's boyfriend, a very tall, thin blond young man, Alex, whose parents don't want him, as in so many cases, to consider emigrating for fear of never seeing him again. I wondered who Alex was. As they say he did not "look Jewish" but it was clear that Misha trusted him completely. As I was leaving I noticed on the wall of Misha's apartment a sticker that read Housatonic Community College, located in Bridgeport, Connecticut. I asked how he had received this. He then told me about Michael Stein, a photographer from Orange, Connecticut, who had been to visit him. Misha then gave me the names of some people who had visited whom I knew, Rabbi Alex Shapiro z"l and Rabbi Israel Dresner. I promised that I would send regards to all of them. At about midnight Misha escorted me out into Leningrad's White Night. He flagged down a passing car moonlighting as a cab, told him where I was going, and negotiated a price of five rubles. The "cabby" had a Toyota sticker on his dash. We started talking about Toyotas. He joked that his Russian Zhigulli Fiat was his Toyota.

Misha met us the next day at the Lenin Square / Finland Station stop on the metro. He had with him the photographs of the important documents. Having photographed and developed them, he put them back in the canister, a bit of film hanging out, so it looked like a new and unused Ektachrome film. He put it back in its original box with the American instructions and sealed the box so it looked like a new box of film. Having that film in my possession enabled me later in the day to burn Lev's letter, flush it down the toilet, and do the whole spy trick. To be doubly sure, I had dictated the letter into the microcassette which Ingrid brought home on her person from Russia. Misha was an invaluable help to secret agent 0018.

Misha then took us to where his daughter was selling tickets for a boat trip on the canals of Leningrad. Knowing the ticket seller, we went to

the head of the line with no Russians objecting. I took some Polaroid pictures, which Russians were agape at and spent the entire day with Misha.
The trip on the canals was exceptionally hot and steamy, with a high point
when we passed the gate at which Misha had been a doorman. We walked
along Nevsky Prospekt. Ingrid saw a lot of sidewalk painters and Misha kept
telling me how important it was for Ingrid to see that as an artist. I used my
newfound ability as a "Russian" to go into the Europeskya to get three bottles
of warm mineral water and bring them out. I knew my sources. We sat outside in a little park and nibbled some more cheese sandwiches that we had
brought from breakfast. Misha noted that we had passed, while viewing the
sidewalk artists, a number of members of *Pamyat* (Memory), the anti-Semitic
Russian group devoted to ridding the Soviet Union of Jews and Jewish influence. We then walked to the St. Isaac Cathedral, the Museum of the History
of Religion and Atheism, which was very plush inside. We found a *menorah*
(candelabrum) there which wasn't called a *menorah*. In terms of the entire
exhibit, the space allocated for Judaism was minuscule. We went to another
cathedral that was magnificent. A rainstorm struck while Misha and I went
upstairs in the cathedral to view Leningrad from on high and Ingrid remained
in the gardens outside. Toward evening we left Misha, agreeing to meet him
the next morning with Victor. I told Misha that I had forgotten to take the
pictures of Victor and Leah's wedding that I had traded for a picture of Rachel,
Rebecca, and me standing on the Mount of Olives with Jerusalem in the background, and a picture of Rachel in army uniform. Misha said he would tell
Victor. Since he had been the photographer at the wedding, he had some
pull.

  We returned to the hotel, dressed quickly, and took a cab to the
Kirov theater.

> INGRID: I found at the Intourist office that they sold theater tickets to
> tourists. You never knew if you could get anything to ballets because
> they always told you that they were sold out for all kinds of groups
> way ahead of time. The only tickets that they might have would cost
> $40 each for the Kirov. I found that when I was at the Kirov theater,
> I got my tickets for a lipstick since the man was selling some tickets
> that he could not use. He didn't have any change for my rubles so
> the lipstick did the job. Just about the highest price was three rubles
> and fifty kopecs, about $5.00. Those were the best seats in the house—
> from $40, down to $5.

We got tickets to the ballet, sat down inside in these lovely arm-chairs in the orchestra. Ingrid went through the program which seemed, strangely, rather long and tried to decipher what was there. *Swan Lake* seemed to be there. Tchaikovsky's name appeared a suspiciously large number of times in Cyrillic letters, but we weren't quite sure. Finally the curtain went up and there we saw a picture of Lenin, a red star, a hammer and sickle, and a whole presidium of people sitting on the stage. We wondered what was going on. It was the *graduation ceremony* of the Kirov Ballet School. After about an hour of ceremony and speeches and awarding diplomas, each of the graduate students came out and did his or her graduation ballet recital. That explained the multiple appearances of Tchaikovsky's name. We had excellent seats and it was an interesting though rather long experience. The cab we got back from the Kirov, a moonlighter, had an empty tank of gas. He stopped at a gas station which was closed. He then stopped a fuel truck. The two drivers, one empty of fuel, the other with a surfeit, yelled at each other a bit and our guy gave him a jerrycan, apparently agreeing to meet later and have some "people's" gasoline transferred to his private use. On the way back to the hotel we commented on what a nice city Leningrad was and he responded, "Yes, nice for you." He asked if we would pay with a couple of dollars since he was collecting hard currency to buy a VCR.

On Sunday morning, Victor and Misha took us to visit an oddball artist, living in a very sparse apartment/studio, by the name of Zev Chernoy. We were told that when we came to the courtyard we should not talk at all and certainly not English since he was afraid of being harassed. The apartment was furnished with several very rickety chairs, a bed that was made of wood with a thin mattress. Zev himself was an unusual looking person with long earlocks coming out from under his hat. He turned out to be a bicyclist who found our story of the thirty-five-mile bike trip around the five boroughs of New York City awe inspiring. He gave us a couple of his cards, one of which is going to be our New Year's card. In addition to the Jewish work that he does, he also does work that concerns itself with the rights of other small obscure ethnic minorities, some groups having no more than fifteen people.

> INGRID: What I remember about Zev is that he was in a very sparse apartment, though not terribly small for one person, considering Russia. Even his bed was hard. He had made all kinds of drawings that related to Israel in some way and they were all tacked up way out of eye level which I thought was sort of strange. He showed us samples of his work

by showing us postcards that had been either drawn or reproduced. He was also very interested in archeology and would like to have archeological books about Israel.

Later Sunday, Victor and Misha wanted to take us out to eat. On the way, as we were walking along looking for a place to eat, a man came up and asked Victor and Misha for a light. I noticed immediately that he, Victor, and Misha had gotten into a confrontation. This man had spotted them as Jews and started to make snide, anti-Semitic remarks. Victor positioned himself on one side of this man and Misha on the other. Later on, after the man left rather dejectedly, they spoke of other people whom they had had to "beat up" for such things. Victor is a person who will take nothing untoward from anybody. I asked Victor and Misha how this man knew that we were Jews. They offered, "The Russians can tell that without any problem at all." When we finally found a restaurant that was open, after a number were closed, the restaurant refused to serve us though it was totally empty. Victor and Misha said something to the person in charge and suddenly we were inside the restaurant. We asked if it was possible to get any watery Russian beer and were told, "*Nyet*," that there was no possibility. Yet, shortly thereafter, the beer showed up. A can of pineapple juice was brought to the table, some smoked salmon, and some chicken salad. Victor, of course, washed before he ate and they then paid outlandish prices for having taken us out.

We walked on in the heat, finally arriving at the Leningrad Summer Garden, a park with endless statuary from Czarist times. Sitting there we emptied what remained in our bags, giving it all to Misha and Victor, including some of Irwin Peck's jewelry, and granola bars which Victor rapidly devoured. I don't remember if it was Victor or Misha who said how uncomfortable they were receiving *tzedakah* (charity). I noted that what we were giving them was not, in any shape, manner, or form, *tzedakah*. They were on the front lines, bringing Jewish life up from out of the concrete of Russia, nourishing it, strengthening it, doing everything they could to have it grow. We were not in the front lines, but were providing the supplies to enable that to happen and in no way should they think of it as *tzedakah*.

We headed back to the hotel. Victor and Misha waited outside the hotel while we went in. We packed everything else that we had into a suitcase. We went down to the hard currency bar, picked up a can of Coke and a can of Sprite, and went out to give them what we had which was virtually everything in the room including my camera covering and my flash since Misha could use that. Misha, who had insisted on giving us something, had given us a small Russian box. Misha asked me if we had a slide machine, which we do but never use, and gave us slides of portraits from the Hermitage. They drank the Coke, the first one that they ever had. They said that they would be back at 9:00 P.M. with the pictures of Victor's wedding and that they would call into the hotel. I didn't want them to take that risk, so I was sitting outside the hotel around 9:00 wondering whether I would indeed get the picture, when I saw two figures trudging along, one with the distinctive blue "Sun Country" hat and a shorter figure with him. They were coming with a bunch of flowers for Ingrid. I went in to call her down. We stopped again at the hard currency bar and picked up another Coke and a bottle, apparently from Finland, that said *Jaffa Aurinchko* on it. Victor and Misha gave Ingrid the flowers. Victor gave me a Georgian hat.

The next morning, bright and early, Intourist had our regular black Volga sedan take us to the airport. Unfortunately, they pulled their first boo-boo that day by taking us to the domestic airport instead of the international one. It is hard to believe how dilapidated the domestic Leningrad airport is, but a lipstick and an eyeshadow later, we were at the international airport in line with a group of tourists. Our bags, containing all that illicit material, were passed through without inspection. The Aeroflot plane was much like everything else in Russia, rather down in the mouth. As we touched down in Ireland, we had a special feeling of being free again and having everything that we had, ourselves especially, being safe and sound.

Index

identity
of American Jews, 21
blessing and, 215–216
[Either/Or] thinking and, 180
healing power and, 232
of individual, 115
ideomotor activity, 236
Igud Hamorim, 296, 305, 307
Ile de France, 5
ill congregants, visiting, 223–267
image of God, 156
Imber, Rebecca, 48
immigration
to Israel, 296, 313
to United States, 5
immune system, 227–229, 259
implied causative, 257–258
impulse expression, 121
indirect communication, 245–
250
individual, identification of, 115
influential others, 234
"Inner Dynamics of the Rabbinate,
The" (Bloom), 85
inner strengths, of rabbis, 153–
167, 189
Institute for Religious and Social
Studies, 42
intentionality, 202
Internal Revenue Service (IRS), 6
International Hotel (Moscow),
305
internship
of author, 75–76
for rabbinical students, 195
Intourist Hotel (Moscow), 295
intrapersonal difficulties,
114–115
involvement, by clergy, 116–117

isolation, 107
Bowers on, 116
of clergy, 107–108
Minnesota Multiphasic
Personality Inventory
(MMPI) results about,
114
of rabbis, 67, 80
set-apartness, 115–119
symbolic existence of rabbis and,
191
Israel
immigration to, 296, 313
military, 297
Partition Day, 26–27
trip by author (1953), 31–34
Zionism, 11, 31, 314
Israel, Rabbi Richard, 286
Israel Defense Forces, 297, 314
[I–Thou] relationship, 87, 167,
215–216
with congregation, 183
segregation and, 289

Jackson, Al, 289
Jackson, Edgar N., 271, 272
Jeremiah, 100–101
Jewish Community Center (Fort
Lee, New Jersey), 29
Jewish Community Center
(Ramsey, New Jersey),
52–53
Jewish education, 58, 77
Jewish Education Committee (New
York City), 13, 24
Jewish home
keeping a, 103–104
rabbis and, 146–148
Jewish law, 209

ABOUT THE AUTHOR

Rabbi and Clinical Psychologist, Jack H Bloom is one of a handful of rabbis who is a full member of both the Central Conference of American Rabbis (Reform) and the Rabbinical Assembly (Conservative).

Dr. Bloom has become known as a rabbi's rabbi. In addition to his private practice at the Psychotherapy Center in Fairfield, Connecticut, Dr. Bloom serves as Director of Professional Career Review for his Reform colleagues, for whom he created a program to assist rabbis seeking to shape their futures. Working closely with Conservative rabbis, he mentors and teaches regularly at the Rabbinic Training Institutes sponsored by his alma mater, the Jewish Theological Seminary of America.

Dr. Bloom earned a BA at Columbia College, a BHL, MHL, and rabbinical ordination at the Jewish Theological Seminary of America. For ten years he was rabbi of Congregation Beth El, Fairfield, Connecticut, during which time he completed an STM in Pastoral Counseling from New York Theological Seminary.

Dr. Bloom earned a Ph.D. in Clinical Psychology from Columbia. Dr. Bloom's dissertation "The Pulpit Rabbi as Symbolic Exemplar" was the first of his extensive writings on "what it's like to be a rabbi."

In 2001 an honorary doctorate was awarded to Dr. Bloom

> in recognition of the enormous contribution you have made to improving the personal and professional lives of Conservative and Reform rabbis. You have placed a concern for colleagues at the center of your professional life. Your love and respect for the work of your colleagues has made you the quintessential rabbi for rabbis.

Dr. Bloom and his wife, Ingrid, a German teacher, reside in Fairfield. They are the parents of four children and the grandparents of five.

Order a copy of this book with this form or online at:
http://www.haworthpressinc.com/store/product.asp?sku=4855

THE RABBI AS SYMBOLIC EXEMPLAR
By the Power Vested in Me

_____ in hardbound at $49.95 (ISBN: 0-7890-1865-9)

_____ in softbound at $29.95 (ISBN: 0-7890-1866-7)

COST OF BOOKS_____	☐ **BILL ME LATER:** ($5 service charge will be added)
	(Bill-me option is good on US/Canada/Mexico orders only; not good to jobbers, wholesalers, or subscription agencies.)
OUTSIDE USA/CANADA/ MEXICO: ADD 20%____	
	☐ Check here if billing address is different from shipping address and attach purchase order and billing address information.
POSTAGE & HANDLING_____ (US: $4.00 for first book & $1.50 for each additional book) Outside US: $5.00 for first book & $2.00 for each additional book)	
	Signature_____
SUBTOTAL_____	☐ **PAYMENT ENCLOSED: $_____**
in Canada: add 7% GST____	☐ **PLEASE CHARGE TO MY CREDIT CARD.**
STATE TAX____ (NY, OH & MIN residents, please add appropriate local sales tax)	☐ Visa ☐ MasterCard ☐ AmEx ☐ Discover ☐ Diner's Club ☐ Eurocard ☐ JCB
	Account # _____
FINAL TOTAL____ (If paying in Canadian funds, convert using the current exchange rate, UNESCO coupons welcome.)	Exp. Date_____
	Signature_____

Prices in US dollars and subject to change without notice.

NAME_____

INSTITUTION_____

ADDRESS_____

CITY_____

STATE/ZIP_____

COUNTRY_____ COUNTY (NY residents only)_____

TEL_____ FAX_____

E-MAIL_____

May we use your e-mail address for confirmations and other types of information? ☐ Yes ☐ No
We appreciate receiving your e-mail address and fax number. Haworth would like to e-mail or fax special discount offers to you, as a preferred customer. **We will never share, rent, or exchange your e-mail address or fax number.** We regard such actions as an invasion of your privacy.

Order From Your Local Bookstore or Directly From
The Haworth Press, Inc.
10 Alice Street, Binghamton, New York 13904-1580 • USA
TELEPHONE: 1-800-HAWORTH (1-800-429-6784) / Outside US/Canada: (607) 722-5857
FAX: 1-800-895-0582 / Outside US/Canada: (607) 722-6362
E-mail: getinfo@haworthpressinc.com
PLEASE PHOTOCOPY THIS FORM FOR YOUR PERSONAL USE.
www.HaworthPress.com

BOF02